Prof. Dr. Wilfried Böhler
Dipl.-Kfm. Michael Hinck

Wirtschaftsenglisch

Business Cases • Know-How • Soft Skills

Merkur
Verlag Rinteln

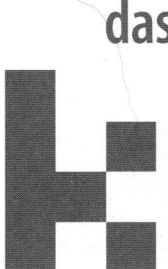

das Kompendium
herausgegeben von Christian Jaschinski

Verfasser:

Prof. Dr. Wilfried Böhler
Professor für Wirtschaftsenglisch an der Universität Paderborn

Dipl.-Kfm. Michael Hinck
Lehrer für Englisch und BWL an der Privaten Wirtschaftsschule Bayreuth

Das Werk und seine Teile sind urheberrechtlich geschützt. Jede Nutzung in anderen als den gesetzlich zugelassenen Fällen bedarf der vorherigen schriftlichen Einwilligung des Verlages. Hinweis zu § 52a UrhG: Weder das Werk noch seine Teile dürfen ohne eine solche Einwilligung eingescannt und in ein Netzwerk eingestellt werden. Dies gilt auch für Intranets von Schulen und sonstigen Bildungseinrichtungen.

2. Auflage 2003
© 2003 by MERKUR VERLAG RINTELN
Gesamtherstellung:
MERKUR VERLAG RINTELN
Hutkap GmbH & Co. KG, 31735 Rinteln
E-Mail: info@merkur-verlag.de   info@das-kompendium.de
Internet: www.merkur-verlag.de   www.das-kompendium.de
ISBN 3-8120-**0622-7**

Vorwort des Herausgebers

Liebe Leserin, lieber Leser,

Wirtschaftswissenschaft ist ein umfassendes und faszinierendes Fachgebiet. Wissenschaft und Praxis sollen einander befruchten und der Fortentwicklung des Wissens und somit dem wirtschaftlichen Erfolg zum Wohle aller dienen. Dem trägt die Buchreihe **das Kompendium** Rechnung, indem sie den Spagat zwischen wissenschaftlichem und praktischem Anspruch wagt.

Ausgerichtet auf eine generelle Anwendbarkeit ist der vorliegende Band umfassend und ausgewogen in seiner Themenabdeckung, gleichzeitig interessant aufgemacht und sicherlich ein Medium, das man regelmäßig und gern nutzen wird.

das Kompendium ist ein idealer Wegbegleiter für Studierende sowie für Praktikerinnen und Praktiker ein Manual der Wirtschaftswissenschaft, das für die tägliche Arbeit und qualifizierte Weiterbildung unverzichtbar ist – somit ein Tool, das man nicht mehr missen möchte.

Haben Sie Fragen, Anregungen oder Kritik – Lob und Tadel gleichermaßen –, lassen Sie es mich wissen. Nur so können wir die Bücher für Ihre Ansprüche weiter optimieren. Sie erreichen mich unter **info@das-kompendium.de**. Weitere Informationen auch zu anderen Bänden der Reihe finden Sie unter **das-kompendium.de**.

Ich wünsche Ihnen viel Erfolg bei der Arbeit mit diesem Buch!

Christian Jaschinski

Vorwort der Autoren

Das vorliegende Lehrbuch hat für den Bereich Wirtschaftsenglisch eine bedeutsame Schnittstellenfunktion. Es richtet sich an Studierende, die über Grundkenntnisse der englischen Sprache verfügen und jetzt eine Kompetenz im Bereich Wirtschaftsenglisch erwerben möchten. Darüber hinaus richtet sich dieses Buch auch an Praktiker und Fachkräfte, die ein Referenzwerk zum Lernen und Nachschlagen benötigen.

TEIL A bietet interessante und wichtige Beiträge zu Themen wie *Presentations, Telephoning* und *Meetings*. Ferner wird der immer stärker werdenden Bedeutung der so genannten „Soft Skills" Rechnung getragen – der „sozialen Kompetenz", welche neben den fachlichen Qualifikationen oft über den Geschäftserfolg mitentscheidet.

Die Übungen im Teil A orientieren sich an praxisnahen Geschäftssituationen und stellen ein gutes Training für den Umgang mit dem gängigen Geschäftsenglisch dar.

TEIL B vermittelt in 14 Kapiteln die geschäftsfeldbezogenen Lehrinhalte, u. a. Finanzierung, Kostenrechnung, Marketing, Personalmanagement, Qualitätsmanagement und rechtliche Grundlagen. Dieser Teil richtet sich dabei durch die prozessorientierte Betrachtung der betrieblichen Funktionen in erster Linie an Fachhochschulen und Universitäten. Jedes Kapitel beinhaltet einen Fachtext aus dem jeweiligen Themenbereich, einschließlich Vokabular, *„Knowledge Check"* und praktischen Aufgabenstellungen.

Das methodische Konzept orientiert sich an nordamerikanischen Managementansätzen und -praktiken und betrachtet die unternehmerischen Prozesse aus betriebs- und verhaltensorientierter Perspektive. Zentraler Bestandteil ist dabei der Einsatz von Fallstudien, die im Rahmen der Veranstaltung diskutiert und bearbeitet werden können. Der Einsatz von Fallstudien bietet die Möglichkeit, das zuvor erarbeitete Vokabular in einem praxisbezogenen Kontext einzusetzen, die eigenständige Umsetzung der Terminologie zu trainieren und den Ausdruck eigener Situationsanalysen und Lösungsansätze erheblich zu verbessern. Er fördert darüber hinaus die Fähigkeit, Problemstellungen systematisch und strukturiert zu analysieren.

TEIL C behandelt den Bereich der Geschäftskorrespondenz. Von „A" wie „Anfrage" bis „Z" wie „Zahlung" werden alle praxisrelevanten Geschäftsfälle abgedeckt. Die Themen umfassen u. a. Angebote, Bestellungen, Beschwerden und Mahnungen. Jedes Kapitel behandelt das erforderliche Vokabular, Redewendungen und zahlreiche Aufgaben zum Üben des kaufmännischen Schriftverkehrs.

Aufgrund der Orientierung an nordamerikanischen Managementansätzen wird im Teil B des Buches *American English* verwendet, während in den Teilen A und C *British English* verwendet wird. Das im Teil C dargestellte Layout für die Geschäftskorrespondenz orientiert sich an den Empfehlungen der *London Chamber of Commerce and Industry* (LCCI).

Ergänzt wird das Buch durch ein **Glossar der 500 wichtigsten Wirtschaftsbegriffe**, jeweils mit englischer Definition und deutscher Übersetzung. Das Glossar eignet sich hervorragend als Nachschlagewerk und für die Bearbeitung der Fallstudien.

Die **2. Auflage** wurde um zahlreiche Lösungsvorschläge ergänzt, um eine effektive Kontrolle für das selbstständige Lernen zu bieten. Darüber hinaus wurden einige Fallstudien in Teil B und mehrere Schaubilder überarbeitet. Zudem verfügt die Neuauflage über einen Index, um ein schnelles Auffinden der Inhalte zu ermöglichen.

Paderborn im Sommer 2003   Wilfried Böhler
                                                        Michael Hinck

Important Abbreviations

am	in the morning (*ante meridiem*)	vormittags
asap	as soon as possible	sobald wie möglich
attn	for the attention of	zu Händen
Ave	avenue	Straße
B/E	bill of exchange	Wechsel
B/L	bill of lading	Konnossement, Seefrachtbrief
c/o	care of	zu Händen
Cat No	catalogue number	Katalognummer
cc	carbon copy	Kopie an
COD	cash on delivery	per Nachnahme
CWO	cash with order	Kasse bei Auftragserteilung
D/A	documents against acceptance	Dokumente gegen Akzept
D/P	documents against payment	Dokumente gegen Zahlung
dept	department	Abteilung
E&OE	errors and omissions excepted	Fehler und Auslassungen vorbehalten
ea	each	jeder, jedes, jeder
EE	errors excepted	Irrtümer vorbehalten
eg	for example (*exempli gratia*)	zum Beispiel
Enc	enclosure, enclosed	Anlagen
ie	that is (*id est*)	das heißt
incl	including	einschließlich
L/C	letter of credit	Akkreditiv
Ltd	private limited company	Gesellschaft mit beschränkter Haftung
NB	note (*nota bene*)	Bitte beachten, Hinweis
p&p	postage and packing	Porto und Verpackung
pa	per annum	pro Jahr
plc	public limited company	Aktiengesellschaft
pm	in the afternoon (*post meridiem*)	nachmittags
PO Box	post office box	Postfach

pp	per procurationem		in Vollmacht, in Vertretung
PTO	please turn over		Bitte wenden.
qty	quantity		Menge
Rd	road		Straße
ref	reference		Bezug, (Ihr/Unser) Zeichen
RSVP	(*répondez s'il vous plaît*)		um Antwort wird gebeten
St	street		Straße
T&CB	terms and conditions of business		Geschäftsbedingungen
VAT	Value Added Tax		Mehrwertsteuer

The 13 Incoterms

EXW	Ex-Works	Ab Werk
FCA	Free Carrier	Frei Frachtführer
FAS	Free alongside Ship	Frei Längsseite Schiff
FOB	Free on Board	Frei an Bord
CFR	Cost and Freight	Kosten und Fracht
CIF	Cost, Insurance, Freight	Kosten, Versicherung, Fracht
CPT	Carriage Paid to	Frachtfrei
CIP	Carriage and Insurance Paid	Frachtfrei versichert
DAF	Delivered at Frontier	Geliefert Grenze
DES	Delivered Ex Ship	Geliefert ab Schiff
DEQ	Delivered Ex Quay	Geliefert ab Kai
DDU	Delivered Duty Unpaid	Geliefert unverzollt
DDP	Delivered Duty Paid	Geliefert verzollt

Inhalt

Vorwort des Herausgebers		5
Vorwort der Autoren		6
Important Abbreviations		8
The 13 Incoterms		9
Inhalt		10
A	**Managing in the Global Marketplace**	**17**
A 1	Planning Meetings	20
	Checklist – Meetings	21
	Exercise – Scheduling reservations	22
	Exercise – Calling a meeting	23
A 2	Conference Centres	24
	Exercise – Deciding on a conference venue	25
	Exercise – Requesting information	27
A 3	Presentations	28
	Checklist – Presentations	29
	Exercise – Arranging hotel reservations	30
	Exercise – Booking a hotel room	31
A 4	Telephoning	32
	Key vocabulary	33
	Key phrases	33
	Checklist – Leaving messages on an answering machine	35
	Exercise – Scheduling job interviews	36
	Exercise – Arranging an interview	38
A 5	Business Skills	40
	Exercise – Making a reservation	41
	Exercise – Finalizing details	43
A 6	Conversation Skills	44
	Exercise – Selecting a supplier	45
	Exercise – Delegating tasks	47
A 7	Business Etiquette	48
	Exercise – Processing orders	49
	Exercise – Problems with deliveries	51
A 8	Customer Service	52
	Exercise – Managing performance records	53
	Exercise – Requesting resources	55
A 9	UK Airports	56
	Exercise – Organizing the collection of guests	58
	Exercise – Changing arrangements	59

B	**Learning English for Business Management**	61
	Introduction: Learning English for Business Management	63
	SWOT-Analysis	64
	SWOT Case: STMicroelectronics – Testing the Fabric of a Doughnut Structure	67
B 1	Society, Business, Government, and the Global Network Economy	72
B 1.1	Principles – Models – Practices	73
	Economic Goals and Measurements · Economic Fundamentals in the Global Network Economy (GNE) · Competitive Aspects of the GNE · Regulatory Challenges of the GNE	
B 1.2	Knowledge Check	77
B 1.3	Keywords	77
B 1.4	Case Study Approach	78
B 1.5	Strategy Case: Nortel	79
B 1.6	Mindset Management	83
B 1.7	The Linked Mindsets Framework	84
B 1.8	Experiential Case: Feeling Sidetracked	85
B 2	Theory of the Firm	88
B 2.1	Principles – Models – Practices	89
	The Objective of a Firm · Transaction Costs and Vertical Integration · Transaction Costs and Opportunistic Behavior · High Transaction Costs · Specialized Products · Changing Market Conditions · Monitoring Costs	
B 2.2	Knowledge Check	94
B 2.3	Keywords	94
B 2.4	Strategy Case: Enron Corp. – Out-of-the Money	94
B 2.5	The "Intrapreneurial" Mindset	98
B 2.6	Experiential Case: The Stress-Challenged Manager	99
B 3	The Constitution of Business	102
B 3.1	Principles – Models – Practices	103
	Structural Trends · Expanding Web of Services · The Company of the Future · Legal Forms · Sole Proprietorships · Partnerships · Corporations	
B 3.2	Knowledge Check	108
B 3.3	Keywords	108
B 3.4	Strategy Case: KirchMedia – Game over?	109
B 3.5	The "Executive" Mindset	113
B 3.6	Experiential Case: The Temperamental Networker	114
B 4	The External Environment and Corporate Culture	116
B 4.1	Principles – Models – Practices	117
	The Environmental Domain · Survival of the Fittest · The Structure of the Corporate Environment – Layered Structure · Adapting to the Environment · Structural Variety · Ownership · Influencing the Environment · Corporate Culture · Cultural Types	
B 4.2	Knowledge Check	122

B 4.3	Keywords	122
B 4.4	Strategy Case: Iridium LLC – Steering into a Descending Orbit	122
B 4.5	The "Advocate" Mindset	126
B 4.6	Experiential Case: The Group Decision	128
B 5	Business and the Law	130
B 5.1	Principles – Models – Practices	131
	Taxes · Company-Related Laws · American Court System · Law of Torts and Product Liability · Agency · Property Transactions · Bankruptcy	
B 5.2	Knowledge Check	137
B 5.3	Keywords	137
B 5.4	Strategy Case: Dimon Inc. – Treading Carefully	137
B 5.5	The "Coaching" Mindset	140
B 5.6	Experiential Exercise: Giving and Receiving Feedback	141
B 6	Top Management Direction	144
B 6.1	Principles – Models – Practices	145
	Official Goals · Generic Strategies · Operative Goals · Goal Content · Managing Multiple and Conflicting Goals · Organizational Effectiveness · The Control Function	
B 6.2	Knowledge Check	150
B 6.3	Keywords	150
B 6.4	Strategy Case: Expedia Inc. – Courting a Virtual Third Party	151
B 6.5	The "Administrator" Mindset	155
B 6.6	Experiential Case: Skilled Incompetence	156
B 7	Decision-making Processes	160
B 7.1	Principles – Models – Practices	161
	Individual Decision-making · The Rational Approach · The Decision Support System Approach (DSS) · Bounded Rationality · Group Decision Making in Organizations · The Political Model · The Incremental Decision Process Model · The Intuitive Model · Contingency Framework for Decision-making	
B 7.2	Knowledge Check	164
B 7.3	Keywords	165
B 7.4	Strategy Case: CEMEX – Global, Nimble … & In the Money	165
B 7.5	The "Auditing" Mindset	170
B 7.6	Exercise: Memo "Please report to work on Saturday"	171
B 8	Human Resource Management	172
B 8.1	Principles – Models – Practices	173
	Contextual Framework of Human Resource Policies · Staffing · Lifelong Employment · Up-or-Out Flow · Unstable In-and-Out System · Mixed Flow Patterns · The Reward System · The Work System · The Integration of HRM Policies	
B 8.2	Knowledge Check	176
B 8.3	Keywords	176
B 8.4	Strategy Case: Pharmacia – Merging People, not Firms	177

B 8.5	The "Visionary" Mindset	181
B 8.6	Experiential Exercise: Creativity-Relevant Skills	182
B 9	Control Concepts for Quality and Productivity	186
B 9.1	Principles – Models – Practices	187

Production Efficiency · Materials Management · Quality Assurance · Production and Operations Management (POM) · Compatibility Testing · Production Planning · Routing · Scheduling · Follow-up and Control

B 9.2	Knowledge Check	190
B 9.3	Keywords	191
B 9.4	Strategy Case: Smithfields Foods – Sensing a Gut Feeling	191
B 9.5	The "Entrepreneurial" Mindset	196
B 9.6	Experiential Case: Negotiating Objective Criteria	198
B 10	Accounting	200
B 10.1	Principles – Models – Practices	201

Financial Accounting · Fundamental Concepts · Financial Analysis · The Certification of Financial Statements · Trend and Ratio Analysis · Management Accounting · The Role of Budgets · Scorecharting

B 10.2	Knowledge Check	208
B 10.3	Keywords	209
B 10.4	Strategy Case: Elan Corp.	209
B 10.5	The "Informating" Mindset	212
B 10.6	Experiential Exercise 1: Organizational Design Preference	213
B 10.7	Experiential Exercise 2: Corporate versus Professional Identity	214
B 11	Financial Management	216
B 11.1	Principles – Models – Practices	217

The Financial Plan · Risk Management · Internal versus External Financing · Short-term versus long-term Funding · Debt versus Equity · Managing Cash and Marketable Securities · Managing Receivables and Payables · Managing Inventory · Capital Budgeting

B 11.2	Knowledge Check	222
B 11.3	Keywords	223
B 11.4	Strategy Case: Egg plc – Not Fully Hatched Yet	223
B 11.5	The "Risk-Managing" Mindset	227
B 11.6	Experiential Exercise: The Confrontation Meeting	228
B 12	Marketing	230
B 12.1	Principles – Models – Practices	231

The Rationale of Marketing · Marketing Management Process · Market Research · Market Segmentation · Marketing Mix · Product · Product Life Cycle · Market Portfolio Matrix · Product Portfolio Matrix

B 12.2	Knowledge Check	239
B 12.3	Keywords	239
B 12.4	Strategy Case: The Algonquin Hotel – Executive Suite?	240

B 12.5	The "Pro-active" Mindset	245
B 12.6	Experiential Exercise: ACME Role-Play	246
B 13	Global Competition	248
B 13.1	Principles – Models – Practices	249
	The Growth of Global Corporations · The Global Trade and Investment Environment · Basic Entry Decisions · Structuring the Global Company · Framework for Global Competitive Advantages · Growth Factors in Global Competition · Traditional Barriers to Globalization · Cultural Barriers · Administrative and Legal Barriers	
B 13.2	Knowledge Check	253
B 13.3	Keywords	253
B 13.4	Strategy Case: Tesco – Ever on Piling High & Selling Cheap?	254
B 13.5	The "Collaborative" Mindset	259
B 13.6	Experiential Exercise: The Glass Cubicle	259
B 14	Integrating the Total Concept	264
	Framework of Internal and External Competitive Forces · Process Organization · Diagnostic Model for Integrating Reflection and Action · Aligning Mindsets for Performance · Switching Mindsets · Managing Individual Outcomes · Integrative Case: Cadbury Schweppes – Growing for Value or Rank?	
C	**Business Correspondence**	**281**
	Layout of business letters	283
	Tips for writing business letters	283
	Example of layout	284
C 1	Anfragen (Enquiries)	286
	Key Vocabulary	286
	Key Phrases	286
	Sample letter – Enquiry	288
	Exercises 1–3	289
C 2	Angebote (Offers)	290
	Key Vocabulary	290
	Key Phrases	290
	Sample letter – Offer	292
	Exercises 1–3	293
C 3	Bestellungen (Orders)	294
	Key Vocabulary	294
	Key Phrases	294
	Sample letter – Order	296
	Exercises 1–3	297
C 4	Zahlung (Payment)	298
	Key Vocabulary	298
	Key Phrases	298

	Sample letter – Acknowledgement	300
	Exercises 1–3	301
C 5	Versand und Transport (Despatch and transport)	302
	Key Vocabulary	302
	Key Phrases	302
	Sample letter – Enquiry about collection and delivery	304
	Exercises 1–2	305
C 6	Verzögerungen (Delays)	306
	Key Vocabulary	306
	Key Phrases	306
	Sample letter – Complaint about delay in delivery	308
	Exercises 1–3	309
C 7	Mangelhafte Lieferung (Bad delivery)	310
	Key Vocabulary	310
	Key Phrases	310
	Sample letter – Complaint about defective goods	312
	Exercises 1–4	313
C 8	Mahnungen (Reminders)	314
	Key Vocabulary	314
	Key Phrases	314
	Sample letter – Reminder	316
	Exercises 1–4	317
C 9	Memos	318
	Layout of memos	318
	Exercises 1–5	319
C 10	Berichte (Reports)	320
	Layout of reports	320
	Tips for writing reports	320
	Example of Layout	320
	Exercises 1–2	321
C 11	Bewerbungen (Applications)	322
	Sample Cover Letter	322
	Sample Curriculum Vitae (CV)	323
	Sample Resume	324
C 12	Die 13 Incoterms	326
D	**Answer Key**	329
E	**The "Handy 500": Glossary of 500 fundamental Business Terms**	371
F	**Index**	413

A

Managing

in the

Global Marketplace

Preview – Part A
Managing in the Global Marketplace

1	Planning Meetings • Scheduling reservations
2	Conference Centres • Deciding on a conference venue
3	Presentations • Arranging hotel reservations
4	Telephoning • Scheduling job interviews
5	Business Skills • Making a reservation
6	Conversation Skills • Selecting a supplier
7	Business Etiquette • Processing orders
8	Customer Service • Managing performance records
9	UK Airports • Organizing the collection of guests

A   Managing in the Global Marketplace

Today, companies of all sizes in a <u>multitude</u> of product and service industries are <u>competing</u> in the world's markets. This development is driven by spreading <u>affluence</u>, the <u>increase</u> in global travel, the revolution in global communications, as well as by privatization and deregulation of government monopolies. Simultaneously, falling <u>trade barriers</u> and the need to find new markets <u>reinforce</u> the increasing globalization. This raises a large number of <u>issues</u>. It creates <u>opportunities</u> for businesses to expand and to grow, encouraging companies to look abroad for new customers or suppliers. Big companies set up <u>subsidiaries</u> abroad in large numbers and even smaller companies maintain at least a foreign sales outlet. As efficient foreign competitors enter previously protected markets and challenge local companies, the lesson is that no market position is secure without constant innovation and attention to customer satisfaction.

> **multitude** – Vielzahl
> **to compete** – im Wettbewerb stehen
> **affluence** – Wohlstand, Reichtum
> **increase** – Anstieg, Zunahme
> **trade barrier** – Handelsbarriere
> **to reinforce** – verstärken
> **issue** – Thema
> **opportunity** – Möglichkeit
> **subsidiary** – Niederlassung
> **r & d** – F & E

Multinational enterprises (MNEs) like Coca-Cola, McDonalds, Sony or IBM play an important role in the global market. These "Global Players" maintain a world-wide network of suppliers, production facilities, <u>r & d</u> teams and sales outlets. Even small and medium-sized enterprises (SMEs) often operate outside of their home market.

Not only the business itself but also the workforce of the company is affected. Globalization leads to changes in the workplace and working in a global marketplace involves a huge variety of different situations, e.g.

- making travel arrangements and preparing business trips,
- finding a suitable hotel, deciding on a venue and booking a conference room,
- organizing presentations and meetings,
- and dealing with customers and suppliers.

Effective communication is essential to success in the international business world. Therefore, it is important for the manager to develop a new set of skills in order to meet the requirements of today's international communication and business.

A 1 Planning Meetings

When planning a meeting a variety of points have to be considered:

You should have an extensive knowledge of your manager's business associates and should be aware of how to contact them. One has to consider where the meeting is to take place and how long the meeting will last.

Contact people as early as possible in advance and offer alternative dates to cover any eventualities that may arise. Having contacted the people concerned, it is vital to seek confirmation and make any necessary adjustment to the schedule by phone.

a variety of – eine Vielzahl an
extensive – umfassend, ausführlich
business associate – Geschäftspartner
to consider – berücksichtigen, bedenken
eventualities – Eventualitäten, Möglichkeiten
vital – unerlässlich
confirmation – Bestätigung
necessary – erforderlich, notwendig
adjustment – Anpassung
schedule – Zeitplan, Terminplan

Take into consideration where people from outside your firm are travelling from in order to coordinate when best to commence the meeting. Internal staff should be approached as soon as you are aware of any meeting involving them. This allows them time to alter their schedules. It is a advisable to be familiar with the schedules of the firm's key people.

In the event of someone not being able to attend, ascertain whether other methods may be employed, like telephone, web, or video-conferencing. Contact the departments concerned for any relevant material required for the meeting, such as files, reports, figures, data and so on. Ensure that any equipment needed is available at the venue, e.g. projector, screen, flipchart and the like.

In advance of the meeting see that suitable refreshments are provided. Your arrangements with all the people concerned must be convenient to your superior as his/her schedule is your main priority.

An agenda for the meeting will also be required, stating who is attending and what topics are to be addressed. The agenda should be sent out to all participants in advance of the meeting.

to commence – anfangen, beginnen
to approach – Kontakt aufnehmen
to ascertain – herausfinden, ermitteln
to employ – verwenden, einsetzen
department – Abteilung
required – erforderlich, benötigt
to ensure – sicherstellen
equipment – Zubehör
agenda – Tagesordnung
participant – Teilnehmer

Planning Meetings | **A 1**

Checklist – Meetings

Before calling a meeting, ask yourself the following questions:
- ✔ Does the <u>matter</u> require support, <u>consensus</u>, or discussion?
- ✔ Could the <u>issue</u> be handled without a meeting?
- ✔ Could it be managed with a memo or phone call?

Decide why the meeting is being held.
- ✔ decision-making
- ✔ <u>persuasion</u>
- ✔ information exchange
- ✔ brainstorming
- ✔ motivation
- ✔ delegation

> **matter** – Angelegenheit
> **consensus** – Konsens, Übereinstimmung
> **issue** – Problem, Angelegenheit, Sachverhalt
> **persuasion** – Überredung, Überzeugung
> **to stick to** – sich halten an, bleiben bei
> **kindly** – freundlich
> **to appreciate** – schätzen, würdigen

Tips for organizing and conducting meetings:
- ✔ Start and stop on time.
- ✔ Consider starting at odd times – for example 8:10 or 9:20. This tends to increase punctuality.
- ✔ Try to avoid typical one-hour meetings. Ask yourself: Would thirty/forty/fifty minutes do?
- ✔ Not all meetings have to be formal.
- ✔ Remember to bring extra copies of the agenda.
- ✔ Always <u>stick to</u> the agenda. Distribute the time efficiently.
- ✔ Only one person can speak at a time.
- ✔ Don't let one or two people dominate the discussion.
- ✔ Stop side conversations by saying <u>kindly</u> – "I'd <u>appreciate</u> your input. Is there something you're saying we need to know?"
- ✔ Stop talking and look at talkers. When they stop, you talk.

A1 | Planning Meetings

Exercise – Scheduling reservations

Background

You are employed at the *Conference Centre Cork*. During the planning meeting with your manager, *Declan Burne*, arrangements are being made for the reservations.

We are full on 6 April 2003. This morning, *Aran Mills* phoned to reserve the *Munster suite* for their fashion show. *Irish Crystal* would like the *Leinster suite*. *Patricia* should take that one. They are launching their new range. It will start at 2 o'clock. *Kelly's Brewery* are having their AGM in the *Ulster suite*. It begins at 10 am. They wanted the *Connacht suite*, but *Tara Books* have reserved it for a press reception. *Christina* hasn't done a press reception yet, has she? It'll be a good experience for her. As they don't start till 9 o'clock, we have ample time to prepare the rooms. *Patrick* can look after *Aran Mills* and *Kelly's Brewery*. *Aran Mills* starts at 1630 hrs.

Assignment

Complete the reservation plan and list the customers in alphabetical order.

Bookings for 6 April 2003

Customer	Event	Suite	Staff	Time

Planning Meetings | A 1

Exercise – Calling a meeting

Background

Ihr Unternehmen plant eine Umstrukturierung der Geschäftsbereiche *(restructuring of business units)*.

Assignment

Schreiben Sie als Geschäftsführer ein Memo an alle Abteilungsleiter *(Department Heads)* und laden Sie diese zu einem Meeting am 28. des nächsten Monats ein.

Das Meeting beginnt um 14.10 Uhr und wird voraussichtlich 1 $^{1}/_{2}$ Stunden dauern. Es findet in Raum 19 im 3. Stock statt.

Bitten Sie die Teilnehmer darum, pünktlich zu erscheinen und den letzten Quartalsbericht *(quarterly report)* mitzubringen. Eine vorläufige Tagesordnung ist beigefügt.

Falls jemand nicht teilnehmen kann, wird um eine kurze Nachricht gebeten.

Memo

To:

From:

Subject:

Date:

A 2   Conference Centres

Conference centres provide a business-focussed <u>environment</u>. These <u>facilities</u> can be used for a variety of events: product introductions, press conferences, training seminars, motivational meetings, and new product launches. Conference centres <u>provide</u> accommodation, ensuring your guests or staff are all in the same location. Meals and refreshments are part of their services, <u>dispensing with</u> the need for caterers.

Using these <u>venues</u> ensures you have all the technology you need to host any business occasion. <u>Equipment</u> available includes high-speed internet access, satellite video conferencing, and other means of audiovisual presentation and communication technology. These services are an extension of your office. The required equipment will be set up and a support team is on hand in the event of any technical problems. Additional equipment can be rented, e.g. mobile phones, notebooks and so on. Trained staff are present to ensure everything runs smoothly. A conference service manager works with you and sees to all details, allowing you to focus on your event.

environment	– Umgebung, Umfeld
facilities	– Einrichtungen
to provide	– bieten, zur Verfügung stellen
to dispense with	– überflüssig machen
venue	– Tagungsort, Treffpunkt
equipment	– Ausrüstung, Ausstattung
attendee	– Teilnehmer
requirements	– Anforderungen, Erfordernisse
to enable	– ermöglichen

Most conference centres are within easy access of airports and stations. Some centres provide transport for your <u>attendees</u>, for instance a shuttle to and from the airport. Leisure and entertainment are not overlooked. Centres have bars and restaurants with meals of a very high standard and the chefs are prepared to devise extra menus for other special occasions. Sports facilities are also in-house, including gyms, swimming pools, and saunas. Outside sports are catered for at some of the bigger centres and include team builders like rope climbing and orienteering, volleyball, basketball, and of course golf.

Depending on your needs, centres will negotiate a price package, incorporating your <u>requirements</u> and the size of your group. This is beneficial as it means you can arrange the event to your specific needs.

There are a lot of advantages to using conference centres. You don't have to arrange accommodation, catering, transport, and the hiring of technical equipment. Staff from the conference centre will deal with any problems that occur. It saves you time, as you are dealing with just one company. It is more likely to be efficient, as your own employees are free to concentrate their expertise on your event.

Conference centres <u>enable</u> you to project a positive image of your company. Their staff are trained to set up these events and are experts in this field, giving you the opportunity to host a successful meeting, without the stress.

Conference Centres | A2

Exercise – Deciding on a conference venue

Background

Your company needs to find a suitable conference centre for its delegates.

	Benner's	Meadowlands	Oakfield Arms	The Brandon	Horan's
meeting rooms	11	29	16	21	6
largest room (amphitheatre)	–	170	80	120	–
largest room (ballroom)	180	550	390	400	650
computer labs	–	2	–	1	–
guest rooms	70	110	100	150	140
guest suites	–	10	6	–	–
PC workstation	✓	✓	✓	✓	–
internet access	–	✓	✓	✓	–
lounges	–	2	1	1	–
fitness room / gym	–	✓	✓	✓	✓
sauna	–	✓	–	✓	–
pool	–	✓	–	✓	–
office services	✓	✓	✓	–	✓
video conferencing	–	✓	✓	✓	✓
notebook rental	–	✓	✓	–	–
mobile phone rental	–	✓	–	–	–
car rental	✓	✓	✓	✓	✓
car parking	300	780	480	610	650
distance from airport	8 miles	4 miles	5 miles	2 miles	2 miles
shuttle service	–	✓	–	✓	–
RATING	** (2)	***** (5)	**** (4)	**** (4)	*** (3)

A 2 | Conference Centres

Assignment

Look at the table and answer the questions with a single word or figure.

1. Which centre has the largest amphitheatre?
2. How many centres have a computer lab?
3. How many centres have a pool?
4. Which centre has more guest rooms than *Horan's*?
5. How many centres don't provide internet access?
6. How many hotels have parking for 500 cars?
7. Which center has the largest ballroom?
8. How many centres provide office services?
9. How many centres have fewer than 15 meeting rooms?
10. How far is the *Meadowlands* away from an airport?
11. Does the *Oakfield Arms* have more meeting rooms than *Horan's*?
12. Which centre doesn't offer video conferencing?
13. Which centre is farthest from an airport?
14. Does *Horan's* have a lounge?
15. Which centre has the lowest rating?
16. How many centres offer a shuttle service?
17. How many centres rent mobile phones and notebooks?
18. Which centre doesn't provide office services?
19. How many centres have more than 100 guest rooms?
20. Could you rent a notebook at *The Brandon*?

CONFERENCE CENTRES | **A 2**

Exercise – Requesting information

Background

Sie haben die Aufgabe, weitere Informationen über geeignete Tagungsorte zu beschaffen.

Assignment

Schreiben Sie eine E-Mail an das *Conference Centre Cork* (info@ccc.ie) und fordern Sie eine aktuelle Broschüre und Preisliste an.

New Email	
To:	
CC:	
BCC:	
Subject:	

[Send] [Cancel]

A 3 Presentations

<u>Prior</u> to your presentation, give yourself <u>ample</u> preparation time. It is essential you understand the topic you wish to present. Find out in advance, what the person <u>assessing</u> your work feels is important and which points to focus on. Ensure all your information is up-to-date and relevant to your topic. Avoid textbooks, as the information given may not be suitable for many reasons, e.g. no longer relevant, companies referred to are no longer in business, theories are <u>outdated</u>. Good sources of suitable data are the internet, journals, and current business magazines. Other possible <u>sources</u> are the media and the financial press.

prior – vor, bevor, vorher
ample – ausreichen, genügend
to assess – beurteilen, bewerten
outdated – überholt, veraltet
source – Quelle
to simplify – vereinfachen
concise – präzise, prägnant
vital – unerlässlich, wesentlich
brief – kurz
spelling – Rechtschreibung
unable – nicht in der Lage

Work out which are the most important points of your presentation, and <u>simplify</u> them. Aim to keep it as short and <u>concise</u> as possible. Ideally it should be 15 to 20 minutes long, as people tend to lose concentration after this time.

Construct your ideas in a way that they follow on from each other and don't use charts and tables. Only use them if necessary, as they are time-consuming and complicated. It is <u>vital</u> to the success of the presentation to stay within your time. Allow 1 to 2 minutes for an explanation on each slide. You shouldn't have more than 5 to 6 key points per slide. Your key points should be presented on slides, you are there to communicate the details. Avoid complicated backgrounds, as these are distracting.

On average, one would use 10 to 15 slides for a 20 minute presentation. Explain <u>briefly</u> to your audience the form your presentation will take. Remember to check the <u>spelling</u> on your slides.

Ensure you have a back-up, in case you are <u>unable</u> to use PowerPoint (problems with the PC or the projector) and provide yourself with a back-up copy of your slides for an OHP (overhead projector). Be prepared to use the board to list key points.

Always appear enthusiastic, use positive body language and keep eye contact with the audience. To put the presentation across confidently, you must be able to talk with ease about your ideas. Practise with friends or at home, in front of a mirror. Avoid reading from cue cards and don't fidget. This leaves the audience with the impression you don't know what you are talking about and people find it very distracting.

At no point during the presentation sit down. Stand in a comfortable position. Don't pace or sway.

Checklist – Presentations

Ask yourself the following questions:
- ✔ What is the purpose of the presentation?
- ✔ Who is my audience? Why are they here?
- ✔ What questions might arise?

Before the presentation:
- ✔ PREPARE, PREPARE, PREPARE
- ✔ Know much more, than you'll ever say.
- ✔ Memorize the first and the last two minutes of your presentation.
- ✔ Arrive early and socialize with the audience as they arrive.
- ✔ Check out the equipment.

During the presentation:
- ✔ Immediately establish eye contact with the audience and smile.
- ✔ Speak at a fairly rapid pace to keep the audience's attention.
- ✔ Don't read your speech. Remember to smile. It relaxes you and your audience.
- ✔ Speak only after you have established eye contact.
- ✔ Don't lean on or hide behind the podium.
- ✔ Don't apologize or make excuses. It decreases credibility and brings the problem to the top of the participants' minds.
- ✔ Never say "Before we take a break …". You'll lose your audience.
- ✔ Don't give handouts before your presentation.
- ✔ If you ask for questions and there are none, have one closing thought prepared so you can formally close on a positive note and won't be left hanging.

Handling hostile questions:
- ✔ Repeat or paraphrase questions in a positive way. This will give you time to think.
- ✔ As you respond, gradually shift your body language and eye contact away from the hostile questioner.
- ✔ Continue with next point in presentation.

A 3 — Presentations

Exercise – Arranging hotel reservations

Background

You work in the office of a consulting firm and are responsible for hotel reservations.

You have received the following message on your answering machine:

"*Kate* is looking into things at *ITC Ltd* in *Galway*. Steve needs to stay for a night at *Benner's* in *Limerick*. He is paying *OfficeLine* a short visit, first thing on the 8th. *DataTec* has specifically asked for *Declan*. He must have left a good impression the last time he was there. He will stay at the *Brandon* in *Tralee*. *John* will need 5 days at *Bewley's* in *Dublin*. He would like to stay the four nights at the *Oakfield Arms*. He has to leave again on the 26th as he has an assignment in *Cork* for the 27th. *Kate* has to be there by the 17th. I suppose she'll need 3 nights, so book her into *Horan's*. *Declan* wants to get there on the 4th, but he reckons that 2 nights will do."

Assignment

Complete the table and list the companies in alphabetical order.

Hotel Reservations

Company	Town	Hotel	Arrival	Departure	Consultant

Exercise – Booking a hotel room

Background

Sie haben die Planung abgeschlossen und nehmen gegenwärtig die Hotelbuchungen vor.

Assignment

Schreiben Sie eine E-Mail an das *Oakfield Arms* Hotel (bookings@oakfield-arms.ie) und buchen Sie ein Zimmer für *John O'Sullivan* vom 22. bis zum 26. des Monats. Teilen Sie dem Hotel darüber hinaus mit, dass ein Mietwagen bereitgestellt werden soll. Bitten Sie um eine Bestätigung per Fax.

A 4 Telephoning

In today's business world it is <u>likely</u> you will have phone contact with English speaking <u>customers</u> and <u>suppliers</u>. Telephoning in a foreign language is less <u>daunting</u> if you try to relax – so don't panic! Always remember, the person you are speaking to will understand that your English is not <u>word perfect</u>. They probably deal all the time with other people who are not native speakers. It is also safe to <u>assume</u> that they cannot speak all languages.

likely – wahrscheinlich
customer – Kunde
supplier – Lieferant
daunting – beängstigend, erschreckend
word perfect – perfekt auswendig gelernt
assume – annehmen
notes – Notizen
advisable – ratsam
to look up – nachschlagen, nachschauen
phrase – Redewendung

When making these calls, think about what you want to say and why you are calling. Makes <u>notes</u> before the call with references to the conversation. It is <u>advisable</u> to <u>look up</u> any vocabulary you will be using during the conversation. Learn the typical key <u>phrases</u> and when to use them in the conversation.

It is important to speak clearly and be <u>articulate</u>. <u>State</u> who you are and the <u>reason</u> why you are calling, e.g. "This is .... I am calling about ....". When talking to native speakers it is natural for them to speak at a normal speed. <u>However</u>, this may prove too fast for you. Control the call by asking them to <u>repeat</u> what they have said, asking them to speak more slowly, and to <u>spell</u> words you are not <u>familiar</u> with. And if you don't know the English alphabet, learn it. By asking these things you will <u>avoid</u> any misunderstandings, which – remember – neither of you want. <u>Confirm</u> important details immediately, especially any dates or addresses given. Listen carefully to the phrases and vocabulary that are being used. It is likely you will be able to use the same phrases later in the conversation. This shows the other person that you are listening to what they are saying and they, in turn, will make more of an <u>effort</u> to help you understand. It also creates a positive atmosphere which is important to the impression you leave.

articulate – verständlich, deutlich, artikuliert
to state – angeben
reason – Grund
however – jedoch
to repeat – wiederholen
to spell – buchstabieren
familiar – vertraut, bekannt
to avoid – vermeiden
to confirm – bestätigen
effort – Anstrengung, Bemühen, Mühe

Begin and end your call politely. "I would like some more information …" sounds much better than "I want some more information …". And don't forget to thank them for their help.

Key vocabulary

area code – Vorwahl
country code – Ländervorwahl
directory enquiries – Auskunft
directory/phone book – Telefonbuch
extension – Durchwahl
to hang up – auflegen
to hold on – am Apparat bleiben
to take a message – eine Nachricht entgegennehmen
to leave a message – ein Nachricht hinterlassen
to call back – zurückrufen
to put through – durchstellen, verbinden
yellow pages – Gelbe Seiten
local call – Ortsgespräch
long-distance call – Ferngespräch

Key phrases

Ein Gespräch entgegennehmen (Answering the phone)

Good morning/Good afternoon, ... speaking.
This is .... speaking.
Who's speaking, please?
Who would you like to talk to Sir/Madam?
How can I help you?

Nach jemandem fragen (Asking for someone)

Good morning, this is .... calling from ....
I'm calling about ....
I am returning your call.
I'd like to speak to ...., please.
Could you put me through to ...., please?
Could I speak to someone who is in charge of ...., please?
Could I speak to someone who is responsible for ...., please?
Could I speak to someone who deals with ...., please?
Am I speaking to ....?

A 4 | Telephoning

Schwierigkeiten (Difficulties)

Say again, please.
Could you repeat the address, please?
Could you give me the address again, please?
Sorry, I didn't catch that.
I can't hear you very well.
Could you speak up, please?
I'm sorry, but you must have dialled the wrong number.

Den Anrufer verbinden (Putting the caller through)

I'll put you through to ....
I'll put .... on the line.
One moment please, I'll see if .... is available.
I'm sorry, there's no reply from ....
Just a moment, please. I'll put you through.
I'm sorry, the line is engaged.
I've tried to get through several times, but it's always engaged.
I'm afraid he's away on business.

Den Anrufer bitten zu warten (Putting the caller on hold)

Just a moment, please.
Hold on, please.
Hold the line, please.

Den Anrufer bitten noch einmal anzurufen (Asking someone to call back)

I'm sorry, ... is in a meeting.
I'm afraid she's not in the office today.
Could you call back later in the day?
Would you like to call back later?

Eine Nachricht entgegennehmen (Taking a message)

Can I take a message?
Can I give him/her a message?

Would you like to leave a message?

Can I take your details?

I'll tell him that you've called.

I'll give her the message as soon as possible.

I'll make sure he calls you back as soon as possible.

Can she call you back when she gets in?

Could you spell that, please?

What was your name again, please?

At what number can you be reached?

Could you give me your number, please?

Eine Nachricht hinterlassen (Leaving a message)

I'd like to leave a message for ....

Could you ask him to call me back later/tomorrow/in the afternoon?

My telephone number is ....

Das Gespräch beenden (Ending the call)

Thank you for your help.

Thank you very much. Goodbye.

You're welcome. Goodbye.

Checklist – Leaving messages on an answering machine

- ✔ Make clear who is calling by giving your full name, company, and position.
- ✔ Always give the date, time and day of the week.
- ✔ Give your phone number clearly, and then repeat it slowly, so the other person is not forced to listen to the whole message again.
- ✔ Leave detailed messages so that a response isn't always necessary.
- ✔ Don't forget to thank the other person at the end of your message.
- ✔ Never delete a message until you have successfully returned the person's call.

A 4 | Telephoning

Exercise – Scheduling job interviews

Background

You work as a personnel manager for a small company. You are discussing the current job applications with your colleague Helen.

Helen: I can see you have the new applications …

You: Yes, just reading through them …

Helen: Do you plan to interview next week?

You: Yes, I have arranged them for Wednesday.

Helen: Can you do all the interviews, or do you need me?

You: I could do the first four, starting at 9 am. Can you do the last two?

Helen: If we allow half an hour each and break for coffee after the third interview for quarter of an hour, we should finish before lunch.

You: Do you want to go over them?

Helen: Yes, good idea. Well, we have *John O'Shea* and *Bridget Connell*. Both sound suitable for the job and they are both the same age, 25. And then there's another woman. She is two years younger than them.

You: Can I see?

Helen: Of course. Here you are. *Ann Caffrey*, she is with *OfficeWorks* with *John O'Shea*.

You: Who else do we have?

Helen: There are *Maureen Sullivan* and *Noel Casey*, both work at *Parker Smyth*. Noel is 21. *Maureen* is five years older than him.

You: And finally there's *Mary O'Donovan* who is 22. She is presently without a job.

Helen: I will arrange the interviews in alphabetical order, using the surnames, if that's okay.

You: That's fine. Wait … Noel doesn't work for Parker Smyth anymore. He's now with *TrendLine*. How could I forget … he send me an email last week.

Helen: Where does *Bridget Connell* work?

You: She's used to work at *OfficeWorks* but is now with *Giles*.

Telephoning | A 4

Assignment

Use the information from the conversation to fill in the interview schedule.

Interview Schedule

Applicant's Name	Age	Present Employer	Starting Time

A 4 | Telephoning

Exercise – Arranging an interview

Background

Sie haben den Zeitplan für die Interviews erstellt und müssen nun die Bewerber zum Vorstellungsgespräch einladen.

Assignment

Schreiben Sie eine E-Mail an Bridget Connell (bridget.connell@webmail.com) und laden Sie die Bewerberin zu einem Gespräch am Mittwoch, dem 9. April 2003 um 10.00 Uhr ein. Bitten Sie Bridget Connell alle relevanten Zertifikate mitzubringen. Schicken Sie darüber hinaus eine Kopie der E-Mail an Ihre Kollegin Helen Smyth (helen.smyth@pc-company.ie).

New Email
To:
CC:
BCC:
Subject:
Send   Cancel

A 5   Business Skills

In order to advance and succeed in business, there are certain skills you need to develop. **Leadership** is the most obvious skill you will need. To lead, you need strength of character, integrity, and conviction. You must be willing to take risks and accept responsibilities for these actions. The ability to motivate people to work towards a common goal is essential. Lead by example, which will determine your ability to inspire.

to advance	– vorankommen, vorwärts kommen
to succeed	– Erfolg haben
to develop	– entwickeln
conviction	– Überzeugung
to determine	– bestimmen, entscheiden
familiar	– vertraut
to benefit	– nutzen, von Vorteil sein

You cannot advance in business today, without **technical expertise**. Technology is the driving force of the economy and all businesses need to use it. Become familiar with your firm's technology. Keep up with new technologies and innovations that could benefit the company in the future.

Communication is an ability which is acquired by proper listening. Many people forget that fact, logical as it is. How can you introduce new ideas, if you do not listen to your staff? Good communication is multifaceted. Eye contact, patience, and a versatile vocabulary are essential to this skill. Speak with clarity and confidence to deliver your message. An expert communicator can make up for deficiencies in other areas – so maximize on this skill!

To succeed in international business, **language skills** are essential. A second or third language is a powerful asset to your business dealings. Popular choices in the corporate world today include English, Spanish, Mandarin, and Japanese.

Another essential trait is **business savvy**, which is the collection of knowledge about your industry and company. What is the driving force of the industry? Who are the major players and how do they interact? Read a variety of business publications to keep up. It is crucial to familiarize yourself with the company beyond your department. How do main business functions operate? How does information flow? Talk to the people who decide on the fate of your firm. Never hesitate ask a relevant business question.

ability	– Fähigkeit
patience	– Geduld
versatile	– vielseitig
deficiency	– Defizit, Mangel, Unzulänglichkeit
savvy	– Sachverstand, Wissen
crucial	– entscheidend
fate	– Schicksal

Financial knowledge is vital to the success of your firm. Revenue is what determines the survival of a company. Without it, a company will fail. The goal is to achieve a profit. The problem is that some people are so removed from this aspect of business, they lose touch with the bottom line. This is a common syndrome with a company's IT department. An IT manager is so preoccupied with system maintenance, he loses sight of the profit needed. Keep in mind the financial health of your company. Think of ways to bring money into the company.

Learn to solve problems. The ability to devise a solution to a major problem will set you apart from others. Find out what the most common problems are. Is it a lack of staff communication, a technical issue, or an information bottleneck?

Solution detection is a skill you must exercise and publicize. The most driven people set everything aside to tackle major problems. Don't become complacent. Make something happen and get noticed.

Exercise – Making a reservation

Background

Helen O'Brien, a colleague of yours, who is currently on business in Ireland, has to visit a number of customers in Cork.

SouthBridge Investments plc
12 Kingsway
London WC2B 6XF

Phone: 020 7648 7410
Fax: 020 7648 7400
Email: enquiries@southbridge.co.uk

I'm almost finished in Galway and have to go on to Cork now.
Book me into the Meadowlands - a single room with bath and shower.
I'll get there about 7 in the evening on the 21st.
I'm staying for two nights and I'll need a car and internet access.
Their fax number is 00353 21 377 855.

Thanks
    Helen

A 5 | BUSINESS SKILLS

Assignment

Use the note to fill in the hotel booking form for your colleague.

Hotel Booking Form

COMPLETE IN BLOCK CAPITALS

Hotel _____   Fax _____

Town _____

Name _____

Company _____

Address _____
_____

Telephone _____

☐ single room   Check-in _____
☐ double room   Check-out _____
☐ twin-bedded room   Other requirements:
(Please tick)   _____
                       _____
                       _____

Date _____
Signature _____

Exercise – Finalizing details

Background

Das *Meadowlands* Hotel hat sich mit Ihnen in Verbindung gesetzt, da man weitere Details zum gewünschten Mietwagen benötigt (Typ, Versicherung etc.).

Assignment

Schreiben Sie eine Kurzmitteilung (SMS, maximal 160 Zeichen) an Helen O'Brien und teilen Sie ihr mit, dass sie sich mit dem Hotel in Verbindung setzen soll, um die Details zu klären. Die Rufnummer des Hotels lautet 021 377 888.

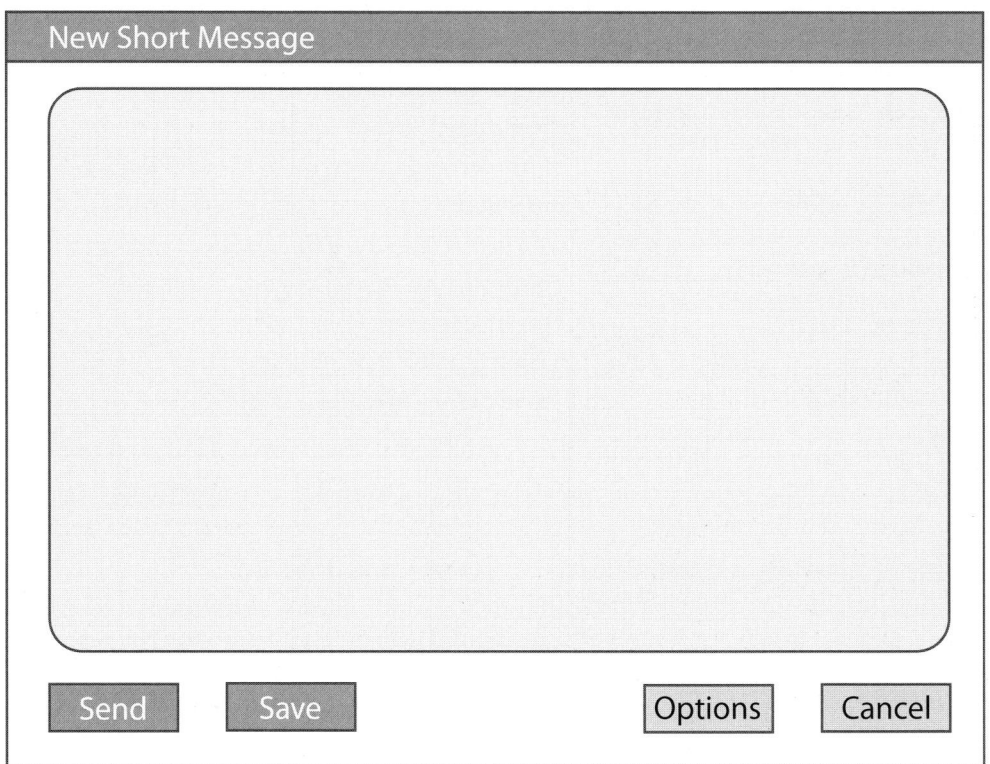

A 6   Conversation Skills

Conversation is about good social contact which is <u>essential</u> to successful business. All things being equal, people prefer to do business with friends. All things being unequal, people still prefer to do business with friends.

Within the business world today, you will <u>encounter</u> business people from abroad. It is generally accepted when <u>conducting</u> business with English speaking people to adopt a more friendly <u>approach</u>. It is normal practice to introduce yourself using your first and last name. You will find on the introduction being returned, first name use will be <u>suggested</u>, e.g. "Hello Mr Murphy. I am Ann Doyle, but please call me Ann". If people use your first name don't continue to use their <u>surname</u>.

After you have been introduced the <u>opportunity</u> for conversation arises. It is best to stick to safe <u>topics</u>. Ask about their flight or journey. Offer refreshments to create a more relaxed atmosphere. Talk about where your guest is from and where you come from yourself. Suggest places of interest or any events taking place while the person is visiting. These are good ways to keep the conversation flowing. It gives you the opportunity to learn more about the person you are dealing with. Listening is very important and will help you interact more effectively with the other party.

essential	– unentbehrlich, wichtig, erforderlich
to encounter	– begegnen, treffen
to conduct	– führen, leiten, betreiben
approach	– Haltung, Vorgehensweise
to suggest	– vorschlagen, empfehlen
surname	– Nachname
opportunity	– Gelegenheit, Möglichkeit
topic	– Thema
appropriate	– passend, geeignet
to avoid	– vermeiden

British people consider politeness very important and are not as direct as other cultures, e.g. after seeing a presentation they would not say "I didn't like it". They would soften it by saying "I am not sure about it". To help you with the conversation ask "open questions" that are not simply answered with "Yes" or "No". Answer questions fully and add any <u>appropriate</u> comments. Know when you have worn out a topic and introduce a new one.

Bring the conversation to a close politely, e.g. "Nice to have met you" or "I will see you at the meeting tomorrow".

Subjects to <u>avoid</u> are personal issues (as you are in danger of sounding insincere or overly flattering), religion (as it is such a diverse subject and usually considered private), politics (because it is either very interesting or extremely boring), and internal affairs (as you have no way of knowing where the person stands on these issues).

Be friendly, relaxed and always be positive when remarking on their country or culture.

Exercise – Selecting a supplier

Background

Your company is looking for a new supplier.

Supplier	nearest delivery outlet (miles)	established	delivery time (days)	discount (per cent)	credit period (days)	staff
StarLine plc	3	1962	7	3	90	52
Smyth & Co	7	1970	5	10	90	11
SilverStar Ltd	10	1953	2	7	30	16
ITS Ltd	4	1921	7	2	14	27
Murhy & Sons	2	1992	7	5	0	14
Boyle & Co	15	1980	10	3	30	9
RCS Ltd	8	1967	2	0	14	22
Smith & Co	12	1920	1	2	0	10
TMT Ltd	9	1998	14	5	0	18
NewLine plc	6	1972	3	0	0	43

A6 Conversation Skills

Assignment

Look at the table and answer the questions with a single word or figure.

1. How many suppliers are listed?
2. Which supplier offers a better discount than SilverStar Ltd?
3. How many suppliers deliver in less than 7 days?
4. How many suppliers have fewer than 20 staff?
5. Has TMT Ltd been in business for over 10 years?
6. How many suppliers offer a shorter delivery time than StarLine plc?
7. How many suppliers offer a larger discount than TMT Ltd?
8. Has RCS Ltd been established longer than Smyth & Co?
9. Is ITS Ltd the oldest supplier?
10. How many suppliers are a public limited company (plc)?
11. Which supplier has the longest delivery time?
12. How far is the nearest delivery outlet of ITS Ltd?
13. How many suppliers have more than 15 staff?
14. Which supplier guarantees the shortest delivery time?
15. How many suppliers are a private limited company (Ltd)?
16. How many suppliers offer no credit period?
17. RCS and ITS offer the same credit period. Is this true?
18. Which company offers the largest discount?
19. How many suppliers offer more than 5% discount?
20. How many firms give a credit period of more than 2 weeks?

Exercise – Delegating tasks

Background

Sie haben sich für *Smyth & Co* als neuen Lieferanten entschieden.

Assignment

Schreiben Sie an den Einkaufsleiter (*purchasing manager*), *John Carrol*, und bitten Sie ihn, einen Termin mit *Smyth & Co* für die nächste Woche zu vereinbaren. Die Rufnummer von *Smyth & Co* lautet 061 322 749 55.

Memo

To:
From:
Subject:
Date:

A 7 Business Etiquette

Being part of the business world today <u>requires</u> us to have some knowledge of cultural differences. How other nations approach business and what is <u>expected</u> in a social environment. It is normal practice for the British and the Americans to conduct business in a more sociable way. Both, British and Americans consider politeness very important and expect a certain standard of <u>behaviour</u>.

The British are considered a reserved nation and dislike physical contact. It is not common to shake hands when being introduced, as it is for example in Germany, unless you are offered a handshake. The British have a relaxed way of conducting business and are <u>renowned</u> for their sense of humour. During a meeting they will tolerate a certain amount of facts and figures, but will want to come to the point sooner than their European counterparts.

to require	– erfordern
to expect	– erwarten
behaviour	– Verhalten
renowned	– bekannt, berühmt
to appreciate	– schätzen, würdigen
to admit	– hereinlassen, Einlass gewähren
to reorder	– neu bestellen, nachbestellen

When scheduling a meeting in Britain, do not arrange it before 9 am, as it is considered too early. British people tend not to use titles, e.g. doctor or professor. When dealing with Americans always be well prepared. They are a very direct nation and do not like to waste time. Americans business people like to conduct their meetings through tough negotiation and their interest will lie in the end result, not with how this result was achieved. They will <u>appreciate</u> the fact you have not wasted their time with unnecessary details.

There are some points to remember regarding Americans. They do not like to refer to the 'toilet' – they prefer 'bathroom' in a private house or 'restroom' in hotels and restaurants. If you are invited to someone's home, offer to bring dessert or salad. Otherwise you could bring a box of chocolates or something from your own country. Do not bring flowers as you would in Europe. Do offer to help with anything, e.g. the washing-up, and be positive when referring to their country and your visit.

In both countries a dress code is expected. Regardless of whether your meeting is taking place in a hotel, restaurant, or office. A tie is definitely required as certain clubs and restaurants won't <u>admit</u> you without one. In the US and especially in Britain when entering a building hold the door for the person following you. If you are considering giving a gift, ensure it is suitable and tasteful. When it comes to social occasions, there are a few points worth noting. Always ask any ladies present what they would like to drink first. Do not start yours until everyone has their drinks. Wait for the other person to finish their drink before you <u>reorder</u>. When attending large dinner parties, it is acceptable to start your soup or other courses before everyone has been served. This only applies when hot food is being served.

The rule is simply common courtesy that makes for better relationships with other cultures.

Exercise – Processing orders

Background

You have just received the following email from one of your customers:

---

from: thomas.harp@pcplanet.ie
to: orders@pcperfect.com
cc:
bcc:
subject: urgent order - pc equipment
date: Tue, 25 March 2003 11:04:00

We urgently need some PC equipment for our Dublin stores.

Please send us 20 printers - including cables. The cables are EUR 3.50 each and have the catalogue no CA8801. Furthermore, we need the SilverLine Office software (cat no SO3648). 30 should do, I suppose.

We definitely need some recordable DVDs, as well. There are 20 in each box, aren't there? So 40 boxes should be enough this time. The DVDs have the item no ME4486 and are EUR 38.90 per box.

The printers have the number PR1219 and are EUR 169.00 each. The software package is EUR 49.90, if I remember correctly.

Send half of the order to each of our two stores in 8 Grafton Street and 47 Henry Street. And deliver the items on the Friday, as it's usually fairly busy on Saturdays.

Just put the order on our account no 7109224.

Thanks

Tom

A7 | BUSINESS ETIQUETTE

Assignment

Complete the delivery note for the *Henry Street* store.

PC Perfect
27 Baggot Street
Dublin

DELIVERY NOTE

COMPLETE IN CAPITALS

Company   _____

Account No   _____

Ordered on   _____
(date)

Ordered by   _____
(name)

Delivery Address   _____
  _____

Delivery Date   _____

Payment Method   cash ☐   credit card ☐   cheque ☐   account ☐
(please tick)

Catalogue No	Description	Quantity	Unit Price in €

Business Etiquette | A 7

Exercise – Problems with deliveries

Background

Beim Zusammenstellen der Lieferung stellen Sie fest, dass Sie den gewünschten Drucker nicht mehr vorrätig haben.

Assignment

Schreiben Sie eine E-Mail an Thomas Harp (thomas.harp@pcplanet.ie) und teilen Sie ihm mit, dass der gewünschte Drucker (PR1219) zurzeit nicht vorrätig ist und Sie ersatzweise ein anderes Modell (PR1239) zum gleichen Preis liefern werden. Falls ihm die Geräte nicht zusagen, kann er diese in der nächsten Woche selbstverständlich umtauschen.

A 8   Customer Service

All companies are in business to sell their products or <u>services</u>. The customer wants high-quality products at a fair price. To <u>achieve</u> good customer relations, <u>provide</u> good value and make the consumer feel valued.

Deliver what you promised and when you promised it for. <u>Reliability</u> is a key factor to <u>retaining</u> your customers. Your company's image counts – first <u>impressions</u> are <u>lasting</u> impressions and you will not get a second chance to make a first impression. If you don't pay attention to the customer, <u>eventually</u> the customer won't pay attention to you. The main reasons customers stop coming are <u>indifference</u> and bad service.

The majority of customers won't tell if they are unhappy – they just won't come back. According to research, the average person who has a bad-service experience tells at least nine others about it.

Make it a point to take a step back and look at the business from the customer's point of view. Ask yourself: Can we improve our service? Are our opening times <u>convenient</u> for the customers?

Staff training is vital to good customer relations. Your staff represents your company. They are the image that is presented to the customer. Your employees must be able to deal with all kinds of people. When serving customers, use their names and remember to listen to their needs and wants. You are helping people to make decisions – so find out what information they need.

The customer is always right. They <u>vote</u> with their wallets every day. It is worth remembering that they have the power to decide whether you stay in business or not. When dealing with customers' complaints, never argue or blame the customer. Explain how you intend to resolve their problem. Listen to what the customer has to say – whether or not your suggestion is acceptable to them. The most angry customer will find it difficult to maintain anger when dealing with someone who is being helpful and friendly. Thank your customer for bringing your attention to any possible defect in your product and for their feedback. Everybody likes to feel special. You should try to individualize customers. Aim to give a more personal service. Positive word of mouth is your best advertisement.

services – Dienstleistungen
to achieve – erreichen
to provide – liefern, bieten
reliability – Zuverlässigkeit
to retain – behalten, halten
impression – Eindruck
lasting – dauerhaft, anhaltend
eventually – schließlich
indifference – Gleichgültigkeit
convenient – bequem, günstig
to vote – abstimmen, wählen

Customer Service | A 8

Exercise – Managing performance records

Background

Your firm organizes computer training seminars for employees of other companies. A group of 8 participants has just finished a 2-week course on office applications.

A colleague has sent you the following memo:

All of them have finally finished their examinations, well, Patrick didn't turn up for his spreadsheet exam, but that wasn't really a surprise after he failed both of the other exams, word processing and presentations.

Brian Gallagher wasn't bad either. Just missed a distinction in data base but got it in both, word processing and presentations.

Mary Burke did two, word processing and spreadsheets, and passed both with credit.

Pat was the most successful candidate which JTS Ltd has ever sent. Three distinctions and a credit in data base, she's really excellent. She didn't take the word processing exam, as she got that the last time she was here.

Fiona Doyle just took the word processing. And passed, of course.

Ted O'Neill tried the data base, but he failed. Well, it is after all the most difficult exam. Maureen O'Brien tried it as well, and didn't make it either. But she got a credit in the internet one and even a distinction with the presentations.

Mike was quite good, I suppose. Got a credit in presentations, but missed the distinction with the word processing and just managed to get through the spreadsheets.

So we had 20 exams in total, didn't we?

A 8 | CUSTOMER SERVICE

Assignment

You are responsible for maintaining the training records. Use the information from the memo to complete the following training report.

TRAINING REPORT

Company _____

Course Title _____

Course Length _____

D = Distinction
C = Credit
P = Pass
F = Fail
A = Absent

Candidates	Modules					Exam Results
	WORD PROCESSING	SPREADSHEET CALCULATION	DATA BASE	PRESENTATIONS	INTERNET AND EMAIL	
Michael O'Donnell						
Ted O'Neill						
Maureen O'Brien						
Mary Burke						
Patricia O'Leary						
Patrick O'Carroll						
Brian Gallagher						
Fiona Doyle						

Exercise – Requesting resources

Background

Ein Unternehmen möchte bei Ihnen kurzfristig Prüfungen zur Mitarbeiterzertifizierung durchführen lassen.

Assignment

Schreiben Sie an den Leiter der Ausbildungsabteilung (*training officer*) und bitten Sie darum, dass für nächste Woche Donnerstag ein zusätzlicher Prüfungsraum zur Verfügung gestellt wird. Es werden 12 Plätze benötigt und auf allen PCs müssen das Betriebssystem (*operating system*) Windows XP und das Softwarepaket Office XP installiert sein.

Memo

To:

From:

Subject:

Date:

A 9 UK Airports

BAA (British Airports Authority) owns 7 UK airports: Heathrow, Gatwick, Stansted, Glasgow, Aberdeen, Edinburgh, and Southampton. They have contracts with 11 airports outside of the UK, for example Indianapolis in the USA , Naples in Italy and 6 airports in Australia.

Their airports handle almost 200 million passengers worldwide, including 118 million in the UK. Almost 20 % of the international passengers travel through their UK airports.

contract	– Vertrag
links	– Verbindungen
to let	– vermieten
retail facility	– Einzelhandelsgeschäft
currency exchange	– Devisenumtausch
car hire	– Autovermietung
to contribute	– beitragen, beisteuern
destination	– Bestimmungsort, Reiseziel

BAA have developed Stansted as their base for low cost European airlines. They have established the Heathrow Express and Airport Express, securing excellent rail links for their London airports.

They let and manage all the retail facilities in their airports, incorporating foreign currency exchange, car hire, car parks, catering outlets, and shops. They contribute £ 10.2 billion to the UK's Gross Domestic Product per year.

Heathrow, BAA's largest airport, is named after the village of Heathrow where Terminal 3 stands today. It began as a small village in 1946, serving 18 destinations, making 9,000 flights a year. The first departure from Heathrow was to Buenos Aires, via Lisbon, opening up Britain's first air link with South America. The flight took place on 1 January 1946.

Heathrow is the world's busiest airport, handling 64 million passengers in 2000/01. Heathrow averages 1,250 flights a day. With over 90 airlines, serving 160 destinations worldwide. Their busiest routes are New York, Paris, Amsterdam, and Dublin. The USA is the most popular destination. On their busiest day, 29 July 2001, 213,000 passengers passed through the airport.

Heathrow has four terminals, with a fifth presently under construction. Terminal 1 was opened in 1969 by Her Majesty the Queen. It is home to 13 airlines; 24.6 million passengers used the Terminal in 1999.

Terminal 2 was opened in 1955 for short haul flights and was Heathrow's first terminal. It was originally known as the 'Europa' Building. In 1999, 8.2 million passengers passed through the terminal. Today it is used by 28 airlines.

Terminal 3, formerly known as the 'Oceanic' building, was opened in 1961 for long haul flights. It is home to 41 airlines and handles 15.5 million passengers a year.

Terminal 4 was opened in 1986 by the Prince and Princess of Wales. It is home to 6 airlines and averages 14.2 million passengers a year. Terminal 4 is connected to Terminal 1 by an underground transfer tunnel.

Each year over 80 million items of baggage pass through Heathrow. The Lost Property Office receives 200 phone calls per day. An average of 20 mobile phones are lost every day. In their duty free shops they sell over 400 different perfumes. Chanel No. 5 is currently the most popular. Heathrow's perfume sales total almost 10 % of the UK's perfume sales. Whiskey is their best selling spirit. On average one bottle is sold every seven seconds.

Lost Property Office	Fundbüro
currently	gegenwärtig, zur Zeit
to total	sich belaufen auf
facilities	Einrichtungen
runway	Landebahn
to issue	erteilen, herausgeben
fare	Flugpreis, Fahrpreis
government	Regierung
approval	Genehmigung, Zustimmung
to incorporate	vereinigen, verbinden
demand	Nachfrage
increase	Anstieg

Over 26,000 cups of tea, 6,500 pints of beer, and 6,500 sandwiches are sold every day. Over the last five years £ 960 million have been invested in airport facilities. An average of £1 million has been invested every day at Heathrow.

Gatwick, BAA's second biggest airport in the UK, is the sixth busiest international airport in the world. It is the busiest single runway airport in the world. Over 31 million passengers pass through Gatwick every year, a quarter from which are traveling to and from North America. Gatwick is home to around 100 airlines and serves around 200 destinations worldwide. They serve more destinations in the USA, Canada, and the Caribbean than any other UK airport.

Gatwick began as a small flying club and was opened in 1930. It was sold in 1933 to Morris Jackaman for £ 13,500. In 1934, the air ministry issued the first public license for commercial aircraft. 1936 saw Gatwick's first scheduled flight, which was to Paris. The fare cost four pounds and five shillings (equivalent to £ 160.22), including the first class train fare from Victoria.

In 1952, the government gave approval for the development of Gatwick as an alternative to Heathrow. Building began on the new London airport in 1956. It cost £ 7.8 million to build and took 2 years and 9 months to complete. It was opened by Her Majesty the Queen in 1958. Gatwick was the first airport to incorporate air, rail, and road transport as a single unit.

Stansted is BAA's third biggest London airport and their newest in Britain, with a steadily growing demand of airlines wanting to fly from Stansted, and an increase of passengers. Stansted is one of the fastest growing airports in Europe.

Stansted has one terminal and is home to 15 airlines, serving 93 destinations. Presently Stansted handles 13.9 million passengers a year.

A 9 | UK Airports

Exercise – Organizing the collection of guests

Background

You work at the *Westwood Hotel* where you have to organize the collection of guests from the airports. Your manager has given you tomorrow's agenda.

"Five people have to be picked up during the day. *Ted Murphy* is on flight *EI 698* from *Cork*, arriving at 0830 hrs at *Gatwick*. He called earlier to inform us that his colleague, *Mary Lynch*, is going to be delayed in *Milan*. She will not arrive at *Heathrow* at 11 o'clock on *BA 5869* as expected. He said she would phone later to confirm her new time of arrival.

There are two guests to be collected from *Heathrow*. They are *Anne McCarthy*, arriving from *Dublin* at 4 pm and *Owen Carrol*. He is flying in from *Frankfurt*, on *LH 412*, due in at 1400 hrs. Anne's flight number is *EI 502*.

Our last pick-up is at *Stansted*, at 1030 hrs. *Pat Mahony* arriving on flight number *TW 8346* from New York. He would like to be collected an hour later, as he has business at the airport.

Mary Lynch just phoned. She'll arrive at *Luton* at 8.20 pm on *RA 704*."

Assignment

Complete the list in order of pick-up time.

Airport Arrivals

Pick-up Time	Guest	Flight	From	To

UK Airports | **A 9**

Exercise – Changing arrangements

Background

Aufgrund einer Verzögerung in *Mailand* kann *Mary Lynch* nicht wie geplant um 11 Uhr in *Heathrow* landen (Flug *BA 5869*). Sie wird stattdessen mit dem Flug *RA 704* um 20.20 Uhr in *Luton* ankommen.

Assignment

Schreiben Sie eine Kurzmitteilung (SMS, maximal 160 Zeichen), welche *Mary Lynch* an den zuständigen Koordinator im *Westwood Hotel* schicken kann.

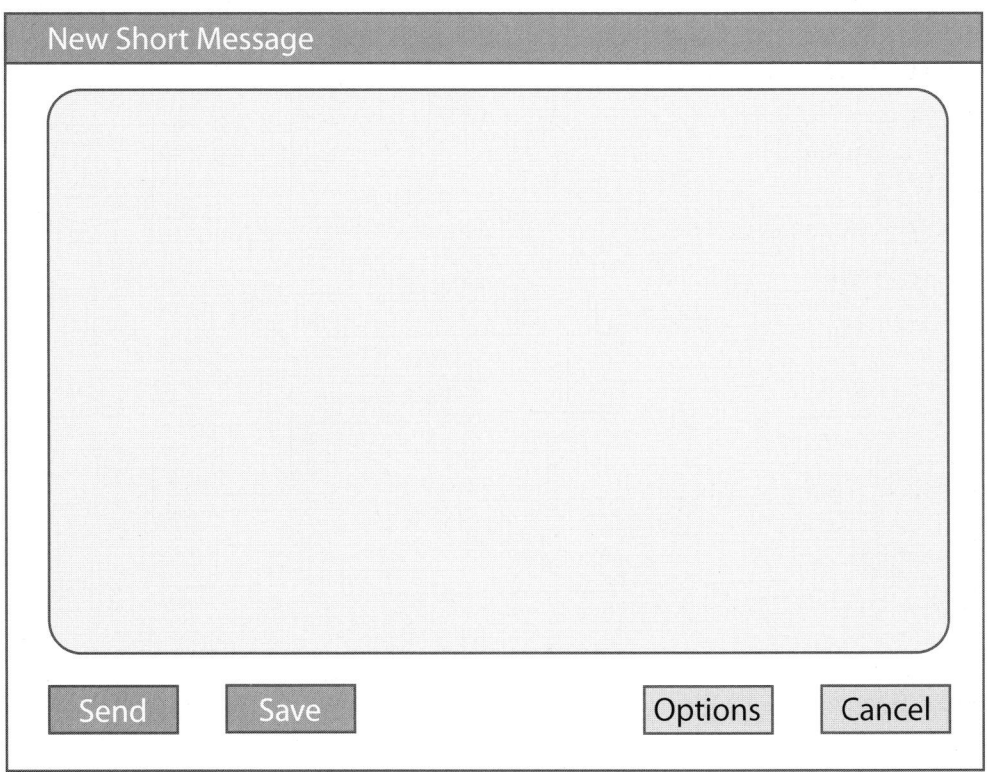

B

Learning English for Business Management

Preview – Part B
Learning English for Business Management

1. Society, Business, Government, and the Global Network Economy
2. Theory of the Firm
3. The Constitution of Business
4. The External Environment and Corporate Culture
5. Business and the Law
6. Top Management Direction
7. Decision-making Processes
8. Human Resource Management
9. Control Concepts for Quality and Productivity
10. Accounting
11. Financial Management
12. Marketing
13. Global Competition
14. Integrating the Total Concept

B   Introduction: Learning English for Business Management

"America's Business is Business!" President Coolidge's famous dictum from 1925 would not seem out of place in the ongoing globalization debate. More than ever, American corporations are leading the world economy. In the year 2002, 197 U.S. firms made it into in the Fortune Global 500 rankings. De facto, U.S. based organizations and institutions are setting worldwide standards for leadership and debate. This primacy is reflected in universally accepted management models and concepts, such as Economic Value Added, the Value Chain, the Balanced Scorecard, and Ethics in Corporate Governance.

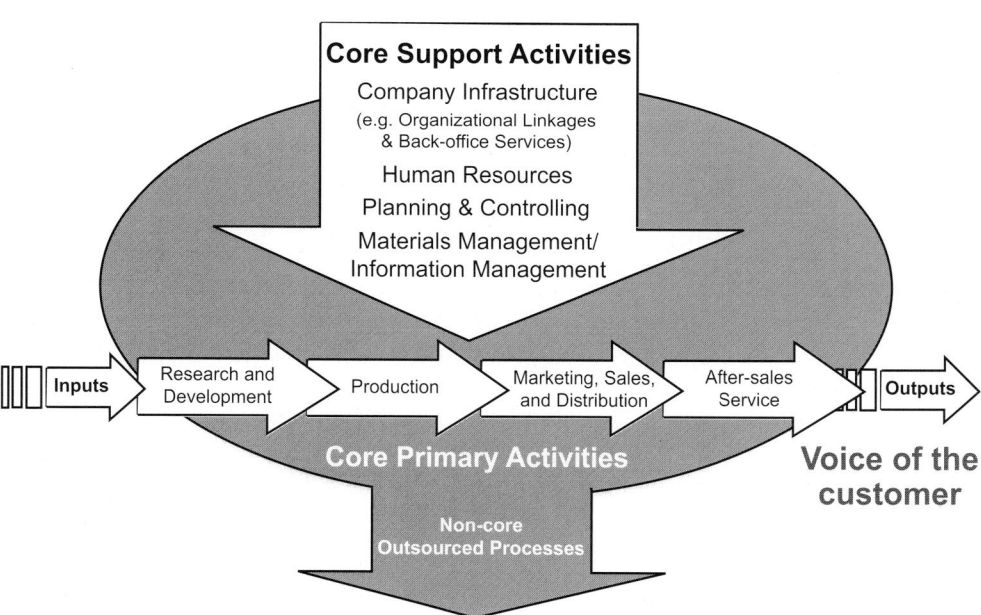

But, while many American CEOs have achieved celebrity status, the collapse of the Bubble Economy in 2000 has also humbled many formerly admired business leaders. The reversed outcomes suggest that a "manager for all seasons" must maintain an open mind to identify and respond to subtle signals of change. In an increasingly complex environment, the sensing of opportunities and imminent threats is closely linked with the ability to the big picture, and to deploy different categories of knowledge – be it in arts, sports, fashion, or science.

> **B** | INTRODUCTION: LEARNING ENGLISH FOR BUSINESS MANAGEMENT

SWOT-Analysis

To an outsider, the reasons for a company's success or failure often seem self-evident. Relative to a company's objectives, an analyst or consultant can easily tell that the company is over-borrowed, that the product pipeline needs to be replenished, or that the changing legal environment is seeding class action.

Accordingly, when an unprejudiced opinion has identified the key issues, it is a sign of professional mastery to set down the main reasons for the widening gap between a company's vision, goals, and SWOTs (i.e. strengths, weaknesses, opportunities, and threats), preferably in the space of one page. For, in confronting organizational slack, a concise analysis is more persuasive and more likely to spur action than a lengthy dissertation, which would cloud the big picture through a blizzard of data and high theory.

The first aim of a business analysis is to build up a picture of the internal strengths and weaknesses of the organization. These would relate to resources, programs and structure in key areas, such as:

- vision, goals, strategies,
- products, operations, quality,
- planning, financing, controlling,
- marketing, sales, distribution.

Furthermore, the external threats and opportunities which may impact a company must be assessed. For example:

- the industry sector, where structural changes may be occurring;
- the labor market which may be changing due to demographic or social factors;
- new competitors who may be creating threats or opportunities;
- new technologies which may transform processes, consumption patterns;
- Investor relations which are subject to changing trends and fashions within the financial community.

As the business analysis aims to present a contingent framework for decision-making, it is necessary to bring together the two dimensions of problem finding and problem-solving techniques. These are the SWOT analysis and a fitting management concept, such as the value chain.

Once the issues and means have been analyzed, alternative solutions bundling a range of possibilities should be developed, among which a final solution will then be recommended to form the basis of a realistic strategic plan.

The SWOT analysis below is designed to illustrate the picture building technique. The analysis is based on an identified purchasing issue in an aerospace company. The analysis relates to the fact that the company is reliant on a sensitive component obtained from a limited supply source.

SWOT Analysis
(Applied to a Supplies Situation)

	Strenghts	Weaknesses
Internal ⮕	– Centralized procurement – Regular demand – Reliability	– Hi-tech imported components
	Opportunities	**Threats**
External ⮕	– Alternative design – Joint venture – Virtual integration with a lead supplier	– Few suppliers – Exchange rates – Legislation

By applying the management model of the value chain, the SWOT analysis will lead to the formulation of strategies at the corporate level (such as developing inter-firm supply chain management), at the business level (such as implementing contingency planning), and at the functional level (such as optimizing the design-to-market process).

Learning Sequence

In this brief introduction we would like to illustrate the unique traits of American business terminology as a special branch of English for Special Purposes (ESP). Frequently, second language learners are preparing for a selected range of professional situations that require command of a professionally accepted body of English firmly rooted in North American business culture. Such focused ESP learners accept that they will practice in a global business environment steeped in North American management practices – with a focus on results and pragmatic problem solving.

With this need in mind, the authors intend is to enact "Business English" as a communication tool for goal-oriented, competitive agents, who will soon be planning, and supervising international business projects. Consequently, the learning sequences in Part B, are committed to the pragmatic intent of making sense of the management context before linguistic sophistication.

B | Introduction: Learning English for Business Management

Phase 1: Terminological Preparation

The content-oriented introduction into new subject knowledge and skills is meant to serve as a platform for new or unfamiliar vocabulary which will be needed in later phases of a course module (e.g. for paraphrasing ideas). The aims of this "semantic" phase are:

- to refresh the language they already know within a business context;
- to focus on the terminology and parts of language used by the student which will be required for the further parts of the course module and forthcoming modules;
- to arouse interest in the new topic by drawing on students' experience and knowledge of the subject area.

Phase 2: Elaboration

The ideas, thoughts and subject-specific terminology from the semantic phase will be applied in tasks and activities (e.g. question-discussion/presentation phase).

Phase 3: Consolidation

The results of the second phase will now be organized and structured by the students in a wider and more concrete application of the results from phase 2. Two methods are used in this course:

- Transferring and applying the results into a different situation or example, specified in a text-based business case.
- An experiential task in which the students apply the results of the previous phase in a new context (e.g. from the perspective of a specific managerial mindset).

Disclaimer:

Management concepts are not checklists or simple rules: they are tools for evaluating opinions and assessing behavior, and each scenario demands its own interpretation and analysis. Consequently, the outcome will be a personal, and not a universally valid solution.

The series of cases below are drawn from situations faced by international managers. The cases are designed to represent "messy" real-life information mosaics. As such, they contain some redundant data, and lack a clear structure.

Using the concepts and techniques in the chapters to analyze and evaluate these situations will sharpen analytical and conceptual language skills that can be transferred to future work scenarios. Hence, the cases are intended as a basis for debate rather than to illustrate effective or ineffective handling of specific management situations.

SWOT Case: STMicroelectronics – Testing the Fabric of a Doughnut Structure

2001 turned out to be the worst year in the history of the semiconductor family. But not, it seems, for all players. For STMicroelectronics (ST), it seemed, the constellation was favorable, with its star shining brightly. As Pasquale Pistorio, President and Chief Executive Officer, stated proudly in March 2002, ST had distinguished itself by starry results. While the total industry suffered a revenue loss of 32% and – in ST's industry sector – a loss of 24% ST's revenues merely declined 18.6% on a year-over-year basis. However, compared with previous years, the outcome does not quite reflect a starry performance.

Company Background

In 1987, two loss-making state-owned semiconductor companies, SGS Microelettronica of Italy and Thomson Semiconducteurs of France entered into a merger of equals, eventually regrouping as STMicroelectronics. In the aftermath, the revitalized company grew from a dull 5% market share and a poor 17th rank in chip sales to become the world's Nr.3 chipmaker behind Intel and Toshiba corporations by 2001. Subsequently, in 2002, ST's net revenues were $6.32 billion and net earnings were $429.4 million. According to analysts' rankings for 2002, ST finished among the top five semiconductor manufacturers worldwide for the second consecutive year. At this point in time, the group was offering over 3,000 main types of products to more than 1,500 customers. It had evolved into a transnational company, employing 43,000 people, maintaining 16 advanced R&D units, 39 design and application centers, 17 main manufacturing sites and 88 sales offices in 31 countries.

Post-merger Integration

From its inception, the merger seemed a natural fit. Both companies had advanced technology and experienced management. However, as separate entities locked into their domestic markets, they lacked scale and realized that they could never achieve sustained profitability if they did not move out to source specialist knowledge and deep market understanding in a global reach.

For a time ST maintained dual headquarters, in Paris and Milan. However, dual locations soon proved inefficient. In order not to offend any party, a decision was reached to move headquarters to Geneva, Switzerland, where it now occupies several floors in an office building next to the airport. Although this compromise helped to create a very lean corporate center, many executives felt that it merely succeeded in making Italian and French managers equally unhappy.

At first sight, the Geneva office lacks atmosphere and excitement. Even the executives for whom it is home seldom stay there for an extended period. For instance, they may be teaching or training at a large campus in Agrate, Italy, or at a campus in Crolles, near Grenoble. Or, they are just as likely to be monitoring projects in Seoul, Tapei, Sao Paulo or Izmir. These disparate locations are not peripheral outposts, for the company's facilities in them are ST's distributed functional core. While technology R&D is centralized in Agrate and Crolles, product development is localized in order to be close to the customers around the world.

Although the immediate post-merger phase was conflict-laden, the combined company had many strengths to rely on, among which stand out its deep engineering expertise and empathic partnering skills. Before the merger, SGS and Thomson had already worked together in a strategic alliance to develop and produce a type of chip that retains data even with the power switched off. Also, many top executives had previously worked for big US chip producers such as Texas Instruments Inc. and Motorola Inc. This helped forge a common professional mentality. Equally important to the merged company's future was the deep expertise in analogue technology, the devices that process continuous rather than digital electronic signals. Far from being an obsolete remnant of the pre-digital age, analogue technology pointed the path to a gleaming future.

Product Focus

Essentially, analogue chips are required to manage power, radio frequency transmission, sound and graphics. The proliferation of cellular telephones, wireless computers, and consumer electronics products has created a resurgence of demand for analogue devices in the 1990's, which ST was well positioned to exploit. ST recognized the opportunity to combine analogue functions, such as sound, graphics and power management, together with digital circuitry, such as logic and memory, on a single chip. ST's system on a chip is now ubiquitous, albeit invisible to the average customer. So great is the percentage of ST content in some branded consumer products that many of the company's best customers treat it as a trade secret.

But, in spite of its strong positioning in the analogue industry, ST quickly recognized that it could not exploit its advantage through traditional arm's length relationships with its customers. Because it had to combine its silicon know-how with the customer's system know-how, the traditional buy and sell relationship was transformed into a co-design relationship, based on the willingness to exchange technology. Consequently, each customer can get a custom product.

Partnering Strategy

Flexibility and the ability to partner are keys to maintaining ST's status as a pure chipmaker. Unlike Motorola or many Japanese semiconductor manufacturers, ST has no product line that might compete with that of its customers. And, after many of its competitors have gone "fabless" (i.e. have fully outsourced manufacturing), ST retains the ability to supply customers with complete solutions.

Based on its unique combination of technology and strategy, ST has been able to capture a large percentage of the value-added activities in many markets it serves. Significantly, the company's increasing importance to many of its customers has eroded the boundaries of the supplier/customer relationship. For example, ST has to share component inventories with customers because in many cases it is the sole supplier of a chip that may constitute 90 % of the finished product's technology content.

Because ST was compelled to partner early and intimately with consumer electronic manufacturers in order to convince customers to replace their clunky circuit boards with its system-on-a-chip, it learned to handle the possibility of conflict of interest by establishing effective firewalls between design teams.

Close cooperation and single sourcing of critical components also require ST's customers to make cultural and structural changes. Companies that once relied on their vertical integration and the depth of their engineering capability now depend on linking up with ST for their systems design, manufacturing and packaging. And because sharing proprietary information with, and outsourcing systems development to ST requires trust, the company pursues a gradual approach to partnerships, enhancing confidence by increasing both the percentage of ST content in the customer's product and the closeness of the relationship over years.

Working for Nokia over a period of 10 years, ST evolved from a simple supplier, to a premium supplier, to one of 10 partners. By then, the two companies recognized they had compatible cultures and values, enabling them to set long-term goals and following SOP's together. A governance committee made up of executives from Nokia and ST meet regularly, like a virtual board for the evolved virtual company, and the operation's performance is evaluated just as if it were an independent company. And there are frequent meetings of teams from both companies in development, marketing and purchasing.

ST perceives its suppliers as seamless extensions of the company. To upgrade its manufacturing skills, it cultivates joint development agreements with its own premium suppliers, such as Canon Inc. Through these alliances, ST's engineers are able to ensure that their specific needs are designed into succeeding generations of manufacturing equipment. These alliances have enabled the company to access and assimilate complex knowledge from disparate sources.

Like all chip companies, ST has moved labor-intensive assembly processes (so-called back-end operations) to developing countries like Brazil and Malaysia. On a smaller scale, it has also moved high-value-adding activities, like product development there.

Fostering a Nimble Learning Organization

To facilitate continuous development, ST has made a learning culture central to its strategy. Learning at ST is a distributed, continuous process, in which the company seeks innovative thinking wherever it is based, while pursuing a more formalized and central process with its in-house ST University and adjunct development centers spread out among campuses in southern France, in Sicily, Singapore and Phoenix, Arizona. Furthermore, all employees are required to train regularly at the company's plants around the world.

Linked by Intranet and Web-based collaboration tools, employees do not require a common location to share a project. In addition, ST coordinates development efforts across multiple time zones is through the promotion of virtual teams. For the employees, the price to be paid for working in a virtual environment is the cell phone ringing at any time, day or night at any place. To cope with this exacting schedule, some managers have trained themselves to sleep in three-hour shifts, even when at home, because they never have time to adjust for any single time zone.

When ST identifies a need, or a gap in its knowledge, its policy is to move quickly to place people where that knowledge can be found. Knowing from experience, that unusual ideas can bubble up at unexpected places, only to fall victim to the "not-invented-here-syndrome", ST has established a company-wide award system with ongoing top management support. The company's technical, marketing and manufacturing strengths are matched and further enhanced by a zealous commitment to Quality and Environmental Management (QEM) that has earned many prestigious awards around the world.

One such highlight was the winning of the Malcolm Baldrige Award (MBQA) in 1999. Because gaps in planning and execution quickly transmute into competitive disadvantages in the fast-paced semiconductor field, the judges commended ST's "top-down, bottom-up" strategic planning process. ST primes the process by taking its cues from its customers. Subsequently, the strategic planning process is initiated at the corporate level. In a sequential order, every business unit and sub-unit prepares a headline plan which displays vital targets and performance indicators that are established during the iterative, company-wide review of the plan. In reverse order, lowest-level headline plans roll up to support each successively higher level. The bottom-up cascade culminates with a concise, integrated summary of the entire group's progress toward goals in three major categories: financial, growth, and social.

Structural Risks and Uncertainties

In spite of the many excellent benchmark ratings, some investors are concerned that the lean central organization, which resembles a doughnut in the sense that a ring of porous fabric is built around a hole in the middle – is able to deal with future market disruptions. For example, ST did not participate in the mass lay-offs that most semiconductor companies conducted during the industry downturn of 2001 to save costs. Although new orders did not materialize for almost six months, ST maintained its production capacity – according to the company view – in order to support employee motivation, when business would accelerate again.

Nevertheless, many analysts are concerned that the centerless structure may yet become a liability for this company that has grown so fast from a small regional player to a global leader. In addition to factors discussed above, unfavorable changes resulting from the cyclical demand conditions facing the semiconductor and electronic systems industries might easily cause excess or obsolete inventory.

The breathtaking pace of technological change is a relentless challenge for the chip industry. Technological change could easily result in a new disruptive product development by key customers that in turn could benefit newly emerging or more diversified competitors. In addition, ongoing reengineering efforts of key customers might lead to changes in order patterns that would favour low-cost suppliers for standard components. The communication and information industries are maturing in ways that will affect technology component suppliers for years to come.

The industry, according to some industry executives, has entered "the post-technology era". The steady advances in chips, disk storage and software mean that the focus is no longer on the technology itself, but on how people and companies can use it. As a result, the balance of power is shifting away from technology suppliers and toward their corporate customers. At the same time, the use of lower-cost building blocks of component hardware is spreading, making it easier for companies to share data, using industry standards rather than depending on one or two main suppliers. These trends would mean increased pressure on prices and profits for corporate customers, for their component and system suppliers, and – in funding decisions – a very tricky time for investors. Many fear that in the coming years gross profit and gross margin will be relentlessly squeezed by a combination of intense pricing pressure, a weakening dollar, and a shift in demand to standardized components.

Mr. Pistorio must now ponder for how long a policy of achieving glowing reports from incremental improvements in manufacturing efficiencies will stave off investors' calls for a more ambitious vision.

B 1 Society, Business, Government, and the Global Network Economy

- Economic Goals and Measurements
- Economic Fundamentals in the Global Network Economy (GNE)
- Competitive Aspects of the GNE
- Regulatory Challenges of the GNE
- Case Study Approach
- Strategy Case: Nortel
- Mindset Management
- The Linked Mindsets Framework
- Experiential Case: Feeling Sidetracked

B 2 Theory of the Firm

B 1 Society, Business, Government, and the Global Network Economy

B 1.1 Principles – Models – Practices

Economic Goals and Measurements

At the turn of the century, all economic indicators were signaling an era of uninterrupted economic growth. And, with China, the world's most populous and fast-growing country, joining the World Trade Organization (WTO) in December 2001, the trend to globalized growth seemed irreversible. But, just three months later, the relationship between the world's biggest trading partners had reached a crunch point. Exacerbated by a sudden economic downturn, the USA introduced "safeguard" tariffs on foreign steel, thereby triggering a tit-for-tat debate on possible protectionist and retaliatory measures. That verbal escalation gave an ominous warning that free trade and the multilateral system of dispute settlement were secondary issues when they collided with national moods and domestic political pressures.

In every society, seemingly contradictory strands in economic debate reflect the history, traditions, collectively held beliefs, and vested interest of its members. And, although each has society different values, civic institutions, and commercial traditions, many concepts have been developed to compare the success of different economic systems in quantitative terms. The basic standard measure of an economy's performance is gross domestic product (GDP) – the monetary value of all the final goods and services produced by an economy over a given period of time.

> **gross domestic product** – Bruttoinlandsprodukt
> **benchmark** – Vergleichsgröße
> **scope** – Umfang, Reichweite
> **bribery** – Bestechung
> **bidding** – Preiswettbewerb
> **small scale** – kleinere, in kleinem Umfang
> **to barter** – tauschen
> **to estimate** – schätzen

However, GDP as a benchmark may lead to many misinterpretations. For example, the relative level and changes in the environmental quality of life are not included, and also the value the underground economy is not reflected in the figures. For example, the scope of bribery in bidding for contracts is left out, as are unreported small-scale transactions between individuals. Furthermore, the value of bartered goods and services can only be estimated because money is not used in the transaction. However, in most societies, the unreported payments of the "underground" economy represent a substantial portion of GDP.

Economic Fundamentals in the Global Network Economy (GNE)

All economic theories feature needs, scarcity and competition as the basis of human action. Because resources are scarce, individuals – solitary actors or collectively organized – are required to make economic choices in order to grow or, at a minimum, to survive.

Achieving a competitive advantage is vital, because, in the global marketplace, the chances are that someone else will be trying to market something similar. And, as potential customers are free to buy where they please, there will be competition for those customers' business on price, quality, or innovation.

C. E. Wilson, a former chairman of America's biggest automotive company, once coined the memorable phrase that what was good for General Motors was good for the United States. Indeed, one generation ago, vested business interests were represented forcefully by long-established companies like Exxon, Coca-Cola and GM. Today, there are many "global players" that did not even exist in 1975 – for example, media giants like Time-Warner-AOL, IT champions like Microsoft and pioneering biotech firms like Celeron and Biogen.

What apparently distinguishes these companies from their predecessors is that their primary product is mobilizing ideas on a global scale, or, in economic terms, leveraging distributed intellectual capital. Because traditional accounting rules tend to downplay the value of intangible assets like brand recognition, or the knowledge generated in research departments, the so-called "network" companies often have a high market value relative to the book value of their equity. Complicating the matter, a large number of long-established companies in mature industries also claim to have successfully transformed their organizations into nimble global network structures, thus boosting their market value.

intangible – immateriell
assets – Vermögensgegenstände
equity – Eigenkapital
shareholder value – Aktienwert

Taking into account the symbolic dimension of global corporations as indicators for the health of international business, C. Wilson's maxim could be rephrased, as follows: "if it's good for the Globally Networked Corporation, it's good for the world." Therefore, it would seem appropriate to reward top managers with incentive schemes that would create a bias towards optimism and risk-taking. However, structures geared to reward performance also attract individuals who are more concerned to enrich themselves than to develop the business. The results are undue risk-taking and poisoned relationships between those at the top and the lower tier employees. Furthermore, a perspective of shareholder value that is based on biased value assessments will attract the attention of regulators. Thus, in 2002, in the wake of pervasive corporate accounting fraud, the Public Company Accounting Oversight Board (PCAOB) was established in the USA to sanitize the auditing process.

Competitive Aspects of the GNE

Among economists, there is substantial agreement about what makes the GNE different for purposes of regulation. The disagreement arises over what should be done to ensure that the GNE works to the benefit of consumers. Companies, as a rule, are not permitted to <u>fix prices</u> with competitors. Economists agree that such collaboration is bad because the result <u>distorts</u> output at the expense of consumers. For example, in the case of <u>mergers</u>, economists argue that the efficiency gains need to be weighed against the greater market power of giant companies. There is also widespread agreement that the <u>antitrust laws</u> are sufficiently flexible to address property rights issues raised by the GNE.

to fix prices	– Preise absprechen
to distort	– verzerren
mergers	– Fusionen
antitrust law	– Kartellgesetz, Kartellrecht
economies of scale	– Größenvorteile
pace	– Geschwindigkeit
to undermine	– schwächen, untergraben
viability	– Leistungsfähigkeit, Erfolgsaussichten
incentive	– Anreiz
possession	– Besitz

In general, GNE companies are knowledge-based. They profit from <u>economies of scale</u> in fields protected by patents and copyrights. In software, for example, it usually requires a large initial investment to produce a prototype, but just small marginal costs to produce further units.

Another GNE characteristic is that the value of a product increases as other related products are developed. For example, as more software applications are written for a computer operating system, the more valuable the operating system becomes to consumers.

A less familiar feature of GNE products is economies of scale in consumption – a phenomenon sometimes referred to as "increasing returns", or "network effects". For example, adding another person to a cellphone network typically makes the network more valuable to other users, if the extra user does not create congestion.

An important social outcome of GNE companies is the accelerated <u>pace</u> of change. Because their activities are based on developing and licensing proprietary information, GNE companies are driven to innovate in ways that <u>undermine</u> the <u>viability</u> of competitors. Ultimately, this intense competitive pressure also leads companies to accelerate revenues and to overstate profits by creative misapplication of accounting rules to the newly evolving business models. Generally, these manipulations involve pulling future revenues forward, valuing expenditures for research as capital expenditures, and overstating licensing revenues.

As the GNE is based on producing and communicating knowledge rather than on manufacturing efficiency, it operates on different principles than the traditional economy. The <u>incentive</u> to produce is to achieve <u>possession</u> of temporary monopoly power – because otherwise the price will be bid down to marginal cost and the high initial fixed costs cannot be recovered. Accordingly, the unrelenting <u>pursuit</u> of that monopoly power becomes the primary goal of the GNE players. In addition, the creative destruction of established structures becomes the essential <u>spur</u> of economic growth. In the resulting "winner take all" markets, the pressure that drives the winners to ever greater efficiency is the <u>threat</u> of the next breakthrough or "killer application" – not the worry that competitors will learn to make the same products at less costs per unit.

A company that is intent on securing a dominant position in the market will often charge a low price, so that it can attract customers. Yet, even after attaining a dominant position, it is unlikely to charge the profit-maximizing price that would be appropriate in a static economic scenario. This price restraint is aimed at maintaining customer goodwill. The company's dominant market power will be unlikely to last unless it maintains a large customer base that is willing to absorb the output of its costly innovation efforts.

> pursuit – Streben, Verfolgung
> spur – Anreiz
> threat – Gefahr, Bedrohung
> to entrust – anvertrauen, beauftragen
> task – Aufgabe, Auftrag
> collusion – Absprachen

Regulatory Challenges of the GNE

The current rise of winner-take-all markets poses a huge challenge for regulating bodies <u>entrusted</u> with the <u>task</u> of identifying and terminating misuse of monopoly power and accounting rules. For, if competition in a GNE industry generates only a single industry champion, it is hard to assess whether the competitive behavior was in line with the ethics of an open society.

One theory frequently used in support of government intervention is that GNE markets have a tendency to "tip". Although a market may initially be easy to enter for competitors, once a company gains a significant lead in sales the market will tip in its favor and give the dominant company market power for a sustained period.

The non-interventionists argue for restraint in regulating GNE markets. They focus on measures of dynamic competition, placing less reliance on market share and mechanical definitions of markets. Non-interventionists explicitly recognize that some activities traditionally viewed as anticompetitive could be good for all stakeholders – consumers, employees and investors – if they trigger a virtuous cycle of linked sales, as in telematics.

Similarly, many economists are open to arguments that consumers and investors benefit from <u>collusion</u> among companies aimed at setting industry-wide standards.

These non-interventionists differ on how to deal with GNE companies that long to dominate a market. They are for examining these issues on a case-by-case basis, giving the dominant company the benefit of the doubt if there are clear benefits to consumers.

And, even when they <u>acknowledge</u> that competition has failed, they resist intervention unless there are good reasons to believe that the <u>remedies</u> would do more good than <u>harm</u>.

Furthermore, non-interventionists argue that GNE markets have a social structure, <u>embodied</u> in long term relationships, <u>mutual trust</u>, and obligations.

acknowledge – eingestehen, bestätigen
remedies – Mittel, Heilmittel
harm – Schaden
embodied – eingebettet
mutual trust – gegenseitiges Vertrauen
reliable – zuverlässig

In general, companies can only maintain an information advantage if they maintain <u>reliable</u> contacts in places where useful information arises. Litigation, in contrast, will promote a general risk-aversive climate marked by defensive behavior and innovation-stifling secretive procedures throughout the industry. This loss of transparency would also lead to a loss of confidence in the capital markets.

Based on the logic of interest groups, on the other hand, it is also predictable that the social networks arising from preferred business relationships will restrict the freedom of companies to choose among other relationships. Therefore, regulators must consider whether to unbundle giant GNE corporations like Microsoft on a merit basis in order to optimize performance within each of several well-defined sectors, or to impose standardized regulatory rules. Also, firms should be required to explain to investors the impact of their accounting system, and to immediately disclose any changes in their business outlook.

B 1.2   Knowledge Check

(1) Explain what an economic system is.
(2) State the object of antitrust policy.
(3) Identify four realities of the GNE.

→ **See Answer Key for solutions.**

B 1.3   Keywords

Economic system; entrepreneur; gross domestic product (GDP); antitrust laws; economics of scale; network effect; congestion; incentive; "winner take all" market; game theory; marginal cost of production; customer base; interventionist; tipping point; collusion

B 1.4 Case Study Approach

Case Study Approach to Problem-Solving

Step 1: Identify the Problem

(a) Assert Claim: Ask yourself, *"What point is being made?"* and accordingly state symptoms for concern or deviation from plan that require immediate attention.

(b) Establish Grounds: Ask yourself, *"What do you have to go on?"* and accordingly identify the fundamental issues and causal factors giving rise to these symptoms or variances.

Step 2: Find Warrant for (i.e. Analyze, Justify) the Identified Problem

Ask yourself, *"What justifies making the connection between your claim and your grounds?"*. In this step you first need to review the information you have about the problem. You may need to make some inferences to fill in gaps, but you must clearly denote what is inference and what is factual. Clearly state the assumptions you are making to fill information gaps. Next, analyze the cause of the problem. Consider appropriate theoretical concepts, models, and analytical approaches that point to feasible solutions.

Step 3: List and Evaluate Alternative Courses of Action

At first, be creative. Then, look critically at the alternatives you came up with. List advantages and disadvantages of each alternative in terms of criteria that seem appropriate (perhaps based on a SWOT analysis).

Step 4: Draw Conclusions, Recommend a Solution

Select the alternative you would recommend and explain/justify your choice. Include specifics about the implementation of your recommendation: who should do what, when, and how.

Step 5 (optional, depending on assignment):

Propose a realistic timeline for implementing the recommended solution. Also, analyze unforeseen problems, and propose a contingency plan.

Suggested Performance Criteria for Grading:

- Rhetorical persuasiveness
- Structure/Consistency
- Analysis/Logic
- Judgement/Creativity

B 1.5 Strategy Case: Nortel

Nortel's Challenge – Transforming the Organization through Supplier Alliances

On 2 Oct 2001, Nortel Networks, based in Brampton, Ontario, announced that they would cut another 10,000 jobs through the sale of businesses, thus shedding more than half the employees they had at the beginning of 2001.

The company, a global supplier of communications equipment, had already announced 30,000 job cuts since problems in the industry began to worsen at the beginning of the year. It began the year with 94,500 employees and expected to have 45,000 after the downsizing.

In addition to the job cuts, Nortel's board announced that it would replace the CEO John A. Roth with Frank A. Dunn, the chief financial officer who had worked at Nortel for 25 years.

Nortel's problems surfaced early in that year after the frenzied construction of communications networks for Internet traffic had slowed down abruptly. Especially the telecoms that had been large buyers of Nortel's switches and fiber optic gear had suddenly come under financial strain. Accordingly, Nortel's sales to carriers that operated "long haul" continental and worldwide communications networks declined from $2.1 billion in the last quarter of 2000 to only about $300 million in the second quarter of 2001.

History

Founded in 1892, Canada's Nortel Networks Inc. produced the switches and other electronic hardware that long distance carriers and local telephone companies used to route voice calls over copper wire. This was considered a stable business in which sales growth was correlated to population growth, or about 3 percent a year.

Nortel had a traditional divisional structure with five product units, acting as semiautonomous companies, each with its own profit-and-loss responsibility. The value chain was vertically integrated, linking processes from raw semiconductor components to circuit boards to finished products. From a competitive perspective, Nortel's competitors, mostly subsidiaries of other telecommunications companies, had similar structures.

In 1997, Nortel's senior management embraced the vision that the future belonged to fiber-optic rather than copper-wire-based telecommunication networks. Nortel saw an opportunity to gain a lead in the emerging Internet market. Their traditional competitor, Lucent Technologies Inc., remained firmly committed to the old telephone networks, and the booming Cisco Systems Inc. was primarily regarded as a maker of equipment for managing LANs.

The customers for this new fiber-optic market were mostly Nortel's old telecom customers, determined not to miss an historic market shift. In addition, a fast-growing customer segment of IT-startups emerged. But it was a market in which Nortel could not hope to become a leader if they continued operating as a traditional manufacturer. Already, aggressive competitors, such as Cisco, were outsourcing heavily, while expanding their product portfolios by an aggressive policy of acquisitions.

Nortel made a strategic choice to model themselves on Cisco's business model. Having achieved revenues of $20 billion, Nortel decided to become $40 billion company within 24 months. The strategic decision to imitate Cisco meant switching from vertically integrated operations to virtual integration and engaging in acquisitions to maintain a technological lead over competitors. Furthermore, Cisco was heavily involved in M&A deals targeted at acquiring innovative technology and intellectual assets, rather than in manufacturing or distribution. For those functions, Cisco drew on their web of alliance partners – suppliers, distributors, contract manufacturers, and commerce and infrastructure services providers.

Imitating the Cisco model, Nortel began aggressively to transfer their production facilities to contract manufacturers like Solectron Corp. and Flextronics, entirely reverse-engineering their production and supply chain management processes from customers to suppliers.

Nortel had traditionally maintained arm's-length relationships with their component suppliers. But to enable a speedy transition to the new business model, these suppliers had to become strategic partners. Nortel would continue selling equipment, but the core competence would reside in their proprietary technology, not in manufacturing. For manufacturing, Nortel have now come to rely on their network of subcontractors.

Initially, Nortel's strategy appeared to be working: They won a 43 percent share of the expanding market for optical networking equipment, which was reckoned to triple, from $31 billion in 1999 to $90 billion by 2003. Analysts said this result mirrored Cisco's optical revenues. But Nortel's total revenues were higher, as their activities still included traditional electronic telecommunications equipment, a market in which Cisco did not participate.

Fragmenting the Vertical Structure

In 1999 and 2000 Nortel spent more than $11 billion in nine months to acquire a bundle of technology companies. Their objective was to buy proprietary technology and talented people, rather than production capacity. In the course of those two years, the company also divested 15 manufacturing sites and transferred 9,000 employees to contract manufacturers.

While much of their manufacturing capacity was sold to contractors, Nortel kept in-house production of most proprietary components, such as semiconductor lasers. In this way, contract manufacturers allowed the company to increase production exponentially without huge capital outlays or massive new construction.

As a large original equipment manufacturer (OEM), Nortel had long outsourced tasks like circuit board assembly to subcontractors. But their relationships with these suppliers were largely tactical. For the new processes to work, Nortel's communication with their suppliers had to become much more frequent and open.

Within the old Nortel model of five lines of business a customer like AT&T had to deal with five different product units. Within the new customer-centric model, each major customer has its own dedicated supply chain management team, which Nortel calls an order house. The order house is a virtual unit, in that team members are typically geographically dispersed and there is no physical plant. The order house works closely with customers to understand their current and future needs, and forwards this information online to all critical suppliers. Nortel shares customer data online with its key suppliers, and meets them face-to-face at the senior executive level at least quarterly.

In the old model, the procurement team acted on purchase orders from the sales team. In the new model, account managers work directly with network deployment staff at the customer to get an early perception of customer needs. This information is given to the order management team, which shares it with key suppliers.

Intelligent Supply Chain Resting on Strategic Partnerships

Major suppliers have experienced a rapid and substantive change in their relationships with Nortel. Their supply chain profited from the knowledge-sharing, enabling them to anticipate Nortel's needs and accordingly align their own mix. This new relationship pattern contrasted starkly with the very bureaucratic and unresponsive the old Nortel.

Within these strategic partnerships, Nortel took an active role in developing e-business tools and service offerings. It was a founding partner of "e20pcn", a Web-based supply chain portal for the telecommunications industry. It also uses a variety of packaged e-business tools in its interactions with suppliers, including programs from Ariba, I2, and Calico. These programs, known as third-party tools, help Nortel's buyers manage component orders and aid Nortel customers in configuring systems. But Nortel's day-to-day, real-time interaction with customers and suppliers was still managed by a proprietary program developed by Nortel's own software engineers.

For more long-term strategic communications, Nortel have instituted a twice-a-year suppliers' forum, featuring the company's senior management, product development teams, and experts from outside. The forum is an occasion for suppliers to gain first-hand information about the company's plans, to give Nortel feedback from their customers, and for the participants to network among themselves.

Formerly, suppliers used to meet only with purchasing managers, or maybe the head of procurement. Under the new rules, suppliers met with the head of the business, thus enabling them to make their own entrepreneurial judgements.

Measures of Success

Nortel have used a variety of workflow metrics to measure the success of their new supply chain management process. For example, the time between receiving a purchase order and generating a shipping date was reduced from two weeks to 48 hours. Day sales outstanding, a measure of outstanding receivables as a proportion of sales, has dropped from 114 at the end of the second quarter of 1999 to 80 in the comparable period in 2000.

The number of suppliers has also dropped. Whereas in 1996 Nortel had 40,000 active suppliers, in the fourth quarter of 2000, 90 percent of their material purchases came from fewer than 200 suppliers. Suppliers still numbered in the thousands, but have been reduced by a factor of 10.

Nortel also had vastly fewer people working in the supply chain management function, down to 950 from 2,000 people, with the 950 people representing totally different individuals and different skill sets.

However – in this dynamic and volatile business – Nortel have not succeeded in significantly reducing inventory levels, which remain at about two months. The company has been able to respond more quickly to unexpected demand by shifting about half of its inventory from the factory floor to 41 logistics centers located around the globe. Better communications with customers, allowed delayed configuration on a large scale.

Reacting to the Crisis

The unfolding crisis in the telecommunications industry has transformed Nortel from a technology powerhouse with $30 billion in sales a year ago into a company that could conceivably have just half that revenue in the next four quarters.

Nortel's loss in Q4 included charges of $750 million for obsolete inventory, $750 million for provisions related to customer financing and receivables and $400 million for the decline in value of investments. Nortel were also taking charges of $815 million for costs related to employee layoffs and $240 million for reducing capacity in their fiber optic components business.

Intent on countering such charges with cash generating measures, Nortel were proceeding with the sale of several businesses to other technology companies and leveraged buyout firms.

Still, the corporation said speculation about the possible sale of their enterprise unit to Cisco Systems, the leader in this domain, was unfounded. Their aim was to implement a plan that would allow them to earn profits at lower revenue levels.

→ See Answer Key for suggested case solution.

B 1.6 Mindset Management

Driven by global competition, most management models emphasize the need for flexibility and responsiveness. Business stories abound of "fast movers" outclassing "reactive imitators", rather than the "big players" crowding out "small niche players". As work generally involves play and exploration, the most thrilling work experience is on the borderline with the unpleasant. Accordingly, in order to cope with dynamic changes in workplace climate some organizations may emphasize structure through top-down control, whereas in another context they would cope through empowerment and consensus building.

A basic insight of organizational behavior is that people experiencing the same events live entirely different realities that are shaped by their own needs and motivations. Until the person exercising authority learns how the other person interprets events and thinks about them, management is only about power games and manipulation. It is people's mindsets – their distinctive viewpoints, needs, and agendas that determine how they actually see and respond at work. Mindsets are the points of origin for all workplace behavior. Therefore, no task briefings should take place without engaging the interests and motives of the people who are expected to fulfill the work assignments.

To perform credibly, managers at all levels (a) need conceptual skills for diagnosing and resolving organizational problems connected with the external environment, (b) have to understand their role in the work process, and (c) master the task skills involved in performing the job. To help managers cope with the flow of this complex and volatile work process:

- formal authority empowers the manager with position status (or legal authority) to perform in a proactive, i.e. directing and producing mindset;
- authority and trust facilitate certain cooperative mindsets for the manager, such as coaching and mentoring;
- analytical mindsets, such as coordinating and information processing, in turn, process information needed to maintain these interpersonal mindsets;
- authority, trust and access to information, place the manager at a central position in the organizational decision-making process.

B 1 Society, Business, Government, and the Global Network Economy

B 1.7 The Linked Mindsets Framework

Many of today's managerial perspectives evolved during an early management movement together with the development of assembly-line work; the academic discipline of business management was not needed or even known before the maturing of the corporation. Understanding this historical background would help recognize why approaches that were developed in earlier times do not necessarily work today.

Effectiveness criteria for assessing human action in organizations are: *focus on internal operations, focus on the external business environment, emphasis on flexibility,* and *emphasis on control*. These dimensions exist *concurrently*, but obviously not all receive equal priority. For example, the manager in a new, small organization that concentrates on establishing itself within a competitive environment will give less emphasis to developing employees than to finding a market niche in the external environment.

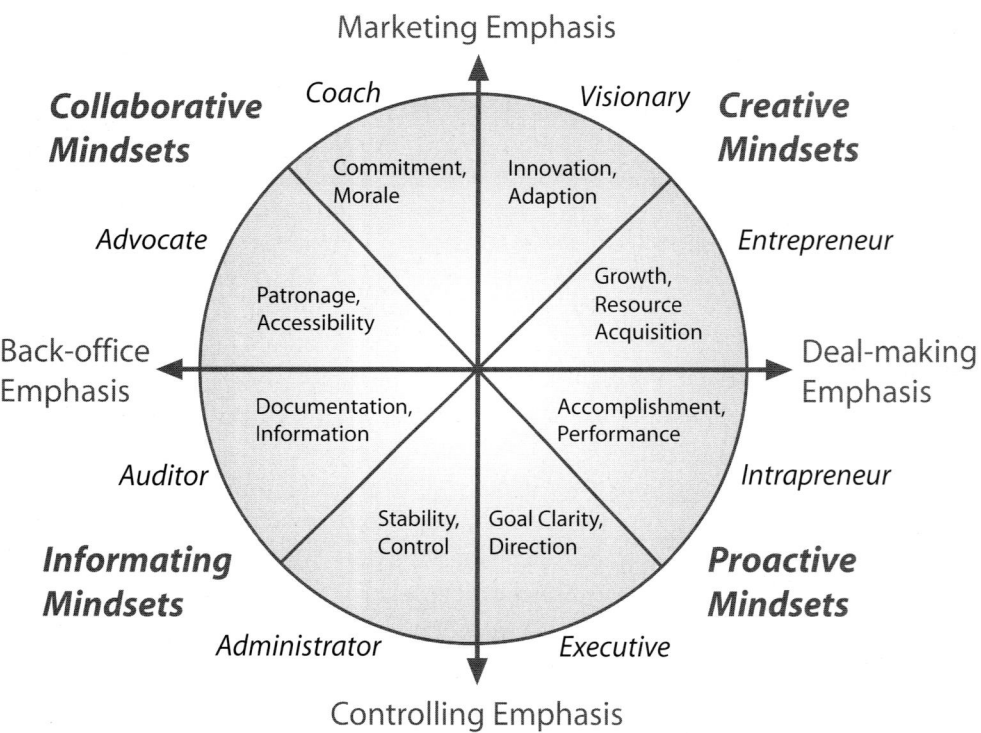

The linked mindset framework combines the effectiveness concept of the "rational" model (with the emphasis on goal achievement) with the efficiency goal of the "internal process" model (with the emphasis on efficient use of resources and harmonious internal functioning). By connecting each mindset to the contingent set of skills and motivational drives, the linked mindset framework illustrates the need to continuously align diverse values and interests to control and guide action.

The linked mindset framework offers a more realistic model of managerial work than a one-dimensional view of behavioral roles. In work situations, generally, the creative mindset mode and the information mindset mode are more closely connected to the individual whereas the cooperative and the action mindset modes relate more closely to the inter-group relations within and outside the boundaries of the firm. A given business situation may prompt managers – by which we mean all empowered employees within an organization – to adopt a specific mindset mode. But, to perform successfully in an organizational setting, these managers must also work through the three remaining mindset modes. For example, a manager's action in response to new information will only have a meaning for the organization if it generates a new perspective that influences other participants to become active in their turn. Similarly, leaders may be people-oriented, but to succeed they must also convey a sense of mission and stimulate action.

In general, at the individual level, managers need to mobilize creative skills by being innovative and resourceful and by communicating skillfully, whereas at the organizational level, managers must coach, build successful teams, and, in addition, set goals and motivate people.

Which of these mindset modes and performed social roles will predominate in the workplace and thereby characterize an organizational culture is a prime leadership issue.

B 1.8 Experiential Case: Feeling Sidetracked

When Marge Javel graduated with an honors degree in business studies from Zion University and became a research assistant in a charity more than eight years ago, she was confident that she would make a career there.

In her first years, she developed and promoted a variety of research topics related to the economics of fundraising and the social returns on charity activities. She considered herself to be a hard worker and a fast learner, successful in helping to build up a team and working closely with her colleagues. The engagement with donors, charity personnel and beneficiaries provided her with many exciting opportunities to demonstrate her presentation and communication skills. After four years she was promoted to a research analyst position, responsible for providing independent guidance and advice to donors.

When the position of a senior client development executive became vacant, Marge felt confident enough to apply. But, she was devastated when the board turned down her application, selecting instead a research analyst with more seniority. She felt aggrieved because she had worked with the successful applicant and was convinced he was not fit for this position. In their joint projects, it was Marge who consistently took on all the difficult assignments, based of her robust, assertive and forthright approach to building relationships. Given her track record as an articulate and creative "hands-on" operator who always met her deadlines, Marge judged that it was she who should really have been put in charge. She began feeling sidelined and didn't know how or where to take action.

To prepare for the next opening in two or three years time, she went to her coach to learn which competencies she should improve. She was told that the new executive was expected to take a strategic view and to establish a more efficient control structure and to lead the introduction of new audit approaches. The answer seemed ambiguous at first, but as the veiled message began to sink in, it caused her great anguish.

In her years as research assistant, she thought she had coped well with the assigned responsibilities, gaining a good deal of expertise, and benefiting in the regular bonus payments. But lately she felt discouraged and depressed. If she stayed late, it was only out to get something done that needed doing.

Whereas all others in her team seemed to be forging ahead, Marge had no idea where she was going. Still, she was reluctant to move elsewhere because she would lose what seniority and retirement benefits she had. Recently, she had turned down an attractive offer from a NGO, because she thought there would be too little opportunity for advancement.

Marge felt totally lost. Would it have been better after all to move on? Idly sifting through her notes from a recent self-assessment seminar she was struck by the following graph:

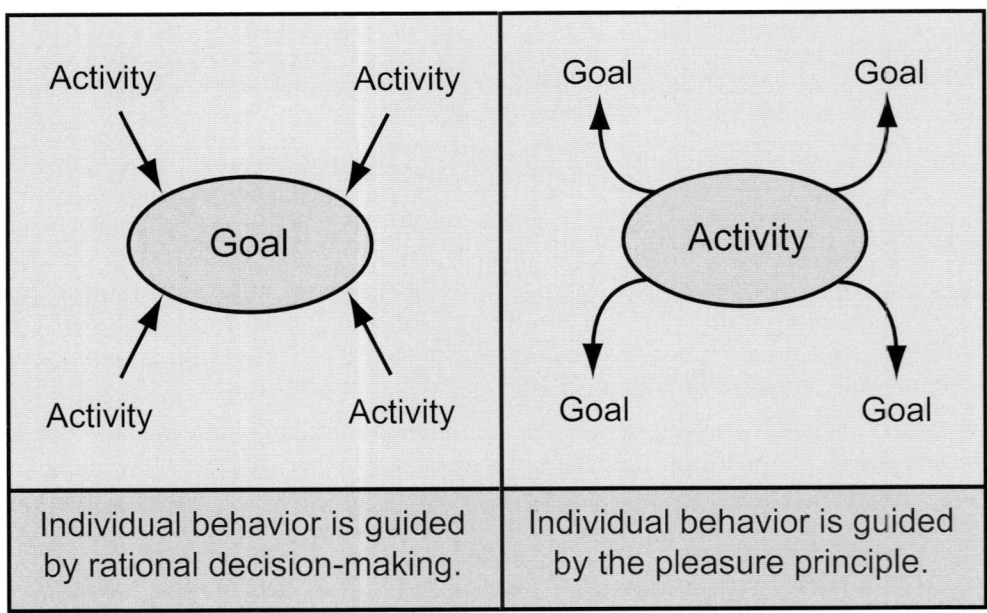

Alternative Motivational Modes

B 2   Theory of the Firm

- The Objective of a Firm
- Transaction Costs and Vertical Integration
- Transaction Costs and Opportunistic Behavior
- High Transaction Costs
- Specialized Products
- Changing Market Conditions
- Monitoring Costs
- Strategie Case: Enron Corp. – Out-of-the Money
- The "Intrapreneurial" Mindset
- Experiential Case: The Stress-Challenged Manager

B 3   The Constitution of Business

B 2 Theory of the Firm

B 2.1 Principles – Models – Practices

A firm is a business organization that transforms inputs (i.e. resources it purchases) into outputs (the valued products that it sells). It gains the difference between what it earns as revenue and what it spends on resource inputs. For instance, a pharmaceutical firm builds a plant, hires workers, purchases raw materials, and then produces and sells drugs. The firm decides the quantity of resources to buy, how to combine the resources to make drugs, and how and where to sell them. The firm makes a profit if it sells its drugs for more than the cost of producing and selling them. Accordingly, the profit-maximizing objective of most firms requires that they are run efficiently and that managers and workers do not deviate from that objective.

A firm's success is related to performing only those actions that it is good at, and relying on external contractors (i.e. the market) for other essential actions. The market and the firm are alternative means of providing goods and services. If the costs of doing business with other firms are high, a firm will perform more tasks internally. In printer manufacturing, for example, the relative costs of dealing with other firms changed substantially, due to rising labor cost differentials and currency movements. So, Canon, for instance, went from purchasing critical components from other firms to producing them internally. Offsetting a firm's aim to become larger to avoid the cost of doing business with other firms is the cost involved in monitoring its own managers and employees to ensure that they operate in the firm's interest. The optimal size of a firm depends on this trade-off.

objective – Ziel
to deviate – abweichen
contractor – Vertragsunternehmer
to offset – ausgleichen
trade-off – Kompromiss
unlike – im Gegensatz zu
entitled – berechtigt
to solicit – werben um
donation – Spende
to deduct – abziehen
contribution – Beitrag
constraint – Beschränkung

The Objective of a Firm

Although most firms are organized to make profits, there are many "nonprofit" firms such as charities, religious organizations, non-government organizations, and educational institutions. A firm with nonprofit status does not have to pay corporate income tax. Unlike ordinary firms, nonprofit firms do not have owners who are entitled to share the profit. As a rule, they are legally restricted from distributing any excess revenues to others.

Many nonprofit organizations, such as charities and colleges, raise funds by soliciting donations. Donors may deduct their contribution from their income tax. Without the non-distribution constraint, donors would have no assurance that their donations would be used to achieve the charitable objectives of the nonprofit firm.

B 2 | Theory of the Firm

The standard assumption in most economic models is that the primary objective of the manager of a company is to maximize the company's profits. However, managers may have objectives other than profit maximization. For example, if managers want to control a large company, they may maximize sales rather than profits. Similarly, managers may spend the company's money on lavish office furnishings, executive jets, and other amenities that reduce the profitability of the company but benefit managers directly.

However, various forces keep managers from deviating from profit-maximizing behavior. If a company is run inefficiently and unprofitably, rival companies may drive it out of business that do maximize profits. Managers who lose their jobs when their company is forced to downsize or who are fired for inefficiency or inaction find it difficult to obtain new jobs. Incentives, such as stock ownership and other bonuses, are specifically designed to motivate managers to maximize profit. In this way, the market works to eliminate inefficient, unprofitable managers.

Transaction Costs and Vertical Integration

Companies strive to use the least costly approach. For some goods and services, a single company may carry out many of the necessary steps; for others, a different company is responsible for each step. When a company relies on itself rather than others to produce input, it is said to be vertically integrated. That is, if a single company can perform most of the necessary steps less expensively than if it relied on other companies, it will do so. Which approach is more cost effective depends on transaction costs, or the costs of trading with others apart from price, such as writing and enforcing contracts and searching for the lowest price.

> **assumption** – Annahme
> **lavish** – üppig, verschwenderisch, großzügig
> **amenities** – Annehmlichkeiten
> **to strive** – anstreben
> **to rely on** – sich verlassen auf
> **apart from** – außer
> **to enforce** – durchsetzen
> **to negotiate** – verhandeln
> **agreement** – Vereinbarung, Abkommen
> **contingency** – Eventualität

Transaction Costs and Opportunistic Behavior

A major reason why it may be less expensive to produce internally, rather than rely on markets, is that companies incur transaction costs in using the market. Transaction costs include the initial cost of negotiating an agreement as well as the ongoing costs of enforcing the agreement. Because no agreement can specify all possible contingencies, modifying agreements to deal with unforeseen events is an important transaction cost.

Anytime two unrelated parties agree to a transaction that would be completed in the future, each might engage in such opportunistic behavior which means taking advantage of another. When circumstances allow, each side may try to interpret the terms of the contract to its advantage, especially when terms are vague or even missing. If the contract covers a standard transaction, then opportunistic behavior is unlikely. However, a signed contract may contain provisions that turn out to be undesirable to one of the parties. Also, in complicated contracts, it may be impractical to specify all possible contingencies.

This implicit incentive for opportunistic behavior can be avoided if activities are organized within a company rather than between companies in the marketplace. In a single company, if one division tries to behave opportunistically towards another division, the manager can act to ensure that such behavior does not reduce overall profitability. Also, conflicts are often easier to resolve within a company than between companies. Legal action to resolve conflicts between companies may be inadequate and expensive compared to hierarchical control.

circumstances – Umstände
provision – Bestimmung, Klausel, Verordnung
to resolve – lösen, beseitigen
inadequate – unzureichend
to penalize – bestrafen
source – Quelle
equipment – Ausrüstung, Zubehör
purpose – Zweck
vulnerable – angreifbar, verwundbar

High Transaction Costs

A company chooses to perform activities itself rather than to rely on the market when transaction costs are likely to be high. These tend to be high when it is difficult to write a contract that penalizes opportunistic behavior. Transaction costs are likely to be especially high when products are specialized, market conditions are changing, and information is sold.

Specialized Products

A product is asset specific if it is specialized or customized, and if a buyer who signs a contract with a single supplier for such a product has only one source for immediate supply. But the supplier would also find it difficult to sell the specialized product to another buyer. In addition such products often require specialized equipment that may be worthless to the supplier except for making the specialized product. Such costs incurred for capital goods that cannot easily be used for other purposes are called "sunk costs". Buyer and seller – because of their limited options after the contract is signed – are vulnerable to opportunistic behavior.

The ownership of specialized production facilities is often used to prevent problems of opportunistic bargaining. For instance, a resort hotel typically owns its restaurant rather than contracting with catering company. Similarly, chemical plants often own specialized vehicles, rather than negotiating for transport. In cases where ownership is not used, one would expect to see detailed long-term contracts. Otherwise, once an initial investment has generated "sunk costs", opportunistic bargaining would become an attractive option for the counterpart.

Influence of Transaction Costs on the Organization of the Firm's Value Chain

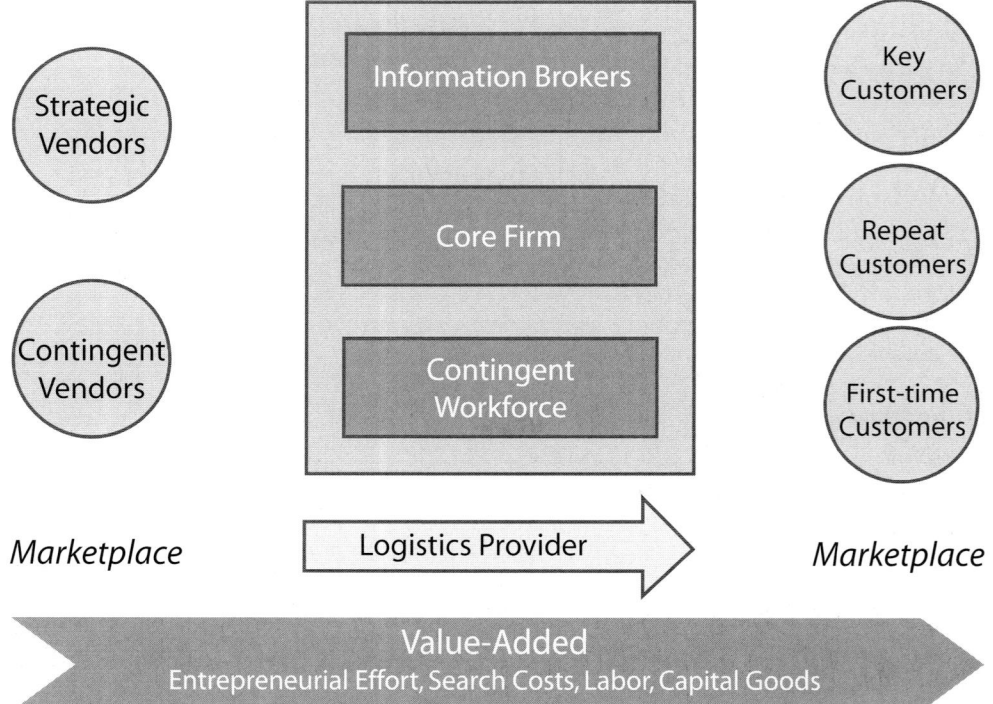

Changing Market Conditions

No contract can take all potential contingencies into account. The more unpredictable the future, the harder it is to specify contractual terms. If the parties fail to specify how terms should adjust over time, both buyer and seller are at risk each time the terms are renegotiated. Even complicated price formulas are unlikely to allow the flexibility required for efficient responses to changed circumstances. Moreover, a buyer who dislikes risk may not sign a contract at unknown prices, even if they are to be determined by a known formula.

Monitoring Costs

If transaction costs are lower for a company that produces its own resources instead of buying them on the market, the question <u>arises</u> why it would not be more efficient to eliminate the marketplace and consolidate all activities in one big company? The answer is that sometimes the <u>allocation</u> of resources within a company costs more than in a market. A company may hire its outside accountant as an employee, but he may not follow instructions any better than as an independent agent. An accountant with complete job security might even work less hard.

An employee on a fixed wage whose output is hard to monitor may not have the same incentive to work hard or minimize costs as a self-employed operator would. If workers' efforts cannot be easily distinguished from those of their co-workers, they are unlikely to be rewarded for their extra hard work, and hence will work less. Companies must therefore spend resources both on incentives and on supervision to maintain internal efficiency. The larger the company, the greater are the number of interactions between employees that are necessary to coordinate their activities. And, as the size of the company increases, the number of these internal interactions can <u>eventually outweigh</u> the benefits of allocating resources within the company.

to arise – auftreten, entstehen
allocation – Zuteilung, Zuweisung
eventually – schließlich
to outweigh – überwiegen
to evolve – sich entwickeln
adversely – ungünstig, nachteilig
artificial – künstlich
previously – zuvor, vorher
to achieve – erreichen, erzielen

The multidivisional organization structure evolved to help owners and managers monitor and control their employees' actions efficiently. Incentive and control systems are designed to ensure that managers follow company policy rather than defecting or pursuing opportunistic goals that would <u>adversely</u> affect other important stakeholder groups, such as customers, and suppliers. Moreover, many market transactions include detailed monitoring provisions, and large companies also set <u>artificial</u> prices (or transfer prices) to allocate goods among divisions.

If companies operate inefficiently, competitors will enter their field, or acquire and run them more efficiently. A merger and acquisition (M&A) may take the form of a vertical merger, where a company combines with its supplier, a horizontal merger, where companies within the same industry combine, and a conglomerate merger, where companies in unrelated businesses combine. By integrating plants and spreading fixed costs over a greater output economies of scale may be realized. With superior technical knowledge, and financial resources <u>previously</u> available to only one of the firms, economies of scope (or synergy) may be <u>achieved</u>.

B 2 | Theory of the Firm

B 2.2 Knowledge Check

(1) Explain the factors driving and limiting a company's size.
(2) Which monitoring and controlling activities help secure a company's effectiveness?
(3) How does a company secure the loyalty of its managers?

→ See Answer Key for solutions.

B 2.3 Keywords

Asset specific product; charities; conglomerate; contingency; defection; division; economies of scale; economies of scope; external contractor; horizontal merger; marketplace; merger and acquisition (M&A); monitoring costs; multidivisional structure; offset; opportunistic behavior; sunk cost; takeover; transaction costs; trade-off; transfer prices; vertical integration.

B 2.4 Strategy Case: Enron Corp. – Out-of-the Money

Enron Encounters the Limits of Disintegration

In November 2000, Kenneth Lay, CEO and founder of Enron Corporation, was first choice for the position of Secretary of Energy in the new Bush Administration. But, he turned down this offer to pursue his career as leader of a Fortune top-ten company. The stock market reacted on a positive note, raising the value of the company to $60 billion.

With revenues reaching new heights in the fourth quarter of 2000, Enron announced a new vision. Having transformed itself from a regional gas pipeline concern into the world's biggest energy trader, it was now committed to revolutionizing the concept of the global corporation. Enron's master plan foresaw the disintegration of the value chain into a web of autonomous businesses. This concept posed a direct challenge to integrated energy companies such as Exxon, which had just announced a quarterly profit of over $4 billion.

However, when the IT bubble burst in Q2, 2001, commodity and stock prices tumbled. In the wake of collapsing markets, it was not the model of the integrated corporation that disintegrated, but Enron. On 2 December 2001, the company filed for Chapter 11 bankruptcy.

Early History

Enron emerged in 1986 from the merger of two natural gas giants.

Faster than his competitors, Ken Lay realized that with the advent of deregulation, energy production, trading, and distribution were being integrated into a global marketplace. Barriers that once separated producers, suppliers, distributors, retailers, and investors were becoming permeable, and linked by information networks. He visualized the web of natural gas pipelines intersecting the United States as a connected system, capable of shipping gas from any gas field to any local gas company. And, while most gas utilities were looking for ways to defend their vested interests, Enron was pioneering spot markets for gas.

Global Network Strategy

Lay was a strong believer in the decentralized pattern of information flows in a liberalized market. Accordingly, he decided to build a strong entrepreneurial culture in direct contrast to the entrenched bureaucratic culture in traditional utilities. To realize this strategy, Lay created several new publicly quoted companies, recruiting aggressive, well-compensated traders to accelerate growth.

With its new approach, Enron succeeded in reducing the cost of gas for some utilities by 30% to 50%. With success came more ideas for new products, services, types of contracts, pricing options. Lay pioneered the use of gas as a fuel in electric generation plants, a technology that was prohibited under the old federal regulations. In order to demonstrate the superiority of this technology, Enron built and operated its own gas-fired power plants in Texas, showing that it could compete economically against coal-fired plants, and with far less pollution. By his single-minded pursuit of a contrarian strategy, Lay created a huge new market for natural gas as the preferred fuel for generating power.

In line with its business concept of interconnected distributed networks, the company began expanding overseas by completing the building of a 150 megawatt plant in Hainan Province, China. Enron also entered into asset-heavy businesses overseas such as the Dabhol power project in India and Wessex Water in Britain. It bought and sold contracts on gas and electricity on a global basis and led the market in financial derivatives related to the energy markets. In North America, Enron became a dominant market maker in the energy trading business, accounting for 15–20% of gas and power trading.

In the last decade, besides becoming the world's largest trader of electricity and natural gas, Enron had also slipped into the role of a telecommunications company, an investment firm, a paper and lumber producer and an insurer. With more than $100 billion in revenue last year, it had evolved into a highly diversified conglomerate. In line with its maverick image, Enron single-handedly created the market for treating telecommunications bandwidth – the transmission capacity used to carry voice and data on communications networks. Even after its broadband business reported large losses earlier this year, Enron remained the world's largest bandwidth trader.

Early Warning Signals

As the transition from a one-company-show into a multilateral market was proceeding, Enron's problems came to surface. Customers began to defect to other energy traders and independent brokers, such as Amerex, also based in Houston. Several of Enron's larger competitors in energy trading, like Dynegy, and the El Paso managed to poach some of its bandwidth trading business.

Enron responded to these reversals by migrating into purely financial products, including credit derivatives. In effect, the giant energy and financial trading business had transformed into a hedge fund with ancillary gas pipeline operations. However, there were few barriers to entry left in energy trading. Attracted by Enron's success, dozens of rivals moved into trading, hiring away Enron's skilled employees in droves.

An early warning of Enron's growing difficulties was indicated by the declining returns on extra revenues. Revenues had grown by $10 billion from 1998 to 1999, and then by another $60 billion in 2000, peaking out at $100 billion. Profits before tax, meanwhile, had only risen by $1 billion in 1998, and by less than $500m in both 1999 and 2000. Enron's return on capital, however, was only 6.6% in 2000, underperforming rivals such as Williams and Dynegy.

The company attempted to boost its margins by selling fixed assets – such as generation plants – and booking the gains as operating revenues. In spite of these creative accounting efforts, the firm's trading margins were driven down from 5.3% in early 1998 to less than 1.7% in Q 3, 2002.

The Crisis Unfolds

Attempting to make up for lower margins Enron began extending its brand into new areas. It grew to have contracts with some 8,000 counterparties, in hundreds of business lines ranging from credit insurance to metals trading. In practice, this meant taking increasingly bigger risks, such as trading in telecoms bandwidth futures. Compounding its systemic hedging risk, Enron took net long positions, just as gas and electricity prices plunged. Hedging strategies work well in rising markets, but may break down disastrously when prices fall.

First doubts about Enron's liquidity arose among its business partners as rumors of irregularities began proliferating. The company reacted by restating its accounts for the past five years, in the process erasing nearly a fifth of the total profits. The news triggered an investigation by the Securities and Exchange Commission. Still, the firm refused to lay open its accounts and off-balance risks to public scrutiny.

Once investors and counter-parties began having second thoughts about Enron's numbers, its survival was at stake. Previously, Enron was able to raise loans because its debt was rated as investment grade; however these loans had clauses attached which required Enron to make additional payments if it was downgraded. As this prospect emerged, customers became wary about raising capital for such a highly leveraged firm.

Few outsiders understood well what Enron did, or were able to form a clear picture of its risk exposure. For example, swaps were created on Enron's balance sheet that would compensate the buyer of assets in the event of an unexpected loss. The quality of the assets sold may have been doubtful (for example, a block of Internet shares); occasionally, the third-party entity would pay using a loan from Enron, which then booked the interest on the loan as income. Enron went to the limit in deciding what constituted a fair price for illiquid assets. It was rumored that about 28 % of Enron's EPS in 2000 came from gains on sales of securitized assets, mostly to third parties connected with Enron.

Like many financial firms, Enron's success depended upon a confidence trick. As long as people believed in its integrity, it could prosper. But as soon as credibility became an issue, its position crumbled. It seems that Enron spent $5 billion in November 2001 alone, paying off clients. That was not enough to stop customers from withdrawing their business.

Enron suffered a mortal blow on 28 November, when Standard & Poor's downgraded Enron's debt to junk status in response to the reluctance of competing firms, such as Dynegy, to take Enron over.

Current State of Affairs

Adding to the creditors' woes, a deluge of lawsuits from Enron's shareholders, employees, and pensioners seems likely. More than half of employees' 401(k) retirement plan assets, or about $1.2 billion, was invested in company stock, and those shares are nearly worthless. Enron filed for bankruptcy on 2 Dec.

The collateral damage is difficult to predict, not least because of Enron's continuing unwillingness to submit its accounts to public scrutiny. Although no other company has yet been downgraded because of its exposure to Enron, it is believed that 1,000 firms are vulnerable as counter-parties. Among energy companies, Dynegy, with $75m, probably has the largest exposure to Enron, but its overall capital at risk is much higher.

Losses among financial firms are even higher. J.P. Morgan Chase is involved with $400m through non secured direct loans and trades, as well as another $400m in loans secured by Enron's gas pipeline subsidiary. Citibank. Now that it is protected in bankruptcy by Chapter 11, Enron can borrow from banks, which know that fresh loans will be senior to old ones. The plan now seems to be to sell what assets it can (the ownership of its main gas pipeline is disputed by Dynegy), so as to keep alive the core trading business and the Internet operation Enron Online, perhaps with a view to selling them to a bank.

The investment community and shareholders are anxiously considering alternatives. Can Enron survive in a lean form? Would it be a better strategy for a prospective buyer to retain Enron's best staff and to start a new business?

B 2.5 The "Intrapreneurial" Mindset

Organizations recruit new members by promising them rewards for their participation. In turn, the organization prospers by finding and developing its niche in the larger society. Ultimately, all organizations are founded on shared meanings as the basis for coordinated action toward a common goal. Counteracting the confusing variety of images, signals, forecasts, and alternatives confronting the members, it is a manager's role to articulate an easily understood vision of the future – in effect acting as an "intrapreneur", or entrepreneur within the boundaries of the firm.

Personal Productivity

High-performers in organizations who are driven by a sense of personal mission to "manage" – that is to accomplish, to be in charge of, to have responsibility for, and to influence both action and opinion – will most likely think in terms of measurable results. They will display the dual capacities of self-management and team mastery. To reduce stress, high performers tend to value internal goals and intrinsic rewards most, and to care a great deal about the tasks they perform. These managers avoid uncalculated risk-taking, and consistently search for opportunities to pursue moderately ambitious goals. In their quest for group effectiveness, they respond to challenge by emphasizing outcomes, results, and solutions, rather than striving for perfection. Feeling secure in their perception of mastery, high performers are well equipped to balance work, private life and social activities.

Motivation

In general, employees invest a lot of effort in fine-tuning methods to achieve the level of performance expected from them. Managers can use this human need to achieve accepted goals by making an effort to gain the employees' trust and in the process creating high performance expectations that subordinates will strive to fulfill.

Furthermore, employees will typically compare the performance level expected by the manager with the likelihood of a reward. The manager can address this concern by making certain that employees are aware of all the possible outcomes that will result from performance, and by making certain that they know what outcomes are important to their employees.

Stress Management

A certain level of stress at work is needed to create excitement and goal satisfaction. But higher levels of stress will lead to anxiety and defensive behavior, lowering the productivity of managers and the people they lead. Even though stress is linked to negative attitudes or emotions, its consequences are distinctly physiological. As the body does not distinguish between real and imagined threats, the physiological responses are identical.

In an organizational setting, stress often occurs in the form of frustration, because interference by other people gets in the way of achieving of one' own goals. A possible solution would be to capitalize on, rather than be sidetracked by the frequent interruptions and intrusions of other members of your organization, for instance by initiating cooperative projects and extracting information from informal gossip.

Successfully managing stress at work involves knowing when and whom to accommodate, and to avoid inefficiencies caused by confusing priorities. In this sense, personal productivity is closely connected with the skill to get the system working for oneself rather than vice versa. For example, the most significant factor in sustaining a fast-track career with bearable stress is the ability to nurture a constructive influence with senior managers.

The following rules set useful guidelines in effective stress management:

With tasks of similar urgency and importance, it is best to address the most difficult first.

The most important items should be done during the most productive time of the day.

Any tasks someone else can do should be delegated.

Meetings that do not have a clear, useful purpose should be avoided.

Documents should be skimmed before reading and those with a low "return on investment" thrown out.

Whenever a subordinate presents a problem, more than one solution should be offered.

At least one significant task bringing a sense of accomplishment should be achieved daily.

Long-range planning and short-range priority setting should be aligned to avoid crises.

A secluded place should be found for uninterrupted work on important tasks.

To prevent a creeping downward goal tolerance, efficiency in managing stress should be monitored continuously and schedules frequently adjusted.

B 2.6   Experiential Case: The Stress-Challenged Manager

On his way back from the espresso machine, Frank, a senior analyst who was assigned to complete a report for the principal analyst, stopped at Bella's desk. She had been on leave for training, and they spent several minutes reviewing what had been going on there and in the office.

Back at his desk, he found a memo detailing new policies concerning non-business or personal use of the Internet during office hours. Frank felt unsure, and asked Jo about privacy issues. It was 9:45 before Frank returned to his cubicle.

At 10:30 the principal analyst called to instruct him to find a report detailing "hold stock" recommendations over the last four years. The principal analyst also expressed his dissatisfaction with the new Internet policy and discussed possible implications for employee morale. It was actually Bella's job to retrieve the report, but she was in the middle of an Equal Employment Opportunity meeting. Frank attempted to find it himself, but was unable to understand Bella's database structure. After 20 minutes he decided to wait for her return to the office. It was already 11:30 am, and there was not enough time to begin any major project before lunch. Frank cleaned up his in-basket instead, preparing himself for a productive afternoon.

Returning to work at 1:00 pm, Frank quickly glanced over the newsletter to shareholders, and then became absorbed in some busy work. It was 1:30 pm before he remembered to ask Bella for that report. A few minutes later she forwarded him two different reports. One compared "hold" recommendations over the last year, the other "hold" recommendations over the past five years. There was no four-year compilation, and Bella stated that there never had been one. Frank asked her to search again.

When Bella still couldn't find the report, Frank called the principal analyst back. The secretary said he was out in a meeting. After Frank left a message, he and Bella each returned to their previous work.

Frank's assignment wasn't due until the end of the month, and since it was meanwhile 3:00 pm, and the remaining two office hours were not enough to make much progress on the report. Also, sooner or later, Bill Harris would come wandering over with a new offering of lottery tickets. The disciplinary implications of the Internet policy for his gambling operations must have upset him, and he always proceeded very cautiously when he felt threatened. Frank could see Bill fidgeting across the office, and he made a mental note to reserve a large block of time for the report later in the week.

(1) What are some of Frank's "stressors" that he has to change?
(2) What is the best way to deal with a superior who frequently
    (a) interrupts your work schedule with non-work-related matters?
    (b) withholds information or gives imprecise information?

B 3 The Constitution of Business

- Structural Trends
- Expanding Web of Services
- The Company of the Future
- Legal Forms
- Sole Proprietorships
- Partnerships
- Corporations
- Strategic Case: KirchMedia – Game Over?
- The "Executive" Mindset
- Experiential Case: The Temperamental Networker

B 4 The External Environment and Corporate Culture

B 3 The Constitution of Business

B 3.1 Principles – Models – Practices

Structural Trends

In recent decades, the relative balance between goods-producing and service businesses has <u>shifted</u> in such a way that far less labor is involved in <u>assembling</u> and manufacturing than in finding out what an individual customer wants, then designing products for and servicing this individual customer (the essentials of Customer Relationship Management.)

Also, for many years, small businesses have been losing ground to larger competitors, such as the department store chains and franchise outlets dominating the shopping malls. The most dramatic change has been the evolution of some chains and hypermarkets into network structures linked together by information technology. The rise of services reflects a growing trend among producers to outsource services that the producers <u>formerly</u> performed themselves. Instead of having its own legal staff, for example, a company might prefer to obtain outside legal expertise. While foreign producers with access to inexpensive labor are taking over much of the world's manufacturing, over half of the economic activity in advanced economies now consists of creating and processing information.

> **to shift** – verschieben, verlagern
> **to assemble** – zusammenbauen, montieren
> **formerly** – früher, ehemals
> **insurance** – Versicherung
> **real-estate broker** – Grundstücksmakler
> **haulage** – Transport, Güterverkehr

Expanding Web of Services

The financial-services sector contains an even mix of large and small businesses. On the one hand, there are giant <u>insurance</u> companies and banks with operations around the world; on the other, there are webs of independent insurance agents, <u>real-estate brokers</u>, and local banks. As in financial services, deregulation has impacted formerly stable industries such as shipping, and telecommunications, while new logistical concepts have revolutionized <u>haulage</u>. As transport, power transmission, and telecommunications are all capital-intensive industries, large firms tend to dominate this segment of the service sector.

Meanwhile, the service area that is growing the most rapidly is the heterogeneous group of "other" services that includes such diverse businesses as beauty parlors, repair shops, private schools, health services, hotels, theme parks, movie theaters, and professional services. The most important factor of production is labor, often supplied by the owner of the business. As the barriers to entry are relatively low, there is fierce competition in this sector.

The Company of the Future

As companies are restructuring, it is often difficult to define where the firm begins and ends, with customers, suppliers, and allied companies linked into a highly adaptive "network organization". The vertically integrated company, which prefers to run and own its whole value chain, is considered an outdated concept. The modern concept of lean management calls on every organization to define its core and its surrounding partnerships, the overall aim being to balance long-term relationships and spot contracts.

outdated	– überholt, veraltet
surrounding	– umgebend
aim	– Ziel
sole proprietor	– Einzelunternehmer

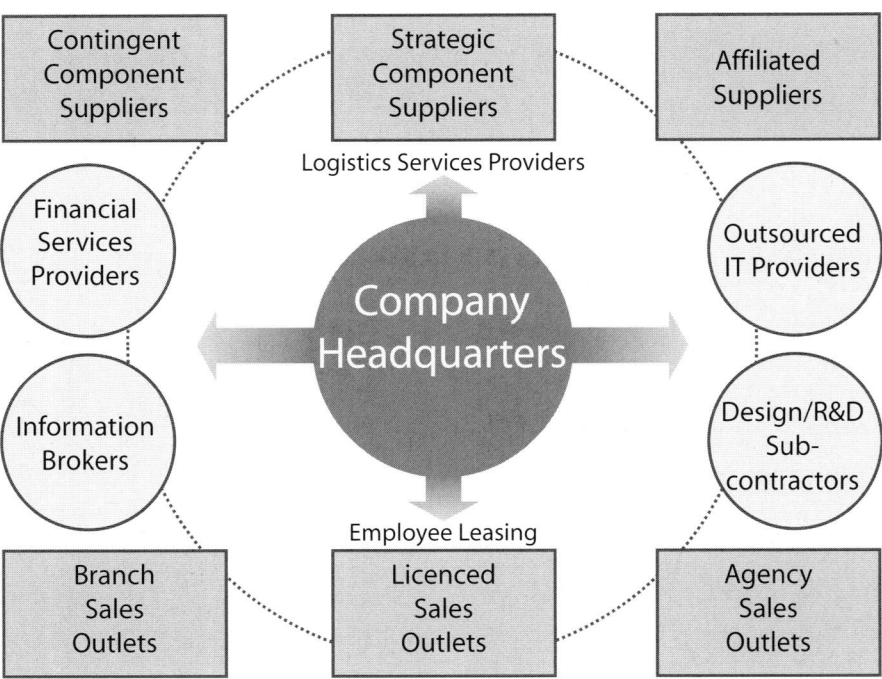

A Network Organization

Legal Forms

The structural changes have been accompanied by changes in the ownership of many companies. The three most common forms of business ownership are sole proprietorship, partnership, and corporation. Corporations tend to be large-scale operations, accounting for the major share of total receipts in all of the economy's industrial sectors. However, sole proprietorships are more numerous, particularly in the service sector. Each form of ownership has a characteristic internal structure, legal status, size, and environmental constraints.

Sole Proprietorships

A sole proprietorship is a business owned by just one individual. Few formal procedures are required. A possible disadvantage is that the proprietor has unlimited liability which means that he/she is personally responsible to the full extent of private wealth for all debts. However, in capital intensive businesses the need for a big capital investment in conjunction with high start-up costs limit the number of sole proprietorships. Also, when the proprietor dies, so does the business, unless the owner prepares for a partnership or a corporation.

Partnerships

A partnership is a legal association of two or more persons as co-owners of a business. The partners share profits and losses and often the management responsibilities, too. Partnerships range in size from two-person operations to international businesses. Whereas, in a general partnership, all partners are legally equal and are liable for the business's debts, in a limited partnership one or more individuals act as general partners and managers. The others are passive investors whose liability is limited to their capital stake. For professionals in fields such as accounting, law, and business consultancy, there is the prospect of starting as an employed associate, and eventually becoming a partner with an investment of their own in the business.

---

liability – Haftung

debts – Schulden

in conjunction with – in Verbindung mit

general partnership – OHG

limited partnership – KG

capital stake – Kapitaleinlage, Beteiligung

takeover – Übernahme

litigation – Rechtsstreitigkeiten

trait – Eigenschaft, Merkmal

endowed – ausgestattet

A partnership can generally raise money more easily than a proprietorship because there are several people to share the risk of unlimited personal liability. In fact, many mergers and acquisition specialists operate through limited partnerships, which can raise vast sums for investing in leveraged buyouts and takeovers. But currently, the risk of interpersonal conflicts and external litigation is driving many professionals to incorporate.

Corporations

General Characteristics

Corporations are defined by five distinct traits: (a) they are artificial persons, endowed with a specific legal standing; (b) they enjoy an unlimited life span; (c) in accordance with their legal charter, they are empowered to carry on a specific business; (d) they are owned by shareholders (stockholders); (e) their shareholders are usually liable for damages only to the extent of their equity stake (i.e. limited liability). Since ownership and management are separate, the shareholders may vote to remove the managers. Because shares of the company may be transferred to someone else, the company's ownership may change fundamentally while the company and its management remain intact.

> **subsidiary** – Tochtergesellschaft
> **partially** – teilweise
> **parent company** – Muttergesellschaft
> **voting right** – Stimmrecht
> **governance** – Steuerung, Herrschaft
> **emphasis** – Betonung, Schwerpunkt
> **participation** – Mitwirkung
> **auditor** – Wirtschaftsprüfer

The giant companies are almost all publicly held corporations in the sense that they are owned by large numbers of the public. In contrast, private corporations withhold their stock from public sale, preferring to finance any expansion out of their own earnings. Thus, top managers who own the majority of the stock are able to secure complete control over operations and at the same time spoil any takeover attempts.

However, not all corporations are truly independent entities. Subsidiary (or affiliate) corporations, for example, are partially or wholly owned by a parent company, which supervises their operations. If the parent acts as a holding company, though, it will exercise little operating control over the affiliate, merely "holding" its stock as an investment.

Corporate Structure and Governance

Because it is impractical for the shareholders of a large corporation to run the company, they elect a board of directors to represent them. The directors, in turn, select and monitor the top officers, who actually manage the company.

Shareholders: their influence varies, with some people owning stock that carries no voting rights, while others own shares that are worth one vote each. Institutional investors, such as pension funds and insurance companies often hold the largest blocks of shares. Their main interest is maximizing shareholder value by increasing the long-term return and value of the shares.

Employees, whose main concerns are pay and job security, are also becoming more involved in corporate governance. This means the exercise of hierarchical power with special emphasis on the relationship between managers and shareholders. Employee participation is secured through employee stock ownership plans (ESOP) which encourage employees to buy and own shares of stock in the company for which they work. Shareholders elect the board members at an annual general meeting (AGM). They also select an auditor for the company's financial statements, and vote on other business. Absent shareholders can vote by proxy, authorizing a third party to vote on their behalf.

Board of Directors: is responsible for guiding corporate affairs and selecting officers. The board has the power to vote on major management decisions, such as building a new factory, hiring a new president, or buying a new subsidiary. The real power in a corporation often lies with the chief executive officer, or CEO, who is responsible for establishing the policies of the company, and acts as the chairman of the board. In big companies the president of the corporation assists the CEO (in small companies the two functions are combined). The board often includes non-executive directors who may vote on major policy decisions but are not involved in running the corporation.

Advantages of Corporations

No other form of business ownership can match the success of the corporation in bringing together money, resources, talent, in accumulating assets and in creating wealth. Although a corporation can assume tremendous liabilities, it is the corporate entity that is liable rather than any of the private shareholders, who are liable only for the amount of their investment. Through security trading, corporations can raise large amounts of equity capital. But, to provide market transparency and defend investors' interests, publicly owned companies are required by law to publish information about their finances and operations.

Establishing Ownership and Control

On the corporate level, many organizations are restructuring to create value by pooling resources. The rebuilding process may involve (a) one company acquiring another, (b) divestitures, where one company sells some parts of its business to another company, and (c) leveraged buyouts (LBO), where individuals purchase the company with borrowed funds (usually high interest, high risk junk bonds) and using the assets of the targeted company to guarantee the loan. After the takeover, the loans are repaid through the sale of assets.

The two basic methods used to launch a hostile takeover are the tender offer and the proxy fight. In a tender offer, the corporate raider offers to buy shares of the corporation at a price that is generally above the current stock price. The raider hopes to buy enough shares to take control of the corporation and replace the existing board and top management. In a proxy fight, the raider launches a contest for shareholder votes to achieve this aim.

Disintermediation and Re-intermediation

The advent of the Internet and the WWW has changed and continues to change network organization structures. Internet sites now fulfill many functions which were traditionally the domain of functional departments, such as Sales or Purchasing, and many intermediaries (e.g. wholesalers, factory outlets) sell directly to businesses and consumers. Moreover, new non-conventional intermediaries (such as Priceline and eBay) have appeared.

An Airline Distribution Network

```
Web Site Airline "A"      Alliance Partner Airlines      Web Site Airline "B"
                          (e.g. Air Canada, Lufthansa)

        Online Intermediary    Central Reservation    Online Intermediary
        (e.g. Travelocity)     System (e.g. Galileo)  (e.g. Expedia)

              Wholesaler       Online Travel          Wholesaler
              (e.g. Amexco)    Agency                 (e.g. Rosenbluth)
                               (e.g. DER)

                       Travel              Travel
                       Agency              Agency

                              Customers
```

B 3.2 Knowledge Check

(1) Discuss the two main types of partnerships.
(2) Explain the legal identity of a corporation.
(3) List the four groups governing a corporation, and describe the role of each.

→ **See Answer Key for solutions.**

B 3.3 Keywords

Annual general meeting (AGM); board of directors; broker; chief executive officer (CEO); corporation; divestiture; corporate governance; employee share ownership plan (ESOP); entity; general partnership; heterogeneous; holding company; hostile takeover; institutional investors; junk bonds; labor-intensive business; leveraged buyout (LBO); limited partnership; liquidity; parent company; partnership; private corporation; productivity; proxy vote; proxy fight; service business; shareholder; sole proprietorship; stock; subsidiary; tender offer; unlimited liability.

B 3.4 Strategy Case: KirchMedia – Game over?

The Kirch Group at a Crossroads

The Kirch Group which controls a big share of commercial programs on German television has survived many challenges in its 42-year history. This resilience was needed again in December 2001. The core business of the Munich-based group was experiencing a slowdown and major obligations were falling due. As a result, the Kirch Group has to cope with the load of € 6.5 billion of debt.

Company Background

In 1999, Leo Kirch, sole proprietor of a closely held media empire, had contemplated an eventual flotation on the capital market. With this perspective in mind, he had split his company into three subgroups – KirchMedia, KirchPayTV and KirchBeteiligungs GmbH – all under a central holding company, KirchHolding.

Investor relations were not considered a priority. Thus, no financial information was published for KirchHolding, and there was no publicly available overview of the entire group's profits, cashflow or debts. The only one of the three sub-groups to publish any financial information was KirchMedia. As of 30 June 2001, this affiliate (excluding ProSiebenSat.1) booked bank loans of € 1.4 billion.

At year's end 2001, this intricately woven financial net began unravelling as several investment banks were threatening to withdraw their support. Thus, Dresdner Bank, a big lender to KirchMedia, one of the three main pillars of Kirch's empire, had refused to extend a secured € 460m loan and asked the group to repay the funds by 31 December. Only after the bank had obtained additional security did it give KirchMedia extra time to find the money – and then only in form of a bridge loan.

Dresdner Bank's action came as an unexpected shock. The additional security that the bank demanded was KirchMedia's 25 % stake in Telecinco, a Spanish broadcaster. To repay Dresdner Bank, KirchMedia could sell this stake for around € 500m, about half of its value of the year before. However, before Dresdner Bank's move, some analysts had hinted that the Telecinco stake would be sold to settle another of KirchMedia's major obligations – one of two put options.

Hold or Divest?

Dresdner Bank's manoeuvering was a cruel blow for Kirch Media. Kirch had been considering an initial public offering (IPO) for June 2002 as part of a proposed merger with ProSiebenSat.1 group, in which KirchMedia owned 52.5 % of the shares and 88.5 % of the voting rights. In effect, KirchMedia would use the deal to take over ProSiebenSat.1. As Kirch had voting control of both ProSiebenSat.1 and KirchMedia, he could guarantee the merger. His problem would be to attract new shareholders to provide new cash.

But, Kirch's bankers, already worried by the steep decline in the current value of all media assets, were skeptical about KirchMedia's financial performance. In the 18 months leading up to June 2001, all of KirchMedia's pre-tax profit of €364m came from free-to-air TV broadcasting, through ProSiebenSat.1 and Telecinco, whereas the other KirchMedia businesses reputedly suffered losses. Profits from the trading of film rights, the origins of Kirch's empire, would be offset by debt-interest payments, and by losses at DSF, a sports channel, and from assorted new-media ventures.

Compounding the bad news, ProSiebenSat.1, which had captured around 45% of the television-advertising market in Germany, suffered a slump in advertising. The company issued a warning that its pre-tax profits for 2001 would be 55% lower than the year before. Its current total market value was down to €1.2 billion, from €6.2 billion in January 2000. Axel Springer Verlag, Germany's largest newspaper-publishing group, had an option to sell its 11.48% stake in ProSieben-Sat.1 to KirchMedia for €767m in cash 2002. Although neither company commented on the option, exercising it was obviously in Axel Springer's interests.

Kirch held a 40% stake in Axel Springer through KirchBeteiligungs GmbH, but the Springer family retained voting control. Even if Kirch managed to negotiate the timing of the payment, KirchMedia would still have to supply the cash. New cash source might be generated by a sale of new shares in KirchMedia – if investors' confidence could be secured.

In this dire situation, Kirch Group executives suspected that Rupert Murdoch of NewsCorp, perhaps in league with John Malone of Liberty Media, was contemplating a hostile acquisition. In July, NewsCorp's BSkyB disclosed that KirchPayTV needed more money and that, if banks declined to provide it, a shareholder (i.e. other than BSkyB) had agreed to provide a temporary loan until June next year. However, true to form, Kirch would not comment on any aspect of its relationship with its bankers.

When it bought its 22% stake in KirchPayTV, BSkyB had negotiated an option to sell the stake back to KirchHolding for €1.8 billion if there was no flotation of KirchPayTV by 1 October 2002. Rupert Murdoch went on record to say that BSkyB intended to exercise its option. Furthermore, BSkyB cast doubt on KirchHolding's ability to pay by warning that it was uncertain whether the resources of Kirch Holding were sufficient to service the put option if exercised. The stake in Kirch and the option were acquired two years ago by the satellite broadcaster BskyB in which the News Corporation was the biggest shareholder. BskyB could use the option in October 2002 if Premiere failed to meet growth milestones laid down in the original contract.

Nonetheless, acquiring Kirch would give the buyer a broad range of entertainment and sports programming, including a huge library of movies and broadcasting rights to F1 auto races and the World Cup soccer tournament. KirchMedia had long-term contracts with most of the big Hollywood studios for free-TV and pay-

TV rights in Germany. In the year 2000, almost one-third of its revenue from these rights came from one of its corporate cousins, KirchPayTV, which bought from it the pay-TV rights module.

However, in March 2001, KirchPayTV was supposedly burdened with € 3.6 billion of future commitments under long-term film and programming contracts; most of this sum was owed to KirchMedia. Were KirchPayTV to default, KirchMedia would have to honor the bill. Accordingly, investors in KirchMedia would have to trust KirchPayTV's solvency.

Potential partners would realize that KirchPayTV, which was selling its services under the Premiere World name, was the biggest loss-maker in Kirch's empire. BSkyB, partly owned by Rupert Murdoch's News Corporation, and others had invested € 2.5 billion in this operation the year before. These funds were already spent for paying off debts and financing massive trading losses of at least € 2 billion since the start of 1999. In June 2001, the subscriber base stood at 2.4m, only 200,000 above the previous year. One reason for the modest growth has been that pay-TV was considered a luxury in Germany, as some 90 % of households receive 30 analogue channels via cable or satellite.

Liberty's Bid for Leadership in European Cable TV

In this situation, Malone, whose Liberty Media controlled a globally distributed cable network came on stage. Preliminary negotiations revolved around the question of licensing programs.

In a well-timed move in Sep 2001, Malone had spent € 5.5 billion to buy six of the nine regional German cable systems that Deutsche Telekom had been forced to shed by regulators. One month later, he bought further cable networks that, under Germany's fragmented system, would link many of the former Telekom connections through the "last mile" into German homes. Together, this deal gave Liberty 5 million directly billed cable subscribers, and a further 5 million billed through other operators – in total, over half the German cable market. Were Malone to gain control of the other European cable firms in which he already has an interest – he would create Europe's biggest cable operation.

In America, Malone had been using his control of distribution pipelines to invest in a clutch of young content companies (though rarely owning them outright) and to promote their programming. Some, such as Discovery Channel, have become global brands.

But Europe and America had different media cultures. Free satellite TV, for instance, was a stronger competitor in Europe than in America. On the other hand it would be difficult to achieve economies of scale in the fragmented, multilingual European market. As Europeans increasingly wanted local versions of American TV productions, such as Disney's or MTV's, the content deals were more complicated – and the content was more costly to produce.

In this precarious situations Kirch only had few lines of defense. The most effective was regulatory: in the past, competition authorities in Germany and at the European Commission have often blocked media alliances, including deals involving Kirch and Germany's cable systems. They would certainly take a hard look at any combination involving Kirch and either the News Corporation or Liberty Media.

Hollow Formula 1 Ownership Control

Further adding to the problems of KirchPayTV, was Kirch's investment SLEC Holdings, a group of companies that held commercial rights to Formula One (F1) motor racing. Kirch's 58.3 % stake in SLEC, acquired through KirchBeteiligungs in the first quarter of 2001in cost some € 1.9 billion, € 1.7 billion of which was borrowed. But Kirch could not draw on his share of F1's cashflow to service his debts, until SLEC had repaid the remaining € 1 billion of a € 1.4 billion bond issued in May 1999. This might not happen until 2005. The debt also restricted capital spending, thus obstructing Kirch's ambitious plans for the F1 business.

Kirch intended to transfer to KirchMedia some of the debt it took on to buy its SLEC stake. However, KirchMedia was not robust enough to carry all of Kirch's F1 debt. The question was: would a stock market flotation of KirchMedia provide the funds to repay the debt? Would an outright sale of the SLEC stake be sufficient?

Ominously, the major automobile makers were fretting under Mr Kirch's control of F1. As they were the main sponsors of F1, they wanted more control over its operations. Another contentious issue was the big share of F1's revenues allocated to SLEC. SLEC paid the teams only 47 % of F1's gross television revenues and retained all the highly profitable fees paid by promoters to stage grand prix events. The car manufacturers wanted more of these revenues for the teams. If a rival Grand Prix series would be established under the aegis of the automakers, the F1 brand would be virtually worthless.

Such a move would greatly reduce the value of Kirch's stake in SLEC. There seemed little chance of resolving this uncertainty prior to an eventual IPO of KirchMedia.

Kirch's Dilemma

Although Kirch has not been successful in selling Premiere World direct to consumers, its large library of film and sports pay-TV rights contained content that any rival pay-TV operators in Germany would also need. A stop-gap measure might be to sell this content on a wholesale basis to Germany's new cable operators rather than an outright sale of KirchMedia. But would this deal be worth giving up control of the media empire's crown jewels?

B 3.5 The "Executive" Mindset

Trust is the essential lubricant required in all deferred business transactions. To achieve a general climate of trust it is essential to choose a course of action, stick to it, and be willing to accept friendly help. Credibility is enhanced by grooming a reputation for energetic and positive approaches to tasks, and by focusing on clearly specified and attainable goals.

On the emotional level, the executive mindset demands a high degree of self-awareness and collaborative intuition to persuade others to follow. In this context, self-awareness means knowing that one might fail, and shedding a strategy that has failed. In searching for a new approach, it would be misleading to look primarily for hard facts and data, as they would only reflect current preoccupations. Putting trust in "gut" feelings and intuition can generate new perspectives, and getting input from colleagues and persons of trust will also help reduce uncertainty. The quality of decisions will be enhanced by considering an appropriate number of alternative solutions. Focusing on "the big picture" might even involve playing the role of "devil's advocate", and developing skills in delaying decisions to keep options open.

Goal Setting

Goal setting takes place at all levels in the organization. At the CEO or general manager level, there is strategic goal setting, centered on an organization's fundamental decisions, such as the choice of missions, strategies, objectives, policies, programs, goals, and major allocation of resources. Taken together, these strategic choices, will shape the organization's overall future.

At the middle management and supervisory level, goal setting tends to be more tactical, with a primary emphasis on implementing and carrying out decisions made as a part of strategic planning. An effective approach for this level is Management by Objectives (MBO). This involves connecting the process of joint goal setting between members of two adjacent levels of supervision with periodic measurement and comparison of actual performance against agreed-upon goals and objectives.

Delegating Effectively

To draw on the work potential of others, an executive must first specify precisely what is to be done. In assigning the task, therefore, it is important to communicate in explicit terms – setting deadlines and time horizons, and asking questions to see if the task is fully understood. In this stage it is important to show trust in other people's abilities in order to motivate them. But it would be demotivating to hold such high expectations that people would most likely fail. A generally successful approach is to project a supportive attitude, keeping the communication channels open, and being available for consultation and discussion.

To make empowerment credible, it is necessary to hold the person responsible for the work done and any difficulties that may emerge. In checking on the task progress, it would be a mistake to take control at the first sign of failure. A better approach would be to jointly explore what was going wrong, and – if asked – to assist the employees in developing their own solutions. On the other hand, ignoring employees' efforts can also be extremely demotivating. Therefore, a habit of recognizing what has been done, and showing appropriate gestures of appreciation reflects good executive practice.

In setting well-specified job objectives it is important to consider the following traits:

- Identify specific key result areas, beginning with an action verb preceded by the word "to", for example: to sell..., to prepare..., to increase..., to lower..., to complete.
- Set realistic targets within the limits of individual jobs.
- Identify a relevant key result area that is the target of performance accomplishment: reports, orders, accidents, inventory, attendance, customer service, etc.
- To verify their degree of achievement, state a performance indicator. Indicators can be quantitative or expressed in qualitative terms subject to judgment.
- Provide a time frame for producing the key result.

Brief Examples of Objective Statements:

Action Verb: To reduce
Key Result Area: turnaround time
Indicator-Measure: by 20 %
Time Frame: in 6 months

B 3.6 Experiential Case: The Temperamental Networker

Ed Gleick, computer specialist with Megatronics, Inc. strode into the office of Project Manager Frank Cesno and announced that he was "through", "finished", and "absolutely determined to leave the company." He asked to have his final paycheque ready in an hour, and without waiting for a response, headed for the door.

Cesno tried his best to imaginize possible scenarios that had caused this outburst. Gleick had been sent to this site some 500 miles from the home office to run tests on a recently installed Local Area Network. The test was important because the work of this project group could not continue until Gleick had completed his tests.

During the test Gleick was accountable to Brad Evans, who had been sent to Cesno's facility along with Gleick. Brad Evans' job was to supervise Gleick and coordinate his work with that of Cesno's project group. On several occasions in the past two weeks, Gleick had told Cesno that Evans was demanding too much of him, constantly putting him under pressure, and having him work overtime and on weekends. Gleick had complained that Evans hardly knew how to design and install a network system on his own and had little appreciation of the stress and strain he (Gleick) was under.

Cesno also reflected that he had talked with Brad Evans about this matter just two days before and had been told that Gleick was one of those freaky, out-of-touch computer whizkids who had been privileged in their jobs all along. Evans had stated that with the deadline to complete the tests less than a week away, Gleick was going to finish these tests on schedule even if he had to take a sleeping bag with him.

(1) Which of the five steps for taking initiative are illustrated in this case?
(2) Which are used effectively/successfully? Why?
(3) Which could have been used more effectively? How?

B 4 The External Environment and Corporate Culture

- The Environmental Domain
- Survival of the Fittest
- The Structure of the Corporate Environment – Layered Structure
- Adapting to the Environment
- Structural Variety
- Ownership
- Influencing the Environment
- Corporate Culture
- Cultural Types
- Strategy Case: Iridium LLC – Steering into a Descending Orbit
- The "Advocate" Mindset
- Experiential Case: The Group Decision

B 5 Business and the Law

B 4 The External Environment and Corporate Culture

B 4.1 Principles – Models – Practices

From an evolutionary perspective, the company is a dynamic and open system that must interact with the environment to survive. Its adaptive quality is applied in acquiring inputs from the environment, in transforming them, and in discharging the outputs to the external environment. The specific functions needed for organizational survival are performed by the subsystems for management, boundary spanning, production, maintenance, and adaptation.

The Environmental Domain

In a broad sense, the macroenvironment is infinite and includes everything outside the company – the natural environment, the economic environment, and society. The corporate environment is more narrowly defined as all elements that exist outside the boundary of the company, to which it is sensitive and must respond to survive.

This relevant environment includes all elements existing outside the boundary of the company that have the potential to affect the company in a particular situation, such as competitors, resources, technology, and economic conditions.

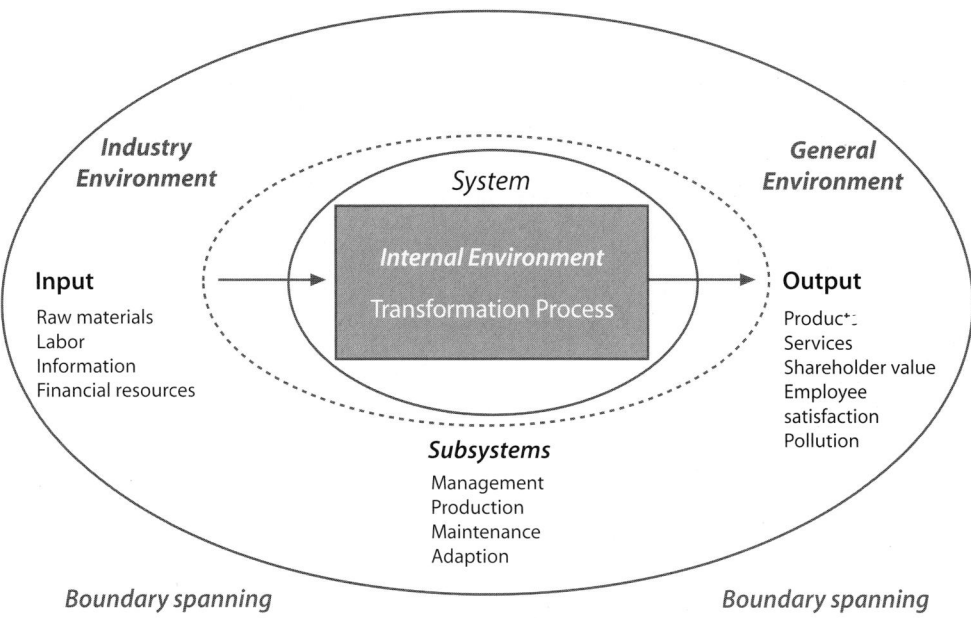

Survival of the Fittest

The assumptions with which managers interpret the environment will influence the way the company will react to cope with risk and uncertainty. For example, if managers believe that there is hidden information waiting to be found, they will employ boundary spanners – such as market research and legal experts – to discover and measure the relevant elements. If they think their understanding of the environment is limited, they will try to imitate successful competitors. But, if they assume that they can impose their perspective on the environment, they will ignore external obstacles, and enact their plans.

assumption	– Annahme, Vermutung
to influence	– beeinflussen
uncertainty	– Unsicherheit
market research	– Marktforschung
obstacle	– Hindernis
downfall	– Untergang
overdue	– überfällig
to encompass	– umfassen, einschließen
layer	– Schicht
dispersed	– verstreut, verteilt

From a historical point of view, the same factors that create success for a company can bring about its downfall. Thus, craftsmanship may emerge as an obsession for detail, entrepreneurial growth as empire building, and innovative product policies as aimless drifting. Even successful companies arrive at an average life span of only 40 years. When long overdue changes are implemented, many incumbents will succumb to internal inertia, while new, better-adapted competitors emerge out of nowhere to occupy their niche.

In a simplified model, the evolutionary selection process encompasses three stages: (1) variation, by which changed system elements create replicas of themselves, (2) selection according to "fitness" criteria, and (3) retention, or "hard-wiring" of the direction taken by the organization. As new companies proliferate, some new features (i.e. variations) will find a niche and help acquire the resources from the environment necessary to survive, while others are eliminated. Only the best-adapted companies survive, are institutionalized, and in time become a dominant part of their environment.

The Structure of the Corporate Environment – Layered Structure

For analysis, the corporate environment can be visualized as having three layers: general, task and internal environments.

The general environment is the more widely dispersed outer layer, and affects companies indirectly. It includes social, demographic, and economic factors that influence all companies about equally. Increases in the inflation rate, for example, are part of the company's general environment.

The task environment is closer to the company and includes the sectors that conduct day-to-day transactions with the company and directly influence its basic operations and performance. It is generally considered to include competitors, suppliers, and customers.

The company also has an internal environment, comprising the elements within the company's boundaries. The internal environment is composed of employees, production technology, organization structure, physical facilities, and also corporate culture.

For practical analysis, the sectors manufacturing, raw materials, relevant markets, and human resources would constitute the task environment, whereas the general environment would encompass government, social, cultural, and economic conditions, technology, and financial resources.

Adapting to the Environment

If the company faces increased uncertainty from the environment (such as competition, customers, suppliers, or government regulation), managers can use several strategies to adapt: e.g. increasing specialization; adopting a more flexible structure; putting more emphasis on planning and forecasting, combining forces with other companies, or abandoning the domain.

to constitute – darstellen
emphasis – Betonung, Nachdruck
to forecast – prognostizieren, voraussagen
to abandon – verlassen, aufgeben
domain – Bereich, Gebiet
predictable – berechenbar, voraussagbar
conversely – umgekehrt
rigid – starr, fest
to enhance – steigern, erhöhen, verbessern
competitive advantage – Wettbewerbsvorteil
linkages – Verbindungen
autonomy – Unabhängigkeit

Structural Variety

A company's structure should enable it to respond effectively to external changes. In general, an "organic" or loosely coupled structure works best in an uncertain environment and a bureaucratic or "programmed" structure is most effective in a predictable environment.

The organic structure makes for a flexible organization that has few rules and regulations, encourages teamwork, and decentralizes decision-making to the front-line employees. Conversely, the bureaucratic structure characterizes an organization programmed by rigidly defined tasks, rules, procedures, a strong hierarchy, and centralized decision-making.

Ownership

To enhance their competitive advantage, companies try to find a balance between linkages with other organizations and their own autonomy. When companies fear that valued resources might become scarce they will attempt to influence or control other organizations rather than acting in isolation.

<u>Asserting</u> ownership control in the form of mergers or acquisitions is a major form of intervention. It may be <u>supplemented</u> by indirect forms of control, such as cooptation (whereby influential people are recruited into top management) and <u>interlocking directorates</u> (whereby a board member from one company sits on the board of another company).

Long-term contracts, licensing agreements and joint ventures are used to reduce uncertainty. An interlocking directorate, on the other hand, is meant to establish a binding relationship with another company. Both forms represent temporary strategic alliances of two or more companies, typically occurring when the project is too complex, too expensive, or too risky for one company to <u>proceed</u> alone.

Influencing the Environment

The other major strategy for handling environmental uncertainty is to <u>seize</u> the initiative and control those elements causing problems. Given the impact of government on business, companies have responded by trying to influence government and public opinion. The most common <u>approaches</u> are to create lobbies to <u>persuade</u> legislators to <u>vote</u> according to special interests and to influence governing parties by <u>donating</u> money.

to assert	geltend machen, durchsetzen
to supplement	ergänzen
interlocking directorate	Schachtelaufsichtsrat
to proceed	durchführen, fortfahren
to seize	ergreifen
approach	Ansatz, Methode, Vorgehensweise
to persuade	überreden, überzeugen
to vote	stimmen, abstimmen
to donate	spenden

Corporate Culture

The corporate culture represents the prevailing climate in a business organization. It encompasses the set of shared opinions and informal norms that bind organization members together. As the culture reflects the will of the organization to survive in a changing environment, managers should reinforce the values that employees need to have and need to act on for the organization strategy. For instance, if the strategy emphasizes timeliness in project completion, cultural values should reinforce decision-making and planning processes.

Cultural Types

Based on the degree of environmental uncertainty associated with the company's strategic decisions and the speed, with which the company receives feedback from the environment about the decision's success, four cultural categories emerge:

(a) the **win-lose** (or **macho**) **culture** is characterized by high-risk decision-making and fast feedback, as is common practice, for instance, in the media and in the real estate business;

(b) the **win-win** (or **work-hard, play-hard**) **culture** is also characterized by rapid feedback, but decisions are weighed carefully, with managers making many small rather than a few big decisions, thus creating an internal culture for people to be active, and to celebrate success;

(c) the **high-stakes** (or **bet-your-company**) **culture** is characterized by risks which involve high stakes and long time lags before players can assess their success; this dependence encourages strong links with the environment, as in the oil business or in research dominated fields like aerospace;

(d) The **due process culture** is characterized by low-risk decisions and little or no performance feedback to employees, but emphasizes compliance with rules and procedures.

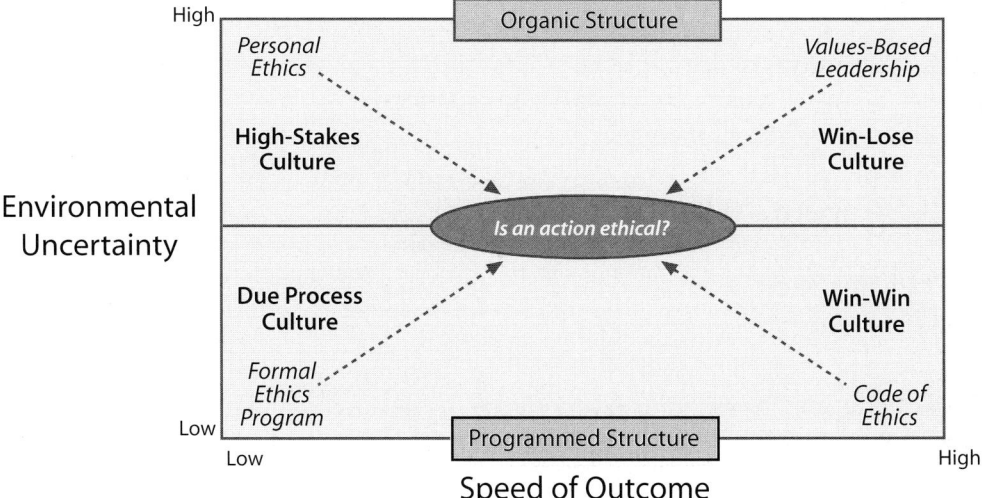

When a company's culture is not in alignment with the environment, changes must occur in norms and values to support the transformation process. Effective managers are also skilled persuaders, articulating and reinforcing a vision for change through public speaking and symbolic acts.

An ethical issue arises when behavior within the organization transgresses the bounds of legal requirements or socially accepted norms. Because business practices reflect the values and behavior patterns within organizations, unethical behavior cannot be attributed entirely to an individual. Contingent on structure and strategy, leaders should either use formal rules (as embodied in a code of ethics) and formal systems (such as ethics committees and disclosure systems, like whistle-blowing) – to shape ethical values, or they should integrate ethics into the organizational culture through supporting words and actions.

B 4.2 Knowledge Check

(1) Explain (a) how a company can predict environmental changes, and (b) how a company can achieve an environmental fit.
(2) List suitable actions for controlling the environment.
(3) Recommend a strategy for survival in the process of "natural selection".

→ See Answer Key for solutions.

B 4.3 Keywords

Boundary spanning; cooptation; corporate culture; differentiation; domain; environmental complexity; imitation strategy; interlocking directorate; interorganizational linkages; programmed structure; niche; norms; organic structure; resource dependence; retention; selection; symbolic management; task environment; time lag; uncertainty; values; variation.

B 4.4 Strategy Case: Iridium LLC – Steering into a Descending Orbit

Iridium Invokes Chapter 11

Until it was rocked by the financial crisis in August 1999, Iridium LLC (i.e. limited liability company) enjoyed significant achievements as the pioneer in handheld satellite communications. Their network of 66 satellites provided global communications capability for mobile telecommunications. The Iridium service was used in the most remote locations under the most extreme weather conditions. Their customer base ranged from pilots in Alaska to pipeline workers in Brazil, from ranchers in Australia to fishermen in Peru. Iridium was now an essential tool of their trade. First movers in a new industry, however, face unique challenges, and Iridium made some mistakes in launching their service.

A first sign of serious trouble was the slow rise in subscribers. Iridium responded by cutting budgets on the operational side. When the losses continued, the board of directors came under pressure from their largest investors – among them Motorola and Nippon Iridium Corporation. To regain initiative, a new top management was appointed under the leadership of John Richardson, and a new marketing focus established. The leadership change has underlined the scale of the crisis. Responding to perceived customer needs, the emphasis was put on reduced, simplified service and equipment pricing. In a bold move to offer added value for their customers, the company introduced newly developed, specialized products and accessories targeted at specific industries such as maritime, aeronautical and remote operators.

At the end of Q3, 1999, the $5bn investment faced financial meltdown. Iridium had debts of more than $3bn, annual interest payments of $250m and satellite maintenance costs of $550m a year, only offset by the trickle of income from its relatively few subscribers. It was therefore imperative for them to reduce the burn rate and to increase their subscriber base. In an effort to conclude a comprehensive financial restructuring under an orderly, court-supervised process Iridium LLC filed for Chapter 11 reorganization. In this way, Iridium was able to remain in business, and to continue providing its global telecommunications service without interruption.

Company History

The Iridium project began in 1985 when Motorola, the US electronics group, embraced the idea of a mobile phone that could be used anywhere in the world. Initially, seventy-seven low-earth orbit satellites, each with a life span of between five and seven years, were to constitute the system backbone. This configuration was symbolized by the name Iridium, the 77th element. Although the required number was eventually brought down to 66 satellites, the name remained.

Reflecting the operational complexity of the project, 15 gateways were planned around the world, where satellite phone signals would be channeled on to terrestrial phone networks.

From the start, Motorola was keen to share the project's high costs and risks. It therefore brought in companies and consortia as owners and operators of the gateways. They agreed to pay to build the ground-stations, and became investors in the project itself. The range of gateway operators was very broad, but doubts about whether the gateway partners were able to contribute significant technical expertise were suppressed in the interest of maintaining the network density.

Diversified Financial Backing

In its first round of funding in 1993, Iridium raised $800m from its strategic investors. At that time, the Motorola business plan forecast 2m users by 2002, with profits flowing even earlier.

By the end of 1996, Iridium had raised $1.9bn from investors and moved into a $750m property financed by Chase Manhattan and Barclays Bank. All partners were happy to increase their funding as long as forecasts for the new market continued to be favorable. The risks seemed acceptable, as these projections came not only from Iridium and Motorola, but also from several other rival projects that were being planned. In an attempt to broaden the capital base, Iridium went public in 1997.

By the time the Iridium service was ready for launch in 1998, Motorola had diluted its equity stake to just 18 percent. It had also received $3.6bn in payments from Iridium for the satellites and associated services. Motorola's own investment amounted to just over $2bn.

Strategy Shift

In the face of massive changes in the technological and economic environment of mobile telecommunications, Iridium decided that it would partner cellular operators. Initially, the satellite group had planned to compete directly with the terrestrial cellular operators. Now, it seemed, cellular operators had a solid advantage in capacity, as well as on price. At the time of the service's launch during 1998, Iridium handsets were calculated to retail for about $3,000, while call rates would average $7 a minute.

At this stage of the product-life cycle, the cellular market was experiencing exponential growth. From the perspective of the individual firm, it was marked by technological advances, and cutthroat competition, reflected in tumbling handset prices and call rates.

Yet, Iridium remained convinced that international business executives would be willing to pay a significant premium for the benefit of being able to make calls from anywhere in the world from their mobile phones.

Deteriorating Competitive Situation

Despite its worldwide ambitions, Iridium revealed a parochial orientation when it failed to buy into the European GSM system as the coming international standard for cellular operators. This system was gaining market share around the world with the exception of North America. In combination with this seamless global reach, "roaming" agreements enabled users to use their GSM mobile phones abroad, thereby undermining Iridium's use-anywhere advantage.

Iridium's other advertised advantages also looked increasingly tenuous. For example, the offshore oil and gas industries were once touted as an important source of revenue. However, a search in the industry journals reveled that worldwide were less than 300 active seismic crews operating in the oil and gas industry. But Iridium maintained its optimistic forecast, predicting that the cash flow would be positive by the end of its first year of operation. By 2002, when Iridium expected to have a three to four million subscribers, it stated that it would repay $3bn of debts and still have $3bn free cash flow to spend on its next generation of satellites.

Technical Troubles Cause Financial Deterioration

But then a series of technical failures followed that shook investors' confidence. First, two Iridium satellites failed in orbit. Subsequently, Iridium announced it was pushing back its launch, planned for 22 September, for six weeks due to "technical problems". Compounding this bad news, Iridium's great rival Globalstar lost one-fifth of its satellites in a launch explosion.

During the period from Sep to Dec 1998 it was vital for Iridium to raise additional long-term debt. The company required almost $1bn of additional funding to survive the next 12 months of operations. However, its dwindling share price ruled out raising further capital in the stock market. Also, the rating agencies had become cautious.

Apart from this financial squeeze, Iridium was facing further technical problems. While prototype handsets had been shipped, commercial versions had not been delivered by October. In addition, Kyocera of Japan which together with Motorola was one of Iridium's two handset contract manufacturers was experiencing software problems.

Meanwhile, some gateway operators and service partners sent out warnings that they were not ready for Iridium's launch. For instance, some had not received training in the use of the handsets and many lacked promotional material. When demand picked up slightly during the summer of 1998, handsets immediately went into short supply. Some of the gateways and service providers also showed themselves unprepared. Finally, complaints were voiced online that the phones did not work indoors and many other technical difficulties. The large European service providers were not actively promoting Iridium products because they could not guarantee for the security of the network.

While sorting out these problems, Iridium was delighted that an advertising campaign had produced more than 1m sales inquiries. Yet those leads produced only 10,000 customers. And the auditors calculated sunk costs of $14,000 per subscriber.

Tough Financial Covenant

In December 1998 the company signed a banking arrangement, again led by Chase and Barclays, with ambitious subscriber targets as covenants. The $800m loan was supposed to secure Iridium's survival over the next 12 months. However, the loan was contingent on Iridium fulfilling specific objectives, such as signing on 52,000 new subscribers.

Given that Iridium only had a total of 10,294 subscribers at that point in time, and was also experiencing severe delivery problems, it was a risky decision on the part of the company and the banks to agree on such ambitious targets. While refusing to comment publicly, Iridium's bankers admitted that the covenants were based on the company's own projections, and not on investors' inflated expectations.

Iridium was now facing several lawsuits for allegedly failing to keep investors informed of the obstacles ahead.

Company Outlook

It would be an extremely challenging task for the new management to turn Iridium around. Investors and bondholders would be asked to accept substantial cuts in the value of their holdings. Investors would also asked to contribute additional $600m in cash to fund the new marketing plan.

In the meantime, Iridium has cut prices on handsets to $1,500 per phone and has lowered tariffs to compete with the GSM providers. The sales force was being beefed up and gateway operators were being provided with more technical support. But, for the turnaround to succeed, the financial backers – investors, bondholders, suppliers and customers would have to be persuaded that a compelling sales idea from 1985 was still a profitable proposition in 1999.

B 4.5 The "Advocate" Mindset

Empowerment

Planning and auditing activities in organizations are doomed to fail if the needed information is not exchanged and discussed in a friendly, supportive atmosphere. In situations, where there is reciprocal dependence among individuals, a trusting two-way communication is vital. The most effective way to enhance communication is to have a committed person adopt an advocate mindset to introduce a project or proposal in informal discussions and face-to-face meetings. The meetings should be conducted in a way to encourage input from everyone, keeping members enthusiastic and energized.

In general, group discussions bring out a wide range of values and perspectives, as they can draw on greater knowledge or expertise than a single individual. Also, from a motivational perspective, employees will feel committed to implementing a decision in which they were involved. They understand the reasons behind the decision, and are well placed to identify potential obstacles to implementation as well as ways to overcome them.

But, if group meetings are not well structured, individuals with the appropriate expertise may allow those with little or no knowledge to dominate the discussion.

Group Exercise – "Nonstop Point-Point Flight"

The following exercise involves group decision-making in estimating the relative distances of 18 destinations from Frankfurt/Main. Each group is to employ the group consensus method in reaching its decision. This means that the group members must agree upon the position of each of the 18 destinations before it becomes a part of the group decision.

Distance from Frankfurt/Main	Personal Ranking	Personal Deviation	Optimal Ranking	Group's Ranking	Group's Deviation
Athens					
Baghdad					
Budapest					
Cairo					
Dubai					
Helsinki					
Istanbul					
Karachi					
Kuwait					
Moscow					

The External Environment and Corporate Culture | B 4

Distance from Frankfurt/Main	Personal Ranking	Personal Deviation	Optimal Ranking	Group's Ranking	Group's Deviation
Nairobi					
Nice					
Oslo					
Rome					
Sao Paulo					
Seoul					
St. Petersburg					
Vienna					
Total					

Discuss:

If the group decision turns out to be better than that of the best group member, does that outcome reflect the higher knowledge of the group or the central tendency of averages?

> **Here are some guides to reaching consensus:**
> (1) Avoid arguing for your own individual judgments. Approach the task on the basis of logic.
> (2) Avoid changing your mind if it is only to reach agreement and avoid conflict.
> (3) Avoid "conflict-reducing" techniques such as majority vote, averaging, or trading.
> (4) View differences in opinion as help rather than a hindrance in decision-making.

Increasing Meeting Effectiveness

Effective meeting management begins by inviting individuals who are affected by, or have an important stake in, the outcome of the decision. It is important to invite participants with the intent of maximizing knowledge and perspective diversity. Preliminary decisions, such as selecting the time and venue, will influence the outcome. For example, holding a meeting in a manager's office will carry a very different message than holding the meeting in a conference room. Efficient administration, such as distributing an agenda in advance, increases the likelihood of accomplishing the meeting objectives.

In conducting the meeting, care should be taken to start on time, to organize the taking of minutes, and to review the agenda to check if there are any adjustments necessary. To create a relaxed climate, new participants should be introduced in a personable way.

In following through the agenda, active participation by all should be encouraged. In the event of some individuals dominating the discussion, they should be asked to give others an opportunity to contribute. Those failing to contribute should be asked for their opinions or suggestions without causing embarrassment.

In concluding the meeting it is helpful to review the decisions and assignments made, and, if appropriate to schedule the next meeting. In the follow-up, it is good practice to periodically contact individuals about their progress.

Conflict Management

Conflicts in organizations are inevitable, and should sometimes be encouraged in order to allow new ideas to surface and to create positive forces for innovation and change.

Each of the following conflict management approaches has advantages and disadvantages that make it more or less appropriate for a given situation:

- adopting an assertive stance when quick, decisive action is vital;
- a compromising approach when goals are important, but either not worth the effort or when opponents with equal power are committed to mutually exclusive goals;
- avoiding a conflict if the issue is trivial, or when there is no chance of achieving one's own aims at that stage;
- accommodating others' wishes when issues are more important to them than to oneself and to maintain cooperation by building social credits for later issues;
- collaborating by merging different perspectives for an innovative solution, especially when both sets of concerns are too important to be compromised. When using a collaborative approach, it is important to keep in mind this maxim: confront the conflict; confront the problem; do not confront the person!

B 4.6 Experiential Case: The Group Decision

Dave Simpson, the office manager of a call center, attended a weekend management seminar focused on group discussion and group decision-making techniques. The key message was that employees with different levels of responsibility, if given the opportunity, would jointly design breakthrough changes enthusiastically embraced by everyone involved. Working together as a group would lead to more effective decisions than working in isolation if the group were held accountable as a functioning unit within the larger organization.

At work, Simpson decided to practice some of the principles that he had learned. He called together his 22 call center operators and told them that higher demands for service required a review of the workflow standards established two years previously, prior to the installation of automated support systems. He gave the operators a chance to discuss and to decide what the new standards should be. Simpson was convinced they would commit themselves to higher standards than he himself would have dared to propose.

After an hour of discussion, Simpson was informed of the unanimous vote that the standards were already too high. He still remained convinced that standards could be raised to achieve the planned productivity increase with the newly installed system. But, under these circumstances, it was obvious that his refusal to accept the group's decision would be very damaging for morale. Before deciding on a course of action, Simpson decided to review his notes from the seminar.

(1) Was Simpson's style of participatory decision making appropriate for the situation?

(2) What would you suggest that Simpson (a) do now, (b) in future?

B 5 Business and the Law

- Taxes
- Company-Related Laws
- American Court System
- Law of Torts and Product Liability
- Agency
- Property Transactions
- Bankruptcy
- Strategy Case: Dimon Inc. – Treading Carefully
- The "Coaching" Mindset
- Experiential Exercise: Giving and Receiving Feedback

B 6 Top Management Direction

B 5 Business and the Law

B 5.1 Principles – Models – Practices

A significant factor for a company's success is its ability to work with government bodies and to use the law to its advantage. The process of managing government relations is complicated by the fact that a company has to <u>monitor</u> the actions of local, regional, and possibly foreign governments within an increasingly complex web of laws and restrictions.

Although it is in the government's interest to support business, the two sides have frequently <u>clashed</u>. For example, when the actions of business mobilize other voters, government is under pressure to pass laws and regulations to <u>curb</u> the controversial practices.

Taxes

The most controversial area of government activities has always been raising taxes both for revenue, and for providing <u>incentives</u> or disincentives for individual and collective behavior. An investment tax credit which is <u>deductible</u> from the taxable income, for example, is designed to <u>encourage</u> companies to invest in capital equipment. Both individuals and businesses often make decisions mainly to obtain special tax breaks.

to monitor – überwachen	
to clash – kollidieren, aufeinander prallen	
to curb – einschränken, beschränken	
incentive – Anreiz	
deductible – abzugsfähig, absetzbar	
encourage – ermutigen, fördern	
taxable – steuerpflichtig	
corporate-income-tax – Körperschaftsteuer	

Personal and Corporate Income Taxes

In partnerships and sole proprietorships, profits are considered as the personal income of the owners, <u>taxable</u> at personal-income-tax rates. The personal income tax is a graduated or progressive tax, which means that the levied tax percentage increases with the income. Corporations pay taxes on their profits as individuals pay taxes on their income. The <u>corporate-income-tax</u> rate of a region is an important factor for the decision to operate there.

Property Taxes

Companies who own property pay higher rates on their land and buildings than private owners do, thereby contributing significantly to a community's property tax revenues.

Sales Taxes and Value Added Taxes

In general, merchandise sold at the retail level is subject to a sales tax, with companies functioning as tax collectors. Although companies are exempt from paying the tax on merchandise they buy for resale, sales tax increases the prices customers have to pay. Sales tax is a major source of revenue in the USA, while value-added tax (VAT) is important in Europe. VAT is assessed along the length of the value chain of a product or service, based on the difference between the cost of inputs (adjusted for prior tax) and the price outputs are sold for.

Excise Taxes and Tariffs

A number of items are subject to excise taxes – taxes originally raised to suppress potentially harmful practices. Excise taxes are usually imposed on gasoline, tobacco products, alcoholic beverages, and luxury items. Although they are imposed on the manufacturer or retailer, it is ultimately the consumer who pays.

Tariffs (or customs duties) were originally intended to raise revenue, but are now used mainly to protect domestic business against foreign competition, or to achieve goals in foreign policy.

Company-Related Laws

One of the most pervasive ways that government affects business is through the legal system: through legislative action (statutory law), through administrative rulings (administrative law), and – in Anglo-Saxon law – through customs and judicial precedents, i.e. court decisions that serve as a model for deciding a later case (common law). In legal proceedings, all three forms of law overlap.

Contracts

In legal terms, a contract is an explicit or implied exchange of promises enforceable by law. Intent or purpose is the essence of a contract between competent (i.e. being of age and legally responsible) parties.

---

merchandise – Waren
retail – Einzelhandel
sales tax – Umsatzsteuer
exempt – befreit
value-added tax – Mehrwertsteuer
value chain – Wertschöpfungskette
excise tax – Verbrauchsteuer
suppress – unterdrücken
tariff, customs duty – Zoll
pervasive – weit verbreitet, beherrschend
custom – Brauch, Sitte, Gewohnheit
precedent – Präzedenzfall
enforceable – durchsetzbar, vollstreckbar

American Court System

Highest Courts of Appeal

U.S. Supreme Court
The U.S. Supreme Court decides which cases it will hear. However, it is obliged to hear certain rare mandatory appeals and cases specified by the Constitution.

State Level: Supreme Courts of Appeal
These are the final courts of appeal for the majority of state cases. However, a party may appeal to the U.S. Circuit Court of Appeals if a case implicates a right protected by the Constitution.

Intermediate Courts of Appeal

State Intermediate Courts of Appeal
40 states have ICAs. These courts are the first court of appeals for the majority of cases. In 10 states the state Supreme Court is the only court of appeals.

U.S. Circuit Courts of Appeal
There are 12 circuit courts spread over the USA. Each court reviews cases from the U.S. District Courts in its Circuit, appeals going to the U.S. Supreme Court.

U.S. Court of Appeals for the Federal Circuit
This court reviews civil appeals involving minor claims against the U.S. government; appeals in patent-right cases and cases involving international trade disputes.

Trial Courts

State Trial Courts
In general, cases involving state, civil and criminal laws are initially filed in state or local trial courts (e.g. Municipal, County, District, Circuit or Superior Courts).

Appeals from the state trial court usually go to the state intermediate court of appeals.

About 95% of all court cases involve state trial courts.

U.S. District Courts
The 94 federal district courts, which handle criminal and civil cases involving:

- Federal statutes
- The U.S. Constitution
- Civil cases between citizens from different states involving more than $ 75,000.

Most appeals go to the U.S. Circuit Court of Appeals; some go to the U.S. Court of Appeals for the Federal Circuit.

U.S. Court of International Trade
Specializes in cases in the field of international trade. Appeals go to the U.S. Court of Appeals for the Federal Circuit (CAFC).

U.S. Claims Courts
For federal cases involving claims over $ 10,000 and cases involving some government contractors.

Appeals go to the CAFC.

For a contract to be <u>valid</u> and enforceable:

- an oral or written offer must be made and communicated to the intended party or parties.
- an offer must be accepted. There must be clear intent (spoken, written, or by action) to enter into the contract. The acceptance must also be <u>conveyed</u> to the other party or parties.
- a contract is legally binding only when the parties have bargained with one another and exchanged something, called <u>consideration</u>. Consideration may be in the form of a payment of money, a delivery of goods, or a performance of services.
- a valid contract must be free of <u>fraud</u>, <u>duress</u>, <u>undue influence</u>, and even mistake.

When one party fails to live up to the terms of a contract, the other party may claim <u>breach of contract</u>. It may <u>sue</u> in <u>court</u> for <u>damages</u> or negotiate to settle out of court. The damages awarded reflect the amount of profit lost and often include court costs as well.

Companies may create a product warranty, or guarantee, by explicitly making or even by just implying a promise about the product. A company will be in breach of warranty if the product does not perform as specified.

Law of Torts and Product Liability

Torts are non-criminal acts (other than breach of contract) injuring a person or property. Intentional torts are willful acts resulting in injury, even though there might be no intent to cause harm. An example is <u>maligning</u> another's reputation through in writing (<u>libel</u>) or in speech (<u>slander</u>).

One of the most controversial areas of tort law is <u>negligence</u>, a failure to use a reasonable amount of care necessary to protect others from unreasonable risk of injury.

Developing out of tort law, <u>product liability</u> law holds companies responsible for their products on the grounds of negligence and strict liability (i.e. liability without fault). For example, a company can be held liable for injuries caused by a defective product because of poor design, improper construction, improper assembly, or negligent advertising. To avoid

---

valid – gültig, rechtswirksam
to convey – mitteilen, übermitteln
consideration – Gegenleistung
fraud – arglistige Täuschung, Betrug
duress – Nötigung, Zwang
undue influence – unzulässige Beeinflussung
breach of contract – Vertragsbruch
to sue – verklagen
court – Gericht
damages – Schadensersatz
to malign – verleumden
libel – (schriftliche) Verleumdung
slander – (mündliche) Verleumdung
negligence – Fahrlässigkeit
product liability – Produkthaftung

litigation, a company must perform reasonable tests and must use reasonable care when inspecting a product. As a company may be held liable for injury caused by a defective product even if it used all reasonable care in the manufacture and sale, it is also advisable for companies to warn consumers about the possible dangers of using their products.

A company may even be sued, although it did not produce the item that caused the injury. Market share liability shifts the burden of proof to the defendant who is held liable for a percentage of the damages equal to its share of the market at the time – causing many firms to withdraw from high-risk areas.

Agency

Agency exists when one party, known as the principal, authorizes another party, known as the agent, to act on his or her behalf, and when the principal has the right to control the conduct of the agent in whatever activity is delegated. The principal usually creates this relationship by explicit authorization, either orally or in writing. In some cases (such as property transfers) the authorization must be written in form of a document called power of attorney. In others, an "implied agency" may be created.

Agency is important to business because the principal is liable for any contracts made or wrongdoing committed by an agent as long as the agent is acting within the scope of his or her authority.

Property Transactions

Property represents the rights of one person with regard to any object and all other persons. The law recognizes two types of property: (1) Real property as land and everything permanently attached to it. (2) Personal property, or chattels as all other property. It may be tangible (such as cars, or anything having a physical existence) or intangible (bank accounts, stocks, insurance policies, and intellectual property – including trademarks, patents, and copyrights).

Two types of documents are important in obtaining real property. The landlord transfers real property to a new owner through a deed, whereas a lease or a rent contract is used for a temporary transfer to a tenant.

---

litigation – Rechtsstreit, Prozess
burden of proof – Beweislast
defendant – Angeklagter, Beklagter
agency – Handlungsvollmacht, Vertretung
principal – Vollmachtgeber
agent – Bevollmächtigter
power of attorney – schriftliche Vollmacht
liable – verantwortlich, haftbar
chattels – bewegliche Güter
tangible – materiell
intangible – immateriell
trademark – Warenzeichen
lease – Mietvertrag, Pachtvertrag
tenant – Mieter, Pächter

A permanent transfer of tangible or intangible personal property is technically a transfer of title, or ownership. Any loss before the transaction is the seller's, and any loss afterward is the buyer's. But when property is purchased COD (<u>cash on delivery</u>), the title is not transferred until the goods are accepted and paid for. <u>Installment buying</u> is even more complicated, the title passing when the buyer takes possession of the property, although weekly or monthly installments still have to be paid.

> cash on delivery – per Nachnahme
> Installment buying – Ratenkauf
> debt relief – Schuldenerlass
> obligations – Verpflichtungen
> debtor – Schuldner
> creditor – Gläubiger
> proceeds – Erlös
> lawsuit – Klage, Prozess
> takeover bid – Übernahmeangebot

Bankruptcy

Bankruptcy is the legal system of <u>debt relief</u> for individuals or businesses who are no longer able to meet their financial <u>obligations</u>. Voluntary bankruptcy is initiated by the <u>debtor</u>; involuntary bankruptcy by <u>creditors</u>. In the United States, under Chapter 7, the debtor's assets are liquidated, and the <u>proceeds</u> divided equitably among the creditors. By entering Chapter 11, a company is allowed to reorganize. It gains time to cut costs and to improve operations while stopping regular payments to creditors and delaying <u>lawsuits</u>. Occasionally, companies merely use bankruptcy law to avoid unpleasant obligations or to defend against <u>takeover bids</u>.

Citing United States Laws (i.e. "the Law")

Example: 22 USC § 1501 (a)

- The leading digits represent the Title number, in this case, "22". U.S. Laws are divided into numbered Titles.
- The "USC" represents United States Code
- The symbol, "§" signifies Section
- The next number indicates the Section Number

Citing Code of Federal Regulations (i.e. Implementing "the Law")

Example: 15 CFR § 122 (b)

- Federal Regulations are divided into various Titles. The leading digits represent the Title number, in this case, "15".
- The "CFR" represents the Code of Federal Regulations.
- The symbol, "§" signifies Section.
- The next number refers to the Section Number.
- The parentheses indicate a particular paragraph within the section, in this case "(b)".

B 5.2 Knowledge Check

(1) State how (a) government affects business, and (b) companies influence government.
(2) List five revenue-raising taxes and two regulatory taxes.
(3) State the difference between statutory and common law.
(4) Name (a) six areas of law relevant for businesses; (b) the key elements of a valid contract.
(5) Distinguish between real, personal, and intellectual property.

→ **See Answer Key for solutions.**

B 5.3 Keywords

Administrative law; agency; bankruptcy; breach of contract; common law; consideration; contract; customs duties; deed; excise taxes; intellectual property; lease; market-share liability; negligence; personal property; power of attorney; prior tax; private law; product liability law; property; public law; real property; statutory law; strict liability; tort; value-added tax; warranty.

B 5.4 Strategy Case: Dimon Inc. – Treading Carefully

The last decade was tough going for the U.S. tobacco industry. The turbulence was reflected in the blizzard of product liability claims against the major cigarette manufacturers adding up to several hundreds of billion dollars. Compounding these legal troubles, militant anti-smoking groups were lobbying for classification and regulation of tobacco as a drug by the Food and Drug Administration (FDA). Adding to the pressure, Congress and many state legislatures were considering ever more stringent bans on smoking and tobacco advertisement. Also, the Clinton Administration was considering a severe new excise tax on cigarettes to fund public health care reform. On the trading side, the tobacco merchants were struggling to cope with oversupplies in many key markets as a new federal law limited the foreign-grown tobacco leaf content of U.S.-made cigarettes to 25%.

Despite these threats and disruptions, the industry remained extremely optimistic about the fundamental health of the business. Expanding markets in the Far East, the former Soviet Union and other parts of the world were more than making up for the declining business in the United States. Moreover, the continuing market trends towards light blends were favoring the U.S. tobacco industry.

One of the world's largest tobacco suppliers, Dimon Inc., a Fortune 500 company with headquarters in Danville, Virginia, is engaged in two international businesses, the purchasing, processing and selling of leaf tobacco and the purchasing and selling of fresh cut flowers. Dimon has operations in every major tobacco-producing region of the world, including more than 30 countries worldwide, and handle a substantial share of the world market for internationally traded leaf tobacco. With sales in excess of $2.1 billion in 1996, the company is the second largest leaf tobacco dealer as well as the largest importer and exporter of fresh cut flowers in the world, and employs close to 10,000 full-time and seasonal people worldwide.

Company History

In the 1850s, a tobacco commission merchant by the name of Richard H. Dibrell opened a tobacco business in Richmond, Virginia. It thrived on extensive travel in the search for new tobacco markets, new customers, and the timely acquisition of smaller subsidiary companies.

Overseas operations expanded into the Far East, Africa, and Europe. In addition, the larger domestic cigarette manufacturers began to do substantial business with Dibrell Brothers beginning in the 1930s.

An important era drew to a close when the three founding families passed on the entire executive control to a Board of Directors in 1959.

Adapting to Industry Changes

Consolidation, modernization, and diversification were the themes for Dibrell Brothers during the 1960s. The purchase of Richmond Cedar Works, a manufacturer of ice cream freezers, in 1967 represented the company's first effort to diversify. Dibrell Brothers diversified again in 1969 by entering the home lighting industry with the purchase of American Interiors.

By the early 1970s, Dibrell Brothers had enjoyed considerable success, having paid a dividend to its shareholders every year since 1925. This advance was possible because of the company's geographic spread which helped insulate it from the usual risks associated with agricultural products: political upheaval, bad weather, and import/export restrictions.

During the late 1980s, consumers throughout the world were increasingly opting for low-priced, generic cigarettes. This trend intensified during the early 1990s and signaled a fundamental reshaping of the tobacco industry. Dibrell Brothers was well-positioned for this shift, having imported a sizable amount of inexpensive tobacco for years and thereby enabling it to benefit from the rising popularity of low-priced cigarettes. Dibrell Brothers' management had acted to offset the global trend to lighter blends by moving out of the dark tobacco markets in countries such as the Dominican Republic and Indonesia. Generally, processing occurred in the country of origin.

Flower Operations

In 1987, Dibrell Brothers diversified again by acquiring Florimex Verwaltungs- gesellschaft mbH (Florimex), an importer and distributor of fresh cut flowers in Europe, North America, and Japan. When Richmond Cedar Works was sold in

1990, Florimex became Dibrell Brothers' only non-tobacco business. Dibrell Brothers' stock tripled in value in 1991, driven primarily by the profitability of its Brazilian operations and the remarkable growth of Florimex, which doubled its annual revenue total between 1989 and 1993 to reach $360 million.

Florimex distributed cut flowers through its network of 51 branch offices in 18 countries. Flowers are acquired from more than 300 suppliers located in all five continents. Its primary sources of supply were through auctions in the Netherlands and contract arrangements in Kenya and Latin America. Flowers were transported by commercial and cargo planes, and within hours of cutting passed through distribution channels to flower vendors around the world. Florimex maintained fleets of refrigerated trucks for transporting flowers throughout Europe, where the average consumption of fresh cut flowers was twice that of the USA.

Dimon's management was optimistic about the future of the cut flower business.

Forming of Dimon Inc.

It was evident that the future of the industry belonged to large companies, with large reserves of ready capital and solid global operations. However, the era of small, family-controlled companies was fast drawing to a close. In an effort to remain competitive and to attract new investors, Dibrell Brothers and Monk-Austin Inc. a Farmville, North Carolina-based tobacco company, agreed to consolidate their operations through a merger. Based on this strategic decision, the newly formed Dimon Inc. was established in Oct 1994 as a merger of equals. This equality was symbolized in the new name, forged out of the merging firms' names. From the perspectives of both tobacco industry and the financial community, the merger seemed a logical move. The two companies had traditions of strong leadership; both had experienced operations on every leaf-trading continent; and both companies took pride in their long and rich history.

New Strategic Assessment

In October 1997, Dimon's board was contemplating a major change in its strategy to assure its survival by adjusting to the new, competitive environment. It believed that, in the long run, attention to two basic themes would lead to increasing shareholder value. These were (1) service to customer, and (2) cost efficiency. At Dimon, cost efficiency was addressed by continuously developing low cost sources of supply and continuously finding new ways to leverage the company's investments.

As strategic directions for the future, the board was convinced that Dimon's operations had to be further streamlined to assure greater productivity and also that its overseas expansion program had to continue. China, for example, was already the world's biggest producer and consumer of tobacco, and Dimon was cooperating with Chinese State enterprises to improve the quality of tobacco, their techniques of handling and shipping patterns. Some other rising stars in its sourcing portfolio were Argentina, Malawi and Zimbabwe.

> The board was taking a hard look at the product diversification strategy, especially with regard to the contribution of the non-tobacco activities. In this context, it had to decide whether or not to divest its flower import and export business, Florimex Worldwide and organize itself entirely around the worldwide leaf tobacco industry.
>
> Dimon's main tobacco customers were multinational manufacturers of tobacco products. More than half of the company's consolidated tobacco sales were made to subsidiaries of three holding companies: Phillip Morris Companies. Inc., the state-owned Japan Tobacco Co., and RJR Nabisco Holdings Inc. Dimon has made efforts to develop mutually beneficial partnerships with these major customers. However, this cooperation raised the question whether Dimon might be considered as an accessory to tort claims. Conventional wisdom implied that since Dimon was a tobacco vendor with no direct involvement in manufacturing and selling tobacco products to consumers, it was not at risk from the legal entanglements of the cigarette industry stemming from product liability.
>
> Although top management was alert to changing consumer patterns that were partly the result of anti-smoking campaigns, it was also pondering the riskiness of its gamble on light tobacco blends. To balance this one-sided product strategy, the board was considering the acquisition of Intabex, the world's fourth largest leaf tobacco dealer with annual sales of approximately $700 million. Intabex had over 35% of the world's dark air-cured market. Dark air-cured tobacco was used primarily as cigar wrappers and filler for cigars and cigarettes, and enjoyed a strong market penetration in the Philippines, Indonesia and Latin America.
>
> In a public statement, the board announced that a strategy change had not been decided on yet, and that any definitive acquisition agreement would require board approval and customary regulatory approval.

B 5.5   The "Coaching" Mindset

Every individual – either consciously or unconsciously – exercises some power, and everyone is subject to the power of others. But, power is inherently volatile and transient. In organizations, it must be groomed and guided in order to accomplish goals. Power tends to accumulate around the most important projects in an organization, and around the people who have access to resources required to achieve high-priority goals.

An important part of every manager's job is to build a power base by acquiring knowledge, resources and personal influence from which to act. In this context, poor communication skills often lead to interpersonal and organizational problems. As people begin to experience conflict, they will resist change, and avoid contact with others, resulting both in low morale and low productivity. Therefore, managers who fail to cultivate a power base from as many sources as possible or who shy away from using power are not doing their jobs.

Building influence with subordinates and peers takes a long time, and a lot of patience. But people ultimately respond when they see competent work and realize the manager wants to share the credit with them. As high regard is not a zero-sum commodity, it is advisable for managers to create a "mentality of abundance", an attitude that there is plenty of credit and opportunity to go around. When people are generous and encouraging, opportunities increase in an organization. The paradox of selfishness is that it usually results in a net loss of resources. Productivity in the work unit begins to wilt when people start hoarding information, and withhold recognition, physical resources, and their own energy.

It follows that the most sophisticated form of deploying managerial power is through coaching. This means developing people by providing performance evaluation and feedback. Feedback on performance is one of the most helpful pieces of information that a person can get.

B 5.6 Experiential Exercise: Giving and Receiving Feedback

Directions:

Read the two roles that follow. At the indicated time, conduct a meeting, initiated by the person playing Schulz.

Role for Claus Schulz, Manager

You are a security maintenance manager at a theme park. You are in your early forties and your staff consists of eight full-time park maintenance assistants. You feel committed to this job and feel that you have had considerable success in building up your park's reputation as the most popular theme park in the country over the past eight years.

You are about to have a coaching session with one of your park maintenance assistants, Martin Leiris. Martin has had a lot of experience in the outdoors. He is a diligent and energetic assistant, but recently you have had several complaints from visitors.

It seems that Martin has severely censored several visitors for suspected clandestine smoking on the premises. Although smoking would count as a misdemeanor that should be reported, Martin's approach has been somewhat aggressive.

For example, a few days ago Martin followed a visitor to a restroom, picked up an empty cigarette package as he dropped it coming out of a booth, and brandished it in front of his face. The visitor was quite irate about the incident.

Although you do not think any severe action, such as firing Martin, is presently justified, you do feel the problems you have identified must be resolved.

Role for Martin Leiris, Parks Maintenance Assistant

After you were graduated from high school, you moved to California to live with your older brother. You worked part-time but spent as much time as possible hiking and rafting. When your money ran out, you applied for and got your present job at

B 5 | Business and the Law

the theme park. One of your goals in taking this job was to show ordinary citizens how wonderful the outdoors really are.

You like your boss, Claus Schultz, and you believe he respects your work. But workers at the park have been a little anxious lately. There has been a noticeable increase in violations of park rules by visitors, and there have also been reports of lurking around the restrooms.

This is why it really angers you to see people being careless about littering and violating non-smoking rules. They are endangering the high reputation for cleanliness and safety built up by Claus. And you make sure that they realize their fault by accosting them directly.

You understand Claus' position, but you do wish he would give you more backup support on this. Claus has asked to talk with you this afternoon and you are planning to bring the matter up.

(1) At the conclusion of the role-play, discuss the guidelines. How well was each implemented?

(2) What did you learn from this role-play?

B 6 Top Management Direction

- Official Goals
- Generic Strategies
- Operative Goals
- Goal Content
- Managing Multiple and Conflicting Goals
- Organizational Effectiveness
- The Control Function
- Strategy Case: Expedia Inc. – Courting a Virtual Third Party
- The "Administrator" Mindset
- Experiential Case: Skilled Incompetence

B 7 Decision-making Processes

B 6 Top Management Direction

B 6.1 Principles – Models – Practices

A company is created and designed to achieve some end. The direction setting process typically begins with an assessment of the opportunities and threats in the external environment, including the amount of change, uncertainty, and resource availability. A review of internal strengths and weaknesses then sets the direction of activities. Acting on the envisioned fit between external opportunities and internal strengths, the next step is to define the overall mission and the objectives. Finally, specific operational goals or strategies are formulated to define how the company should accomplish its overall mission.

Many types of goals exist in a company, each performing a different function. It is especially important to identify the officially stated mission and the actually pursued goals.

assessment	Einschätzung, Beurteilung
opportunity	Gelegenheit, Möglichkeit
threat	Bedrohung, Gefahr
uncertainty	Unsicherheit
availability	Verfügbarkeit
strength	Stärke
weakness	Schwäche
to envision	sich etwas vorstellen
objective	Ziel
to accomplish	erreichen
to pursue	verfolgen
purpose	Zweck
legitimacy	Berechtigung, Legitimität
stated	genannt, angegeben
to decline	fallen, sinken, zurückgehen
to develop	entwickeln

Official Goals

The Mission Statement

The company's general statement of its purpose and philosophy is often written down in a mission statement. It describes the company's values, aspirations, and reason for being, and symbolizes legitimacy to external and internal stakeholders. It sets out the official goals, so people know what it stands for, accept its existence, and can identify with the stated goals.

Legitimacy

Companies want customers, competitors, suppliers, and the local community to look upon them in a favorable light. For example, the tobacco industry, driven by the declining legitimacy of cigarettes, developed legitimate and socially responsible goal statements.

Generic Strategies

A generic strategy is a policy setting out how the company can compete. Whereas goals define where the company wants to go, strategy defines how it will arrive there.

Strategy of Low-Cost Leadership emphasizes cost reduction and efficiency. A company using a low-cost strategy would probably champion low-cost production, reduce administrative overheads, and secure cheap supplies of raw materials. The goal would be either to charge lower prices and increase sales, or to maintain normal prices and enjoy high profit margins.

Strategy of Differentiation involves the continued search for innovative product characteristics, special service as well as extensive communication with customers to enhance product sensitivity and loyalty. A differentiation strategy allows a company to charge premium prices for unique product, or service attributes.

Focused Strategy

The selection of specific goals and strategies has important organizational consequences. For example, a strategy of growth, innovation and product differentiation would require a loose, organic structure to foster creativity and marketing flair, whereas a strategy of cost efficiency would require a mechanistic, tightly controlled structure with close employee supervision.

---

to emphasize – betonen

overheads – Gemeinkosten

to enhance – steigern, erhöhen, verbessern

unique – einzigartig

to require – erfordern

to foster – fördern

to spin off – ausgliedern

Operative Goals

The operating procedures explain what the company is trying to accomplish concerning overall performance. Specific measurable goals for tasks provide day-to-day direction for employees within the departments.

The Purpose of Operative Goals

Employee direction and motivation: goals give a sense of direction to company stakeholders, and the way they are set signal to employees what they are working for.

Decision-making: company goals help define the correct decisions concerning organization structure, innovation, employee welfare, or growth. For example, a higher profit goal might provide decision guidelines for closing or spinning-off marginally profitable plants.

Standard of performance: goals provide a standard for assessment. The level of company performance, whether in terms of profits, units produced, or number of complaints, needs a basis for evaluation.

Goal Content

Profitability or overall performance may be expressed in such terms as net income, earnings per share, or return on investment.

Growth goals refer to increases in sales or profits over time and output volume. Growth and volume goals also may be indicators of overall performance, in addition to goals that attempt to specify the delivery of services within specified budget expense levels.

Resource goals may involve obtaining financing for the construction of new plants, finding less expensive sources for raw materials, or recruiting qualified personnel.

Market share goals refer to the market share or market standing desired by the company. Market goals are the responsibility of marketing, sales, and advertising departments.

Training and development goals refer to the training, promotion, safety, and growth of employees. These activities improve morale and help employees develop higher skills.

Innovation goals refer to internal flexibility and readiness to adapt to unexpected changes in the environment. Innovation goals are often defined with respect to the development of specific new services, products, or production processes.

Productivity goals refer to the amount of output achieved from available resources. They typically describe the amount of inputs required to reach desired outputs, stated in terms of "cost per unit of output", "units produced per employee", or "resource cost per employee".

Quality goals imply continuous improvement from the design stage to disposal.

Managing Multiple and Conflicting Goals

As companies face multiple and conflicting environmental demands, success in one goal may mean failure in another goal. For example, lowering quality to enable lower prices may ultimately reduce shareholder value. To resolve these differences, managers typically use:

Bargaining engages managers with different goals to negotiate a workable basis for achieving their joint interests. This process leads to a coalition, which is an alliance among several managers who agree about organizational goals. The term coalition describes the political nature of the goal-agreement process.

Satisficing means companies accept a "satisfactory" rather than a maximum level of performance. By accepting satisfactory performance across several criteria, the company can achieve several goals simultaneously.

Sequential attention means companies attend to important goals for a period of time and then turn to other goals. Sequential attention enables a company to achieve satisfactory levels of performance on one goal before going to another goal.

Priority setting means top management defines a preference order among goals. Giving priority to one goal, such as profit making, does not mean other goals will be ignored; other goals continue to exist, but will receive less emphasis.

Organizational Effectiveness

While company goals define the outcomes it seeks to achieve, **effectiveness** is the degree to which it realizes its goals. Effectiveness is a broad concept that takes into consideration a range of variables at both the corporate level and departmental levels.

Efficiency is a more limited concept that measures productivity, or the amount of resources used to produce a unit of output. It is measured as the ratio of inputs to outputs. A company would be described as more efficient if it can achieve a given production with fewer resources than another. But, efficiency does not automatically lead to effectiveness: a company may be highly efficient but fail to achieve its goals because it makes a product for which there is no demand; conversely, a company may achieve its profit goals but be inefficient.

Effectiveness Approaches

Organizational effectiveness can be assessed in different ways:

Approaches to Measurement of Effectiveness

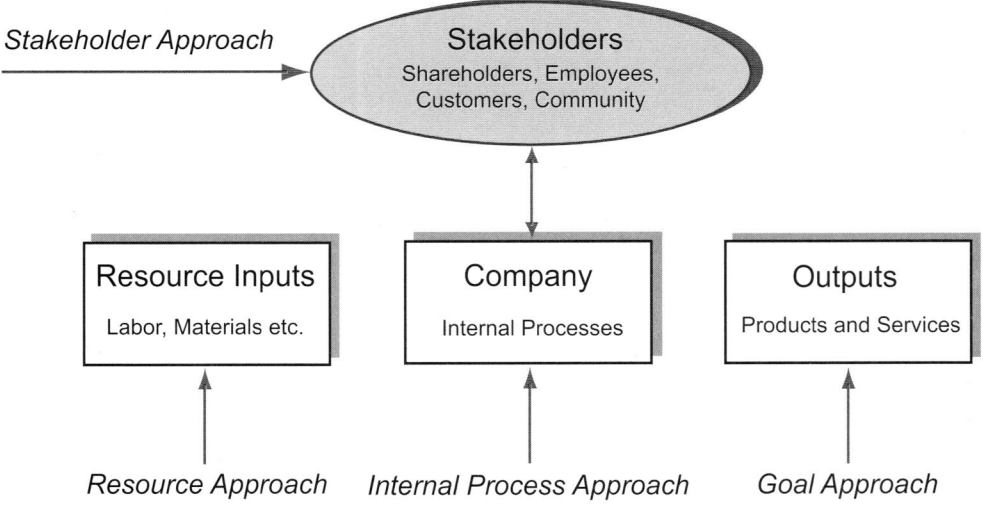

- the **goal approach** identifies a company's output goals and assesses achievement;
- the **internal process approach** measures effectiveness as internal efficiency, whereas efficiency is defined as the use of existing resources to maintain smoothly running internal processes;

- the **resource approach** emphasizes the input side of the transformation process; it assumes companies must be successful in obtaining scarce and valued resource inputs from other organizations; effectiveness is indicated by the ability of the company to exploit its environment in the acquisition of scarce and valued resources;
- the **stakeholder approach** assesses the satisfaction of groups that have a stake in the company's performance, such as creditors, suppliers, employees, and owners as a performance indicator; accordingly, a company which performs poorly in the opinion of one or several stakeholder groups is not meeting its effectiveness goals.

The Control Function

Management must know how it is performing in order to make the most effective uses of scarce resources. The controlling process consists of sequential actions taken by management to establish performance standards, measure and monitor performance, compare standards against actual performance, and take corrective action where indicated.

Instruments for Bureaucratic Control

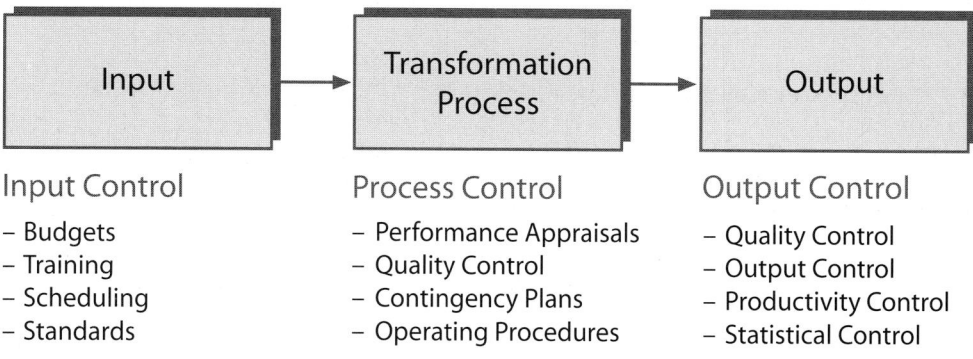

Input Control
- Budgets
- Training
- Scheduling
- Standards

Process Control
- Performance Appraisals
- Quality Control
- Contingency Plans
- Operating Procedures

Output Control
- Quality Control
- Output Control
- Productivity Control
- Statistical Control

Management must decide what performance to measure, when to measure and how to measure. As the measurement of performance is costly, the number and frequency of measurements and cost effectiveness must be balanced. Basically, there are three types of control strategies. Each form of control uses different information, and all three types may be used simultaneously.

- **Market control** measures the profit or loss. Market control is used where product or service outputs can be priced and where competition exists both as a point of reference, and as an alternative for outsourcing activities (i.e. "make-or-buy" decision).

- **Bureaucratic control** is the use of rules, policies, hierarchy of authority, documentation, and standardization to program behavior and assess performance in a stable environment. Bureaucratic mechanisms are used to control administrative functions and departments for which prices and competitive markets do not exist, or to regulate routine activities.
- **Peer-group control** is the use of social characteristics such as corporate culture, commitment, shared beliefs, values, and mental models to control behavior. Peer-group control is important when uncertainty is high – when prices cannot be calculated, and rules and behavior cannot specify every correct behavior. It is used mainly in companies or departments with a strong informal culture, such as in research, where individual performance is difficult to measure.

B 6.2 Knowledge Check

(1) Which steps must a company take to: (a) achieve legitimacy; (b) resolve goal conflicts?
(2) Distinguish between alternative effectiveness approaches.
(3) Discuss the factors involved in the choice of a strategic goal.
(4) Discuss the suitability of different control strategies.
(5) Describe strategies for controlling the sequential stages of the transformation process.

→   See Answer Key for solutions.

B 6.3 Keywords

Bargaining; behavioral control; budgets; bureaucratic control; differentiation; effectiveness; efficiency; focus; generic strategy; goal approach; low-cost leadership; market control; mission; official goals; operative goals; output control; peer-group control; priority setting; resource approach; satisficing; sequential attention; stakeholder approach.

B 6.4 Strategy Case: Expedia Inc. – Courting a Virtual Third Party

On April 23, 1999, Laurent Coppieters and Peter Ingelbrecht, founders of the online travel company Rent-A-Holiday, located in Brussels, arrived at the VacationSpot head-office in Seattle for pre-merger negotiations. VacationSpot was represented by the CEO Steve Murch, and the Chief Operating Officer (COO), Greg Slyngstad. Both companies were in the business of marketing listings in the independent leisure accommodation segment with a focus on villas and bed & breakfasts (B&Bs), and had started operations in 1997.

A Snapshot of the VS-team's first impression, circulated by email:

The negotiations have been going well. Basically, the time was used to get to know each other, and to discuss each company's vision and strategy. The process seemed to be progressing smoothly until the subject of valuation came up on the agenda. Both companies had recently completed a round of financing and it was the view of VS that this status should be the basis for valuation, i.e. a 9:1 ratio based on a $27 million valuation for VS and a $2 to $3 million valuation for RAH. The merger would hinge on retaining Ingelbrecht and Coppieters with long-term management contracts.

A Snapshot of the RAH-team's first impression, circulated by email:

The outlook was promising. There was consensus as to maintaining the momentum of the first-mover advantage, expanding the scope of the-business model, and concentrating on the North American and European lodging market. But, from the Belgian perspective, the valuation given for RAH was unacceptable.

The Market for Independent Leisure Lodging

In 1999, leisure travel – with wide range of services ranging from air travel and car rentals to hotel reservations and package vacations – was a $3 trillion business. With $126 billion revenue in 1998, the independent leisure travel lodging market, comprising condominiums, homes, ski cabins, chalets, villas, and timeshare property units, constituted only a small and fragmented part of the $230 billion worldwide lodging market. At that level, it was not a key market for the existing reservation networks, which were designed for large travel suppliers (airlines and chain hotels). The niche market status was reflected in inconsistent pricing and massive under-utilization of the assets.

And yet, this segment had a growing appeal for to sophisticated consumers. Increasing numbers of business travelers and holiday-makers, turned-off by the standard service at chain hotels, were switching to studio suites and B&Bs.

In 1999, there were several web sites that addressed the independent leisure lodging market segment, but mostly in the format of online classified advertisements. The few sites with advanced search functions (e.g. by amenities, price, availability, or style or real-time online reservation capabilities) were linked to the big hotel chains.

Profile of Expedia Inc.

Expedia Incorporated, based in Bellevue, WA, was an online provider of branded one-stop travel, shopping and reservation services for leisure and small business travelers.

In October 1999 the company operated eight websites that provided real-time access to schedules, pricing and availability information for more than 450 airlines, 40,000 hotels, all major car rental companies and thousands of cruise and vacation options. It sold the travel services under two different business models, the agency model and the merchant model (an accounting method that effectively boosted published revenues by calculating as revenue the entire amount of hotel rooms sold rather than a commission).

The company aimed to achieve market leadership through a dual strategy of internal growth and acquisitions. Its Expedia Global Travel Marketplace was to provide the widest possible selection of worldwide lodging options to customers by bringing everything in travel to everyone everywhere. Small lodging suppliers, for example, would have an opportunity to make their inventory available in Expedia Global Travel Marketplace.

Prior to its initial public offering (IPO), planned for November 1999, Expedia was a wholly owned subsidiary of Microsoft. Following the IPO, it became a separate company, but retained a contractual relationship with Microsoft who also retained a majority control.

Meanwhile, Microsoft has launched an initiative extending its Windows-based applications to build a federation of web services linking related transactions – rental cars, hotels and airlines. The data would be held in a central repository. This proposed system would open big opportunities for sophisticated web-hosting services, such as web-based e-commerce, content distribution, enterprise resource management, and customer relationship management.

History of VacationSpot

The Beginnings

Steven D. Murch, a graduate of Harvard Business School with a Master Degree in Computer Science from Stanford University, decided in 1991 to join Microsoft, at that time, still a medium-sized, but rapidly growing company.

In 1996, while working at Microsoft, Murch realized that contrary to his earlier bias, the business of B&Bs was not actually based on real estate or physical properties but located in virtual reality. The most important elements, he realized, were branding, and information. And the Internet was an ideal medium not only for placing reservations, but also for applying yield-management techniques to manage the pricing and to segment the customer base. The private lodgings represented a sizeable segment within a $3 trillion market in which the average transaction was $1,500.

Murch approached Slyngstad, who had transformed the online travel service Expedia from a CD-ROM product into an Internet site, for advice. Slyngstad suggested that the plan should be modeled on an online, real-time reservation system, and volunteered to become a partner.

Early Development

Murch and Slyngstad established VacationSpot in September 1997. Their strategy was based on a comprehensive range of property offerings, an advanced reservation technology, and a strong distribution channel. After using venture capital financing and their own funds to start up, they approached Microsoft in April 1998 for a long-term distribution deal. This gave them a salient position on Expedia in the accommodations segment for two years in exchange for the usual 20 % of equity. Furthermore, they had access to Microsoft as an Application Service Provider. On the financial side, the company succeeded in raising the required funds from investors in a first round private placement in July.

VS made a total of three acquisitions over a period of six months. One acquired company had developed a Windows-based reservation software product for firms and B&Bs which VS eventually developed into a reservation database management product connecting into the VacationSpot site via the Internet to process reservations. Whereas they had started out with paid listings while expanding their supply, they were now in a position to effectively take a commission on all transactions. Their objective was to get a full 8 % commission of sales on reservations made through their site and a lower 4 % commission on reservations made off their site as a user fee.

VacationSpot in April 1999

The company was increasing its listings by 12 % annually and was receiving more and more booking inquiries. However, the founders were becoming concerned about the quality of the listings and the comprehensiveness of the offering.

A review of the customer request profile revealed a gap in European offerings.

The Dilemma of VactionSpot.com

Although the initial distribution agreement with Microsoft prevented them from entering into other distribution agreements, the acquisitions improved their position with both their "suppliers" (property owners or managers) and potential distribution partners. But to enhance their status with distribution partners, it was necessary to reduce the equity/assets burn rate of 26 % and to achieve an operating profit within a year. VS had already switched from a flat fee to a commission-based system to increase the volume of properties signed-up. The new 8 % fee effectively cut out the existing travel agents, who on average charged 10 %.

But, the founders realized that further growth would whet the appetite of established online travel agents. Was it time to boost market power and technological backup by leveraging the links with Expedia?

Searching for an alternative route, Murch and Slyngstad decided to approach Rent-A-Holiday with a merger proposal.

History of Rent-A-Holiday

The Beginnings

In 1995 Peter Ingelbrecht joined the Boston Consulting Group in Brussels with an MBA-degree from Stanford. On his first project, Ingelbrecht worked with Laurent Coppieters, a three-year BCG consultant with a commercial engineering degree. They found a mutual interest in establishing their own company. On a trip to Spain, Ingelbrecht had remarked a high vacancy rate in private lodgings relative to the hotel chains. A first survey revealed that marketing in this segment was quite unprofessional, with much local advertising and little cross-border marketing. The weak market position forced property owners and tour operators to offer substantial commissions to the travel agents.

When the two decided to establish Rent-A-Holiday (RAH) with their own funds in April 1997, the first focus was on Europe. A subsequent loan in June 1997 resulted in a debt-to-equity ratio of 75 %. At that point, the asset-equity burn rate was 30 %, although the business plan did project a turnaround in the second quarter of 2001.

Early Development

Acquiring listings turned out to be more costly than originally planned, although RAH easily succeeded in recruiting a multilingual workforce in Brussels to build inventory via phone calls or local visits. Once a customer had identified a property she liked, she would submit an inquiry via the RAH web page which would be automatically translated into the supplier's language. The supplier would then contact the prospective customer, by email, fax or telephone, to confirm availability and ask for payment. The development of this translation engine provided RAH with an advantage over their competition.

RAH's founders were intrigued by their potential as an "infomediary" in terms of generating traffic, getting property listings, and brokering consumer Internet data in exchange for vendor concessions on goods and services. However, they had not been able to raise as much money as VacationSpot. Although their business model was similar, the venture capital market in Europe was not as developed as that in the USA.

Rent-A-Holiday in April 1999

By April 1999 RAH had about the same number of property listings as VacationSpot, and was the largest European company in this market. With its translation engine and user interface it maintained a substantial competitive lead over its less technologically advanced competitors. The slow rate of financing, however, slowed down its European acquisition program as a quick path to increase listings. Getting technical people to sign on was still difficult for startups. But the situation was improving. As Belgium and other countries were easing tax rules to make it easier to offer employees stock options.

To take advantage of this positive business climate Coppieters had been toying with the idea of boosting volume and reaping synergy effects by forming a joint venture with a US on-line travel company. A year ago, Coppieters had already contacted VacationSpot to explore possible links. Another possibility was to approach established online travel agents like Expedia or Travelocity, either alone or together with a local partner like VacationSpot.

The Dilemma of RAH

In the current situation, the question was how a potential merger with a US company would affect their status. The two-day negotiation had made it clear to the RAH team that the new headquarters of the merged firm would not be Brussels. Maybe it was better to remain independent rather than to accept a low valuation and the role of a junior partner.

B 6.5   The "Administrator" Mindset

To assure that all employees are productive, fulfilling specified tasks, at the correct time, and at the right locations, managers must be very flexible. Only by maintaining a 360-degree vigilance and a penchant for trouble-shooting will managers achieve a smooth workflow with a minimum of conflict among individuals and work units. Responsive management involves reuniting three interrelated viewpoints: planning, organizing, and controlling. For instance, a network administrator on a busy day cannot base his decisions solely on the daily stream of software-managed information that comes across his desk, but has to trust his gut feeling.

Planning Role

Planning is the organizational response to uncertainty. If the environment is stable, the organization can concentrate on day-to-day-efficiency. With increasing environmental uncertainty, planning and forecasting can soften the impact of a shifting environment. However, under conditions of extreme uncertainty, planning may not be helpful, because future scenarios are too difficult to predict.

Planning revolves around three basic questions:
- **Where are we now?** Which are the forces operating from outside and which resources can be accessed within?
- **Where do we want to be?** Whereto will the search for new concepts lead us?
- **How can we get there from here?** Which sustainable goals are capable of becoming the shared vision of all stakeholders?

Organizing Role

Organizing is the process of dividing the work into manageable components and assigning activities to achieve the desired results effectively. Once organizational plans are set, it must be decided how to allocate and coordinate resources in order to accomplish the goals.

Controlling Role

A major responsibility of managers is measuring operations to determine whether they are on target, and assuring control by correcting or changing activities as needed in four steps:

- Setting performance objectives or standards.
- Measuring actual performance.
- Comparing actual performance against objectives or standards.
- Taking appropriate action.

Control systems will only work if those people who have responsibility for implementing the systems have the ability and willingness to carry through. Because of the inherent emotional impact, implementing and maintaining organizational control systems are often considered to be the more uncomfortable jobs of the administrator. This is partly because, as individuals, we identify with the human desire for autonomy, as well as with the tendency to resist control.

B 6.6   Experiential Case: Skilled Incompetence

Jackie Matthew, in charge of Human Resources (HR) for the regional division of a Fortune 500 agro-business firm, invited two consultants to discuss a new corporate directive.

"As you know, the changing competitive environment within NAFTA is causing a major corporate reorganization. The CEO has come out with a policy directive that all regional divisions must develop and implement a plan to align the workforce with a multidimensional scorecard by the end of the year. The message is that we have to reduce our level of staffing by about 15 percent."

"The policy directive empowers regional personnel offices like ours to support operations managers in assessing workforce needs. My budget authorizes me to hire two additional full-time staff professionals for this project. Now that we are entering new territory, I consider outside consultants to be most qualified for this role."

The remaining time was used to discuss the objectives of the project and the techniques that could be used. Jackie gave assurances to the consultants regarding the cooperation of the operating managers, who would provide data and implement staffing rules. The three agreed a formal contract would be negotiated and investigative work would begin immediately as soon as executive approval was obtained.

The Lean Production Project

Jackie approached the vice-president in charge of the division, Luke Margolies, suggesting the use of consultants to conduct a management audit. Their purpose would be to determine skill needs and ways of better deploying human resources within the restructured divisions.

"You know, Luke, our efforts to become more competitive by designing innovative benchmarks for our human resources will provide a real service to the operating divisions within the region. A skills inventory conducted by the consultants might reveal a lot of slack. We could find out where we had redundant resources, where our gaps are, and which people are best qualified to fill openings."

After listening to Jackie, Luke Margolies agreed and made the following suggestion:

"They have a good deal of excess personnel that according to our new efficiency paradigm must be eliminated. By using the best practices knowledge of the consultants, we could encourage and facilitate new scorecarding concepts. So, Jackie, do bring in your consultants to design a system that provides the necessary information and support for this alignment project."

Jackie met with the consultants to work out the details of the proposal and contract. The project prescribed a top-down audit that would involve managers from three key operating lines. The project title "Designing a Balanced Scorecard for Learning and Growth" would reflect the value-oriented focus of the audit. It would provide decision guidelines for retirements and terminations, promotions, reassignments, new recruiting where necessary, and management training and development.

Obstacles in Getting Access to Line Departments

After the project kickoff, the consultants soon became frustrated with delays caused by Jackie's slowness in scheduling interviews with key executives. She insisted on "positioning" the consultants for each interview, arguing that the sensitive nature of the data and internal competition among the three key divisions required advance preparation. To cut the time-consuming intervals, the consultants began to approach the executives they knew from other consulting assignments directly. In general, the executives were keen to engage the consultants' attention for a variety of workflow management and development purposes. They also suggested ways in which the consultants could enhance effectiveness. All managers agreed that the decision support system was inadequate to help them respond flexibly to disruptive events.

Four Months Later

Jackie is reporting to a visibly upset Luke:

"I've received your mid-project report and discussed it with the consultants. It seems that some of our operations managers think we are interfering. They say that they aren't convinced about scorecarding and are responding to required changes in their own ways. But they do

want to go into greater detail with the consultants on a number of empowerment projects, such as strategic business analysis, capital budgeting, executive succession, manager development, and matrix management. This HR project seems to be out of touch with what operations managers have in mind."

Jackie is groping for an explanation as Luke continues.

"The direction of the consulting efforts seems to diverge from the direction the operating departments want to go. To continue with this plan would lead us into conflict with the division executives. In fact, from their perspective, the problem is about maintaining spare capacity to meet sudden demand surges. Jackie, I assumed you had checked with the operations managers about the need for a substantial workforce reduction.

In the end, we've run up a lot of expenses, with no results in the way of the original brief. Limiting the consultants' access to people have triggered lot of anxiety and conflict. Now we have to explain to the consultants why we must drop the project.

In the meantime, the COO is recommending your temporary assignment as Senior Business Process Research Analyst to our competitively challenged Little Rock poultry plant. I know you will appreciate this transfer as a mark of confidence and another chance for future promotion."

(1) Discuss the difference between HR's interpretation of management needs on the corporate level and those held by management in the operating divisions.

(2) How could HR have secured the cooperation of the operating divisions?

(3) How could the expertise of the consultants have been used more effectively?

B 7 Decision-making Processes

- Individual Decision-making
- The Rational Approach
- The Decision Support System Approach
- Bounded Rationality
- Group Decision Making in Organizations
- The Political Model
- The Incremental Decision Process Model
- The Intuitive Model
- Contingency Framework for Decision-making
- Strategy Case: CEMEX – Global, Nimble … & In the Money
- The "Auditing" Mindset
- Exercise: Memo "Please report to work on Saturday"

B 8 Human Resource Management

B 7 Decision-making Processes

B 7.1 Principles – Models – Practices

At any given time, managers in a company will be identifying issues, analyzing problems and implementing decisions based on a variety of different approaches. These will depend on the situation, the group dynamics, and individual traits, such as the attitude to risk-taking.

Individual Decision-making

To facilitate decision-making, procedures may be programmed if there are well-defined issues with easily specified alternatives and if there is consensus regarding the expected outcome. And not, if a company is facing new problems, and may not know how to respond.

The Rational Approach

The universally accepted rational approach to individual decision-making stresses the need for a systematic problem analysis that will result in a persuasively argued choice supported by an implementation outline. This logical, step-by-step sequence is structured as follows:

a) **Problem Identification Stage**

Managers monitor internal and external information that may indicate deviations from planned behavior by talking to people and reviewing financial statements, performance evaluations, industry indices, competitors' activities, etc. They respond to deviations by identifying essential details of the problem, i.e. who was affected, who was involved; where, when, and how current activities were influenced, and then define the outcomes to be achieved.

to stress – betonen
deviation – Abweichung
current – gegenwärtig, aktuell
to achieve – erreichen, erzielen
to assess – bewerten, beurteilen, einschätzen
probability – Wahrscheinlichkeit
merit – Vorzug

b) **Problem Solution Stage**

The manager identifies alternative courses of action, seeking ideas and suggestions from new sources. This step may involve the use of statistical techniques or personal experience to assess the probability of success. The merits of each alternative are assessed as well as the probability that it will achieve the desired results. The manager then uses his or her analysis of the problem, objectives, and alternatives to select a single alternative that has the best chance for success. Finally, the manager uses managerial and persuasive abilities, and gives directions to ensure that the decision is carried out, monitoring activities as they are being implemented.

The Decision Support System Approach (DSS)

This approach <u>applies</u> mathematics to rational decision-making. Mathematical models can <u>contain</u> a large number of variables, each one relevant in some way to the ultimate outcome, and quickly solve problems that have too many explicit variables for human processing. This system is at its best when applied to problems that are analyzable, measurable, and can be structured in a logical way.

Bounded Rationality

Beyond this systemic <u>constraint</u>, managers are often unable to follow rational procedures due to time pressure, the large number of variables, and the ill-defined nature of many problems. Hence the <u>attempt</u> to be rational is "<u>bounded</u>", or in a sense limited, by the enormous complexity of many problems. Although consistent leaders are generally held in higher esteem than decision-makers who switch from one course of action to another, failure to admit a mistake and adopt a new course of action may also result in blocking out or distorting negative information, and thus <u>inhibiting</u> learning.

Group Decision Making in Organizations

The Political Model

Corporate decisions involve many managers, and a final choice is usually based upon a coalition among these managers.

As a company's goals are often <u>ambiguous</u>, and inconsistent, managers disagree about problem priorities. In order to reach a decision, they must bargain, and build a coalition around the question of which problems to solve. Although individual managers may intend to be rational, they frequently act under cognitive constraints.

> **to apply** – anwenden, verwenden
> **to contain** – enthalten
> **constraint** – Beschränkung
> **attempt** – Versuch
> **bounded** – begrenzt, beschränkt
> **to inhibit** – hindern, abhalten
> **ambiguous** –mehrdeutig, unklar
> **to perceive** – wahrnehmen, erkennen
> **to emerge** – auftauchen, sich ergeben

- In the **problem identification stage** of decision-making, discussion and bargaining are especially important. Unless coalition members <u>perceive</u> a problem, no action will be taken.
- Decisions are made to **"satisfice"** rather than to optimize problem solutions. The coalition will accept a solution that is perceived as satisfactory to all coalition members.
- Managers are concerned with immediate problems and short-run solutions. They engage in **"problemistic search"**, which means they tend to look around in the immediate environment for a solution to quickly resolve a problem. Managers do not aim for a perfect solution, but typically adopt the first satisfactory solution that <u>emerges</u>.

The political model also takes into account that in every organization, irrespective of mission statement and hierarchy, there is a privileged in-group, whose interests set the corporate agenda. Although this core group seldom exceeds five percent of the organization, intensive networking causes the perceived interests of this core to become the focal point of decisions made throughout the organization. Consequently, effective decision-making requires knowing who constitutes the core group, and considering what interests they stand for.

Decision Process in the Political Model

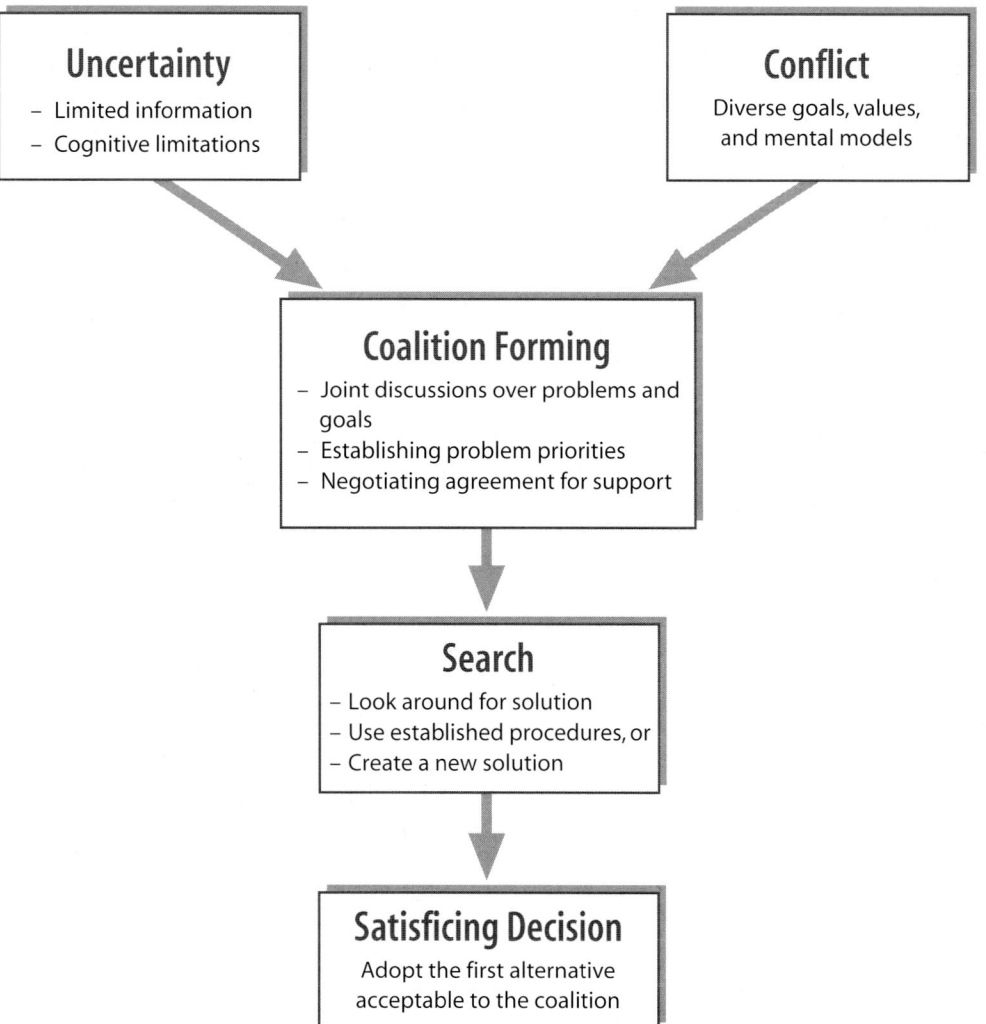

The Incremental Decision Process Model

This decision-making approach emphasizes the learning process in problem-solving. It describes the sequence of activities undertaken from the initial discovery of a problem to its eventual solution. Major choices are seen as a series of small choices that together produce the final outcome. Moving through several decision points, decision makers may encounter obstacles along the way. Such an interruption may mean returning to a previous decision and trying something new. The solution may be very different from what was anticipated.

The Intuitive Model

Both the political and incremental process models describe how companies make decisions when either problem identification or solution is uncertain. But if both parts of the decision process are highly uncertain, companies will apply intuition at the beginning or the end of the decision-making process. Thus, a problem may or may not lead to a proposed solution that may or may not solve things. Occasions for decision-making may arrive when contracts are signed, people are hired, a new product is authorized or when the right mix of participants, solutions, and problems exists.

Contingency Framework for Decision-making

Common goals provide clear standards of performance. Agreement among managers about corporate goals and outcomes is especially important for the problem identification stage of decision-making. When goals are not agreed upon, problem identification is uncertain and managers must concentrate on reaching agreement about goal priorities.

When technology is well understood, appropriate alternatives can be identified and calculated with some degree of certainty. In contrast, when the technology is poorly understood, intuition, judgment, and muddling through become the basis for decision-making. Technical knowledge is especially important to the problem-solution stage of decision-making.

B 7.2 Knowledge Check

(1) Describe the context of (a) the rational approach, and (b) the political model.
(2) Describe the activities in the incremental approach.
(3) Discuss decision-making in a turbulent environment.
(4) Outline an approach for (a) generating acceptance; (b) for avoiding escalating commitment for mistaken decisions.

→ **See Answer Key for solutions.**

B 7.3 Keywords

Authorization; bounded rationality; political model; coalition; complexity; contingency decision-making framework; goal consensus; incremental decision process model; intuitive decision-making; judgment; muddling through; problem identification; problem solution stage; problemistic search; programmed decisions; rational approach; technical knowledge.

B 7.4 Strategy Case: CEMEX – Global, Nimble … & In the Money

MONTERREY, MEXICO, December 13, 2001 – CEMEX, S.A., the third largest cement company worldwide, informed the press that a put option would probably not materialize. Exercising the put option would allow the Indonesian Government to sell a 51 % stake in Indonesia's largest cement maker Semen Gresik. CEMEX, which already held a 25.5 % minority stake, denied that it was considering withdrawing from Indonesia. And CEMEX's President Director Francisco Noriega reiterated that it would use the cash saved to lower its net debt by $1 billion. Over the past 10 years, its operating cash flow (EBITDA) had increased at a compound annual growth rate of 20 % in dollar terms, and this strong operating cash flow generation would enable it to maintain its position as one of the largest and most profitable cement producers in the world.

However, the failed acquisition did raise many eyebrows among institutional investors, given that on October 17, 2001, CEMEX had announced that its bid to acquire a controlling 72.5 percent stake in the Thai cement company TPI Polene was no longer effective either.

The investment community continued raising questions concerning CEMEX future.

History of CEMEX

Founded in 1906, CEMEX had pursued a broad policy of expansion that, by the mid 1980s, had turned it into the leading cement company in Northern Mexico. By that time, it had also diversified into tourism, petroleum and mining projects.

Preempting the increased competition and consolidation that would overtake their industry in the wake of Mexico's accession to GATT in 1985, CEMEX adopted a deliberate strategy to concentrate on its core business: manufacturing, trading and transporting cement. Subsequently, it divested all other operations and reinvested in additional cement assets.

It made a plan to move quickly to acquire the Number 1 and in sequence the Number 2 Mexican cement manufacturers. Having successfully consolidated the domestic market, CEMEX expanded the operations it had bought, notably the marine terminals in California and Texas acquired with its domestic purchases. By that time, CEMEX had become one of the 10 largest cement companies in the world.

Within little more than a decade, CEMEX, had mastered the transition from a regional cement company in Mexico to challenge the established global market leaders. Its strategy was two-pronged. Internally, it created a reliable worldwide tracking, scheduling and rerouting delivery system that successfully managed unexpected demand, Externally, it excelled at making unanticipated acquisitions which upset the stable competition that the established market leaders had produced in the cement markets.

The CEMEX Strategy

The global strategy of CEMEX, was to acquire a geographically diversified asset base that would reduce the volatility of consolidated cash flows. A more predictable stream of steady cash would enable CEMEX to make further investments to increase capacity. With increasing global reach, operations would be better able to optimize and utilize capacity, thus making capital investments more profitable and further increasing cash flows. Furthermore, to level-out the high volatility of cement prices it developed special expertise in transporting cement by sea from areas of glut to those of scarcity.

To undercut its larger competitors, CEMEX initially targeted the minor markets. The acquired CEMEX operations in Spain, formed the base for its subsequent geographic expansion. Next, CEMEX moved towards the integration of South American operations with the 1994 acquisition of Vencemos, the largest cement company in Venezuela and several smaller plants in Texas and Panama. Acquisitions in the Dominican Republic and Colombia – where again two companies were consolidated into one – were followed by purchases of regional manufacturers in other parts of the hemisphere. By 1996, CEMEX had become the most heavily leveraged of all the big cement companies, within the range of 40% debt to asset ratio.

Due Diligence

CEMEX had a strict due diligence policy. Before finalizing a deal, the HR division with the help of local consultants consolidated relevant information on the target company in a manual.

After a briefing on the country and company culture, a due diligence team of highly qualified professionals from the systems division, HR, finance, acquisitions, commercial, operations, administration conducted an on-site analysis of the target company.

A structured post-merger integration process was initiated in every case. The aims were to raise the target's productivity to CEMEX levels, to align the culture in a short period, and to profit from unique features of the target company.

CEMEX Strengths

Before embarking on its expansion strategy, CEMEX had six autonomous plants that rarely communicated with each other. The turnaround began in 1985. During the past 16 years, it had completely changed the processes by which cement companies communicated with and delivered to their customers. The revitalized company based its process redesign on three components: a satellite communications system called CEMEXnet; a Dynamic Synchronization of Operations; and a link of worldwide offices via the Internet.

By 2001, with net sales of US $ 6 billion, CEMEX had grown to become the Number 1 cement trader, and the third largest cement manufacturer and trader in the world. The trading arm was separate from its cement operations, and ran its own fleet of ships as well as renting cargo space. When demand in one country fell, cement could be shipped to a region where demand was booming, thus enabling CEMEX to maintain a stable cash flow.

Its focus on cement and its single-minded pursuit of sales volume in high growth markets also distinguished it from more diversified competitors. Approximately 70 % of its cash flow came from developing markets as opposed to more mature markets like the US and Spain.

CEMEX in Asia

The most promising market for the cement industry was Southeast Asia. The countries of the region fitted the CEMEX template: high government spending on infrastructure needs such as housing and toll roads, and low kilogram per capita ratios of cement consumption of about 200 kg. In Indonesia, consumption was just above 100 kg per capita. This compared favorably with Europe, where on average it was about 800–1200 kg per capita.

Opening Moves

CEMEX spent several years in the mid-1990s prospecting this highly attractive market: It found the asked prices very high, and even so, the local producers were reluctant to sell.

As an alternative, CEMEX built up relations with its existing trading partners, notably the Indonesian producer, Semen Gresik, and entered into trading agreements with companies in Taiwan and Thailand. To explore opportunities for investment in the region it established CEMEX Asia Pte Ltd. 1996 in Singapore.

During this early period, CEMEX, attempted to develop greenfield projects wherever more capacity was needed in partnership with local producers. However, none of these projects was finalized.

Then, beginning with the Asian currency crisis in the summer of 1997, the industry saw a huge reduction in demand – Indonesia by 30 %, Malaysia 37 %, Thailand 35 %, Philippines 17 %. When the value of local companies also began to fall, the multinational players moved in to make their bids.

In 1998, CEMEX sent its acquisition teams into action quickly before prices started to rise again. However, political circumstances caused delays in Indonesia and Thailand. Accordingly, CEMEX bought a minority 30 % share in Rizal Cement in the Philippines, waited for 18 months, and then moved up to 70% by early 1999. It also bought Apo Cement, the lowest cost producer in the Philippines. It was well positioned near a port so it could start exporting to Singapore straightaway.

In Indonesia, CEMEX was named as the preferred bidder for Gresik. The government consolidated three of the five state owned cement producers under Gresik in 1995, so it controlled about 40% of domestic production. By the end of May 1998, CEMEX had done due diligence and planned to take a majority stake, but after strikes and protests about foreign predators, the government backed off. Finally, after a lot of negotiation, it took a 20% stake, paying a premium on the market price because the Rupiah was devalued 10 times.

The Next Asian Expansion

In Southeast Asia, the only major targets left were Siam Cement and TPI in Thailand, and Indocement in Indonesia.

Siam Cement, Number 1 in Thailand, was a more interesting prospect. Given its royal connections, it would probably survive and prosper, once it had restructured and rescheduled its debts. It would resist any acquisition attempt, but it might be interested in a strategic alliance to secure a pan Asian position. On the other hand, CEMEX preferred to control any relationship, which could lead to friction with the culturally sensitive Thais.

Indocement in Indonesia was owned by the Salim family, and was the Number 2 in the market following the creation of SMGR. CEMEX had been talking to it, but could take no decision until Indocement had cut a deal with the government, which held a 20% share, and restructured its US $ 8 billion group debt. Heidelberg Cement and Lafarge were also rumored to be interested in Indocement.

In Northeast Asia, Korea and Taiwan presented possibilities. Both were highly developed nations consuming more than 1000 kg cement per capita already; they were also very protected, mature markets. However, Korea was starting to open up, and Taiwan was running out of limestone reserves. Lafarge had already moved into Korea, and others might be tempted to follow. Japan, although in a recession, was not a profitable prospect. It was a mature market and the Number 1 company, Taiheiyo Cement Corp., was strong both in Europe and the U.S.A.

In general, China appeared to be the best gamble in Asia. However, it did not fit the CEMEX model. There were time-consuming political issues, the cement was cheap and of bad quality, there was an oversupply of subsidized state owned enterprises, and the market was very fragmented.

It was also possible, that India and the Middle East would be the next merger zone. India had not been affected by the recession, and Lafarge and Holcim had already moved in. Finally, there was Bangladesh and Sri Lanka. Due to the complex cultural environment, CEMEX was planning to establish trading operations as a first step.

The Competition

The strategic ambitions of the top four companies were in line with their size, experience in cost control, quality, and access to their own shipping lines. They were all heavily leveraged.

The Number 1 player, Lafarge, was the patriarch of the industry. Its main investments were in Europe, where demand growth was low. This had led it to diversify into other cement products, such as texturized products, or colored cements, and its operating margin was less than that of CEMEX. In 1994 Lafarge established a foothold in China. Soon, all four of the Group's Divisions were operating there. Lafarge expanded throughout Asia (1998: Indonesia and the Philippines; 1999: India and South Korea). Its acquisition of Redland gave it a strong foothold in Malaysia. Its acquisition of Blue Circle, the Number 4 global player, made it the world's leading cement producer. Since the cost of acquiring existing cement plants in a downturn was always less costly than putting up a greenfield plant during a crisis, Lafarge was also intent on expanding through acquisitions.

The Number 2 cement producer, Holcim was part of a family empire that included corporate, financial and real estate interests. The company intended to focus on its core businesses of cement, concrete-additives and concrete chemicals. It was expanding strongly in Africa as well as in Asia. Holcim had taken a long term view of Asia. The Chairman was reported to have asked his Swiss executives to learn Mandarin before embarking on any big purchase in China.

In terms of margins, CEMEX was Number 1 worldwide. However, the rating agencies assesses CEMEX as a risk company because of their emphasis on emerging economies and their strategy of initially purchasing minority stakes in companies while waiting for a crisis-induced sell-off that would enable them to assume majority ownership.

Future Scenarios

The value of assets in the key Southeast Asian markets would increase as the countries recovered their growth. The question was, would these challenges result in a further major consolidation or merely result in a swapping of assets? Further economic growth would raise a need for greenfield projects and capacity expansion, which would again require an ability to invest heavily. This scenario might favor those companies with the deepest pockets. Equally, it might set the stage for an innovative solution.

B 7.5 The "Auditing" Mindset

The auditing mindset is adapted to knowing the true state of affairs in the work unit, sensing when to act immediately and when to plan for later action. To form a realistic picture, the auditor would need to communicate with technical people in terms of physical units and statistical process control, and with upper-level managers in terms of economic value added.

Filtering Information

In order to audit performance it is necessary to observe the performed processes over time and to assess whether variances from the target values are being reduced in a controlled way. Often, individual errors are blamed on "poor performers" when sometimes the system – the procedures and equipment – are the real problems.

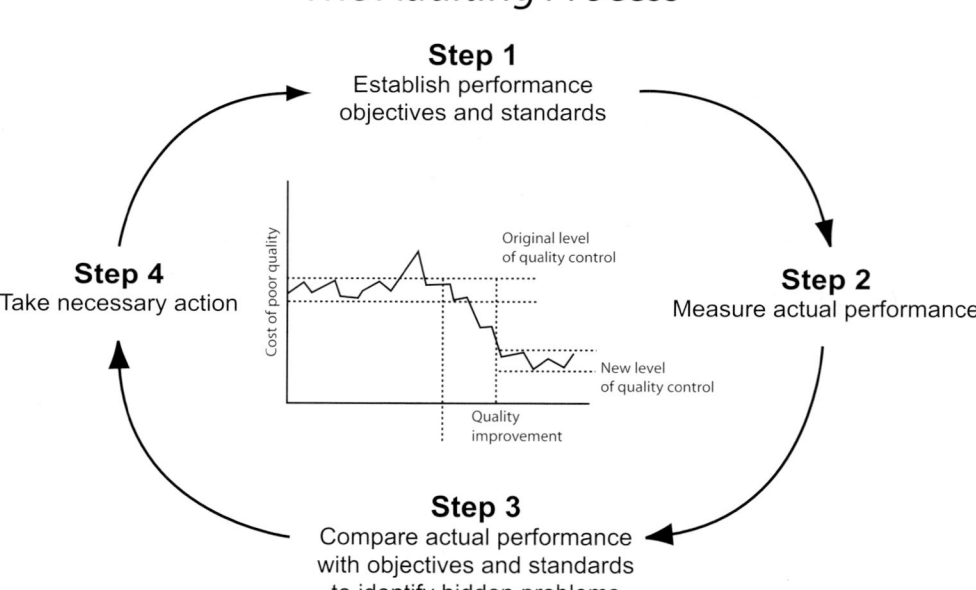

The Auditing Process

Step 1: Establish performance objectives and standards
Step 2: Measure actual performance
Step 3: Compare actual performance with objectives and standards to identify hidden problems
Step 4: Take necessary action

Analyzing Information

What is it that makes different people observe the same phenomenon but "see" different things? The most obvious reason is that people must select their focus in the process of perception. As a rule, there are more stimulants than they can absorb. Accordingly, the characteristics of the perceived object (e.g. size, intensity, contrast, novelty, motion, repetitiveness, sequencing), the characteristics of the situation (i.e. place, social context) and the characteristics of the perceiver (e.g. motivation, past experiences, vision of future) all affect the selection mechanism.

Presenting Information

To be persuasive, a logical structure and a stimulating beginning are vital. In drafting ideas, it is a mistake to allow a critical attitude to surface in the early stage. Conveying a convincing message generally means:

- avoiding the passive voice whenever appropriate;
- making less nouns out of verbs (i.e. endings in -ization, -tion, -ence, and -ance);
- keeping sentences short. A choppy style can be avoided by balancing a series of short sentences with a longer, more complex one;
- repeating words, phrases, or ideas is legitimate when repeating increases clarity.

B 7.6 Exercise: Memo "Please report to work on Saturday"

You are vice president in charge of warehousing at a large athletic equipment retailer, and you have just attended a crisis meeting of the company's executive board. An internal audit of the floor's inventory has revealed dramatic shrinkages in inventory, especially expensive golf equipment.

An anonymous whistleblower had alerted management about these shrinkages. But before the board had even met, a web page "Warehouse Sucks" carried a story about "lax employee morale". Last evening, a reporter for the financial press called the company's information office for details.

The board voted unanimously for an emergency inventory to be conducted on Saturday, 19 May at 9.00 a.m. The plant's union representative was present and approved the inventory, but only after the board agreed to pay for overtime. The board also volunteered to provide lunch. As an additional "incentive", the board agreed to consider favorably vacation requests of those employees who participated in the inventory audit.

Task:

Write a memo to the floor managers based on the information provided.

B 8 Human Resource Management

- Contextual Framework of Human Resource Policies
- Staffing
- Lifelong Employment
- Up-or-Out Flow
- Unstable In-and-Out System
- Mixed Flow Patterns
- The Reward System
- The Work System
- The Integration of HRM Policies
- Strategy Case: Pharmacia – Merging People, not Firms
- The "Visionary" Mindset
- Experiential Exercise: Creative-Relevant Skills

B 9 Control Concepts for Quality and Productivity

B 8 Human Resource Management

B 8.1 Principles – Models – Practices

Companies believe that if they attract and <u>retain</u> the best and most able individuals, they will <u>prosper</u>. Within the firm, they expect their people to <u>align</u> their performance and individual agendas with the established goals, standards and rules. And more, they expect them to take initiative, to manage themselves, to learn new skills, and to respond <u>swiftly</u> to customers'

to retain – halten, behalten
to prosper – gedeihen, florieren
to align – ausrichten, anpassen
swift – schnell, rasch
equitable – gerecht
self-actualization – Selbstverwirklichung

needs. For their part, the employees expect the company to provide <u>equitable</u> pay, good working conditions appropriate to the position and depending on their individual needs for security, responsibility, power, status, and <u>self-actualization</u>.

Contextual Framework of Human Resource Policies

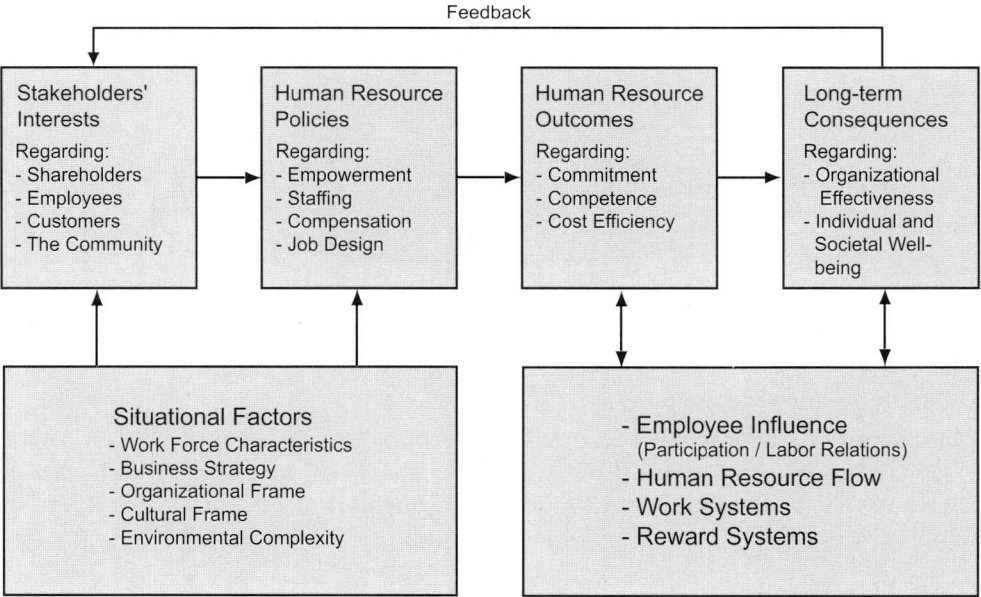

Staffing

A major goal of incentive-contribution schemes is to balance current and future work force requirements with employees' career needs. There are basically three types of HR flow patterns to manage the flow of people and skills in, through, and out of organizations:

Lifelong Employment

Employees usually enter the company at the bottom and stay with the company throughout their careers. To promote loyalty the company will avoid laying off employees.

Up-or-Out Flow

Employees enter at the bottom and move up the organization through planned career paths. A career path is an interrelated sequence of positions, leading to the top rank. Being placed on the fast track means advancement after the minimum required time for a position. Inability to be promoted through any of the ranks usually means that the person has to leave.

Directions of Career Movement

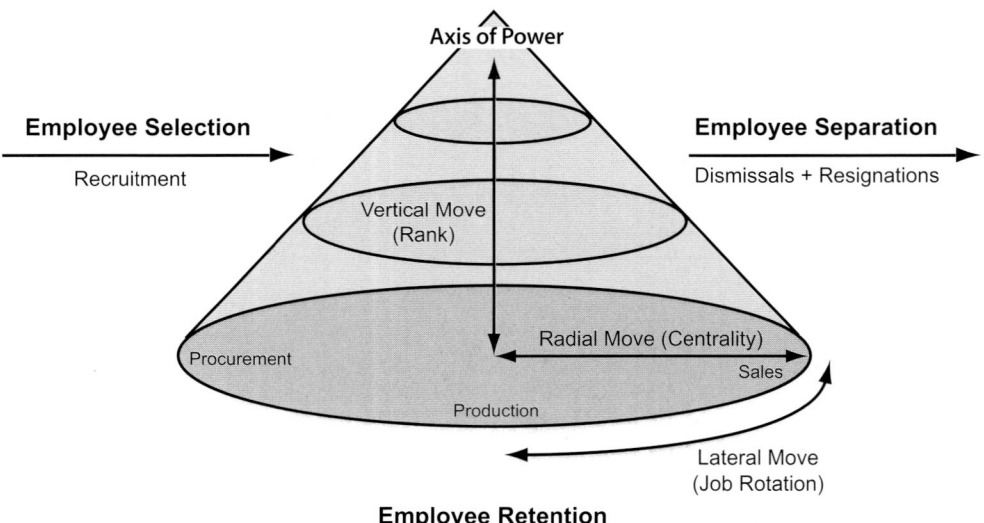

Unstable In-and-Out System

Depending on the company's needs, employees can enter at any level in the organization, and may be asked to leave at any level or point in their career. Alternatively, the contract may specify a given period of duration, or date of termination.

Mixed Flow Patterns

Policies and practices create a human resource flow pattern that has important impacts for outcomes such as commitment, competence, and individual and organizational effectiveness. By requiring employees to remain in each position for a minimum number of years, the company ensures that employees have enough time to gain the skills necessary for advancement, and allows time for improved interpersonal and leadership skills.

Thus, career opportunities open in three directions: (a) vertical movement up or down the hierarchy, (b) radial movement toward more or less influence in decision-making processes, and (c) lateral movement, transferring to different functions, or projects (job rotation).

In controlling this flow, managers should consider that organizational performance is not simply the sum of individual performances. There are <u>numerous</u> factors that cause people to perform above or below their natural levels. First, it is not easy to identify the most able people, and second, <u>innate</u> ability is not a <u>predictable</u> quality. It is the appropriate mix of complementary skills, personal relationships, and leadership that determines effectiveness.

The Reward System

From the company's point of view, the reward system is intended to motivate certain sorts of behavior or outcome. As performance is a function of ability as much as effort, management must attempt to <u>match</u> compensation and individual motivation. But the linkage between compensation and performance is difficult to achieve. It is difficult (a) to develop reliable measures of performance, (b) to gain the employee's acceptance of a performance evaluation, (c) to identify whether extrinsic, monetary rewards or intrinsic job satisfaction are more important for the employee, and (d) to ensure the equitable distribution of rewards.

numerous – zahlreich
innate – angeboren, eigen
predictable – voraussagbar, berechenbar
to match – anpassen, angleichen
job description – Stellenbeschreibung

In order to be motivated, employees must believe that their efforts will lead to acceptable performance levels, and that significant rewards will follow from the achievement of these performance levels. Climate surveys show that people are most dissatisfied with the reward system when appraisals are not directly linked to compensation. Labor action (such as strikes and work stoppages) often result from complaints about the levels of comparative, not absolute pay. Where employees feel undervalued, they will inevitably find ways to compensate for an employer's perceived unfairness.

The Work System

The term work system refers to the way work is organized and managed around the core tasks. Job analysis is used to collect information about specific tasks. Whereas a group of tasks performed by one person makes up a position, identical positions make a job, and broadly similar jobs combine into an occupation. Job analysis data are summarized in a <u>job description</u>.

According to the traditional workflow model, employees perform narrowly defined jobs, stay and specialize unless they are promoted or transferred. They work under close supervision with little opportunity to grow in competence beyond their field of specialization. Compensation is based on the evaluation of the specific job and on individual performance.

The Integration of HRM Policies

The limits of hierarchy as a source of control – embodied in the exit, voice and loyalty options of people – have forced companies to search for new solutions that recognize the legitimate demands of all stakeholders. In empowered workflow models, teams are assigned full responsibility for performing a group of more broadly defined jobs, and employees are rotated through various jobs. Direct supervision is minimized under the assumption that peer pressure is more effective than top-down controls. As the company considers employees to be capable of developing a broad range of competencies, pay is related to work experience and the number of jobs mastered.

Assessing the strengths and weaknesses of the various HR configurations is a complex procedure. In theory, a bureaucratic structure with narrowly defined jobs, and emphasis on internal equity is effective in achieving economies of scale. In contrast, if a company is competing in a highly complex and uncertain environment, it must foster innovation and flexibility through a high-commitment work system and market-related rewards.

B 8.2 Knowledge Check

(1) Define (a) a career path, and (b) a lateral career path.
(2) Explain the phenomenon of career plateauing.
(3) Discuss the unstable in-and-out system of human resource flow.
(4) (a) List the factors that must be considered in choosing a compensation policy.
    (b) Discuss the difference between hourly pay and pay-for-performance.

→ See Answer Key for solutions.

B 8.3 Keywords

Career plateau; compensation; empowerment; equity; fast track; high-commitment; in-and-out flow; job analysis; lateral career path; lifelong employment; pay-for-performance; performance evaluation; position; radial career path; recruitment; staffing; up-or-out flow; self-actualization; vertical career path.

B 8.4 Strategy Case: Pharmacia – Merging People, not Firms

Pharmacia Corporation was created in April 2000 through the merger of Pharmacia & Upjohn with Monsanto Company and its G.D. Searle unit. Pharmacia employed approximately 59,000 people worldwide and has research, manufacturing and administrative sales operations in more than 60 countries.

The decision to merge with Monsanto Co. – and thereby gaining access to its blockbuster arthritis drug Celebrex, and new developments – was only the latest in a series of aggressive moves aimed at catapulting Pharmacia into the top echelon of the drug industry. And provided the merger proceeded smoothly, a combined Monsanto-Pharmacia would be in a strong position to negotiate additional deals.

However, making the Pharmacia-Monsanto merger work would be a formidable challenge. Both companies had research facilities scattered across the globe, and a disparate array of prescription drugs to sell and the product portfolios had little overlap. While blockbuster drugs – defined as earning above $ 1 billion in annual sales – like Monsanto's Celebrex could drive a company's earnings up 15 % or more per year, its agriculture business did not promise such a fast growth. Only a minority of investors believed genetically modified crops had the potential to change the ways people grew and consumed food. In fact, in the long-term, many analysts considered Monsanto a threat to Pharmacia's earnings.

In his two years as chief executive officer of Pharmacia & Upjohn Inc, CEO Fred Hassan had acquired a strong reputation for his mercurial turnaround of a company that was hemorrhaging talent. His reputation was primarily that of a strong leader who inspired loyalty by encouraging new ideas and listening to his front-line people. At the same time, though, he was said to deal ruthlessly with executives who failed to live up to his expectations. Some analysts considered this combination of openness and toughness to be a necessary ingredient for melding Monsanto and Pharmacia into a coherent, effective company in an intensely competitive industry.

Merging Pharmacia & Upjohn

Hassan's skills at uniting colliding interests were demonstrated in 1997 when he resigned from a high-ranking position at American Home Products Corp. to take the helm of Pharmacia & Upjohn (P&U). The company, which was formed by the 1995 merger of Upjohn Co. and Sweden's Pharmacia, was navigating in dangerous currents. Sales were declining, and executives at its London headquarters lacked adequate control over the company's far-flung bases of operation, in Michigan, Sweden and Italy.

Hassan's first act was to hold a press conference in New York City, designed to send a very public message to P&U employees and to gain him time in gaining their trust and in rebuilding their confidence in the organization. He traveled directly from the press conference to Stockholm and Milan and London, where he listened to people's complaints, and gathered information on the company's products. His next destination was Kalamazoo, Michigan (the former Upjohn's hometown), where he wanted to build a rapport with the local workers.

Cross-Border Fighting

P&U, Hassan assessed, it was in complete disarray. There were open disputes between the group's divisions and it was clear employees were drawing battle lines between the European and the U.S. operations.

The overall goal of the merger had been to create a united global sales and distribution force. Combining the companies, however, proved much harder than expected. Each side thought that it could depend on the other's sales force, only to find that each was more interested in promoting its own products. What had been envisioned as three centers (in Sweden, Italy, and the U.S.) working in harmony became three warring factions.

Instead of relying on group meetings, Hassan scheduled many time-consuming one-on-one meetings with P&U managers around the globe. In these private, personal meetings he learned the degree to which distrust was rising and morale suffering. Managers were mounting personal attacks against anyone they viewed as an outsider. One employee charged, for example, that a country manager made hiring and firing decisions based solely on workers' nationalities. Divisional bitterness had all but paralyzed intra-company communication at the most sensitive time in the post-merger integration process.

A Unification Plan

The company's future depended on getting beyond the nationalism that was tearing it apart. That meant creating a mission, a strategy, and a set of values – in essence, a P&U flag to which everyone shared allegiance. It soon became clear to Hassan that the unifying flag was the company's products. P&U needed a systematic way to bring to market quickly best bets for blockbuster success, and to rally people across the firm and around the world to bring about and share in that success.

Beyond using a product with high potential to revitalize team spirit, a process of centralizing and streamlining began in the then highly fragmented institution. Not only were activities organized by country at that time, they were separated by disease as well – areas like oncology, urology, ophthalmology, endocrinology, women's illnesses, and infectious diseases.

With activities separated into these silos the tendency for each group was to maximize its own personnel and resources. Therefore, he concluded that the regional offices and the silos structured around types of diseases had to be dismantled to make it easier to identify the most promising new product developments, and then to channel marketing dollars and sales support toward them.

Focus on Five Engines of Growth

Ultimately, Hassan focused on five "engines of growth" – key products with high-revenue and worldwide potential: Detrol, a bladder incontinence treatment;

Genotropin, a growth hormone; Fragmin, an anticoagulant; Xalatan, a glaucoma medication; and Camptosar, a colon cancer treatment drug.

In a bid to strengthen the company's cancer-drug pipeline, Hassan engineered the acquisition of Sugen Inc. in the first quarter of 1999, after asking top research managers to identify the most innovative biotech companies. The choice fell on Sugen because it was developing an array of promising gene-based cancer drugs.

Even though U&P was strongly in debt, Hassan decided to invest heavily in sales and marketing for the five key products, and to cut back budgets in other areas. In line with this blockbuster strategy, P&U added 600 new sales representatives in the U.S., and began to market Detrol over-the-counter directly to U.S. consumers, rather than just through physicians. This transformed it from an ethical accessory to a mass-market drug. In Japan it severed its distribution contract with Sumitomo for Genotropin, and relaunched the anticoagulant Fragmin in the U.S.

To drive the repositioning, Hassan centralized the marketing function, taking away control of major products from country managers. These "engines of growth" no longer belonged to separate divisions, but were owned by the whole corporation.

Expanding this policy to other areas, Hassan centralized most management functions at P&U. Within the space of a year, he created a top-down structure, reducing the corporate management team from 19 to seven. He also strengthened his own power by personally appointing all executives reporting directly to the CEO. New heads of the finance, legal, and human resources departments were put in charge of operations subject to his control.

Compounding the controversy surrounding the restructuring process, P&U was failing dismally in the U.S. market in the same year. Sales were declining at an annual rate of 7 percent whereas the overall market was growing in the double-digit range. Then, in October 1997, CEO Hassan surprised a corporate audience assembled in London with a bold strategic decision. He announced that P&U would move its headquarters from London to Peapack, New Jersey, given that the major market in the pharmaceutical business was the U.S.

The majority of the assembled managers understood the strategic implications, but many were very unhappy with the implied retrenchment from a global to an international positioning. Europeans, in particular, were not attracted by the prospect of relocating from London to a New Jersey suburb.

But, after a troubled first year, the restructuring process began to bear fruit. Net income more than doubled in 1998, and surged another 14 percent in 1999. Within two years, the stock rose by 40 percent, compared with an increase of 31.4 percent for the Dow Jones pharmaceutical index.

The New Pharmacia Corporation

With the integration of Pharmacia AB and Upjohn barely completed, Hassan surprised the stakeholders and the financial community in February 1999 with the decision to undertake a merger of equals with Monsanto Corporation, based in

St. Louis. This merger seemed to have little in common with the first. P&U and Monsanto were financially healthy, and there were no nationality issues, because both companies were based in the U.S. Replicating his on-hands approach during the P&U merger, Hassan engaged in face-to-face discussions with employees at Monsanto.

Although, there was no crisis feeling tension at both companies was palpable. The press and industry experts were initially hostile to the deal. The analysts asked why a fast-growing pharmaceutical group was joining forces with a company that had a bigger presence in chemicals and agricultural products than in drugs. But, Hassan hoped to tap Monsanto's vast genetic research capabilities for drug development (residing mainly in its Searle drug division) and to acquire Monsanto's new family of pain relievers known as Cox-2.

After Hassan spent much of January and February 1999 ardently promoting the logic of the merger as a merger of equals among journalists and analysts, the financial community and the media began to assess the deal more favorably.

Blending Business Cultures

The improving media view helped reduce the anxieties among employees. Since the merger announcement, Hassan has spent much of his time reassuring the workforce, and making it very clear to the executives whom he values most. The CEO personally called many of the people on a list of valued employees and asked other senior managers to get in touch with the rest. A similar list was drawn up at Monsanto. Then, in February 1999, top research and development people from P&U and Monsanto gathered for a meeting at a neutral location. Everyone made presentations to drive home the importance of collaboration.

But the more pressing challenge was blending the two business cultures. Monsanto was much more decentralized and not as product-driven as P&U. Furthermore, Monsanto's agricultural business was to be spun off in a separate company controlled by Pharmacia.

Growing Anxiety among Monsanto's R&D People

In spite of Hassan's successful track record of an "organic post merger integration process" analysts resumed speculating whether his combination of aggressive and sensitive management styles would work for this second merger.

As the integration of the drug and crop product lines proceeded slowly, many analysts began to question the merger of two distinct businesses serving different markets and customers. In their opinion, the full potential of both companies could only be realized by separating these businesses positions. Accordingly, industry experts concluded that if Pharmacia operated Monsanto's agriculture division as a separate business, it would eventually divest all ownership of the agribusiness.

This opinion was also reflected among the research people at Monsanto, where it was widely believed that Hassan would sell the non-drug business before long to focus on high-growth pharmaceuticals.

However, Monsanto had a long tradition as a life science company. Robert Shapiro who was CEO of Monsanto at the time of the merger had been a major proponent of the idea that drugs and crops were similar businesses that both involved biology. During his tenure, he had promoted a strategy to manage the entire value chain, from seed to crops to food to health and wellness as a coherent system.

Two often-cited reasons for a probable spin-off were the anxiety of the pharmaceutical companies about their ambiguous public image, and the growing public alarm over genetically modified crops. Even as a unit of Pharmacia, Monsanto would probably be a high-profile target for the ongoing biotech crop controversy.

The Ongoing Challenge

But, to realize the full financial potential the combined firm would need to retain Monsanto's talent and know-how that had created the attractive product pipeline in the first place. Ensuring employee commitment could be the greatest challenge of the merger.

B 8.5 The "Visionary" Mindset

One of the greatest challenges facing managers is understanding and achieving a measure of control over unforeseen developments. Adjustment to unplanned change always triggers emotions. Anxiety and stress lower performance where people are uncertain how to behave, or what to expect from others. In addition, unplanned change usually involves a sense of loss. In cases where the need to feel in control is stronger than the reaction to the actual change, even mutually beneficial changes may be resisted if someone else has planned them.

In this situation organizational culture and leadership style are important tools. Because people feel vulnerable during times of unplanned change, it is important to boost self-esteem, for instance by letting people express their emotional responses without negative evaluations.

Change will occur when the forces for change are stronger than the resistant forces, or when the forces against change are stronger than the pressures for change, change will not occur. To analyze the stability of the current force-field it is necessary to examine the forces driving organizational change and those forces resisting organizational change. In general, strategies aimed at diminishing the effect of resisting forces are more effective than increasing the effect of the driving forces, as this often fuels more resistance.

The finals steps, designing how the change should occur, and implementing the change are often more critical than the process of designing what change should occur. Due to the general psychological tendency to project mental states, managers tend to assume other parties share their insights into the need and benefits of a planned change and are prepared to back them with the same enthusiasm.

B 8.6 Experiential Exercise: Creativity-Relevant Skills

Exercise 1 – Breaking Established Thinking Barriers

(1) **The Organization.** To assist in thinking differently about organizations, list on a separate piece of paper as many graphic representations or metaphors used to characterize a specific organization.

(2) **The Department.** A new department for e-commerce is to be established. Which metaphors might spring to mind in characterizing this department?

Exercise 2 – Developing Mental Imagery

According to findings in cognitive psychology, thought processes are constrained and shaped by given sets of images, or schemata. The creative technique of "looking in the mirror", helps managers visualize their respective strengths and weaknesses and imagine new possibilities.

In a workshop setting, people can work in pairs or small groups, developing their own images, and then sharing them with the other participants.

Directions:

Transform each of the follow descriptions into a mental image, immediately rating its clarity according to the following scale: C = Clear; V = Vague; Z = Zero image.

Imagine visually:	Imagine a sensory image:
1. A familiar face	1. Flight path of a volley return at Wimbledon
2. Cars at the scene of a collision	2. Voices in an airport lounge
3. A farmhouse lit by a full moon	3. A dentist drilling a tooth
4. The characteristic voice of a friend	4. The taste of vanilla
5. Your farewell speech to work colleagues	5. Stroking over your hair

Exercise 3 – Using Analogies and Homologies

Identify three pressing problems you currently have at work. Describe each one briefly in writing. Then review the following list of analogies. Try to apply an analogy from this list:

1. Finding your way through the woods at night
2. Going under the shower on a cold winter morning
3. Frying eggs in a pantry kitchen
5. Composing a keynote banquet speech
8. Realizing you have not been invited to an after-work event
6. Surfing on a windy day
7. Imagining your current organization as a Lego structure

Identify the feelings you have associated with each problem, and describe them with an analogy. The use of analogies should help to see the problems from different perspectives.

In a second step, involving the use of homology as a classification tool, compare each situation a similarly structured script from your experience with organizations.

Try to connect the different perspectives that you created on each problem. Use the perspectives to generate possible solutions to the three problems you identified.

Exercise 4 – Using the Nominal Group Technique

The following steps may be used for planning a group session to help reinforce mutual trust and commitment for change:

(1) *Make sure that everyone agrees on the problem definition.*

(2) *Have participants write down all their ideas.* Even ideas that do not seem feasible may give other people ideas. During this time no one should talk, except to ask questions about the problem definition. This step may take anywhere from 10 minutes to 30 minutes.

(3) *Use a round-robin procedure to allow participants to share their ideas.* Have each participant give one idea at a time. Record the ideas on a flip chart so that all ideas are visible to all participants. Again, do not allow discussion as the ideas are being recorded.

(4) *After all ideas are recorded, review each idea one at a time.* Allow participants to ask questions and share reactions about the feasibility and merits of the idea. Keep steering the discussion on course.

(5) *Find the preferred alternative solution.* The voting by a rank vote should be secret. Individually the participants identify their top five ideas. They assign a score of five to their first-ranked idea, four to their second ranked idea, and so on.

(6) *Review the voting patterns.* If one alternative stands out as the obvious preferred choice, then you are ready to decide how to implement that choice. If not, return to step 4, this time rank ordering only on the basis of the top three choices.

Exercise 5 – Competence in Public Communication

In the following case, consider how the speaker relates to his audience. Focus on the assumptions he makes about the beliefs, expectations, and knowledge of his audience. Consider the impact of audience size, and distance between audience and speaker on the matter of credibility.

> **Q3 STATE OF THE CARSON INSTITUTE**
>
> *10 July 2002*
>
> *"The standing of the Carson Institute is strong and is improving every quarter. Our singular mission is to monitor the human clinical trial of a new drug. Validating these*

trials requires careful due-process audits that you, our highly qualified clinical 'monitors', conduct on a monthly basis Here are some of the most important indicators reflecting our strong organizational health:

Staff Survey

We have undertaken the most comprehensive collection of information – approximately 120 responses – in my almost 9 years with the institute. It is a good snapshot of how we are going. Some highlights are:

- 60 % of CMs under contract say that they found out about CI through a colleague.
- 95 % of CMs responding strongly agree or agree with the statement that their application was processed in a smooth and efficient manner and that they were satisfied with the entire contract process.
- 90 % responded that they agreed or strongly agreed with the statement that their project manager is knowledgeable about their monitoring program.
- 95 % responded by strongly agreeing or agreeing with the statement that they were satisfied with the service provided by the project manager, business office and financial office.
- 90 % of the CMs surveyed strongly agreed or agreed with statements relating to relating to the quality of training and development.
- 90 % of CMs surveyed indicated that they would recommend Carson Institute to a friend or colleague.

In all aspects, our survey projects a healthy current state with the potential for a brilliant future, and all of you deserve high marks for contributing to the quality of services and development programs at Carson Institute.

Details of the survey results will be provided to your project heads in time, but this is just the first scene of the first act. These assessment instruments will become a regular feature of our life here at Carson Institute.

Why do I mention that? Continuous improvements are crucial to enhancing the position of the institute. CI must increasingly become a 'knowledge-based institution'. This means that we must collect, process and utilize information and data in our planning and decision-making processes. Gathering that information is the first step and the survey is our first real effort to do this. We will be doing more in the future, and we will want to involve all of you in that effort.

The Bottom Line

Through the three months that ended on June 30, 2002, Carson Institute's financial position continues to reflect positive trends and improving financial ratios. A brief review of this financial performance reveals the following:

The increase in revenues is a combination of several key factors:

- *A 4% increase in monitoring fees for the current fiscal year.*
- *The increase in clinical test centers this year as compared to last.*
- *New data warehouse, technology and monitoring fees.*

The increase in expenditures is directly tied to advertising, facilities, rent and leasing, principally in Everett and Spokane, and an increase in U of Washington certification courses to enhance qualifications.

The net affect of revenues minus expenses results in a net positive income. Congratulations to all of you. Great work!

If the trend I've described remains on track, Carson Institute has the opportunity to produce a positive projected net income as of Sep 30, 2002 – the ending date of our fiscal year.

Call for Action

It is not enough to live in the past – we must live in the present, and we must prepare for the future. This is why there is such a great emphasis on the creation of project plans, business plans and strategic plans. Pay close attention to them, and contribute to them in a timely and effective manner.

With your individual contributions, we can move forward as an institution that provides the highest quality educational experiences for our clinical monitors in the field.

Thank you all for your contributions."

Following these remarks, CEO Rutgers took questions from the staff and clinical monitors present.

Discussion Questions

(1) (a) Is there a credibility issue (i.e. ethical proof based on the perceived quality of the source of the message rather than on logical proof based on evidence, such as hard statistics and examples)?

(b) If so, on which critical dimensions of credibility (i.e. competence, trustworthiness, dynamism, power, goodwill, idealism and affiliation)?

(2) Given an audience that is divided on a topic, how is it possible for the speaker to create a competent relationship with the audience in terms of control, affiliation (i.e. perceived similarity) and goal commitment?

(3) (a) Which persuasive strategies can the speaker use to gain the audience's acceptance of the intended message?

(b) If a speech is stated to be informative rather than persuasive, is it appropriate for the speaker to express an own opinion?

B 9 Control Concepts for Quality and Productivity

- Production Efficiency
- Materials Management
- Quality Assurance
- Production and Operations Management (POM)
- Compatibility Testing
- Production Planning
- Routing
- Scheduling
- Follow-up and Control
- Strategy Case: Smithfields Foods – Sensing a Gut Feeling
- The "Entrepreneurial" Mindset
- Experiential Case: Negotiating Objective Criteria

B 10 Accounting

B 9 Control Concepts for Quality and Productivity

B 9.1 Principles – Models – Practices

Production Efficiency

From a historical perspective, companies have always been alert to improving their skills to survive. Thus, industrial factories producing <u>uniform, interchangeable</u> parts evolved into industrial corporations, when the concepts of specialization and <u>division of labor</u> were applied to manufacturing, as in the <u>assembly line.</u> Now, in the "third" industrial revolution advanced manufacturing technologies are being used to rapidly switch production from one item to another, thereby reducing the relative cost advantages of mass and large <u>batch production</u>.

uniform	– einheitlich
interchangeable	– austauschbar
division of labor	– Arbeitsteilung
assembly line	– Fließband
batch production	– Serienfertigung
replenishment	– Ersatz, Ergänzung
efforts	– Bemühungen, Anstrengungen

For supply chain management (SCM) the demand pattern is the definitive input that drives the inventory, the <u>replenishment</u>, the production and the capacity plans. Marketing activities that affect different points of the supply chain, should be coordinated. Otherwise, pricing or promotion <u>efforts</u> at a manufacturer, for instance, would create bottlenecks at the retailer.

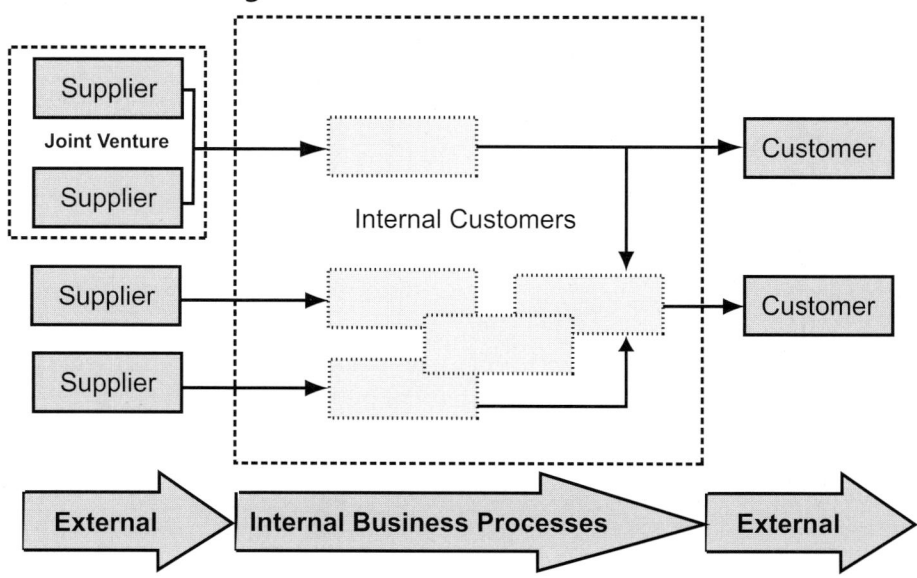

The Total Supply Chain
Linking External and Internal Customers

To obtain optimal results, marketing instruments that affect different points of the supply chain – such as pricing, promotions, order lead-times, product mix, and shelf management – should be coordinated. For example, pricing or promotion efforts at a manufacturer could be wasted if the pricing or promotion efforts at the retailer are not coordinated.

Materials Management

In automated processes the main challenge is to maintain an inventory large enough to keep production going at an optimal pace, yet small enough to keep stocks at a minimum. One aim is to shorten lead times, that is, the periods between the placement of a purchase order and receipt of materials. Flexible manufacturing plants produce only those products already ordered and have little difficulty determining their ongoing inventory needs throughout production.

By implementing an enterprise resource planning system, every department or unit can work with the same data. The software can simulate what might happen in the plant and in the office under various conditions. As the system can schedule each step of production, managers in various branches of the company are able to consult other managers' inventories, schedules, and plans.

Overview of Enterprise Resource Planning

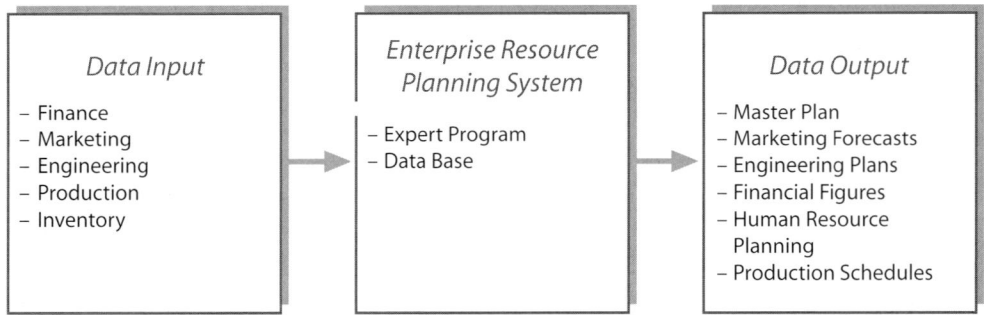

Customer-Driven Quality

Efficiency and productivity as such will not suffice to secure product quality. Quality is meeting or exceeding customer expectations. Before a product reaches consumers, it flows through a chain of many firms and departments in a cross-functional (or horizontal) workflow. Because every decision a manager makes, and every task an employee performs affects quality positively or adversely, a company must understand the impacts of its entire system on quality. Linking quality control with change processes results in efficiency increases: inventories decline, work moves more smoothly, and costs are reduced.

Production and Operations Management (POM)

Production and operations management coordinates a company's resources in the transformation process. The production and operations manager is responsible both for the basic functions of planning, organizing, directing, and controlling, and also for setting up, feeding, and maintaining the value chain from design to distribution.

Production and operations management requires specific information about the company's objectives, the strategies involved, the standards against which the outcome will be measured, the likely demand for the company's products in the future, the product changes probably required to maintain market share, and the resources needed to implement those changes.

Site Selection

One of the earliest long-term issues that must be resolved is the choice of a production site. In the past, access to low-cost resources and transportation dominated, but today such factors as local living standards, qualifications and values of the work force enter into the decision.

Production Forecasting

In the shorter term, top managers must clarify exactly what is expected from production and operations. Using past sales figures and forecasts, management estimates future demand. These estimates are used in turn for planning, budgeting and scheduling the use of resources.

> issue – Angelegenheit, Thema,
> to resolve – entscheiden, beschließen
> accuracy – Genauigkeit
> required – benötigt, erfordert

Compatibility Testing

Production-control procedures vary from company to company. When many resources and complex procedures are involved, production control may become very complicated. For example, in the development of computer software the compatibility of programs written by various people and the accuracy of the accompanying handbook must be coordinated.

Production Planning

Production planning involves listing all the required parts and materials in a list of materials, specifying whether they are to be made or purchased, and placing orders with suppliers.

Routing

Routing, the second step in production control, is the task of specifying the sequence of operations and the path of work through the facility. The methods used depend on the type of product and the layout of the plant: (a) In a process layout, the developing product is sent from one department to another for a certain type of processing; specialized equipment and workers remain in each department; (b) In an assembly-line layout, the developing product proceeds along a continuous line of work stations at which some small task is performed; (c) In a fixed-position layout, the product remains in place, and the resources are brought to it.

Scheduling

Scheduling the production process means setting up a time for each operation to begin and to end. The critical path method (CPM) is a widely used approach for coordinating projects. It focuses on the sequence of tasks that is expected to take the longest time, thus determining when the project can be completed. Other activities are planned around this critical path, and may be delayed up to a point without hindering timely completion of the project. A further issue is dispatching, i.e. the issuing of work orders and the distribution of papers to department supervisors. These orders specify the work to be done and the schedule for its completion.

Follow-up and Control

To reduce downtimes, the production manager must have a system for handling delays and preventing a minor disruption from growing into chaos. Therefore, a successful system is based on good communication between the workers and the production manager and on efficient linkage mechanisms across departments.

Interaction of Technical and Human Needs
(Socio-technical System)

B 9.2 Knowledge Check

(1) Define the goal of advances in production technology.
(2) Cite the four technological advances that made mass production possible.
(3) Explain three innovations in materials management.
(4) Identify the three main production layouts.
(5) Describe a technique for improving scheduling.

→ **See Answer Key for solutions.**

B 9.3 Keywords

Assembly-line layout; automation; critical path method; dispatching; fixed-position layout; inventory control; just-in-time system; lead times; manufacturing resource planning; mass production; material requirements planning; mechanization; process layout; production and operations management; production control; production forecasting; quality control; routing.

B 9.4 Strategy Case: Smithfields Foods – Sensing a Gut Feeling

Smithfield Foods is one of the largest companies in the world to be run by remote control. The chairman, president and CEO Joseph W. Luter III reputedly runs this business with annual revenues of $ 8 billion out of his Manhattan condo equipped only with a telephone, an address book and a pen. Practicing a hands-on management style, he has taken personal charge of the company's strategies, directly approving every acquisition and all capital spending in excess of $ 1m within the 20 divisions.

Smithfield Foods, Inc. is the largest hog producer and pork processor in the world. Throughout the U.S. and abroad in Canada, France, Poland, Japan and elsewhere, their brands set standards for fresh pork and processed meats in the food service, retail and international markets. For example, the company's Smithfield Lean Generation Pork, based on the NPD hog – the leanest hog in large-scale commercial production in the U.S. – was the first branded fresh pork program in the U.S. when introduced in 1994, and it is still the leader.

According to the Federal Reserve Bank of Kansas City, the number of American slaughterhouses for cattle and pigs has dropped by two-thirds since 1980. Mr. Luter has played a part in that process. In the past two years, Smithfield has made 17 acquisitions, giving it 20 % of the domestic processing market for pork. It is interesting to note that American antitrust law was created in 1890 driven by popular distrust of the meatpacking industry.

Contrary to popular perceptions that are reflected and reinforced in the media, the industry is highly competitive. While population growth has provided a positive impulse, Americans have long been spending a shrinking proportion of their income on food. Thus, annual consumption of pork by Americans has been stagnating for decades.

The industry must also deal with environmental concerns. Despite industry claims that concentrating production in large facilities boosts both efficiency of production and waste management, the company is heavily burdened with pollution-related litigation.

As the meat business has become more capital-intensive, Joseph W. Luter III has had to make some bold moves. Intrigued by higher pork consumption overseas in the 1980s, he went to Europe and found the answer: a leaner strain of pigs. So, in

1990, he imported 2,000 British for cross breeding. This was a major step in his effort to integrate vertically and to create a nationwide brand, a strategy already common in poultry. Although this strategy has stabilized Smithfield's profits, it has also antagonized small pig farmers and independent meat plants.

Although Smithfield's profit margins in pork production rarely rise above 3 %. The low margins in combination with environmental restrictions create formidable barriers to entry and forcing less efficient competitors to desert the industry.

For Smithfield, the low margins are tolerable as long as there are prospects for revenue growth, whether through innovation or through acquisitions when opportunities arise. For example, since 1976 Smithfield's net worth has grown by a staggering 31 % annually and its share price by 28 % a year.

In the context of its current strategy, Smithfield Foods is pursuing a Company-wide program to expand high-quality processed meat sales. Rather than simply being a producer and seller of commodity fresh pork, the overall objective is to improve profitability by achieving parity between branded value-added fresh pork and high-value processed meats. In fiscal 1994, the Company's subsidiaries produced about 660 million pounds of processed meats. In fiscal 2000, the total was more than 2.2 billion pounds.

However, as Joseph W. Luter III points out, the future performance is subject to risks and uncertainties that could cause actual results to diverge from those expressed in the statements. The risks and uncertainties include input factors such as availability and prices of live hogs, raw materials and supplies; they also include process-related factors such as live hog production costs, operating efficiencies; furthermore, market-related factors such as product pricing, the competitive environment, market conditions; also financial aspects such as access to capital, the cost of compliance with environmental and health standards must be considered; finally, there are environmental aspects such as adverse results from ongoing litigation and government action.

Technology Issues in John Morrell's Sioux City Plant

The dynamics of these factors are felt strongly at John Morrell and Co. It is a wholly owned and independently managed subsidiary of Smithfield Foods, with four subsidiary companies, offering an extensive product line of processed meats and fresh pork under thirteen regional brands to every segment of the market.

Each regional brand enjoys high brand recognition and loyalty among consumers. It is also the nation's second-largest producer of private-label meat products for retail chains and foodservice distributors. Approximately 6 % of sales are to customers in 25 countries outside of the U.S.

In his continuous drive to increase productivity, to upgrade quality, and to focus on high-margin business, Joseph W. Luter III is in a dilemma. Increasingly, automated meat cutting systems based on robotics are being introduced in meat processing plants to increase efficiency and to facilitate environmental management.

The Sioux City (Iowa) plant of John Morrell, currently employing 1,350 people with a payroll of $33 million, and doing approximately $400 million in annual sales could become a model for automated processing. It is an efficient, flexibly organized plant with a reputation for producing quality products. It is also an employer that brings satisfaction to employees. However, the accelerated dynamics in a formerly stable value chain – as exemplified by online marketplaces – require the workflow to be organized and managed with the concurrent aims of increasing efficiency and reducing cycle time.

In this strategic context, the Sioux City plant manager, Steve Joyce, has a stake in enhancing efficiency, but also must consider that operations became more automated, people would hardly be able to talk to each other. It would be difficult to maintain a team atmosphere in the plant if everyone was hooked up to continuously producing automated equipment liable to break down at any point at any time.

The Pork Conversion Process

A generic slaughterhouse is divided into two separate areas. One area is used to kill and dress animals. The other area is used to cut and prepare finished meats for delivery to customers. Mechanization has developed to the point where carcasses are conveyed entirely by hooks and overhead rails. Workers use mechanical tools for several operations, such as power saws for splitting carcasses and a hydraulic winch to pull off the skin.

The hourly workers on the shop floor are considered semiskilled. Management feels that a loosely run organization brings satisfaction to employees, but is pondering how workers could be organized and managed more efficiently.

The process for converting live hogs into bacon and ham normally requires more than a dozen discrete operations. The dressing sequence begins by stunning, and elevating the hog to an overhead rail where it is stuck and bled. The carcass is dipped mechanically into a scalding tank to loosen the hair and then moved mechanically to the scraping area where the carcasses are scraped clean, partly by hand. Next, the carcass is moved to the singeing area, where the meat's outer layer is darkened, a process that produces skin for good leather quality. Subsequently, the carcass is eviscerated, skinned, decapitated, and split in half with a hand-operated electric saw. At this point the carcass is inspected for disease by a vet and sent to the frosting room.

The hog halves are taken from the frosting room on demand and moved to the meat-cutting area. In this operation, the meat is thawed, and then cut into hams, bellies, and shoulders.

According to standard operational procedures, this meat is then injected with brine to assure a more uniform cure and to reduce the curing time to two or three days. The injection infuses a solution of salt, sugar, nitrates, and a variety of flavor profiles into the meat. The salt acts as a preservative, and the nitrates are used to retain the reddish color of the meat. The solution is injected manually using a series of needles connected to a pumping machine that also controls the rate and pressure of the injection. Bellies are injected twice, with an 8-hour interval. A special blend of ingredients is added to render the meat tender, moist and flavorful, even if it is overcooked.

The injection requires modest skill. Operators are responsible for seeing that the quantity of solution does not exceed the limit set by federal law, and to monitor that the brine is injected uniformly throughout the meat.

After brining, the meat cuts are boned and smoked. The boning operation consists of trimming excess fat and cutting out the bones from hams and shoulders. Great dexterity is required to trim the fat and remove the bone with a minimum of waste and rework. It takes a new worker at least six months to be proficient in this task.

For example, each ham can present specific problems, depending on size and the amount of fat and remaining skin. An operator knows from experience whether a ham will be difficult to work with. After smoking, which is accomplished according to the specified categories, the ham is packed for sale or shipment, and then re-chilled.

The last step in the production sequence is the assembly of customer orders. The order teams assemble items from finished stock, move them to the packing area, check the assembled order against the customer's order, fill cartons with the meat, and arrange shipment.

John Morrell's has an extensive variety of cuts. From bone-in to boneless to seasoned, "Tender N Juicy Fresh Pork". The line of products includes whole primal cuts and further merchandised varieties such as Loin Chops, Spare Ribs, Back Ribs, Boneless Loin Chops, Tenderloins, Pork Butts, Pork Picnics, Fresh Bone-in and Boneless Hams, Boneless Roasts and Rack of Pork.

Jobs in Process Engineering

Currently, an industrial engineering team is responsible for designing, operating and maintaining special equipment for producing an ever-increasing volume and variety of meat products. The work includes studying the production operation throughout the plant, conducting time and motion studies of each task, and suggesting new work procedures. The industrial engineers are also responsible for evaluating new equipment with respect to cost and labor savings.

In this context, (1) Mechanical Engineers are involved in designing and developing new machinery as well as updating current equipment used in the plant's meat processing operations; (2) Electrical Engineers are responsible for supervising the technical aspect of general power distribution, surveying power and electrical needs required for larger energy units and devising electrical maintenance programs; (3) Plant Engineers oversee the physical plant, including the repair, maintenance, modification and installation of equipment, working closely with manufacturing supervisors to remedy problems in processing, packaging and machinery; (4) Environmental engineers perform regulatory compliance audits among various sites, conducting permit writing, engineering design and construction of pollution control equipment, water supply, wastewater, storm water, air emissions, solid waste, hazardous materials and waste minimization.

Driving Factors for Implementing Advanced Technology

A major consideration supporting the change to advanced technology is that automated robot-cutting and artificial vision system can improve the consistent quality of cuts and meat hygiene, and enhance work safety. Another factor to consider is that the expected shortfall of skilled workers makes it necessary to automate some meat processing tasks. For example, a robotic system can remove flank ribs from bellies at a rate of 1,400 pieces per hour.

How does the advanced technology work? Until recently, the complexity of many cutting tasks made it very difficult to mechanize slaughterhouse workstations. A great deal of dexterity and training is required to maintain the uniformity of the cut to produce a consistently high yield. The manual stripping and trimming operations are the cause of many occupational disorders such as bursitis and tendonitis. They also create a higher risk of bacterial contamination.

The robot contains a cutting system equipped with eight double-sided knives and an artificial vision system that can process 700 hogs or 1,400 bellies per hour – the equivalent of the volume achieved by a six-person crew.

An automatic feeder first synchronizes pork bellies on a main cutting conveyor. The bellies then pass a data collecting station with a camera analyzing spatial patterns, and triangulating sections by laser. The resulting cutting parameters are then transmitted to the robot, the entire process taking only two and a half seconds.

The robot changes and sterilizes knives automatically in the course of production. The robot arm is protected by a pressurized wash-down sanitary cover, designed to withstand cold temperatures, changing humidity and high pressure cleansing.

The system can also operate in manual mode, with sub-systems operating independently. In the production mode, the quality of the meat cuts is monitored and controlled continuously. Operators can make certain adjustments, such as the thickness of the meat left on the ribs, without stopping the system.

The CEO's Dilemma

Joseph W. Luter III's dilemma about whether to further automate his plant reflects the increasing complexity of the business. Does it make sense to grow and to acquire new technology to the point where the plant becomes a high-tech CIM operation? Would the new technology be more efficient and reliable than a reengineered assembly-line operation. Within the new work system, would the retrained old employees and newly recruited specialists cooperate effectively? Also, does the plant have the contingent structure and management systems to handle increased growth and automation? Alternatively, if John Morrell Co. do not continue on the path of innovation and enhanced efficiency, they may face decline.

B 9.5 The "Entrepreneurial" Mindset

Understanding Oneself and Others

The importance of understanding one's own motives and behaviors is obvious. Yet, many instances of "groupthink" (as during speculative bubbles) or ethical failures suggest that many people in managerial positions have considerable difficulty understanding themselves.

Applying a developmental model of behavior, people are seen as progressing through a series of stages. In each stage they take on different values and assumptions. One of the early stages is the stage of technician, the most prevalent style of managing. People in this stage are concerned with expertise, technical logic and efficiency. They tend to work closely but impersonally with others, setting ambitious standards, and constantly checking up on details. They tend to be very slow in learning about themselves, and to resist taking feedback about their behavior. The feelings of others do not count as facts.

However, a manager's success depends on the ability to learn rather than on the mastery of specific skills. Specifically, long-term advancement depends on learning how to influence the behavior of others, choosing the right strategy with the right person at the right moment involves knowing one's own values and those of other people.

Apart from naturally endowed emotional intelligence, there are tools and techniques available for managers to help others to learn, to build trust, and to promote empathy. However, there is a paradox involved. The secret of overcoming defensiveness in others is to overcome defensiveness in ourselves.

Active Listening

The most important technique for gaining access to the information we need is listening to others. This is because people can think approximately four times as fast as they can speak. Using the technique of active listening means to refrain from evaluating other people's words, not by assuming a consciously "neutral" position (this would indicate indifference) but by expressively trying to see things from their point of view. This involves:

- sincerely wanting to understand others. This empathy may be signaled by showing interest in the other's point of view, for example by frequently interjecting supportive comments into the conversation;
- reading the nonverbal signals as well as the verbal ones;
- not reacting too quickly to inaccurate statements of fact, and listening carefully for the feelings beneath the statement before intervening to correct facts.

A similarly structured learning approach is also useful in negotiating an agreement. Negotiated decisions should be based on some objective standards or criteria that will help the parties test the reasonableness of a position. This involves

- separating the people from the problem by defining issues;
- focusing on decoded underlying interests, not on declared positions;

- generating a variety of possibilities before deciding on a specific course of action;
- insisting that the result is based upon some objective standard.

Artifact of Persuasion

A negotiator who is skilled at discovering people's motives will tend to use two approaches to give a message a persuasive spin:

(1) making an offer psychologically more attractive (by stimulating intrinsic motivation), or

(2) minimizing psychological resistance to the offer (by stimulating extrinsic motivation).

Changes in attraction and in resistance levels do not necessarily result from rational argument. On the biological level, these motivational adaptions actually correspond to separate neurological systems that control activation and inhibition.

Creating attraction energizes, directs and sustains people's actions. As different people are motivated by different things in different situations, a talented negotiator will address (i.e. activate) these needs rather than stick to a prepared plan.

An empathetic negotiator will also take into account that resistance (i.e. inhibition) is partly "hard-wired" into the brain. Its evolutionary advantage is the ability to detect and avoid cheats. Therefore, directly addressing the "gut" fear of being duped or cheated can be a persuasive approach to reducing resistance. One persuasive ploy in pressing demands, for instance, is to undercut people's defensiveness by specifying a precise (even if arbitrary) sum rather than stating a vague demand.

But, negotiators can only drain resistance temporarily. To the extent that the level of resistance has been lowered, people are motivated to raise it again to be able to counter undesirable changes.

B 9.6 Experiential Case: Negotiating Objective Criteria

Adjuster: We have studied your case and have come to the conclusion that the policy applies. That means you are entitled to a settlement of $7,000.

Claimant: Hmm... How did you arrive at that amount?

Adjuster: Based on generally accepted actuarial standards, that's precisely how much the car was worth.

Claimant: I see your point, but what standard did you use to determine that estimate? Do you know a vendor where I can buy an equivalent SUV for that amount?

Adjuster: Then, how much are you asking?

Claimant: Whatever I'm entitled to under my policy. I sourced a used SUV comparable to mine for $10,900. Adding sales and excise tax, it would come to about $12,800.

Adjuster: $12,800! That's an wildly arbitrary price!

Claimant: It's not that I'm asking for $12,800. I'm just asking for a fair compensation. Would you agree that it's only fair to pay out the sum it takes to replace my SUV?

Adjuster: Fairness is a contractual issue. Indeed, the exact level of compensation is stipulated by the terms agreed on in your insurance policy. I can offer you $8,100. That's the highest sum ACME Insurance will accept.

Claimant: How does the company figure that?

Adjuster: Please, be realistic. $8,100 is a generous offer I'm extending to a valued policyholder, and it's our company's final word.

Claimant: $8,100... I'm not at all convinced. I certainly understand your position if you're bound by company policy, but unless you can specify that amount as being what I'm legally entitled to, I think I might surrender my policy and go to court. Maybe, we should adjourn.

At this point the adjuster is readying for a crunch. In the next phase, the claimant would be confronted with contractually permissible add-ons such as an advisory fee of $40, a service charge of $150 for damage inspection, a surcharge of $80 for weekend service, and a fee of $20 for physical use of the office facilities. But, to keep her options open, the adjuster decides, for the time being, to follow a conciliatory approach.

Adjuster: Okay. I've got an ad here for a 1998 Explorer for $7,900.

Claimant: Really! What does it say about the previous owner?

Adjuster: Is that relevant?

Claimant: Because mine was regularly maintained by a certified dealer. How much does that increase the book value?

Adjuster: Stretching actuarial rules to the limit, $600.

Claimant: Assuming the $8,000 refers to a no-frills SUV, that would bring the figure to $8,500. Does the ad say anything about GPS?

Adjuster: Not in this case.

Claimant: Then, how much value would be added according to your list?

Adjuster: A maximum of $300 under exceptional circumstances.

Claimant: And what about EPS?

20 minutes later, an exhausted, but satisfied claimant walked out with a check for $9,855.

Note, how restrained both parties argued. Keeping the discussion of price focused on objective criteria that were mutually acceptable. By following their respective scripts, each side remained in control of the situation, and impervious to psychological pressure. Each knew their appeal to objective criteria appeared reasonable. For conciliatory individuals, in general, negotiating is an emotional ordeal if they cannot rely on the guidance of a strategy.

B 10 Accounting

- Financial Accounting
- Fundamental Concepts
- Financial Analysis
- The Certification of Financial Statements
- Trend and Ratio Analysis
- Management Accounting
- The Role of Budgets
- Scorecharting
- Strategy Case: Elan Corp.
- The "Informating" Mindset
- Experiential Exercise 1: Organizational Design Preference
- Experiential Exercise 2: Corporate versus Professional Identity

B 11 Financial Management

B 10 Accounting

B 10.1 Principles – Models – Practices

By definition, <u>accounting</u> is the system a business uses to measure its financial performance by <u>recording</u> and classifying sales, purchases, and other transactions. Accounting also <u>provides</u> ways to present this information for <u>evaluating</u> a company's performance. Whereas financial accounting is concerned with preparing information for the outside audience, management accounting is used as a tool to plan and control a company's operations.

Financial Accounting

External stakeholders use accounting information for a variety of reasons: Suppliers, banks, and other <u>lenders</u> want to <u>assess</u> the business's <u>credit standing</u>; investors and shareholders are concerned with the company's profit potential; government agencies are mainly interested in regulating the business and collecting taxes. For all these users the criteria of objectivity, consistency over time, and compatibility with the information from other companies are of utmost importance. Therefore, financial accounting statements must <u>adhere to</u> certain standard formats such as the Generally Accepted Accounting Principles (GAAP) or International Accounting Principles (IAS) that have been established by the professional associations (FASB, IASB) over many years.

> **accounting** – Rechnungswesen
> **to record** – aufzeichnen, erfassen
> **to provide** – liefern, zur Verfügung stellen
> **to evaluate** – bewerten, beurteilen
> **lender** – Kreditgeber, Darlehensgeber
> **to assess** – bewerten, beurteilen
> **credit standing** – Bonität, Kreditwürdigkeit
> **to adhere to** – einhalten, übereinstimmen mit
> **assets** – Vermögensgegenstände
> **liabilities** – Verbindlichkeiten, Fremdkapital

Fundamental Concepts

The two fundamental concepts of accounting are the accounting equation and double-entry bookkeeping:

Assets   = Liabilities + Owners' Equity
$ 100,000 = $ 40,000   + $ 60,000

The relationship of <u>assets</u>, <u>liabilities</u>, and owners' equity remains in balance; in other words, one side of the equation always equals the other side.

The <u>balance sheet</u>, or statement of financial position, provides a "snapshot" image of all the elements in the accounting equation.

> **balance sheet** – Bilanz
> **income statement** – Erfolgsrechnung, G & V
> **miscellaneous** – sonstige, diverse
> **royalties** – Lizenzgebühren

In contrast, the <u>income statement</u> reflects the results of operations over a period of time, usually a quarter or a calendar year (whereby the accrual method is generally used, based on the date of the transaction, rather than the actual transfer of goods and cash). It provides a summary of (1) all revenues (i.e. the amount of money received from sales, and from <u>miscellaneous</u> sources, such as rent, interest, and <u>royalties</u>), and (2) all expenses (i.e. costs incurred in the process of generating revenues). The expenses are subtracted from the revenues to show the actual profit or loss ("net income" or "bottom line").

In addition to the balance sheet and income statement, companies generally prepare a statement of cash flows summarizing receipts and disbursals of cash in three areas: operations, investments and financing. An analysis of the cash flow status provides insights into a company's liquidity, i.e. its ability to honor short-term obligations as they become due.

A Sample Balance Sheet

Assets

    Current Assets
        Cash
        Marketable securities
        Accounts receivable
        Less: Allowance for uncollectible accounts
        Notes receivable
        Merchandise inventory
        Prepaid expenses
    Total Current Assets

    Fixed Assets
        Factory equipment
        Less: Accumulated depreciation
        Less: Accumulated amortization
    Total Fixed Assets

Intangible Assets
    Organization costs
    Trademark
    Goodwill
    Total Intangible Assets

Total Assets

Liabilities and Shareholders' Equity

Current Liabilities
    Accounts payable
    Note payable (short-term)
    Salaries payable
    Taxes payable
    Provisions
    Total Current Liabilities

Long-Term Liabilities
    Long-term note payable (12%)

Total Liabilities

Shareholders' Equity
    Common stock, 200,000 shares
    Retained earnings
        Beginning of the year
        Current year

Total Shareholders' Equity

Total Liability and Shareholders' Equity

A Sample Income Statement

	Net sales	11,341
./.	Operating costs	(10,329)
=	Operating income	1,012
./.	Financing charges	(149)
=	Operating income less financing charges	863
./.	Taxes	(251)
=	Earnings from normal operations after taxes	612
+	Earnings from non-consolidated companies	46
./.	Extraordinary items	(75)
	Earnings before minority interest	583
	Minority interest	(14)
	Net income	**569**

Financial Analysis

Allowing for Different Accounting Methods

Accountants have a certain amount of freedom to act as they see fit, i.e. to act at their own discretion. The subjectivity and discretion involved in accounting techniques make comparisons between companies a matter of interpretation. For example, the method chosen to depict the depreciation pattern of an asset can make a company look more or less profitable. Also, revenues might be recorded when a return can reasonably be projected, or reflect spurious "sales" achieved by transferring inventory to wholesalers and retailers. Furthermore, using the FIFO (first in – first out) or LIFO (last in – first out) methods of pricing inventory, a company can raise or lower its earnings by changing its approach to calculating the cost of goods sold.

discretion – Ermessen
depreciation – Abschreibung
revenues – Einnahmen
spurious – unecht, unberechtigt
wholesaler – Großhändler
retailer – Einzelhändler
earnings – Einkünfte, Ertrag
approach – Ansatz, Methode

Adequacy of Reserves

For almost every company, some accounts receivable will be uncollectible. But the incidence and degree of bad debts are a matter of judgment. Depending on what percentage is used, the company will look more, or less profitable.

Investment funds for pensions are another type of reserve that may be handled in various ways. An example would be the amount a company should set aside to pay employees when they retire. Any solution is questionable, because no one is sure how long a retired employee will actually draw a pension. Unfunded pension liabilities have to be displayed in the liability section of the balance sheet – a method, though not materially affecting a company's cash flow, that makes its liabilities look larger.

accounts receivable	– Forderungen
uncollectible	– uneinbringlich
incidence	– Häufigkeit, Vorkommen, Auftreten
degree	– Ausmaß
bad debts	– uneinbringliche Forderungen
judgment	– Beurteilung
auditor	– Wirtschaftsprüfer, Buchprüfer
unbiased	– objektiv, unbefangen, neutral
disclosure	– Offenlegung, Deklaration
to reveal	– offenbaren, enthüllen, aufdecken
ratio analysis	– Kennzahlenanalyse

Effects of Extraordinary or Unusual Items

A company may also resort to "extraordinary" measures to show an earnings growth. Through a one-time transaction, such as the sale of assets or a switch in accounting methods, a company can create the illusion of continued financial health.

The Certification of Financial Statements

To guard against fraud, independent outsiders, called public accountants or auditors, are required to prepare unbiased reports on the fairness of financial statements. The certified report accompanies the client's published financial statements and indicates whether the statements have been prepared in accordance with GAAP as well as whether any disclosures about uncertainties that would materially affect the client's financial position are necessary. The auditors' report is relevant to anyone who must have a picture of the financial standing of a business, such as creditors, shareholders, investors, and government bodies.

Trend and Ratio Analysis

Trend analysis – a comparison of financial data from several years – can reveal shifts in the nature of the business, and may be used to compare a company's performance with that of competitors or the whole industry. In contrast, ratio analysis compares two elements from the same period's financial statements to reveal how the company is performing in comparison to others.

Often-used ratios:

a) Profitability Ratios

These ratios indicate to what extent the company is making a profit.

$$\text{Return on investment (ROI)} = \frac{\text{income before taxes}}{\text{shareholder's equity}}$$

$$\text{Return on sales ("net profit margin")} = \frac{\text{income before taxes}}{\text{net sales}}$$

$$\text{Earnings per share} = \frac{\text{net income}}{\text{numer of outstanding shares}}$$

b) Liquidity Ratios

These ratios indicate a company's ability to repay short-term obligations, and are of special interest for creditors and lenders.

Working capital = current assets ./. current liabilities

$$\text{Current ratio} = \frac{\text{current assets}}{\text{current liabilities}}$$

$$\text{Quick ratio ("acid test")} = \frac{\text{cash + marketable securities + receivables}}{\text{current liabilities}}$$

c) Activity Ratios

These ratios are a general indicator for the amount of business a company is doing, and how effectively a firm is managing its assets.

$$\text{Inventory turnover ratio} = \frac{\text{cost of goods sold}}{\text{average value of inventory}}$$

d) Debt Ratios ("Coverage Ratios")

These ratios indicate to potential investors the balance of business and financial risk.

$$\text{Debt-to-equity ratio} = \frac{\text{total liabilities}}{\text{shareholders' equity}}$$

$$\text{Debt-to-total-assets ratio} = \frac{\text{total liabilities}}{\text{total assets}}$$

Management Accounting

Management accounting is <u>tailored</u> to the needs of managers in a <u>particular</u> company. Typically, management accounting covers a wide range of financial activities, from recording sales, and sending out invoices to financial planning, which involves forecasting sales, costs, expenses, and profits. It also provides an analysis of <u>operating costs</u>, as a means to control expenses, and provide information for pricing and product decisions. Its overall purpose is to help managers evaluate results, identify opportunities, and <u>allocate</u> resources.

The Role of Budgets

The budget is the financial plan for a company's future activities for a given period of time that estimates proposed expenditures and forecasts how they will be financed. As the budgeting process involves both the projection of future revenues and costs, expenses, and cash flow, it is a controlling as well as a planning operation. The <u>master budget</u> – or operating budget – is based on several component budgets, such as the budgets for advertising, or for research.

Scorecharting

In many cases, meaningful information about a company's credit standing and overall competitive shape can be obtained through an assessment of several key performance ratios. However, a company's performance and competitive position cannot be assessed schematically, in isolation from other trends. Management accountants should also <u>explore</u> qualitative data, inquiring why some factors of success that were important in the past might be less relevant now; also, productivity studies show that measures affect behavior.

> **to tailor** – zuschneiden, anpassen
> **particular** – bestimmt, speziell, jeweilig
> **operating costs** – betriebliche Aufwendungen
> **to allocate** – zuweisen, zuteilen
> **master budget** – Gesamtbudget
> **to explore** – untersuchen, erforschen
> **crucial** – entscheidend
> **bottom line** – Endergebnis
> **to exploit** – auswerten, verwerten, nutzen

In many business sectors highly mobile human capital is <u>crucial</u> to the "<u>bottom line</u>". However, measuring realistically the inputs of brainpower and skills against those of financial capital is not possible in the traditional accounting system. This system was designed for accountability to shareholders, but with managers <u>exploiting</u> "insider" benefits of control (for instance in the form of compensation through stock options) a new "stakeholder" model of accounting is required. In a knowledge- and "service-based" economy this new model would reflect the shift in the balance of power from outside shareholders to top managers, who exercise considerable discretion over the returns received by shareholders.

One measurement system that applies this informed insider effect is the balanced scorecard. The balanced scorecard retains traditional financial measures, but supports a view of the organization from four perspectives: the Learning and Growth Perspective, the Business Process Perspective, the Customer Perspective, and the Financial Perspective. By analyzing the cause-effect relationships between these perspectives, it aims to align business activities to the strategy, and to monitor the corporate governance performance over time. It offers an alternative to the traditional financial indicators, because it describes and explains what has to be measured in order to assess the effectiveness of strategies.

Balanced Scorecard: Cause-Effect Model

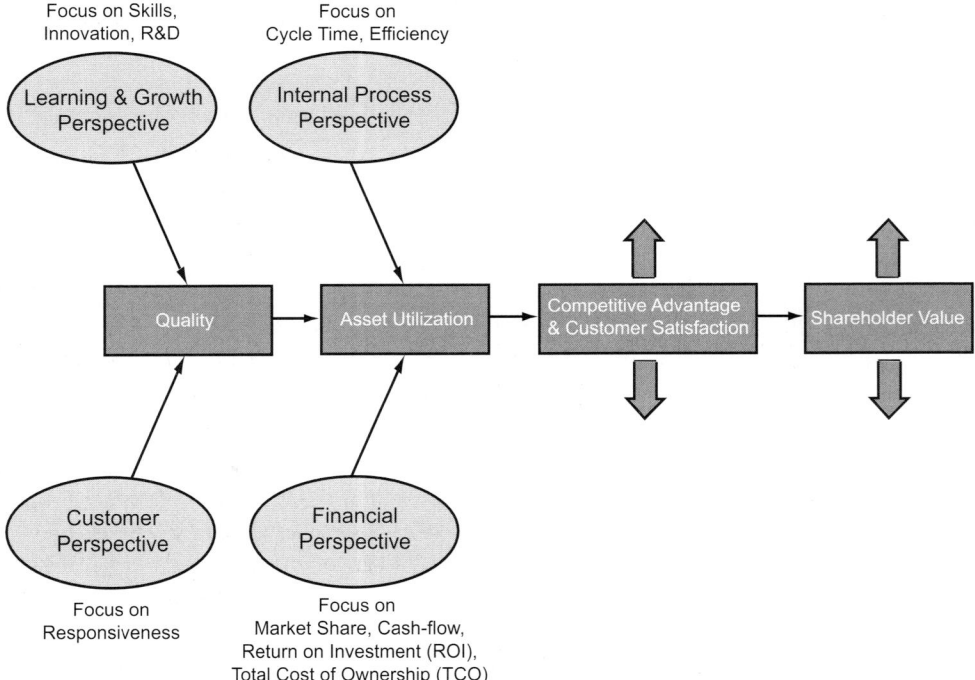

B 10.2 Knowledge Check

(1) Explain (a) the purpose of the balance sheet and identify its three main sections, and (b) explain the purpose of an income statement and identify its three main components.
(2) Define the position of public accountants.
(3) Explain the purpose of the statement of cash flows.
(4) Identify four areas in which accountants may exercise considerable discretion.
(5) List the four main categories of financial ratios.

→ See Answer Key for solutions.

B 10.3 Keywords

Accounting equation; activity ratios; amortization; assets; audit; balance sheet; bookkeeping; budget; certified public accountant (CPA); current assets; current liabilities; current ratio; debt ratios; debt-to-equity ratio; debt-to-total-assets ratio; depreciation; double-entry bookkeeping; earnings per share; expenses; FIFO; financial accounting; fiscal year; fixed assets; generally accepted accounting principles (GAAP); goodwill; gross profit; gross sales; income statement; intangible assets; inventory turnover; liabilities; LIFO; liquidity ratios; long-term liabilities; management accounting; net income; net sales; operating income; owners' equity.

B 10.4 Strategy Case: Elan Corp.

In February 2002, a class action suit was filed in a U.S. District Court against Elan Corp, the world's 20th-largest pharmaceutical company with a market value of about $13.9 billion. The investors involved in the class action suit were seeking damages for violations of federal securities laws on behalf of all investors. The complaint was that the pharmaceutical company used more than 50 joint ventures to hide research-and-development costs and overstate revenues.

History of Growth and Innovation

Elan Corp. plc is headquartered in Dublin, Ireland and employs approximately 4,500 people worldwide. It operates through wholly-owned subsidiaries incorporated mainly in Ireland, USA, and the UK. Elan was incorporated in 1969 to market an innovation – the controlled absorption of a drug by the patient's body. Over the years, it has become a fully integrated biopharmaceutical company. It is considered to be a world leader in drug delivery and special drugs in neurology, pain management, oncology, infectious disease and dermatology. In addition, it is developing drugs for MS and Alzheimer's disease, although the Alzheimer product recently met setbacks and trials were temporarily suspended.

Stellar Financial Performance

The company's reported annual revenue for 2000 was $1.5 billion, up from $323 million in 1996. Earnings per share before other charges rose to $1.46 in 2000 from 48 cents in 1996. Total revenues of $484.3 million rose 24% from the third quarter of 2000, reflecting an increase of 44% in product revenue to $381 million. Elan expected its revenue, mainly from sales in the U.S., to double again in the next four years.

For the third quarter of 2001 the company also reported a strong financial performance with product revenue accounting for nearly 80% of the total. In the view of the CEO, Donald J. Geaney, the significant growth in product revenue and the expansion in the gross margin reflected both the strong product sales performance and the benefits of a stringent product rationalization program.

Focused Product Lines

In May 2000, Elan had acquired Liposome Co., Inc. (U. S.) for approximately $575 million, and, in November 2000, Dura Pharmaceuticals, Inc. for $1.8 billion. This specialty pharmaceutical company was engaged in the marketing and sale of prescription products for the treatment of infectious diseases and respiratory condition. Since then, a major program of rationalization and consolidation of the Elan's U.S. business activities, locations, pipeline and portfolio products has been carried out. Research and early stage development were consolidated in San Francisco, while all other activities, including clinical and regulatory, sales and marketing, and support were relocated to San Diego. As part of this process, the CEO reported cost synergies of approximately $50 million. In addition, the company stated that it was streamlining the pipeline and portfolio of marketed products by focusing on products with the capability of achieving revenue of between $100 million and $500 million. Products that did not meet these criteria were being phased out or disposed of through distribution agreements.

Joint Ventures' Losses

Although these and other reported activities contributed to financial results, they were difficult for investors to evaluate. And, within the network of partnerships, some unusually structured transactions have surfaced. Allegedly, Elan funded many joint ventures with the intention of shifting research-and-development costs off its accounts and to book revenue long before the ventures developed any products to market. For example, the company might invest $40 million in a joint venture. Shortly thereafter, the venture might pay Elan $30 million for a drug license that Elan would book as revenue. However, the sum invested by Elan would not have reduced its reported earnings; it would have been considered as an investment, and would have appeared only as an asset on the balance sheet. In this way, the company would have converted $30 million of funds it already possessed into new revenue.

Elan's policy was to hold a 19.9% interest and its partner the rest. If a company's stake in a joint venture was below 20%, as in Elan's case, it could apply a "cost accounting" approach to investment losses, instead of booking them on its own profit-and-loss statement. Though, as Elan pointed out, if a company had significant influence over the investment, the "equity" method of accounting would be more appropriate. Accordingly, its share of the losses would be booked into its P&L statement, thus reducing its reported earnings.

In this context, Elan confirmed that all of the joint ventures ran losses. But, it was not clear to investors, how these losses affected Elan's earnings. Elan's P&L statements did not break out any losses from the ventures, although, in general, it had veto power over research, 50% board representation and a right to raise its 19.9% financial stake to 50%. In a written statement, Elan elaborated that it "expensed" its share of the operating losses of all business ventures regardless of whether the equity method or cost method was used. Such amounts, it said, were included, in full, in net interest expense.

Arguable Cross Receipt

Elan also stated that the quarterly filings reflected no cash payments because cash was transferred by way of a cross receipt. It said this was a legal mechanism under which amounts owing under different contracts were amalgamated, with the resulting amount then being settled by money transfer. The several ventures – with few or no employees – that were based in Bermuda were not mentioned in this context.

However, critics responded that Elan's approach contrasted sharply from the incremental approach pharmaceutical companies commonly used to link up with small biotech firms. The usual approach was to acquire and increase equity in the smaller firm in line with research advances, and also to secure co-marketing rights to any commercialized drug. However, many joined ventures that bought a license from Elan allegedly had no funds left for research on new drugs. Under these circumstances, Elan would then grant a loan, which the joint ventures would use to contract out research work, often to Elan itself, thus producing more revenue for Elan.

In one case, a joint venture brought Elan revenue twelve months before the partners had even planned a research program. The joint venture reportedly paid Elan a $15 million license fee for drug delivery technology, although the partners did not know which chemical compound they would develop or even which disease they would target. Elan countered criticism by stating that the price of its licenses was based on the value of the technology, not on its utilization.

Further criticism was directed at the accounting of proceeds from Elan's divestments of smaller product lines. These were generally booked as "product revenue", although, under GAAP, they ought to have figured as one-time gains. The critics also drew attention to a letter in which SEC had criticized Elan's taking write-offs for acquired companies' research that exceeded even the acquisition price. The move ensured that "goodwill" – the difference between an acquisition price and the acquired firm's net worth – could never burden Elan earnings.

Issue of Professional Standards

Reacting to these objections, Elan made a small restatement of 1997 earnings. In an ironic twist of events, the SEC ruled in 199 that companies should not immediately book revenue from agreements in which they had continuing involvement, but should book this revenue over the life of the agreement. In response, Elan announced in 2001 a $344 million retroactive charge against earnings. The seemingly adverse SEC ruling had actually enhanced Elan's growth record. Having been forced to reverse the premature booking of revenue, Elan was able to record this revenue as a highly welcome boost to its future earnings.

Irritated by the allegations of systemically inflated revenue, Elan said that its revenue-accounting policy could not possibly have misled investors or analysts because it was known to them and publicly disclosed. It added that its accounting for sales of product lines was correct because it made the sales in steps or retained certain rights.

Related Party or Arms-Length Transaction?

In conjunction with the structured deals, co-optation of current or former Elan employees into the boards of joint ventures was emerging as a further key issue. Such arrangements were not unusual in the pharmaceutical domain. Another common practice was for scientists paid by companies to sit on scientific advisory boards. In this context, the Financial Accounting- Standards Board (AFSB), which creates accounting standards has created the label "Related Party". It recommended that this label should be applied to all transactions with affiliates, owners or management, or wherever one party might be prevented from fully pursuing its own separate interests because of the other party's influence.

Many Elan staff and research people, frustrated by this controversy, were wondering whether a consistent application of this label would have helped investors to evaluate the corporate transactions and allowed them more time to get on with their mission of curing Alzheimer's disease.

B 10.5 The "Informating" Mindset

Informating requires a dual perspective: monitoring and coordinating. Managers require information to interact with other people who, in turn, perform the necessary actions. To manage by informating, therefore, means to act two steps removed from the outcome of managerial work. This classic view of managerial work from the first half of the 20th century has been revived in the so-called knowledge management approach.

Managers devote a great deal of effort to collecting information and guiding its flow within their own organization, and with a number of outsiders with whom they maintain regular contact. Formal information is only a part of this two-way communication. A critical part of every managerial job is "soft" information, such as oral information in the form of gossip, nonverbal information, and unconscious or tacit information.

To function effectively with the people around them, managers have to spend considerable time sharing their information with insiders and outsiders by talking and listening.

The coordinating perspective is connected with formal authority. It represents the managers' efforts to access and deploy information in a directive way inside their units by structuring processes and transmitting information to people so that they can act. At this stage – for example when employees are engaged in designing or problem-solving projects – power typically resides with the persons being coordinated and controlled rather than with the manager, who remains in a passive role.

B 10.6 Experiential Exercise 1: Organizational Design Preference

Instructions

Select the number from the following scale that shows the extent to which the statement accurately describes your views.

> 5 = strongly agree
> 4 = agree somewhat
> 3 = undecided
> 2 = disagree somewhat
> 1 = strongly disagree

"I prefer to work in an organization, where ...
a) employees carry out their tasks as they have been instructed.
b) objectives are clearly defined in quantitative terms.
c) task sequence and procedures are formalized.
d) loyalty and commitment are valued as highly as the ability to do the job.
e) clear lines of authority and responsibility are established.
f) top management direction is visible.
g) career opportunities are announced well in advance.
h) employees are encouraged to specialize.
i) the length of employment is a factor in performance assessment.
j) top management decisions are made unanimously.
k) management is responsible for providing the information needed to do the job well.
l) a chain of command is established in all departments and project groups.
m) rules and procedures are adhered to equally by everyone.
n) employees accept the authority of a leader's position.
o) employees are loyal to their boss in conflict situations.
p) employees clear issues with their boss before referring to a higher level."

Scoring:

Aggregate the scores for all questions.

Interpretation

This questionnaire measures the individual preference for working in an organization structured as autonomously evolved "ad-hocracies" or as highly formalized "machine bureaucracies". A higher score (above 62) indicates a personal preference for a mechanistic structure using more formal monitoring and coordinating systems; a lower score (below 50), a preference for an evolved structure using more informal monitoring and coordinating systems. Scores between 50 and 62 indicate a mixed orientation.

B 10.7 Experiential Exercise 2: Corporate versus Professional Identity

Instructions

Select the number from the following scale that shows the extent to which the statement accurately describes your views.

> 5 = strongly agree
> 4 = agree somewhat
> 3 = undecided
> 2 = disagree somewhat
> 1 = strongly disagree

a) You believe professionals are responsible for making their own decisions about what is to be done on the job.
b) You believe professionals should aim for an advisory position regardless of any income sacrifice involved.
c) You have more interest in solving a challenging problem than moving up the hierarchy.
d) You believe that professionals are evaluated more objectively by their peers than by management.
e) Your friends tend to be members of your profession.
f) You would rather be recognized for your work outside than inside the company.
g) You would feel better making a contribution to your unit than to your organization as a whole.
h) Managers should avoid assigning administrative tasks to professionals.

Scoring and Interpretation

A "professional" identifies with the career profession, and a "corporate citizen" identifies with the employing organization. Total your scores. A score of 34–40 suggests a professional work orientation, of 10–24 a "corporate citizen" orientation, and 24–34 a mixed orientation.

B 11 Financial Management

- The Financial Plan
- Risk Management
- Internal versus External Financing
- Short-term versus Long-term Funding
- Debt versus Equity
- Managing Cash and Marketable Securities
- Managing Receivables and Payables
- Managing Inventory
- Capital Budgeting
- Strategy Case: Egg plc – Not Fully Hatched Yet
- The "Risk-Managing" Mindset
- Experiential Exercise: The Confrontation Meeting

B 12 Marketing

B 11 Financial Management

B 11.1 Principles – Models – Practices

In a market economy, a company's overall financial goal is to increase the owners' wealth. For a corporation, success in achieving this goal is measured by the stock's price per share – in a privately owned company, by the money the owner could obtain by selling or liquidating the business. For companies which rely on the continued inflow of outside funds the timing of financial flows poses a major challenge.

The productive use of borrowed money is called <u>leverage</u>. As long as the company manages to earn a greater percentage of profit on the borrowed money than it costs in interest payments, it is safe. However, leverage is a <u>two-edged</u> tool, and borrowed funds can produce losses as well as gains. The financial manager's problem is to find the combination of funding sources with the lowest cost of capital.

> **leverage** – Hebelwirkung
> **two-edged** – zweischneidig
> **expenditures** – Aufwendungen, Ausgaben
> **surplus** – Überschuss
> **to determine** – festlegen, bestimmen
> **shortfall** – Fehlbetrag, Fehlmenge
> **to postpone** – aufschieben, verschieben

The Financial Plan

To optimize <u>expenditures</u>, the financial manager needs to select the options best able to meet the company's objectives, a procedure culminating in the financial plan. Developing a financial plan for a company involves calculating how much money the company will need, when it will need it, and where it will come from. For each period, the financial plan:

- estimates the flow of funds out of the business;
- estimates the month-by-month flow of funds into the business from all sources;
- compares inflows and outflows. For <u>surplus</u> funds it <u>determines</u> how to use those funds most productively, for <u>shortfalls</u>, it presents ways to reduce outflows and increase inflows;
- analyzes alternative sources of funds and selects the most cost-effective combination;
- creates a system for tracking the flow of funds and measuring return on investment.

The most obvious source of liquid funds is revenues – cash received from sales, rentals of property, interest on short-term investments, and so on. Another likely source is suppliers who may be willing to do business on credit, thus enabling the company to <u>postpone</u> payment. Most companies also obtain funds in the form of loans. In addition, some companies, particularly large corporations, raise long-term funds by selling stocks and bonds to investors.

Obtaining the "right" mix of funds is extremely complicated because there are many funding sources and variables to be considered. The cost of capital, that is, the price a company must pay to raise funds, depends on its financial record, its risk factor, the prevailing level of interest rates, and management's selection of funding vehicles.

Risk Management

The logic of risk diversification is contained in the Capital Asset Pricing Model (CAPM). According to this model, acquiring and investing funds in a variety of uncorrelated capital and money markets leads to lower risk factors, lower required rates of return, and lower costs of capital than "one-stop-financing". Ideally, a policy of global financial diversification should be implemented to reduce volatility.

Credit Rating

Because various companies entail different levels of risk, their cost of money varies. Generally speaking, the companies with high credit ratings – those with the soundest financial position and most promising prospects – can obtain funds more cheaply than their less secure rivals as the lower "beta-factor", reflects a lower volatility. Analysts at the top three ratings agencies (S&P, Moody's Investors Service, and Fitch) give credit ratings on a letter scale ranging from AAA to D (default) to every financial instrument or entity they are asked to assess.

cost of capital	– Kapitalbeschaffungskosten
prevailing	– vorherrschend, gängig
risk diversification	– Risikostreuung
to entail	– mit sich bringen
sound	– solide, einwandfrei, kreditfähig
promising	– vielversprechend
prospects	– Aussichten
to coincide	– übereinstimmen
to renegotiate	– neu aushandeln

For instance, when banks securitice a bundle of credit risks, such as ship mortgages, by slicing the them into layers that carry different levels of risk and selling them as collaterized debt obligations (CDOs), a rating is assigned to each slice by the agencies. Due to the low market transparency, most investors are guided by the ratings.

Interest Rates

Regardless of a company's credit rating, its cost of money will vary over time because interest rates fluctuate. Financial managers may try to time their borrowing to a period of low interest rates, but this is not always possible because a company's needs for liquidity may not coincide with favorable rates. A company may be forced to borrow when rates are high, then renegotiate the loan when rates fall. A variety of innovative financial products has made it easier for companies to "trade in" their old debt for new debt at more favorable rates. In deciding on the balance among these options, financial managers analyze the costs and benefits of internal versus external financing, short-term versus long-term funding, and debt versus equity.

Financial Management | B 11

Internal versus External Financing

Using a company's own funds to cover expenses is superficially an attractive value, because no interest payments are required. For this reason, many companies finance their operations with retained earnings, the money kept by the company after meeting its expenses and distributing a portion of the profits to investors. Most companies, however, depend to some degree on outside financing which, in general, is cheaper than raising equity capital.

Short-term versus Long-term Funding

In choosing between short-term and long-term financing, companies ideally follow the matching principle – timing their borrowing to match the timing of their spending. Accordingly, money borrowed for short-term purposes should be paid back in that time frame to balance the flow of money into and out of the business. Similarly, a project that will take some time to complete should be funded with long-term financing to stretch the repayment schedule.

Debt versus Equity

In choosing between debt and equity, companies consider various factors. When a company is not able to satisfy its capital needs from a single source, it may tap the funds of many individual investors, either by issuing bonds – a corporate debt that obligates the company to repay to the bondholders a certain sum, plus interest, at predetermined dates, or by floating stock. In general, debt is cheaper than equity because companies can deduct the interest on debt from their taxes, whereas dividend payments on stock are not deductible.

However, debt also carries a high degree of risk. Whereas a company that raises funds through stock issues can survive a few lean years by not paying dividends, a company that is unable to meet its loan and bond commitments may be forced into bankruptcy by its creditors. Alternatively, by raising funds through expanding ownership, the original shareholders dilute both their control of the company and their rights to future earnings. Therefore, an attractive funding method, which postpones this dilemma for both parties, is to issue either convertible bonds, or warrants (certificates that merely embody the option to buy stock at a future date).

---

superficial – oberflächlich
retained earnings – einbehaltene Gewinne
debt – Schulden
equity – Eigenkapital
to tap – erschließen, anzapfen
to issue – ausgeben, emittieren
bond – Schuldverschreibung, Obligation
to obligate – verpflichten
predetermined – festgelegt, vorherbestimmt
to float – in Umlauf bringen
stock – Aktien
commitment – Verpflichtung
to dilute – schwächen, verwässern
convertible bond – Wandelschuldverschreibung
warrant – Optionsschein
to embody – verkörpern

On the asset side, the ultimate goal in managing working capital is to minimize the amount of money that is tied up in excess cash, uncollected bills (receivables), and inventory. The trick is to synchronize the amount of money inflows and outflows, and shortening the period between the purchase of resources and the collection of receivables.

Managing Cash and Marketable Securities

An underlying concept of financial management is that all liquid funds should be productively employed. Occasionally, a company will find itself holding excess cash, for example to ride out seasonal business cycles, to meet some large commitment in the near future, or to provide a cushion in case its needs are higher than expected.

Part of the financial manager's job is to ensure that this cash is invested profitably. The challenge is to find a good "parking place" for the funds, an investment that will yield the highest possible return but will create no problem if the company needs to liquidate the investment for instant cash. A number of short-term marketable investments meet these needs because they are relatively low in risk and can easily be converted back to cash.

to ride out – überstehen	
cushion – Polster	
to yield – einbringen, abwerfen	
return – Rendite, Ertrag, Verzinsung	
certificate of deposit – Einlagenzertifikat	
commercial paper – kommerzieller Wechsel	
bill of exchange – Wechsel	
treasury bill – Schatzwechsel	
to redeem – rückzahlen, tilgen	
face value – Nennbetrag	
on maturity – bei Fälligkeit	

The most prevalent securities are certificates of deposit from banks, commercial paper (bills of exchange), and treasury bills, bought at a discount, and redeemed at face value on maturity.

In selecting a portfolio of marketable securities, financial managers must make trade-offs between safety and liquidity versus maximum rate of return. Value-at-risk (VAR) measures are widely used to inform investors of potential shifts in the price of assets, especially futures and derivatives. Because marketable securities are generally viewed as contingency funds most financial managers take a reasonably conservative approach to the management of these securities.

Managing Receivables and Payables

In managing working capital, the main problem is that a company's revenues and expenses are not synchronized. An important item in this context is accounts receivable – the money owed to the company by its customers.

The volume of receivables depends on the financial manager's decisions regarding several issues such as creditworthiness, time frame allotted to trade debtors, alacrity in collecting debts, and discount given for early payment. Typically some 20 percent of a company's assets, might be tied up in bills that have yet to be collected. A systematic analysis of receivables may identify critical payment patterns, and could help focus efforts on collecting. In managing payables – the bills that the company owes – the objective is generally to postpone payment, since payables represent interest-free loans from suppliers. But there are also advantages in paying promptly to be considered, such as cash discounts, or image gains.

> **to allot** – zuweisen, zuteilen
> **alacrity** – Bereitwilligkeit, Eifer
> **payables** – Verbindlichkeiten
> **stockpiling** – Vorratshaltung
> **economic order quantity** – opt. Bestellmenge
> **capital budgeting** – Investitionsrechnung
> **gauge** – messen, beurteilen

Managing Inventory

Inventory also offers opportunities for fine-tuning the cash flow. Many companies carry excess inventory, preferring to have a surplus of stock on hand than to lose customers by running short of a product. However, stockpiling represents capital that is tied up without earning interest. Furthermore, the company incurs expenses for storage and handling, insurance, and taxes. And there is always a risk that the inventory will become obsolete.

Inventory control is achieved by calculating the economic order quantity (EOQ), or quantity of raw materials that results in the lowest ordering and storage costs. The problem is complicated by the fact that frequent orders tend to increase both storage costs, and the risk of disrupting production.

Capital Budgeting

Capital budgeting refers to the process of evaluating and comparing alternative capital investments. These include new facilities or equipment required to expand the business or to replace worn-out equipment, improvements required by law to maintain safety or meet environmental requirements, and other investments such as land, acquisitions, or patents.

In evaluating such projects, financial managers look at both the initial cost of the investment (e.g. by comparing the cost of buying or leasing), and the incremental cash flows that the project is expected to provide over time. But as the future benefits of an investment are often difficult to gauge in advance, there is a good deal of judgment involved in calculating the net present value (NPV) of an investment.

Thus, financial analysts face a fundamental problem: different valuation models, applied to the same investment decision, yield significantly different outcomes. In practice, discounted cash flow (DCF) methods and economic value added (EVA) have become standard methodologies for investment analysis. For example in EVA-based corporate valuation, the key value driver is the spread between the return on existing investments and their average cost of capital (i.e. emphasis on the left hand side of the balance sheet). An alternative method, based on the work of Miller and Modigliani, is the structured finance approach: MM models attempt to identify the impact of financial decisions and shareholder value (i.e. emphasis on the right-hand side of the balance sheet).

Valuing a Growth Option for a Follow-Up Project

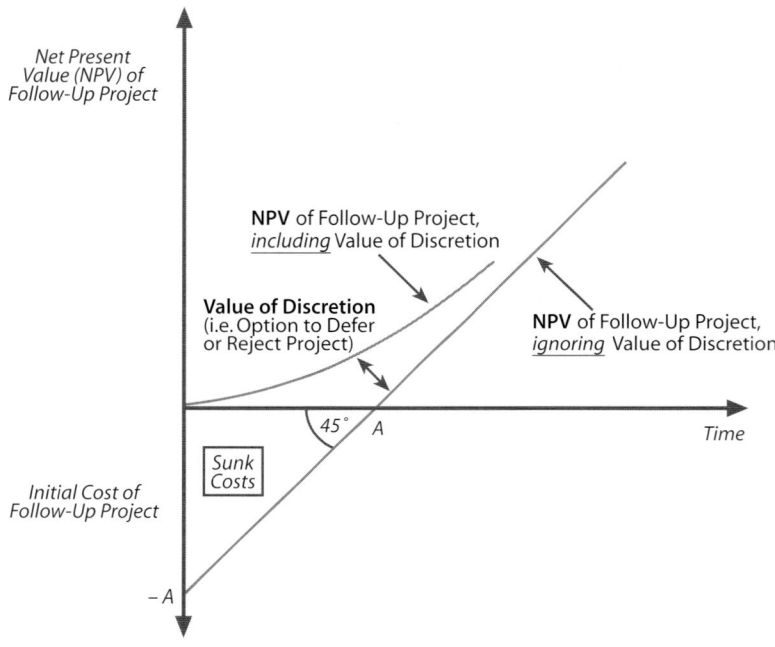

B 11.2 Knowledge Check

(1) List the five steps involved in the financial planning process.
(2) (a) State the matching principle.
    (b) Explain the chief advantages of debt versus equity.
(3) Name three major types of short-term debt.
(4) List four major long-term financing options.
(5) Explain the guiding principle of cash management.
(6) State the financial manager's primary goal in handling receivables and payables.
(7) Define the objective of the capital budgeting process.

→ See Answer Key for solutions.

B 11.3 Keywords

Capital budgeting; capital investment; capital structure; cash flow; commercial paper; common stock; cost of capital; credit rating; economic order quantity (EOQ); financial management; inventory; leverage; loan; marketable securities; matching principle; maturity; payables; receivables; securities; stockpiling; working capital.

B 11.4 Strategy Case: Egg plc – Not Fully Hatched Yet

April 2000 seemed a cruel month for CEO Mike Harris of the UK online bank Egg plc, which was preparing to launch an IPO (i.e. initial public offering). Egg had been established in October 1998 by Prudential plc, a financial services group based in London – with no ties to U.S. companies with the same name. And Prudential had been looking forward to the IPO for an infusion of cash. But, on April 15 the Nasdaq tumbled 355 points. Yet, in line with the company's overall policy of speed and innovation, the board of directors decided to proceed with the IPO. On 12 June 2000, when the shares traded on the low end of the initially forecast range, Prudential sold 20 percent of its stake in Egg for £150 million.

In terms of market penetration, Egg has achieved remarkable growth – acquiring 600,000 net new customers in 2001, principally through its credit card business. In 2001, Egg also managed to raise operating income by 103% to £189.4 million from £93.2 million in 2000. Pre-tax losses were reduced by 43% from £155.3 million in 2000 to £87.8 million. Loss per share was 7.6p (2000: 14.3p). At the end of 2001, the total customers exceeded 2 million. Credit card balances doubled to £1.8 billion (2000: £0.9 billion).

However, the bank still finds itself in a defensive position, with anxious investors in the wake of the burst Internet bubble increasingly insisting that online ventures fulfill their original promises.

Industry Background: the U.S. Online Banking Experience

The first online bank in the world, Security First Network Bank, was launched in the USA in October 1995. Internet-only start-ups were expected to have lower operation costs because they did not need to have physical branches, and could also save operating costs by reducing the inefficiencies of paper-drawn transactions, monthly statements, credit card statements and bills.

However, in practice, low brand recognition and the lack of physical presence were major detractors. Only an estimated 10 per cent of Internet users also used online banking services. To counter the fierce competition from existing banks, US online-only banks had to invest heavily in advertising and IT systems. Many ventures failed to recoup these heavy costs, and were re-incorporated into the banks that established them as independent start-ups, while others teamed up with other businesses to provide a wider range of value-added services.

A further problem was that customer behavior on the Internet was erratic. Demand might surge dramatically in the wake of a successful marketing campaign or after the release of favorable company news. To prepare for such an event the bank's operations needed be scalable to limits far above average usage – generally, ten times or more. It also needed to make accurate demand forecasts and build the necessary infrastructure in time for the expected increases. On the other hand, it would be costly for the bank to over-invest.

The Example of Schwab

Online brokerage firms in the US could illustrate the problems of scalability. Internet trading, even more than online banking, required reliable service and fast, safe, accurate, real-time-transfers of information around the clock. The market leader was Schwab.com, the online trading arm of brokerage firm Charles Schwab Corp. Schwab.com was launched in 1996 and became the world's biggest online brokerage site. Its online-customer assets were US$418 billion in Q1 2000, when online trades accounted for more than 70 per cent of Schwab's total trading volume. It was handling an average of more than 380,000 trades per day for 3.4 million customers.

Because heavy customer traffic at Schwab's Web site occasionally slowed down service, Schwab spent US$324 million or about 12 per cent of its revenue on upgrading its computer systems. But still, within the first two 6 months of 1999, the brokerage firm suffered several site crashes; other online securities firms also suffered similar service disruptions. The incidents made headline news and Schwab poured more money into building a more robust IT infrastructure. The company used to aim to be prepared for traffic peaks of three to four times its daily average volume, but by early 1999 it was already aiming for peaks of 10 times average volume. In 2000, Schwab spent US$409 million or 58 per cent of its overall capital spending on IT equipment. Its total IT expenditures for 2001 were initially expected to be as high as US$800 million.

However, after the stock market tumbled in early 2001, online trading volume at Schwab was down by about 30 per cent; the company's earnings in the first quarter of 2001 fell by 68 per cent compared to the same period in 2000. In March 2001 it announced that it would lay off 11 per cent to 13 per cent of its staff, amounting to some 3,400 jobs. At the same time, all senior managers in the company received salary cuts of five to 50 per cent.

Schwab had also kept its IT expenditure in check: it was removing some of its servers by early and had stopped further investment in its wireless trading product, Pocket Broker. Yet, it had to continue providing new products and better services in order to survive, and that required investing in new technology. The firm was caught in a dilemma of scalability versus investment.

Egg's Performance in Q4 2001

At the end of 2001 Egg offered products and services from four main areas – banking, investments, insurance and online shopping. It described itself as an "opportunistic" company, and some of Egg's products were very innovative. Thus, in June 2001, it was voted best standard variable rate mortgage lender by Moneyfacts; with Egg Invest, it introduced a fund supermarket including Tracker and Balanced ISA products; with Egg Insure, it added home, life and critical illness insurance to its product portfolio.

CEO Harris also emphasized Egg's success in attracting upmarket customers, defined as typically earning £30k per annum and whose Egg Card had an average balance of £1,600 (national average, £900) and an average spending of £2,600 (national average, £1,400).

Reflecting on the synergy potential residing in the customer base, CEO Harris mentioned the growth in cross-holdings which contributed to a strong growth in revenue per customer from £85 on average in 2000 up to £111 on average in 2001. The 450,000 product cross sales in 2001 (compared to 275,000 in 2000) led to a year-end cross-holdings ratio of 1.44.

To further enhance its B2B ambitions in the investment market Egg has recently acquired Fundsdirect, an online fund supermarket. The merger of Egg Invest with Fundsdirect was represented as consolidating two of the UK's large fund supermarkets. The net assets of Fundsdirect at 31 December 2001 were £2.7 million.

A successful performance was claimed for the strategically important Egg Mortgages unit, which grew 18%, reaching £1.0 billion. The Egg Saver mortgage, which offsets interest against people's deposit balances accounted for approximately 65% of mortgage applications since its launch in June 2001.

Advances were also claimed in the streamlining of customer deposits. Despite a small net growth in deposit customers, the average savings balance has fallen to approximately £10,000 per account with the loss of the unprofitable larger balances. The overall net interest contribution from deposits was £15.4 million in 2001 compared to a cost of £3.0 million in 2000.

Egg Insure and Egg Shop have consistently provided positive contributions with total intermediation revenues increasing to £2.5 million (2000: £1.5 million).

Elusive First-Mover Advantage

During the first few months of its existence, Egg took deposits for savings accounts via the telephone, by mail, and over the Internet. Knowing customers are usually reluctant to switch banks, Egg offered a rate substantially higher than that of its traditional competitors and guaranteed that rate through the end of 1999. But early 1999, the field was already getting crowded. Even at the time of its launch, some of the largest High Street banks, such as Barclays, Lloyds TSB, and the Royal Bank of Scotland Group PLC, were experimenting with an online presence, even if they were moving slowly. After an early, small scale experiment with Web banking called B2, Barclays, for example, kept its online service in-house to support its existing businesses.

At the beginning of 2001, the online banking sector in the U.K. included a mix of independent online brands launched by established players (with quirky names like Smile and Cahoot) as well as online services associated with old-line banking names, such as Barclays and Lloyds, that consumers knew and trusted. But, as the number of Web-based banking services has snowballed, user interest has not kept up. The added competitive pressures made the profit payoff more elusive for every player.

When Lloyds TSB began expanding beyond the U.K. market to the rest of Europe, Egg also began developing its international business in France in 2001 through the acquisition of Zebank and associated distribution partnerships. Furthermore, it has established a commercial alliance with Microsoft, offering digital payments services to its 10 million hotmail users in the UK as well as having securing distribution deals for other products, including credit cards.

However, critics maintain that by setting itself up as a clearinghouse rather than just a provider of financial services, Egg has exposed itself to even more competition. Egg's move to becoming a portal and an e-shopping site put them directly up against companies like Yahoo, which already had much experience in this technically intensive business, that required continuous big investment in systems support.

Costly Growth

Persuading bank customers who relied on services such as automatic wage deposit and bill payment to switch banks, was always a costly proposition, especially as Egg did not have any ATMs. So Egg's loss-leader solution was to offer savings accounts with interest rates higher than those of traditional competitors. Loss-leading involved offering such good deals that customers found them difficult to pass up. The company would register losses for a number of years, until it had killed off the competition, and its customers were hooked on its products. Then the company could raise its prices and begin to register profits.

Some growth in new accounts, opened by younger customers, offset the decline in savings revenues. But these customers also had much lower savings balances. The demographic shift caused average deposits per customer to drop. For example, deposits fell by more than 6 percent in one three month period – from £23,200 in December 1999 to $12,350, in March 2000.

Vanishing Online Euphoria

A "click and mortar" competitor, National Westminster Bank PLC was first to sense a backlash against Internet-only banking. It achieved high viewer resonance with a television commercial in mid-2000 featuring an elderly woman who entered her local branch. Instead of tellers and lines, she found herself in a funky coffee bar, and began to sigh that this used to be a bank.

Many stand-alone online banks worldwide were burning cash, in part, because they had overestimated consumers' eagerness for the convenience of banking online, and had underestimated people's desire to have the option to speak in person with tellers and get money from automated teller machines. On top of that, virtual banks' attempts to build market share quickly by offering higher interest rates and lower fees than traditional banks, although effective in attracting customers, have created a strategy expensive to sustain.

Will the Established Banks Prevail?

Egg's founders believed from the start that the company's success required its independence. The IPO proceeds were not the only perceived advantage in separation from Prudential. By creating a new, more entrepreneurial entity, Egg hoped to attract a more dynamic staff. Management thought it could also make decisions more quickly if freed from the bureaucracy, rigid rules and operating procedures of the parent company.

When Egg was formed two years ago, Britain's traditional banks were considered almost certain losers in online banking. The banks were too plodding and cautious, said observers. But HSBC, for example, didn't think so. It opted to build an online service that could be accessed through satellite television. When HSBC first announced its plans, analysts thought the group had committed a serious error. Now, that it seemed clear it might take longer than expected for the PC and wireless mobile banking channels to blossom, introducing a television-based distribution channel seemed like a reasonable move.

Stay on Track, Switch, Make a U-Turn, or Exit?

In response to customer complaints about the time-consuming overhead or because of poor customer service, the board was considering repositioning itself as a dual e-commerce site and as an Internet portal. CEO Harris emphasized that the market was changing so rapidly that the concept of Egg would have to change too, and predicted it would probably change again within the space of a year.

In a virtual reality environment, where appearances dictate perceptions and business models in constant flux, could this be an Egg idea worth hatching? Or might Prudential not be better advised to leverage its IT infrastructure and multimillion-strong customer base to provide Internet-banking performance on demand but without over-investing?

B 11.5 The "Risk-Managing" Mindset

In imaginizing their potential field of action, managers will, either consciously or unconsciously, think through the various dimensions of their organizational mission – concerning the purpose, perspective, and positions of a particular unit to be managed. This conceptual preoccupation may relate to the nature of the firm and its work, such as the products produced, the markets served, the structures and systems designed, and the facilities provided. If the conceptual frame of reference is closely defined, the surrounding mindsets can be aligned and held together tightly. But when the frame is vague, the different issues considered and the different activities performed can diverge in different directions. Then, a clear "vision" in strategic thinking is needed to align, scale and coordinate the unconnected development.

B 11.6 Experiential Exercise: The Confrontation Meeting

Given the difficulty of changing the norms and culture of an organization, ambitious change strategies that cut across organizational functions are often long-term projects. But organizations often face urgent crises that demand speedier changes.

The confrontation meeting is designed to identity and initiate action on pressing problems in one day's working time. Confrontation in this sense means putting aside emotions to solve problems collectively. This technique can be used with relatively large groups (sixty to seventy-five people). It has the advantage of reuniting key managers across levels and functions. The process alternates between general and small-group sessions.

The confrontation meeting typically progresses through five phases:

(1) Climate Setting

The top manager sets the stage, emphasizing the need for fast corrective action. A group facilitator may give a brief lecture on communication or group process.

(2) Divide into Heterogeneous Groups

The total group is subdivided into groups of seven or eight people representing a "diagonal slice" of the organization (a mix of functional and managerial levels). The assignment for each is to think as people concerned about the overall organization for the purpose of identifying current "obstacles, demotivators, poor procedures or policies, unclear goals, or poor attitudes". Groups also are to identity changes in conditions to make the organization more effective and work more satisfying.

(3) Group Reports

Groups report findings to the reconvened total group, flipchart summaries are taped to a wall. Issues are grouped into major categories, such as "meetings", "unclear goals".

(4) Functional Group Action Plans

For the first time members reassemble into natural functional units (sales, manufacturing) to decide priorities and actions for change to improve their areas.

> **(5) Total Group Reporting**
>
> All participants reconvene for reports from each functional area on its agenda and issues to which top management should respond. Management evaluates reports for feasibility and inconsistencies then commits to supportable plans.

The confrontation meeting aims at setting in motion an innovative basis for evaluating, organizing, and carrying out work. After the total group adjourns, top management meets immediately to plan follow-up actions. A month or so later, the total management group reconvenes to review progress and modify plans where needed. In addition to initiating immediate corrective actions, the process tends to reunite organizational members across functional lines and open inter-unit lines of communication.

Through the guidance and monitoring of one or two facilitators, this entire process can be accomplished in one day. Its novelty lies in rotating subgroup membership (between the diagnosis and action-planning phases) and in having all participants share in the data and ideas coming from breakout groups. This restructuring of patterns of interaction is aimed at breaking through the formal hierarchy. Following the last phase of reporting, participants can process debrief personal reflections as to behaviors or actions that helped or hindered the problem-solving effort.

B 12 Marketing

- The Rationale of Marketing
- Marketing Management Process
- Market Research
- Market Segmentation
- Marketing Mix
- Product
- Product Life Cycle
- Market Portfolio Matrix
- Product Portfolio Matrix
- Strategy Case: The Algonquin Hotel – Executive Suite?
- The "Pro-active" Mindset
- Experiential Exercise: ACME Role-Play

B 13 Global Competition

B 12 Marketing

B 12.1 Principles – Models – Practices

The Rationale of Marketing

Marketing is not synonymous with advertising or selling. The American Marketing Association (AMA) defines marketing as "the process of planning and executing the conception, pricing, promotion, and distribution of ideas, goods, and services to create exchanges that satisfy individual and organizational objectives". Hence, marketing comprises more than just promotional activities to enhance sales – communication measures are only a subset of a broad range of necessary processes and procedures.

synonymous with	– gleichbedeutend mit
advertising	– Werbung, Reklame
selling	– Verkauf
pricing	– Preissetzung
distribution	– Verteilung, Distribution
to comprise	– umfassen, einschließen
to enhance	– steigern
subset	– Untermenge, Teilmenge
to involve	– einschließen, umfassen

Marketing Management Process

supply	– Angebot
demand	– Nachfrage
subsequently	– anschließend
to stipulate	– festsetzen, vereinbaren
to achieve	– erreichen
eventually	– schließlich
to evaluate	– auswerten
alteration	– Änderung

Marketing has to be understood as an ongoing, continuous process of managerial activities – the so-called marketing management process. This process involves analyzing the market structure, i.e. competitors ("supply") and customers ("demand"), identifying opportunities and threats, segmenting the consumer market, and selecting potential target markets. Subsequently, appropriate strategies have to be defined, in order to pursue stipulated long-term objectives, and before tactical measures can be decided on to achieve operational goals. Eventually, suggested solutions have to be implemented before evaluating the efficiency and effectiveness of the chosen measures. The feedback has to be used to make any necessary adjustments and alterations to goals, strategies or procedures and, if required, different approaches will have to be taken. This ongoing process of planning, conception, implementation and evaluation has to be managed effectively to achieve optimal results.

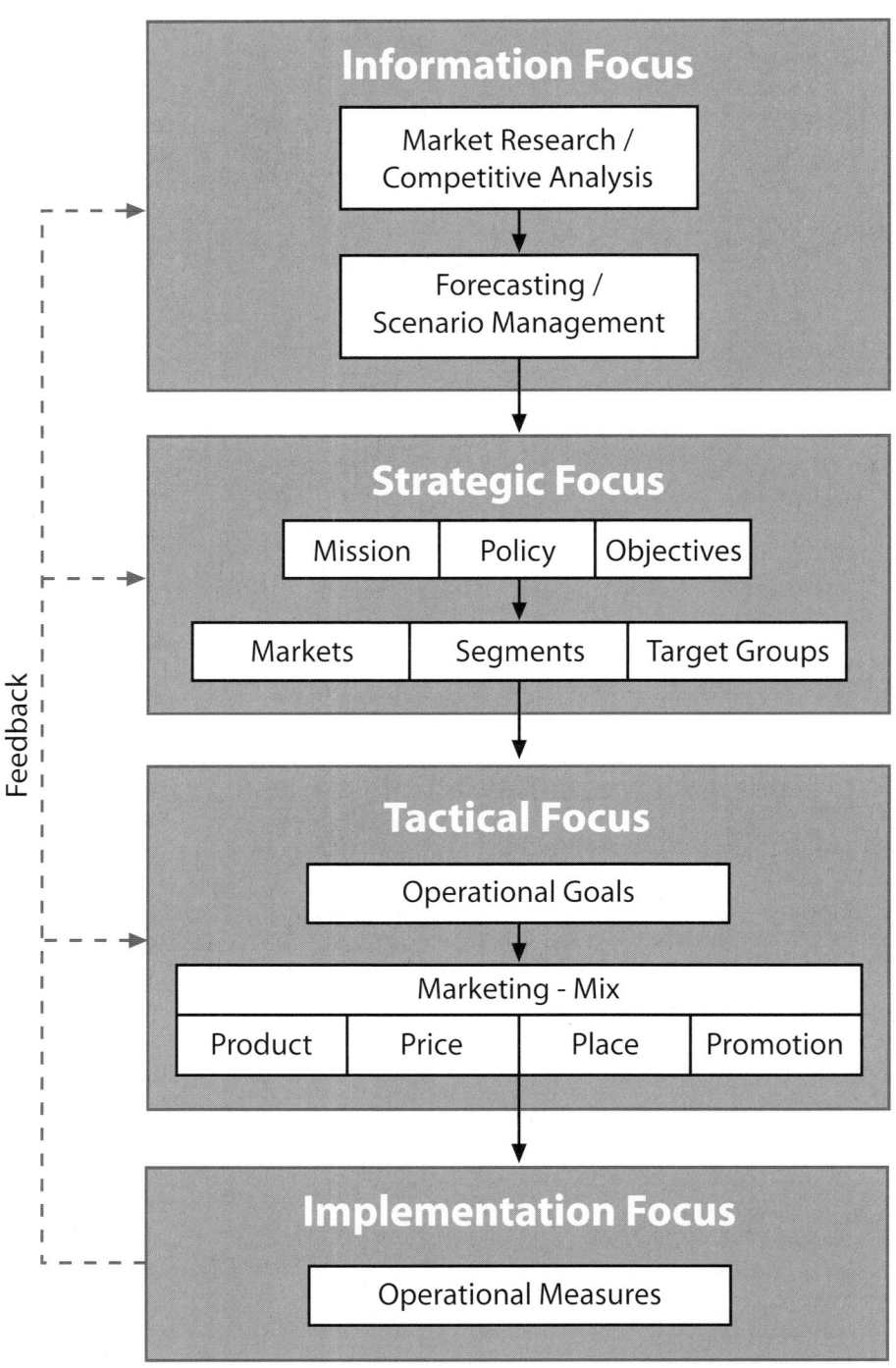

Market Research

Market research is essentially the systematic gathering, analyzing, and interpreting of market-related data. The American Marketing Association (AMA) defines market research as "the function that links the consumer, customer, and public to the marketer through information, which is used to identify and define marketing opportunities and problems; generate, refine, and evaluate marketing actions; <u>monitor</u> marketing performance; and improve understanding of marketing as a process. Marketing research specifies the information required to address these issues, designs the method for collecting information, manages and implements the data collection process, analyzes the results, and communicates the <u>findings</u> and their implications".

In general, two types of market research can be <u>distinguished</u>: desk research and field research. Desk research, also known as secondary research, is the process of evaluating already published and available material. It is usually an inexpensive way of acquiring information, even though it may involve extensive use of mail. The main sources of published information are government statistics, trade associations' publications, magazines, data bases, and a variety of websites on the Internet.

> **to monitor** – überwachen, kontrollieren
> **findings** – Befund, Erkenntnisse
> **to distinguish** – unterscheiden
> **sample** – Stichprobe
> **corresponding** – entsprechend
> **questionnaire** – Fragebogen
> **observation** – Beobachtung
> **to tailor to** – zuschneiden auf, ausrichten auf

Field research or surveys are a more expensive way of acquiring market-related data, as it requires interviewing a number of people, i.e. a <u>sample</u> of the <u>corresponding</u> target market. The most common interviewing techniques are personal interviewing, telephone interviewing, and postal <u>questionnaires</u>. Other means of field research, which is also referred to as primary research, are <u>observation</u> or experimentation.

Market Segmentation

Market segmentation is the process of dividing a market into separate sub markets and identifiable groups, using geographic, demographic or psychographic criteria. Geographic data can be used to segment customers based on their geography or location. Demography is defined as the analysis of the structure, size, and development of human populations. Demographic data provides a means of segmenting customers into groups based on variables such as sex, age, occupation, or income. Psychographics refers to qualitative data such as leisure activities, interests, opinions, views, and tastes.

The purpose of market segmentation is to <u>tailor</u> marketing activities to relevant sub markets and target groups.

Marketing Mix

In order to achieve set operational goals a variety of factors must be considered and appropriate measures have to be taken. To successfully address the target market, the "right type of mix" has to be applied. This marketing mix comprises four essential perspectives – the so-called *4 Ps*: Product, Price, Place, and Promotion.

appropriate – geeignet, passend
measures – Maßnahmen
to differentiate – unterscheiden, abgrenzen
life span – Lebensdauer, Lebensspanne
product life cycle – Produktlebenszyklus

It is vital to take all four spheres into account. If the price is too high, even the best product won't sell. And a low price won't sell a product which doesn't meet the requirements or standards expected by the consumer.

Product

The product perspective involves more than just features, functions, and technical specifications. Being emotional, customers expect more than just plain functionality. It is the additional value which differentiates a product, such as attention to detail and issues such as design, materials used, size, and packaging.

Product Life Cycle

Customers' needs and tastes are likely to change over time. All products have a limited life span, i.e. they go through what is known as the product life cycle. This cycle consists of four stages: infancy, adolescence, maturity, and aging.

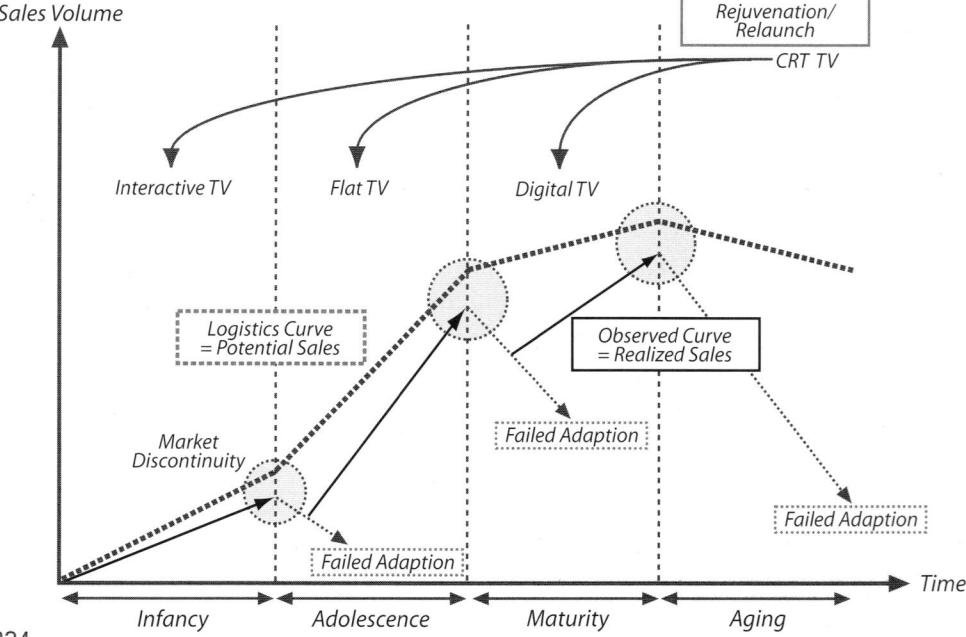

Marketing | B 12

The **infancy stage** is characterized by low sales. The product is not established yet – customers are possibly still hesitant to try the product and it is not stocked by all retailers. Strategic options include penetration and skimming strategies. Use low introductory prices to maximize market penetration, or a high price if the focus is on skimming the consumer's surplus. Moreover, intensive advertising might be required, depending on whether firms pursue a fast or slow introduction.

> **hesitant** – unschlüssig, zögerlich
> **to stock** – im Sortiment haben, führen
> **penetration** – Marktdurchdringung
> **skimming** – Abschöpfung
> **consumer's surplus** – Konsumentenrente
> **to pursue** – verfolgen
> **barriers to entry** – Markteintrittsbarrieren
> **to deter** – abschrecken, abhalten

If customers are satisfied with the product, its reputation will spread, availability will improve, and sales will increase in the **adolescence stage.** Competitors will be attracted and might enter the market. Companies should try to set up barriers to entry, cut prices to deter rivals, or aim to increase customer loyalty.

During the **maturity stage** the established product faces intense competition from substitutes. Sales will level off and market saturation is imminent, resulting in overcapacities and falling market prices. Strategic options include an increased market penetration, market development, and product development or differentiation.

The **aging stage** is the final phase of the product life cycle. The important skill in this stage is to know when to leave the market. Alternatively, a company could try to pursue a cost leadership strategy, extend the life span through alterations or possibly attempt a relaunch with innovative features at a later point in time. Thus, "aged" products with added innovative features may "cycle back" into an earlier phase (i.e. conventional, to digital, to interactive television).

Examples for Global Products Segmentation and Positioning

	Local Market Segment	
Product Positioning	**Universal** (same across countries)	**Unique** (differs across countries)
Uniform (same across countries)	• Marlboro • Swatch • Adidas	• McDonald's • Nokia • Obi
Adapted (differs across countries)	• BMW Mini • Milupa • F1 Racing	• The Simpsons • Esprit • Best Western

At certain points in the product life-cycle, discontinuities in market success will surface, usually in form of a "bump" or a "dip" in sales. These unexpected movements signal the transition from one phase to the next phase. The explanation given is that the phases differ in important aspects and require different marketing approaches in order to avoid a mismatch.

Market Portfolio Matrix

The **Market Portfolio Matrix** illustrates possible strategic options which might be considered by a company. **Market penetration** aims to attract a higher percentage of users of its product, e.g. luring customers away from competitors. **Market development** seeks growth by taking the existing products to new national or international markets. **Portfolio development** refers to product innovation or differentiation to avoid direct competition on the existing market. **Diversification** involves the development of new products for new markets.

Market Portfolio Matrix

	Existing Marketplaces	New Marketplaces
Existing Portfolio	Market Penetration	Market Development
New Portfolio	Portfolio Development	Diversification

Product Portfolio Matrix

The Product Portfolio Matrix, which was developed by the Boston Consulting Group, is a tool to analyze and categorize the performance of products and business units.

Each product in the portfolio, i.e. the range of products, is placed onto the matrix, which seeks to identify those products that generate cash and those that use it, according to the product's relative market share and relative market growth.

The product portfolio matrix is divided into four cells: Question Marks, Stars, Cash Cows, and Dogs.

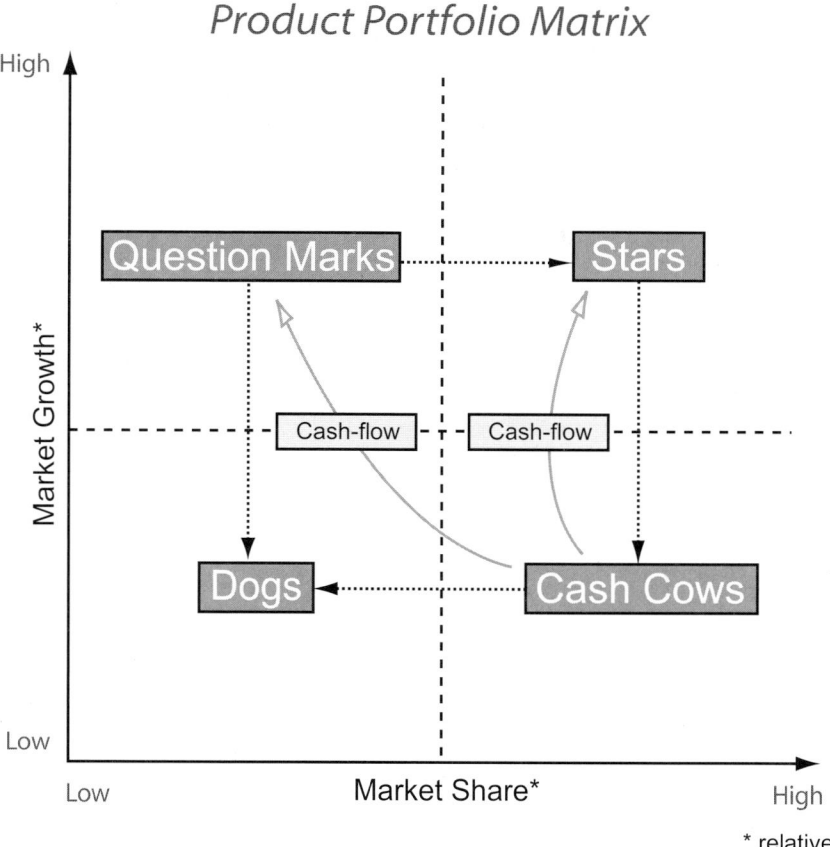

Product Portfolio Matrix

Cash Cows are mature products with a high market share but low growth rate. They are established and do not require a lot of advertising. High earnings and depreciation allowances result in cash surpluses. These products are vital as they generate the funds which are necessary to turn *Question Marks* into *Stars* and to further enhance the development of *Stars*. The recommended strategy for *Cash Cows* is "milk" or "harvest".

Stars are products within the adolescence stage of their product life cycle. They are able to generate ample cash but still require further investments in order to become lucrative *Cash Cows* in future. The recommended strategy for *Stars* is "promote".

Question Marks are generally still within the infancy stage of their product life cycle, enjoying high growth rates. They usually absorb more cash than they generate and might turn into *Stars*, but it is also possible that insufficient market share will turn them into *Dogs*. Hence, the recommended strategy is "observe".

Dogs are typically products within the aging stage of their product life cycle, or products that weren't accepted by the market, resulting in little or no growth and a lack of market share. They often become a "cash trap". Thus, the recommended strategy is "divest" or "eliminate".

Place

The *place perspective* refers to the distribution of products. **Direct selling** involves selling directly to the customer, e.g. retailing, door-to-door, mail order, or e-commerce. Advantages of direct selling include the close contact to customers and the exclusive control over the product range and corresponding decisions. However, direct selling requires storage facilities and sometimes retail premises. When selling products via the Internet, some form of IT infrastructure is necessary.

mail order	– Versandhandel
storage facilities	– Lagereinrichtungen
premises	– Verkaufsräume, Geschäftsräume
drawback	– Nachteil
to recoup	– wiedergewinnen, wettmachen
differential pricing	– Preisdifferenzierung
loss leader	– Lockvogel
to entice	– locken, verlocken

Alternatively, products can be sold **directly to retailers**, i.e. selling to existing retail outlets. Drawbacks are the high administrative costs, as sellers have to negotiate directly with various retailers, requiring sales representatives. Moreover, they will be responsible for the actual delivery to the outlets, resulting in additional costs.

Selling to wholesalers would be another alternative, which would also reduce the need for storage space. The disadvantage being that sellers will possibly lose contact with their customers.

Price

A company has to consider different pricing strategies to achieve the intended operational goals.

Penetration pricing usually means artificially reduced prices to quickly achieve high volume sales with the intention of capturing a large share of the market.

Price skimming involves starting with the highest possible price and successively reducing the price over time. The purpose is to quickly recoup costs and break even.

Differential pricing simply means pricing the same product differently, depending on certain criteria, e.g. reductions for students, discounts for wholesalers, higher prices in more affluent areas, or seasonal offers.

Loss leader pricing involves lowering the prices of some key items in order to attract customers to the shop. The price reductions are used to entice customers to look at other products which are not reduced.

Promotion

The promotion perspective comprises advertising, sales promotion, personal selling and public relations.

Advertising is the most obvious method of promotion. Companies use an array of media for advertisements and commercials. The main **advertising media** are television, radio, newspapers and magazines, posters and billboards, and the Internet.

advertising – Werbung
sales promotion – Verkaufsförderung
public relations – Öffentlichkeitsarbeit
array – Reihe, Menge
billboard – Reklamefläche
voucher – Gutschein
trade union – Gewerkschaft

There are different **types of advertising.** Informative advertising is used to inform the public about the qualities of the product. Persuasive advertising tries to convince the consumer that he or she really needs the product. Competitive advertisements criticize the competitors and highlight the qualities of the own product. Collective advertising is used by small firms to mount a more effective advertising campaign on a larger budget.

Sales promotion comprises a range of measures to enhance the volume of sales, e.g. competitions, lotteries, samples, vouchers, low interest rate financing, and special offers.

Personal selling involves sales men selling to the customer on a one-to-one basis.

Public relations (PR) are concerned with keeping good communications between a firm and various groups that make up the general public, e.g. the local community, trade unions, employees, or the media.

B 12.2 Knowledge Check

(1) What is the relationship between the PLC and the Product Portfolio Matrix (BCG)?
(2) What is the difference between the PLC and the Product Portfolio Matrix (BCG)?
(3) What are the corresponding strategies for the Product Portfolio Matrix (BCG)?

→ See Answer Key for solutions.

B 12.3 Keywords

barrier to entry, billboard, cash cow, cash trap, decline, demand, differential pricing, dog, growth, life span, loss leader pricing, mail order, maturity, observation, penetration, pricing, product life cycle, question mark, questionnaire, sample, skimming, star, supply, voucher.

B 12.4 Strategy Case: The Algonquin Hotel – Executive Suite?

Background of the Deal

Charles Peck, President and CEO of Destination Hotels and Resorts (DH&R), with headquarters in Englewood, Colorado, is proud of his latest acquisition, the illustrious New York hotel, The Algonquin. The hotel is located in the center of midtown Manhattan (59 West 44th Street.) It is on the same street as the historic New York Yacht Club, the Harvard Club, and the Bar Association. Created in the Art Deco style, it has been a famous gathering place for New York's literary set. While there may be grander or more fashionable competitors, there is arguably none, which better personifies both the history, and the literary and show business connections in New York City. In its class, it offers the usual range of facilities extending from intimate boardrooms to grand ballrooms, luxury catering from world class chefs, to organizing exquisite events.

In June 2002, the Algonquin Hotel had been sold to the Denver real-estate partnership Miller Global Properties Fund IV for an undisclosed sum. In a separate deal, the new owners decided that the hotel would be managed by DH&R. The previous owners, Olympus Real Estate Corporation of Dallas had bought the hotel in 1997 for $ 32.6 million, and renovated it in 1998 for $ 5.5 million. With the completion of this transaction, the hotel has changed owners for the third time in 14 years.

The Outsourcing Decision

DH&R is the hospitality subsidiary of Lowe Enterprises, and currently employs over 7,000 people in offices in the USA and in Europe. This rapidly expanding company has increased its assets under management from $ 200 million in 1997 to over $ 3.5 billion in 2001. Its hospitality management subsidiary DH&R is arguably the third largest hotel management company in the U.S. Worldwide the firm operates luxury hotels and resorts valued at more than $ 1.1 billion. It can look back on a history of solid investments and is widely admired by investors for its ability to anticipate market trends.

Its marketing strategy is to promote each luxury hotel on its individual merits, rather than under the identity of a generic brand name. By capitalizing on the unique selling proposition of each property, DH&R aims to target clearly defined segments of sophisticated audiences. To demonstrate its commitment, it initiates appropriate renovations after each purchase. In conjunction with Miller Global, DH&R will immediately begin a wide-ranging three-year capital improvement plan that has been developed for the Algonquin. The plan includes guest room improvements, installation of high-speed internet access in all guest and meeting rooms, and the addition of new technological systems throughout the hotel to meet the needs of the business traveler. At this stage, Charles Peck had also stated that the Algonquin would continue to be marketed domestically and internationally, and that the majority of the staff would be retained.

As Brian Windle, Senior Vice President of Sales & Marketing for DH&R explains, securing the contract for the Algonquin Hotel provides an opportunity not only to enter the New York City marketplace, but also to deploy their distinctive management philosophy while developing and enhancing equity in the Algonquin brand name.

Historical Connection

For a city that claims "to never sleep" the Algonquin constituency is remarkably loyal. Whereas the trendy, fashionable market can be very fickle, there are guests who have been coming to the Algonquin for 40 years and many employees who have been working there for longer. Its worldwide renown was a legacy of the Algonquin Round Table. During the Jazz Age in the 1920s a group of young writers, had taken lunch in the hotel's Round Table Room situated at the end of the wood-lined lobby. In 1925 the New Yorker magazine was created over meals at the hotel, and many of the Round Table regulars went to write for it.

Management upholds the literary tradition with distinction. A plaque on the building celebrates it as a "literary landmark". Readings and talks are held regularly at the Algonquin and the lobby is still a favorite venue for publishers and authors. The literary associations are also a staple byline in middlebrow television shows. Although the hotel offers the standard souvenirs, the lobby is quiet, unlike the famous literati who criss-crossed the tiled black-and-white floor.

However, such associations can also become a liability. Previous to the 1998 renovation the hotel was resting on its laurels and had fallen behind its exclusive competitors. In this context, the President of DH&R was keenly aware of the fact that not all loyal customers were contributing to the bottom line, and vice versa. As a matter of experience, he knew that fussy attention seekers were often less profitable than one-off customers who made fewer demands, but contributed more to revenue.

Strategic Options

Reservations at the hotel were made in several ways:
- pure Transient Tourist or business travelers who made reservations through the national toll-free number. This group usually paid the rack rate (i.e. published rate charge);
- government employees who typically were restricted to a relatively low "per diem" budget;
- contracts with travel agents for tourist groups at negotiated rates;
- corporate groups and association meetings consisting of small exclusive groups that could meet in the suites;
- larger corporate groups and associations attending meetings in the Convention Center or in other hotels;
- contracts with airlines for flight crews;

- weekend packages, including some with special services to make them attractive.

The Marketing Mix

Products

The physical product was fixed by corporate architectural and planning standards as adapted to the specific New York site.

The Algonquin had acquired a reputation for exquisite restaurant facilities with a distinct local flair. Although the hotel was encircled by some of the smartest haute cuisine restaurants in town, the food, like the décor, was very traditional American. The specialty of the Blue Bar (where even the barman used to be a novelist) was turkey club sandwiches and corned beef on rye, chef's salad and cheesecake. The Oak Room and Round Table Room featured more sophisticated but still homely dishes like braised beef short ribs and shrimp, scallop and mussel stew.

Weighing the strengths and weaknesses of opening an own facility or leasing space to a local restaurant with a good reputation, the president of DH&R had to consider whether the food services enhanced the image of the Algonquin with its customers. Perhaps, careful design and positioning could increase their potential to attract customers from outside the hotel.

Price Sensitivities

Together with the airlines, hotels were suffering from diminished business from the general economic slowdown, exacerbated by the events of September 11. Hotels even lost revenue in the peak season encompassing September, October and November 2001.

At this point, business travelers could achieve savings between 20 percent and 60 percent by using the lower prices either to save money, or to trade up to better hotel accommodation than they could normally afford.

The best bargains were at the upper segment of the market. For example, the luxury hotel operator Mandarin Oriental has extended its "Seasonal Choices" campaign by 50 %. The promotional offer included breakfast, late checkout, taxes and service charges. Similarly, the Peninsula has reduced its normal rate for a deluxe room from $ 675 instead of $ 475. The Mark in New York, which was managed by Mandarin Oriental, asked for $ 349 instead of $ 475. A phalanx of other luxury hotels – including the Carlyle, Helmsley Park Lane, Lowell and Plaza, Plaza Athenee and Regent Wall Street – have joined a summer promotion offering up to 40 per cent off until September 15. "Power Packages" with no extras include a deluxe room, airport transport, American-breakfast, free use of high-speed internet access, for single or double occupancy for a seven-day maximum stay.

More than ever, guests who did not accept the rates first quoted were likely to get better or cheaper accommodation.

As the Algonquin represented a unique, local market with different costs and competition market pricing would seem to be appropriate. Accordingly, in the face of ruinous competitive pressure, management was considering the introduction of an upgraded yield management pricing system, rather than deploying a single-price policy. With this concept, first deployed in the air carrier business, all rooms would be booked and, as a corollary, profits maximized. Building on a simple set of pricing differentials, every room might have a different price Monday to Thursday, Friday, Saturday, and Sunday.

As a starting point for the pro forma business plan, there were 52 weekends to consider, with 174 rooms and suites available. Perhaps 25 percent of these would be sold at rack rate. The key issue for the upcoming meeting would be how to price and sell the remaining rooms?

Yield Management in the Hotel Business

As in other domains, hotel guests may be grouped into a wide scope of market segments. A minimum condition in the luxury category is that business and leisure segments have to be served the full range of services if requested. However, as the leisure segment is more price-sensitive than the business segment, it tends to plan and to book far in advance, thus facilitating planning and scheduling activities. In contrast, Business consumers often have to book at short notice, and are therefore more concerned with availability than price. To maximize returns, the hotel must accurately forecast the demand, the revenue and the contribution produced by these segments. In general, lower rates produce low unit-contribution margins, whereas higher rates drive away too many customers.

Extra Service Fees Option

Hotels that are responsive to customer complaints and vulnerable to hardball negotiation tactics – especially during a business recession or in the weak hotel market following September 11 – realise that they have to choose between lowering their rates or eliminating their fees. As the Internet is facilitating the comparison of room prices, hotel managers are under increasing pressure not to raise rates, but to charge for extra services instead.

Hotel chains typically empower product managers to impose fees on a situational basis. In general, vacationers prefer packaged fees to itemised charges, especially when they cover well-defined services. Many business travellers, however, tend to prefer itemisation for expense account purposes. However, many business travellers would welcome a flat fee for frequently demanded services, such as local calls, a high-speed Internet connection, and movie rental. These add-ons might be as low as $1 for an unordered newspaper, but they mostly range from a $5 housekeeping fee to a $20 amenities charge for such privileges as access to putting greens, tennis courts and the hotel fitness centre.

At that point in time, two of the most controversial fees were for departing earlier than planned and for cancelling reservations, which in former times did not carry a penalty. Others included levies for parking in the hotel garage (sometimes even for self-parkers), for receiving faxes, for having baggage transferred, and occasionally for taking an after-hours dip in the Jacuzzi. And with rock-bottom basic prices, there were extreme options, like demanding a fee from conventioneers for the "privilege" of billing to the hotel's own master account – even though the hotel saved the credit card commissions it would otherwise have had to pay.

However, the hotel had to consider that the people who planned conventions and other meetings had the leverage to negotiate prices. They were in a position to say that they were ready to book for 300 people, but would not pay for energy or bellmen and, furthermore, expected all housekeeping to be included.

Although the pricing options may result from the core promotional strategy, the persuasiveness of the hotel managers' arguments would inevitably depend on the prevailing market conditions. These were contingent on industry-specific factors such as the rivalry among competing hotels fighting to maintain revenues and market share, and on layered demand conditions, such as demand from new customers, changing demand from existing customers, or on the bargaining power of travel businesses.

Designing a Strategic Marketing Fit

Charles Peck must now consider whether the Algonquin should remain a premier business hotel, or aggressively target other segments. An opening kick-off for the new strategy must occur shortly. He has already dwelt on the importance of sustaining interest and expanding customer awareness through the rest of the year. This promotional objective requires recognition of the price sensitivities of specific market segments. But even though DH&R has worked out which customers are most valuable, targeting calls for caution. Hotels that do not treat everybody right suffer a high attrition rate in the luxury market. Also, one must bear in mind that today's Lancia driver may one day buy a Ferrari. Basically, must he work out to which extent the luxury market can digest a flexible combination of market pricing national rack rates and highly variable package deals without sliding down the slippery downmarket slope?

Finally, he is wondering how profitability would be affected by improving customer retention rates. Would it be a good strategy to engineer increased customer retention with CRM (or Customer Loyalty Marketing)?

Customer Management Framework

	Low Integration of Customer Requirements	High Integration of Customer Requirements
High Lifetime Value of Customer	**Key Account Marketing** — Knowledge & Customer Proximity Marketing	**Customer Relationship Management (CRM)** — One-to-One Solutions
Low Lifetime Value of Customer	**Mass/Theme Marketing** — Linked Information Systems (Retail, Call Centers, Online Information Systems)	**Target Group/Niche Marketing** — Segmentation; Micro Communication Adaptations

B 12.5 The "Pro-active" Mindset

When managers work from proactive mindsets they are specifying what actions an individual should be taking to achieve the planned results. This means helping individuals accomplish tasks by supplying information about appropriate discipline, sensitivity, skills, techniques, and discrete actions to be taken. Proactive mindset management does not involve changing the thought processes or underlying assumptions that lead individuals to interpret events in a certain way. Rather, it aims to generate situationally appropriate behavioral adjustments, which enables people to see elements of a situation that formerly escaped their attention.

In this situation, motivation depends on maintaining a link between performing competently in a task and taking actions that are personally meaningful. In addition, the outcome must benefit the organization and receive the recognition of other members. In aligning personal and organizational effectiveness needs, managers must apply the insight that organizational life is inherently and unavoidably political. They must be alert to the fact that every organization member has a constant motive to influence how others think about the events in which they are involved.

The most effective method to deal with the inescapable political conflict is therefore to invite the people whose activities managers would like to influence to clarify and to help with the solution.

B 12.6 Experiential Exercise: ACME Role-Play

This role-play brings several motivational approaches into practical use.

(Time required: 80 minutes.)

Background

ACME, Inc., is a widely diversified firm that produces a variety of plastic household products. Top management is concerned about performance in a number of divisions and departments. They assume many work units could be more productive if only employees were more "motivated".

To act on their belief, ACME's management has asked four consulting firms to propose strategies for strengthening motivation. The consultancies were chosen because each is committed to a different theory approach to motivation to guide its intervention.

- **Motivational Dynamics:** oriented toward the theory that unfulfilled needs govern behavior.
- **Power Motives Institute:** devoted to improving power and achievement motives.
- **New Paths to Motivation:** dedicated to the use of expectancies in stimulating goal striving.
- **Behavior Management Associates:** follow the theory that performance is shaped by reinforcement.
- **LMX Institute:** follows the approach, that all organization members belong to either insider or outsider groups, and their performance is accordingly above or below their normal level.

Group Tasks

(20 minutes)

The class should be divided into at least six groups of four to seven people. One group will act as the ACME management-review team and remain available to answer questions raised by the other groups during the planning phase; this group may also make elaborating assumptions. When the presentations are made, this review team will ask questions and offer relevant comments. Each of the other groups will function as one of the four above-named consulting firms.

Each consultant group will prepare to make a presentation to the management team (before the total class) that recommends ways to change employee performance through techniques that are consistent with the presenter's theoretical perspective. The presentation should be four minutes in length and include (a) the premises or assumptions underlying the recommendations; (b) the types of jobs or people to whom the recommendations are applicable; (c) the strategies or recommended techniques for motivational improvement; and (d) the roles or actions ACME management should take to implement the plan.

Suggestion

It may be helpful for consulting teams to think of specific situations – types of jobs, departments, or people – and limit recommendations to these examples. Make any assumptions about ACME (or the nature of work within it) that will help simplify the task. During the 30-minute planning phase, teams may test their assumptions on the ACME management team for clarification.

Presentations

(30 minutes)

Each group will present their recommendations to the class for four minutes. ACME's management team should comment freely or ask questions of the presenting group. Issues to be addressed may include the practicality of a suggestion, the scope of people/positions to whom a recommendation is applicable, the time required before noticeable results can be expected, the proposed method of evaluation, and others. When all presentations are completed, the management team will conduct a discussion among themselves (but in front of the class) to evaluate the four proposals and decide which to accept.

B 13 Global Competition

- The Growth of Global Corporations
- The Global Trade and Investment Environment
- Basic Entry Decisions
- Structuring the Global Company
- Framework for Global Competitive Advantages
- Growth Factors in Global Competition
- Traditional Barriers to Globalization
- Cultural Barriers
- Administrative and Legal Barriers
- Strategy Case: Tesco – Ever on Piling High & Selling Cheap?
- The "Collaborative" Mindset
- Experiential Exercise: The Glass Cubicle

B 14 Integrating the Total Concept

B 13 Global Competition

B 13.1 Principles – Models – Practices

The Growth of Global Corporations

A historic shift is driving businesses that are multinational, but still associated with the government infrastructure of individual nation states toward becoming interdependent worldwide networks, linking companies, markets and transnational government and non-government organizations (NGOs). While this expanding global web of marketplaces is creating vast opportunities for businesses to expand their revenues, and reduce their costs, the increasing number of options and the resulting complexity also creates new challenges and threats.

The Global Trade and Investment Environment

Before expanding into a foreign market, companies have to decide on an <u>appropriate</u> entry strategy. Some options would be (1) to export from their home base or from a third country, (2) to produce and sell in a host country, or (3) to export from there. Furthermore, the internationally operating firms have to decide whether and how to customize their products, <u>align</u> their business strategies, fine-tune their supply chain, and differentiate their marketing and human resource practices to deal with cross cultural issues, differences in language, business practices and government regulations.

To <u>hedge</u> their global risks, these firms must also prepare for a possible stagnation or reversal in the trend to more globalization. For example, a worldwide recession might increase trade tensions, cause a breakdown in major financial markets, by <u>exacerbating</u> the gap between rich and poor nations lead to interventionist policies. Under such <u>circumstances</u>, differences between the interests of global businesses and those of governments would surface.

In spite of worldwide deregulation, companies from specific countries might be prevented from operating in certain markets, or they might be pressured to support investment in other states. Another potential danger might be a partial breakdown of the international dispute settlement system. The resulting rise in transaction costs for global business operations would be compounded by rising agency costs, reflecting a vast number of security and protection concerns. The outcome of this worst case scenario would be a host of cuts and adjustments of the integrated global supply chains, and widespread renationalization of enterprises with strategic value.

> **appropriate** – geeignet, passend
> **to align** – koordinieren, ausrichten
> **to hedge** – absichern
> **to exacerbate** – verschlimmern
> **circumstances** – Umstände, Verhältnisse

Basic Entry Decisions

The lowering of trade barriers and technological advances have made it <u>imperative</u> for larger companies to compete on a global scale. The various modes for entering foreign markets are exporting, licensing or franchising to host country firms, or foreign direct investment (FDI) either in a wholly owned subsidiary, or in a joint venture. The optimal entry mode would be determined by a number of factors such as transport costs, trade barriers, political risks, economic risks (such as a currency <u>devaluation</u>) and competitive strategy. A further possibility to gain immediate market access, would be to establish a strategic alliance based on a limited cooperation with a host country competitor.

Newly established domestic companies may begin their global expansion as exporters. Their <u>rationale</u> would be to gain experience and acquire localized knowledge without a long-term commitment. But at this stage, both the exporting and importing party would first have to trust the other side to fulfill their part of the contract. To provide a measure of transparency, trade practices have been standardized by "Incoterms", represented by acronyms, such as D/P, FAS, FOB, CIF.

imperative – zwingend erforderlich
devaluation – Abwertung
rationale – Grundprinzip, Begründung
intermediary – Mittler, Zwischenhändler
letter of credit – Akkreditiv
bill of lading – Konnossement, Ladeschein
draft – Wechsel
countertrade – Gegengeschäft
to embrace – einbeziehen, umfassen

To substitute for trust, traders often make use of an <u>intermediary</u>, such as a commercial bank. For example, in a deal between a German importer and a Chinese exporter, the importer would obtain the promise of an international bank (known as a <u>letter of credit</u>) to pay the exporter. The exporter, having seen the letter of credit, would dispatch the shipment to Germany. However, the intermediating bank would obtain the title to the product in form of a <u>bill of lading</u>, and in return the bank would pay the exporter, often by discounting a <u>draft</u> or a bank acceptance. The bank would pass the documents (bill of lading, draft, customs invoice, etc.) to the German importer, who would reimburse the bank on presentation.

However, occasionally these standardized means of payment are not an available option, for example in the case foreign exchange restrictions. Then, <u>countertrade</u> might offer a practicable solution. Countertrade <u>embraces</u> a whole range of barterlike agreements, such as build operate, transfer contracts (BOT) for capital intensive investments, and counterpurchase agreements.

Structuring the Global Company

An appropriate global expansion strategy would enable companies to boost their profitability in ways not available to purely exporting domestic enterprises. For instance, international firms can achieve location economies by efficiently dispersing operations and creating a global web of value creating activities. Furthermore, they can realize greater experience cost returns in a larger market by achieving a higher rate of learning effects and utilizing economies of scale.

The multinational enterprise (MNE) – whether it pursues a multidomestic strategy with a localized product and functionally self-contained foreign subsidiaries, or a global strategy based on limited localization and a worldwide product division structure – must review two issues on an ongoing basis. It must reconsider (1) how and where to perform marketing and research and development (R&D) efficiently, and (2) how and where to disperse its manufacturing activities.

To improve decision-making in the face of wide-ranging cultural and economic differences, as well as differences in technical standards and distribution systems, global companies tend both to decentralize and centralize operations in different activities and levels of management. For example, they may set up regional headquarters, which would control operations within specific geographic areas but report to a central executive board. Accordingly, a matrix structure combining regions and product lines would enable a global company to exploit low-cost manufacturing opportunities, while pursuing customized marketing policies which reflect country differences.

A Framework for Global Competitive Advantages

Responding flexibly to this complex environment, the typical global company resembles a loosely coupled multidimensional structure with many centers, few layers of hierarchy, and a unifying corporate culture. Corporate control is maintained indirectly by rotating people into different jobs and countries. Usually headquarters and research facilities are centralized in one country, whereas production and distribution are on an international scale. The goal is to keep close contact with local markets, while achieving economies of scale and scope.

Example of a Global Corporation

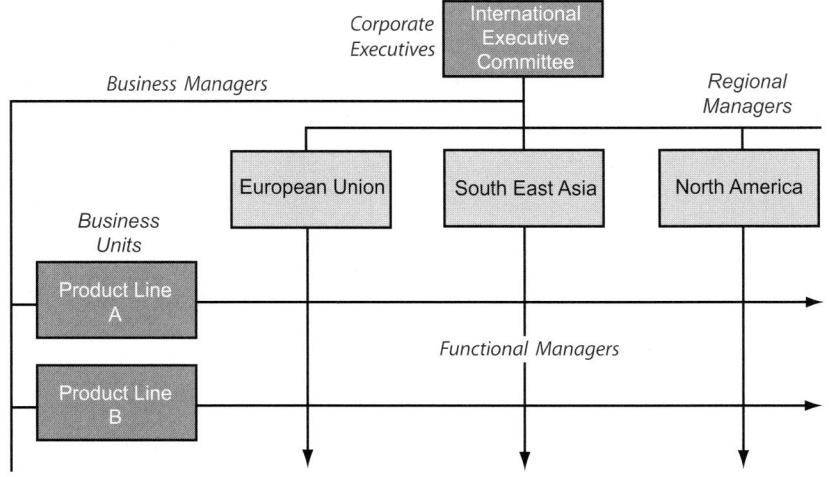

In practice, the dividing lines between the various forms of international activities are not clear cut, and hybrid forms are common. The growth and strength of an MNE depends on the presence of four interacting factors:

- Success in enhancing relative factor advantages: for example a central geographic location, a large pool of professional personnel, and a culturally engrained service mentality;
- Refined demand conditions support product differentiation: For example, the informal US-lifestyle leads to distinct product branding and fast turnaround with little personal service;
- Adjustment of strategy and structure in combination with a high rate of investment: the focus is on establishing a balance between cost leadership and differentiation;
- Developing and upgrading a dense network of relations with industrial customers, suppliers, supporting industries, and research institutions: within this industrial and research clusters the dense networking and positive reinforcement among professionals and experts will result in spillover effects to other sectors.

Competitive advantages will always shift rapidly in a complex and volatile environment. A dramatic example is China. Only a generation ago, the biggest advantage of Chinese companies was their cheap labor. Accordingly, Chinese businesses specialized in producing cheap gadgets. However, as Chinese wage rates have risen over the years, companies have utilized other advantages, such as engineering expertise, production efficiency, and foreign investment capital. By developing these capabilities, Chinese companies have been able to shift their comparative advantage to technologically sophisticated products.

Growth Factors in Global Competition

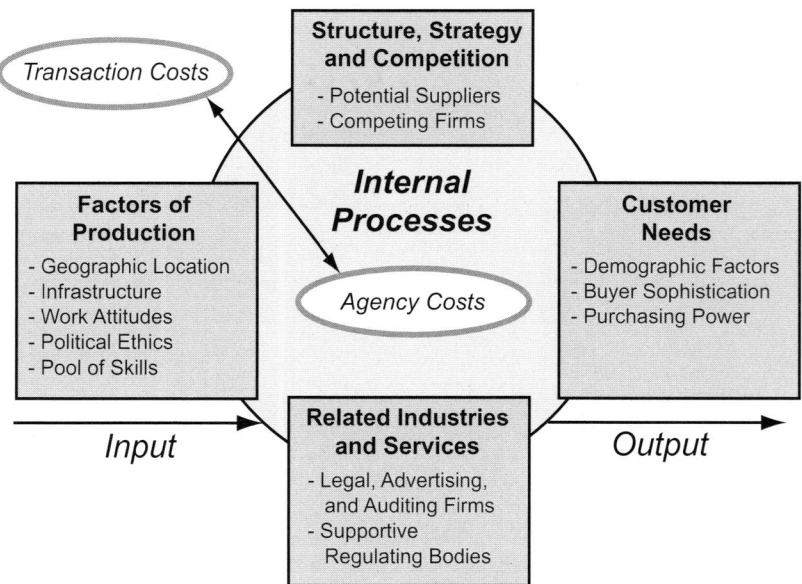

Traditional Barriers to Globalization

Cultural Barriers

The success of many globally marketed brands tends to obscure existing cultural differences. For example, in approaching an Asian businessman, an American would search for clues by looking straight into the counterparty's eyes, would express goodwill through a firm handshake, and would demonstrate commitment by speaking distinctly. However, as people in Japan avoid eye contact, bow rather than shake hands, and speak softly, the American behavior would be considered extremely arrogant and impolite.

In many global markets, product names must be modified to appeal to local tastes; thus, sizes and labeling might have to be changed to conform to the standards used in another country. For example, when Mattel Toys introduced the Barbie Doll in Japan, the toy failed. But when the doll was given smaller chest, shorter legs, and brown eyes, sales expanded dramatically. Adjustment to different cultural conditions will also be necessary inside the company. Thus, competitive incentives that may motivate Western employees may achieve the opposite effect in cultures where teamwork is prized.

Administrative and Legal Barriers

Complex political barriers arise when countries try to protect their own markets from foreign competition. These restrictions which apply to about one half of all world trade may be obvious, such as special tariffs, quotas, and foreign exchange restrictions, or hidden, such as administrative red tape, dumping, subsidies, corruption, and lax law enforcement. Political unrest may be targeted at foreign companies and their employees, as assets are seized, and individuals are harassed or taken as hostages.

B 13.2 Knowledge Check

(1) Distinguish between an absolute and a comparative advantage in global trade.
(2) List five common forms of international business activity.
(3) List and describe three types of international trade pacts.
(4) Identify four techniques that countries use to protect their domestic industries.

→ See Answer Key for solutions.

B 13.3 Keywords

Absolute advantage; comparative advantage; dumping; economic community; licensing; multinational companies; protectionism; quotas; tariffs.

B 13.4 Strategy Case: Tesco – Ever on Piling High & Selling Cheap?

Global Ambitions

April 2002 was a good month for Tesco, the UK supermarket chain, based in Cheshunt, Hertfordshire. The retailer reported a surge in pre-tax profits to £1.2bn for the Financial Year 2001. Since Tesco overtook Sainsbury's as Britain's top supermarket in 1995, it has managed to open up a wide gap over its rivals by keeping prices down, and steadily increasing its market share of the food market to nearly 17 % and to 6 % in the non-food retail market.

Group operating margins reflected the impact of combining current lower margins from international business and the mature margins from the UK business. However group operating margins were expected to improve as the international businesses reached maturity. Total international sales for the year 2001 registered a strong growth of 37.4 % to £4bn, while profits surged 61 % to £119m. They contributed £33 million to Group profits, a 120 % increase over the previous year. Total sales in continental Europe rose by 32 % to £1,063 million, and contributed an operating profit of £24 million, an increase of 85 % over 2000. In Asia, total sales increased by 76 % to £652 million, and contributed an operating profit of £9 million (£2 million in 2000) – although operating profits in Thailand and South Korea were offset by start-up losses in Taiwan.

In 2001, Tesco opened six hypermarkets in Europe and 18 in Asia, giving it a total of 102 outlets overseas. Reflecting a new strategy shift, the company described itself as an international group, as it currently operated in nine countries and had:

- 65,000 staff overseas
- 76 stores in the Irish Republic
- 45 stores in Hungary
- 40 stores in Poland
- 12 stores in the Czech Republic
- 11 stores in Slovakia
- 1 store in France
- 24 stores in Thailand
- 7 stores in South Korea
- 1 store in Taiwan

The company announced that it planned to create 21,000 new jobs worldwide in 2002. The core element of Tesco's international strategy was to export culturally customized versions of its marketing formula for hypermarkets, the popular department store-supermarket combination that sold massive amounts of food and household goods in a single store. By 2003, Tesco's CEO, Terry Leahy, set an ambitious goal for Tesco to have more physical selling space outside Great Britain than inside. About 37 percent of the company's physical floor space was already located overseas.

Company Background

Tesco had earned a reputation as an innovative food retailer who carefully studied its market research and listened to the voice of the customer. The company was committed to delivering a high standard of customer service and a broad range of high-quality products at competitive prices.

In the early 1990s, the company began to accelerate the construction of superstores and to introduce organic food products. The group also launched a wide range of house-brand goods differentiated by price or quality, first under the Value brand, and later under the Finest gourmet label.

In the UK market, Tesco operated 678 stores and was the largest food retailer in the United Kingdom. It has continuously expanded non-food retailing, introducing house brands for value-conscious shoppers. But, operating as a mature business in mature markets Tesco – with 17 % market share in UK food retailing – was close to market saturation.

Tesco's Focus on Emerging Markets

Both Tesco and its main UK rival Sainsbury saw the key to their future prosperity in retailing abroad, where the potential for market share growth seemed much greater. But, the two groups followed different geographic strategies. In 1993, Tesco purchased the French chain Catteau. But the acquisition failed because the combined company didn't have the critical mass to beat the highly competitive French giants, like Carrefour (£ 37.6 bn annual sales), on their home ground, and so Tesco sold Catteau four years later. Subsequently, Tesco's focus was set firmly on emerging markets.

Sainsbury had a longer international experience than Tesco. Its U.S. partnership with Shaw's went back decades. But the US market had far more in common with the UK than the emerging markets targeted by Tesco. Growth, therefore, was likely to be fuelled by in-fill acquisitions, such as its purchase of Star Markets in Shaw's New England heartland.

Other big mass retailers, including the US's Wal-Mart Stores Inc. (17 % sales), France's Carrefour SA (48 % foreign sales) and the Netherlands' Royal Ahold NV (69 % foreign sales), for similar reasons were also expanding into foreign markets worldwide.

Central Europe had a newly affluent population that was perceptive to fresh shopping experiences. And unlike France, the region had few large domestic retailers, leaving the field wide open to foreign competitors. When the government of Hungary approached Tesco in 1994, to purchase a share of Global, an ailing Hungarian supermarket chain, managers saw a very different retail picture than existed in France. In 1994, Tesco purchased a 51 percent stake in Global. The next year, the retailer moved into Hungary in full force, then followed quickly with Tesco stores in Poland, the Czech Republic, and Slovakia.

In 1997, Tesco expanded into emerging markets in Asia. The company believed Korea had the potential to become a significant engine of growth for the group. For the time being, Tesco has limited its regional expansion to Central Europe and Asia, where it now has more than 139 stores.

Cluster Approach

Carrefour had begun to establish itself in Central Europe in the 1990's, too. The French retailer was more experienced in international business than Tesco, and many of its foreign operations were making a profit. Carrefour's strategy was to spread out geographically. With a presence in 25 nations, the company has no more than a 3 percent market share in any one country outside France. In essence, its strategy was to achieve a firm local presence before the competition got too strong, from which it could expand its business when conditions were favorable.

Tesco, on the other hand, was opting for depth – dominating in contiguous countries – rather than dispersing activities. By forming clusters of shared processes, Tesco hoped to build regional economies of scale. Geographic proximity improved efficiency by enabling stores to share resources, even if they did not operate in the same country. Tesco stores in Slovakia and the Czech Republic, for instance, imported up to one-third of their products from each other. The company also calculated that it needed a minimum of 15 stores in any single country to be profitable to spread head-office cost and other overhead.

In comparison with other businesses, retailing was still a relatively local business in most countries. Although consumers worldwide have grown used to global brands, retailers – particularly those that cater to daily household needs – have been slow to respond to consumers outside their own country.

The riskiness of foreign expansion is complexity and increased overhead. The first global companies tried to leverage their brands through standardization as the most cost-effective way to export a domestic quality product to multiple countries at an affordable price. By appealing to local consumers' appetite for prestigious brands, moreover, a multinational corporation can distinguish its products and avoid competing directly with better-adapted local retailers.

Tesco, however, has adopted a contrarian approach to globalization. By seeking to blend into the local scene, Tesco accepted that the overarching consumer thrill was the shopping experience at a hypermarket. Accordingly, Tesco opted for a localized strategy based on a thick understanding of and responsiveness to the cultural habits and preferences of foreign consumers. By 2001, Tesco stocked over 7,000 local products. Local and regionally sourced products could be identified by flags and rosettes depicting country or county of origin, and in some cases even the farm of origin.

Ethical Trading Initiative

In 1997 Tesco introduced a set of Core Values defining the way it aimed to share good business and environmental practice with these new areas, and vice versa.

Based on its Supplier Code of Conduct, for instance, it supported an Ethical Trading Initiative and Fairtrade which stipulated fair terms of trade, local sustainability, better prices, and decent working conditions, supplying customers with tea and coffee bought direct from the grower's co-operatives and other smallholder organizations.

Global Hybrid Online-Supermarket

Tesco's online model, established in 1996, was initially a low-budget operation attached to the back rooms of existing supermarkets. As a comparison, whereas Tesco invested just £56 million to build its online business, Webvan Group Inc. had spent $1.2 billion by the time it went bankrupt. And whereas Webvan raced to enter 24 markets in three years, Tesco, over a five-year period, gradually rolled out its service to about one-third of its 692 stores in the UK. Tesco's online shopping operation – symbolized by the ubiquitous Tesco delivery "vanettes" – was profitable in its first year. It joined online bank Egg.com and online retailer Amazon among the few sites that have prospered in the wake of the dotcom crash.

In 2001, the online revenues reached £307.4 million, and although the Tesco.com unit lost £8.9 million in 2000 because of expansion into new business lines like CDs and videos, its grocery business was profitable.

In June 2001, when most international online competitors had gone bankrupt, Tesco agreed to expand its Internet services abroad in a joint venture with the number-three U.S. supermarket group, Safeway Inc.. Tesco would provide the know-how for running the service. Safeway would also fulfill the orders through Grocery Works, an unprofitable startup that was now a Safeway subsidiary and its exclusive online grocery distribution channel.

As it did with its online initiative in the UK, Tesco took an incremental approach. It invested £15m in return for a 35 % stake. But it closed down three GroceryWorks warehouses to reduce costs, and it introduced the Tesco.com system to only a few stores in 2002.

Tesco also took calculated risks as a solo player. For example, in South Korea, where it had seven supermarkets with plans to open more, Tesco also launched an online shopping service, based on the reasoning that South Korea had a strong base of upwardly mobile consumers and the highest residential penetration of broadband Internet connections in the world.

Net Technology

To improve supply chain management and the coordination between its online and offline businesses, Tesco has implemented a Microsoft point-of-sale system in autumn 2001, based on Windows NT. This standard platform was selected to facilitate online transactions across business lines as well as with customers and vendors. Also, it enabled Tesco to implement a sophisticated network in a short time, using existing tills, avoiding a rip-out-and-replace scenario, while leaving room to migrate. Also, staff members could be moved easily between businesses, for instance from stores to petrol stations without additional training.

In addition, the new system framework would support the communication between central services, stores, and their customers, adding value to cross-selling capability, global sourcing, supply chain management and retailing services. Users would be able to interact with a broad range of smart devices via the Web.

Scale and Scope of Localization

Tesco pushes localization further than companies in other industries or even its own competitors. In Poland, where the company has relationships with 1,300 local businesses, the number of domestic products was over 90 %. Furthermore, more than 90 % of employees in Tesco's foreign stores were local nationals. This pattern was repeated in other countries, including South Korea, Thailand, Malaysia, Hungary, and the Czech Republic.

However, despite Tesco's attention to local culture, the high number of foreign employees has increased complexity for headquarters. Apart from the language barrier and cultural differences, locally recruited staff did not accept the Tesco corporate culture easily. Many had difficulty accepting certain corporate practices and slogans anchored in the Statement of Core Values, such as "ask more than tell", "trust and respect each other", and "enjoy work, celebrate success".

Trading Best Practices

To offset the costs of localization and product diversification, Tesco management has focused on standardizing management methodology to achieve global economies of scale. The stores were designed in a similar look, both in the UK and abroad. They were located mostly on the fringes of cities, to lower costs, and they offered large parking lots for customers' convenience. Tesco also promoted a wide selection of brands and distinctive services at every store, far more than at most hypermarkets. At all its locations, Tesco stressed the same principles of good service, backing them up with training sessions that were controlled from the head office in London.

Tesco has created a virtuous circle by exporting its UK format and fine-tuning it to local markets. Subsequently, it would monitor the relevant strands of that learning and reapply them to the UK.

According to customer surveys, Tesco hypermarkets in the UK have acquired a different touch from Sainsbury's and other competitors. With its highly advertised profile in service enhancements, its aggressive strategy for growth, and its fine-tuned mix of value-priced and specialty items, the company has meanwhile achieved a celebrity status, and replaced Marks & Spencer as the role model for UK-based global retailers.

The question many investors are asking themselves is, whether Tesco's high profile "globalization" blossoms would survive a more cruel April.

B 13.5 The "Collaborative" Mindset

Managers working in this mode aim to change the mindsets of all people involved, including themselves. The underlying assumption is that everyone is involved in an interlocking set of problems in which no appreciable, long-lasting improvement takes place without the participants changing how they see events.

This ongoing mutual learning process involves substantial adjustments in people's thinking – not only about the nature of the organization and the organizational systems in which they are functioning – but also about themselves and about the nature and desires of others.

Learning about the personal competencies, needs and mindsets of individuals with whom managers need to work with collaboratively requires the joint effort of teamwork. The fundamental activity required for promoting teamwork is supporting people to recognize the links between their own self-interests, the needs of others and the needs of the organization.

The basic components of managerial effectiveness are trust and trusting relationships. If there is a lack of trust, any managerial activity will automatically generate defensive behavior, and evoke the solidarity of others. This conspiracy of silence will distort the significance of perceived events. As a result, these left "out-of-the-loop"-managers will make sub-optimal decisions, based on their unbalanced organizational knowledge.

Managers who do not succeed in creating successful teams will face difficulties distancing themselves from poor performers. Rather, they risk being identified with the performance of the people whom they could not reach. An effective strategy for managers to promote a high-performance teamwork mentality is to learn enough about people and their personal competency needs to make themselves indispensable advisers.

B 13.6 Experiential Exercise: The Glass Cubicle

Purpose: To sharpen learner skill as a participant-observer.

Format

Half the participants will be involved in a decision-making exercise while the other half acts as observers in order to develop a better understanding of the group process. Observers will provide feedback first to the group as a whole and then to their individual partners. Decision-makers and observers will switch roles and repeat the procedure.

B 13 | GLOBAL COMPETITION

Procedure

PHASE I

Group Decision-Making and Observations

(40 minutes)

1. Divide the entire group into pairs (with groups of more than twenty, an option would be to divide the class in half before pairing off, thus enabling two groups to perform the exercise simultaneously).
2. One member of each pair will participate in the first round of decision-making exercises; these decision-makers should arrange their seats in a small circle. Their partners will be observers for the first round; observers should seat themselves close to their partners, but outside of the decision-making circle so that they will be able to observe their partners.
3. The decision-making group will be charged with performing Task A, which is to rank order a series of statements concerning factors that influence the effectiveness of a small group. They must arrive at one set of rankings that reflect the group's consensus. (The decision must be reached through discussion and consensus.)
4. Observers should observe both the group processes and their partner's behavior. An optional observer rating form is provided below. Observers should remain silent.

PHASE II

Feedback and Discussion

(Group: 15 minutes. Individual: 5 minutes)

When the decision-making group has completed its task, the observers provide feedback in two stages. The first is feedback on the total group process. The following questions may serve as guidelines for the types of comments that will be useful:

- Which factors helped the group complete its task successfully? Which factors held back the group?
- How did the group spend time discussing procedures?
- Which communication patterns developed, and with which results?
- Which influence patterns emerged; why and with which results?
- Which decision-making procedures were used?

Next, the observers provide individual feedback to each decision-maker in round-robin order, and then the decision-maker comments briefly on the feedback he or she received.

This procedure is repeated until all decision-makers have received feedback.

PHASE III

With the partners switching roles, repeat the procedure for Phase I using Task B for the decision-making exercise.

PHASE IV

Repeat the procedure for Phase II, providing feedback to the new decision making group.

Task A: Group Characteristics Ranking Form

Your task as a group is to rank the following statements that might describe the characteristics of a good team (ranking the statement that indicates the most important characteristic of a good team as 1 and number down to 12 for least descriptive characteristic of a good team).

Dimensions	Observed specific behavior	Impact on group or individual
Referring to the Group		
Communication patterns		
Decision-making procedures		
Content ("task") activities: positive/negative		
Process ("how") activities: positive/negative		
Referring to each Individual		
Task-oriented roles		
Group-maintenance roles		
Self-oriented roles		

The participants must work on the task as a group, and may organize for work in any way.

The statements claim that:
a) there is a healthy competitiveness among members;
b) everyone sticks closely to the point;
c) the group avoids conflict situations;
d) members perform leadership functions;
e) each member gives and receives feeling feedback;

f) the leader suggests a plan for each group meeting;
g) aggression is expressed openly;
h) informal subgroups develop spontaneously;
i) members express negative feelings freely;
j) the goals of the group are formulated explicitly;
k) information is shared freely among members;
l) members' feelings are considered when tasks are performed.

Task B: Manager Characteristics Ranking Form

Rank the following characteristics of a manager (e.g. a project manager assigned to implement workgroup computing) in terms of their importance (from 1 for the most important item, down to 10 for the least important attribute).

He or she:
a) is able to grasp and use the organizational structure of the group quickly and effectively;
b) is able to give precise instructions;
c) keeps all impacted parties fully informed on progress and final actions taken;
d) reconsiders judgments when they prove to be wrong;
e) develops a range of alternatives before reaching a final verdict;
f) is able to grasp instructions quickly;
g) is able to make fast decisions under pressure;
h) is able to delegate effectively;
i) is able to recognize pattern of relations among a variety of items;
j) delays forming an opinion before considering all the facts.

B 14 Integrating the Total Concept

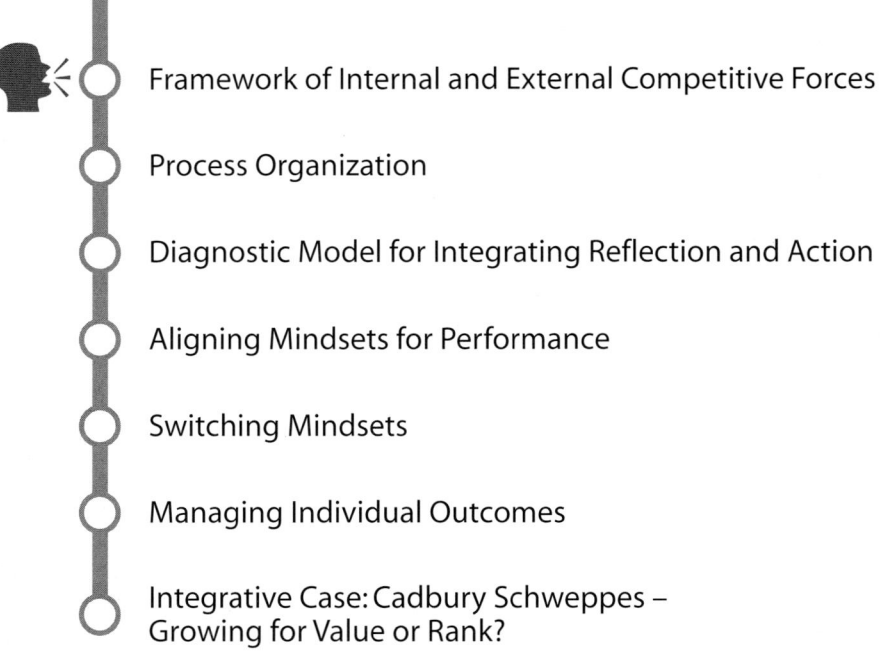

- Framework of Internal and External Competitive Forces
- Process Organization
- Diagnostic Model for Integrating Reflection and Action
- Aligning Mindsets for Performance
- Switching Mindsets
- Managing Individual Outcomes
- Integrative Case: Cadbury Schweppes – Growing for Value or Rank?

B 14 Integrating the Total Concept

Developing a business model, formulating appropriate goals and strategies and deploying within the organization are highly interrelated activities that occur simultaneously in many units and hierarchical levels. In the real business environment, where small chance events and sudden changes in market conditions have a major impact on outcomes, intended strategies are continuously modified by emergent processes in organizations. These modifications are partly orchestrated by top management, and partly the outcome of autonomous action of lower-level employees.

Consistent with the need of organizations o respond quickly to changing circumstances, managers must focus not only on creating a fit between the existing resources of a company and current environmental opportunities, but also on building new resources and capabilities and exploiting future opportunities.

The stakeholder map, extended by the competitive forces in the environment provides an appropriate tool to visualize the competitive force-field in which organizations operate. By "imaginizing" the organization's environment to predict an array of likely scenarios; by generating a shared understanding of the dynamic factors of their task environment, managers at all levels would expand their action horizon. As a result, they would be motivated to design and support breakthrough goals, thereby focusing the organization's attention on building new resources and capabilities.

Consistent with the themes of the previous chapters, management's performance will depend on its ability to identify, analyze and take advantage of opportunities and threats in its external environment. In addition, it must built on its internal strengths and to counter its internal weaknesses.

The task facing managers is to recognize changes in competitive forces occurring, for instance, external threats and opportunities arising from **Five Forces:**

(1) the degree of rivalry in its domain;

(2) risk of entry by potential competitors;

(3) substitute products;

(4) the bargaining power of buyers;

(5) the negotiating power of suppliers.

Changes in the **macroenvironment** may affect these **Five Forces,** such as
- merger & acquisition activities;
- shareholder interests;
- labor relations;
- the goals of government agencies.

B 14 | INTEGRATING THE TOTAL CONCEPT

To compete effectively on performance, top managers would need to identify internal strengths and weaknesses and to concentrate efforts on developing core competencies. Then managers at all levels would need to explore how those competencies might be developed to safeguard existing lines of business and to create new business opportunities, constantly seeking to exceed customer demands. By turning themselves into relentless innovators they will stay ahead of competitors.

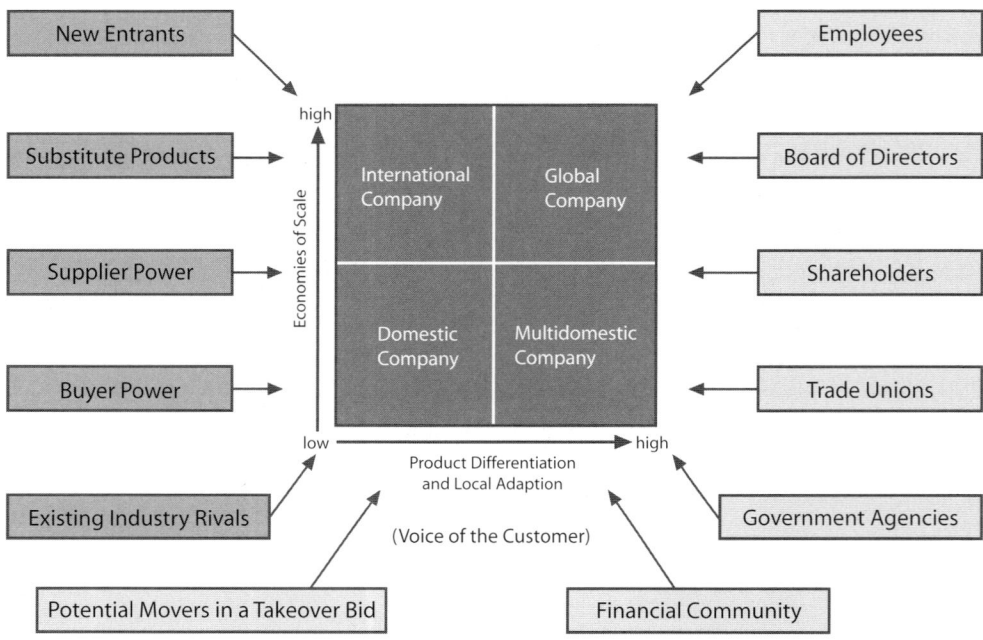

Framework of Internal and External Competitive Forces

However, making changes in more than one area of an organizational system can be a complex task, as the target areas are generally interdependent. Inevitably, changes in one target area will require changes in others, affecting a large number of individuals beyond the original decision area. To be successful, the change process must first overcome the vested interests in maintaining the status quo. This requires identifying possible driving and resisting forces, as well as determining their magnitude. The change can then be implemented in a subsequent stage either by increasing the driving forces, by reducing the resisting forces, or through a combination of these two objectives.

Integrating the Total Concept | B 14

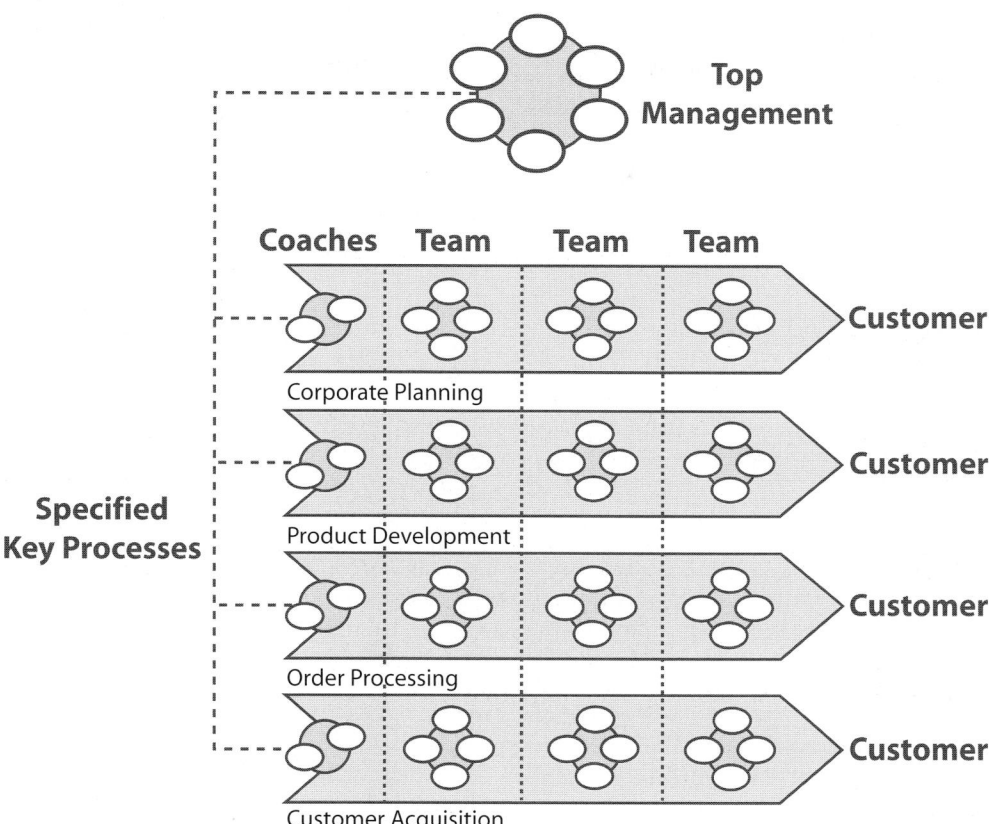

Diagnostic Model for Integrating Reflection and Action

As managers will not necessarily agree about the nature of the competitive forces nor about the strategic responses to pursue, a meaningful analysis could be made in the form of a diagnostic process. The collaborative exploring of the company's competitive context would reflect the different mindsets of the involved parties and result in multiple snapshots of the company's performance. The decision framework could be framed as a set of diagnostic questions, as follows:

Question 1:

Which major organization activity should be the focus of strategic change?

Question 2:

Which perspective should be taken – external or internal?

Question 3:

In which parts of the value chain should changes occur?

Question 4:

What time frame should be used – short or long term?

Question 5:

What standards should be used to benchmark and scorecard?

Aligning Mindsets for Performance

The core assumption of the mindset model is that business management cannot be analyzed exclusively from one frame of reference, such as a functional role or project brief, but must be studied from a holistic perspective. The success and survival of every business depends on obtaining the support of key actors in its environment and neutralizing attackers. To navigate through this ever changing market-space, managers need to understand people's personalities, motivations, skills and psychological preferences.

A person assigned to work on a merger project, for instance, may be highly numerate, but only have experience in working for large bureaucratic organizations, be highly driven by a need for recognition by superiors, and therefore feel frustrated adjusting to teamwork. The co-workers, on the other hand, may prefer unstructured environments, where flexibility and initiative in interacting with other team members is valued.

The holistic view of organizations upholds that each event, activity, and action within an organization has a meaning and sends a message. It is not recorded facts or events that influence behavior at work, but the attribution of meaning by the various participants. Individuals interacting in common purpose, grow a self-organizing pattern of aligned self-interests. These clusters of aligned mindsets control organizational processes, and set the stage for far-reaching decisions concerning profit goals markets, technology, size, and environmental factors.

The central axiom of the mindset perspective is that business management cannot be studied exclusively from one frame of reference such as a functional role or task assignment, but must be dealt with more holistically. It is important to understand people's personalities, motivations, skills, levels of experience, and psychological preferences.

A person assigned to work on a merger project may, for instance, be highly numerate, only have experience in working for large bureaucratic organizations, experience attitudinal problems adjusting to teamwork, and be highly driven by a need for recognition. The co-workers, on the other hand, may prefer unstructured environments, where creativity is extensively used.

The holistic view of organizations upholds that each event, activity, and action within an organization is endowed with meaning. It is not what exists or what happens that counts, but how the various participants perceive this. As individuals interact in common purpose, these personal mindsets will influence one another, depending on the personal knowledge, power, and readiness of those who would be influenced. Ideally, the result is a collection of aligned self-interests that control organizational processes, and set the stage for far-reaching decisions concerning profit goals markets, technology, size, and environmental factors.

As individuals construct reality in an ongoing process based on their experience, interacting mindsets are the engine for all workplace activity. For example, if people have been accustomed to working in a bureaucratic structure, they may have learnt to habitually repress their initiative. In this way, self-limiting beliefs and prohibitions may in time come to dominate the organizational climate. The substance of many outwardly stable companies really consists of skilled incompetence in avoiding action. Always, management activity is bounded by the view of the world that other individuals actually live in.

Switching Mindsets

In aligning their psychological needs with task requirements, people choose either a more goal-oriented, risk-averse or a more thrill-seeking, risk-taking mindset.

However, in line with human nature, the natural tendency of mindsets is to fluctuate continuously between more or less aroused (stimulated) emotional states in a continuous search of wellness and pleasurable experiences.

If people enjoy what they are doing, the activity is felt as stimulating (whereby "the path is the goal"), perhaps even as exciting. When people have attained a high level of excitement, they tend to feel invulnerable and omnipotent (the feeling of "being able to walk on water"). However, inexorably, self-doubts begin to arise, undermining this exalted state. Then these people begin to analyze their situation, and start to calculate their chances. At that point, the high level of arousal will switch into anxiety, at a stroke destroying the sense of wellness.

To overcome the incapacitating effect of anxiety, people will attempt to regain control by blending out arousal-producing factors (for instance, avoiding distractions, and changing their perspective of the former situation). In addition, they will set themselves achievable goals. To the extent that they manage to regain control, they will experience a release from anxiety in the form of relaxation. However, to the extent that circumstances change or satiation sets in, relaxation will switch into felt boredom, and the whole cycle begins again.

In general, sudden switches between wellness levels will occur in response to changing circumstances, frustration or boredom, although people will tend to spend longer periods in the mindset which best fits their personality.

B 14 | Integrating the Total Concept

Managing Individual Outcomes

At work, high levels of commitment, just like low levels, can have negative consequences. If people like a job, they tend to put their currently preferred mindset into all their work involvements. But, while high commitment yields a sense of accomplishment and rewards from the organization, it may also increase resistance to change and trigger unethical activities on behalf of the organization. A low level of commitment, in contrast, will lead to psychological withdrawal (reflected, for example, in absenteeism or a lower quality of work) and in employee turnover. The challenge for managers, therefore, is to understand how other people see and interpret events, and then operate in the appropriate mindset to set the conditions for others to be effective.

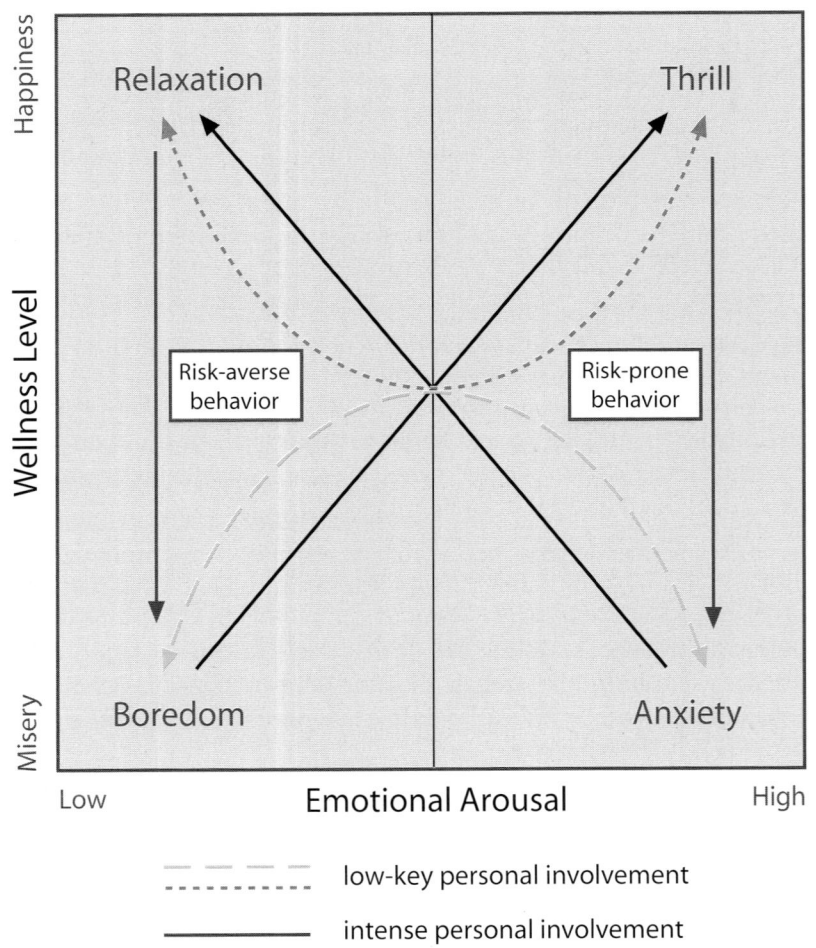

Relationship between Arousal and Wellness Experience

Integrative Case: Cadbury Schweppes – Growing for Value or Rank?

Last Preparations for the Orangina Deal

On a sunny morning in September 2001 a group of top executives convened in the office of the Chief Executive of Cadbury Schweppes plc, John Sunderland, in Berkeley Square in Central London. The only item on the agenda was a final review of the agreement to purchase Pernod Ricard's soft drinks activities. Sunderland used this occasion to summarize the rationale behind this landmark deal, which had been in the making in for two years.

The Cadbury Schweppes Group (CS) was the world's No.3 beverages company, behind Coca-Cola and Pepsi. It manufactured concentrate and syrup, and sold them to its franchised bottlers and independently owned bottling and canning operations. Supporting its global reach, it maintained its own bottling and partnership operations in 13 countries and sales in 149 countries, mainly through licensing and distribution agreements.

Scale and Scope of the Orangina Deal

The current acquisition comprised the Orangina, Pampryl and Yoo-Hoo brands and associated businesses for continental Europe, North America and Australia. The transaction was valued at £700 million. In a separate agreement, Pernod Ricard would take up an option to sell to CS rights for its soft drink activities in all other countries for an additional £35 million. The £700 million sale price would be increased by an indemnity payment of £18 million to compensate for taxation costs linked to the transaction.

As Orangina-Pampryl was the second largest soft drinks producer in France, the deal would double Cadbury's share of the French soft drinks market to almost 19%. Moreover, Orangina was present in numerous export markets, and the Yoo-Hoo brand was the leading chocolate drink in the U.S.

From the perspective of the counterparty, John Sunderland realized, the sale would represent an important stage in the planned re-focusing of Pernod on spirits and wines as its core activity. He knew the proceeds from the sale would be used to fund the announced acquisition of the Seagram brands. Pernod Ricard would be a global corporation in the spirits and wines sector. In this context, he understood the rationale of the agreement that had already been signed between Pernod and Coca-Cola – CS's virtual competitor in the protracted negotiations – for the sale of these activities for $500 million. However, in June, French officials had blocked the deal because they considered Coca-Cola's market power a foreign threat.

Strategic Fit with the Cadbury Portfolio of Brands

For John Sunderland, the deal with Pernod – even at the markup compared to the price which Coca-Cola had negotiated – was only a building block in CS's Value for Growth plan. In the first six months of the ongoing business year, this plan had already led to the acquisition of a number of brands and companies: in the U.S., Slush Puppie (the non-carbonated beverage) and Carteret (a contract packer of Snapple); in Australia, Spring Valley (a juice brand in Australia) and in Argenitna, Mantecol (a confectionery.) The acquisition of La Casera, Spain's third largest soft drinks manufacturer in July, and the acquisition of the ReaLemon and ReaLime brands in the United States followed, set the stage for the purchase of Orangina.

Although the deal with Pernod would cover only the European, North American and Australian markets, CS would use these bases as a platform for its transformation into a global corporation. The beverages operations would be focused on these three profitable markets in which CS already owned the Oasis, Canada Dry and Seven Up brands. The sale of the Dr Pepper and Schweppes operations for $1 billion in 1999 in those countries where CS had only achieved a modest presence and which it did not see as future core markets was part of this strategy and provided the funds required to finance the strategic shakeup.

The assembled executives were optimistic about the value potential of the Orangina brand for the development of the soft drink business in France and in the other targeted markets. The sugary lemonade in the bulbous bottle had epitomized France for a generation of Britons. And, as the resistance of the French regulators to the takeover by Coke had demonstrated, Orangina was one of the quintessential brands of France. The participants were confident that the announcement of its addition to the portfolio of CS's prestigious brands would give the Group's shares a welcome boost.

Strategic Fit with Cadbury's Growth Strategy in Beverages

In his presentation, Sunderland reiterated his commitment to pursue a robust expansion strategy, based on organic growth and acquisitions, while at the same continuing to divest low growth, lower potential assets. During the first half of 2001, overall beverages volumes – before acquisitions – had grown by 2 %. This growth resulted from strong gains in non-carbonated beverages in the U.S. as well from advances in the European and Australian businesses. The confectionery domain also registered improved growth, with a rise in overall volumes before acquisitions by 2 % during the first six months, whereby growth in emerging markets, which represented 25 % of confectionery volumes, was a full 6 %.

In the context of the current deal, Sunderland affirmed his confidence, that CS would contribute its category management skills to create added value for the newly acquired brands. Overall, within the beverage domain, product innovation would focus on increasing functionality to meet a growing trend in consumer taste. In this context, he mentioned Snapple's relaunch of the "Elements" range and the new energy drink "Venom".

Managing the Post-Merger Integration Process

The participants appreciated the fact that the post-merger integration process had already been launched. Robin Longden, IT director for the European operations had selected Kalido Ltd., a global information integration software vendor, to facilitate the migration of Orangina to CS's own reporting and business intelligence standards. The Dynamic Information Warehouse software would be able to deliver integrated information in just two months. This information integration solution would facilitate a speedy integration within the CS beverage portfolio by linking Orangina's key financial information into CS's business intelligence reporting system.

The participants realized that immediate steps would be required to align the strategic planning processes of the newly acquired operations with the GfV philosophy. The management processes and would have to be linked tightly with resource allocation and performance evaluation. The implications of GfV would have to be cascaded down along all levels of the organization to demonstrate to all employees how every activity had a direct impact on corporate and unit performance. In cooperation with Pernod, a first step in securing the commitment of the new employees had already been achieved. Sunderland informed the participants that the deal had received a positive reaction from Orangina's Pampryl's Works Council.

The Key Issue: Growing Strategy

After a short break, Sunderland invited the management team to collaborate in the second phase of the Managing for Value program Program (MfV). The first stage of the program had helped the company to improve its financial performance significantly in the five-year period by reengineering management processes, repositioning the businesses in the market, and improving operational efficiencies. He was adamant in his refusal to adopt the current fashion of short-termism in top management direction, and reiterated his belief that MfV was just evolving from its early stage of development.

In the next stage, the focus of activities would have to shift from a downsizing and efficiency-oriented perspective toward creating value through an innovative elaboration strategy. The strategy mix would involve sharpening and broadening the product portfolio, capitalizing on existing brands, as well as introducing innovations in flavor extensions, packaging, lifestyle focus and new distribution channels. To reflect the emphasis on delivering sustained value for shareholders, the second stage of the MfV program would be renamed "Growing for Value" Program (GfV).

Brief Profile of the Cadbury Group

CS manufactured, marketed and distributed branded beverages and confectionery products, and employed over 36,000 people worldwide. It considered the consumer markets for branded beverages and confectionery as closely related.

In 2001 Cadbury Schweppes was the world's third largest soft drinks company by sales volume and ranked among the four biggest confectionery companies by sales value. It had bottling and partnership operations in 10 countries and licensed its beverages brands in a further 21 countries.

CS chocolate and sugar confectionery was distributed in almost 200 countries. The Group maintained manufacturing facilities in 25 of those countries.

The John Sunderland Leadership

When CS's board of directors had appointed John Sunderland as the successor to Sir Dominic Cadbury in September 1996, they did not expect dramatic changes. CS had become one of the British corporate icons, albeit the share performance did not reflect this positive image. The board was convinced the new CEO would continue to guide the company toward steady growth and international expansion.

But, soon after taking command, Sunderland called for a radical review of existing management processes. He argued persuasively that the old strategy of growing through steady volume increases was no longer valid in a dynamic global environment.

Stretch Performance Standards

The MfV program was designed in a close collaboration between top management and a consulting team, and first implemented in the Trebor Basset confectionery division. In 1997, CS adopted MfV as the official Group Strategy. It set clear financial objectives for 1997 through to 2000 to grow earnings per share by at least 10 % per annum, and to generate at least £150 million of free cash flow. CS would strive to double total shareowner return every four years, although management accepted that achieving this goal was not totally within its control.

At the end of this first four-year period, on average in the four years from 1997 to 2000 underlying earnings per share had grown by 11 %, free cash flow had averaged £252 million and total shareowner return grew by 84 %. Doubling shareowner value in four years was a stretch objective and – despite the shortfall – the board was proud to have come so close to the announced goal.

The Guiding Principles of the GfV Program

Like the MfV program, the design of the GfV program – was guided by the idea of Value Based Management (VBM). It was designed to focus CS's activities on growth markets. By building strong brands, growing by innovation and seeking value-enhancing acquisitions it would succeed in maximizing shareholder value. In a virtuous circle, acting in the interest of the shareholders would secure the future of the business thereby benefiting all other stakeholders in the business: suppliers, customers, employees, consumers, and local communities.

GfV was based on the insight that the growth of shareholder value is connected less with retrospective performance measurement and strategy development processes as on the impact of people's behavior and corporate culture on corporate performance. GfV comprised five closely related elements, which reflected shareholder value maximization. These elements were: Raising Financial Performance, Value Based Management, Rewards, Sharpening the Culture and Leadership Capability.

The Challenge of Sustaining High Financial Performance

The MfV program had started by setting a high hurdle for the organization. It challenged the status quo to create a sense of urgency, and stretched the thinking of managers. Shareholder value objectives were translated into specific financial targets in order to give them meaning and life. Specifically, increasing earnings per share by at least 10 % per year and generating £ 150 million of free cash flow every year were set as further complementary objectives to Sunderland's commitment to double shareholder value within four years.

GfV used economic profit as a proxy for value creation, deducting a charge for the use of capital from the operating profits in the management accounts. By connecting corporate performance and long-term shareholder value creation, GfV provided a tool to monitor performance, and also to guide the development of new value-creating strategies.

As CS entered the next four-year phase of this process it was committed to maintaining the earnings per share and total shareowner return objectives. As a new challenge, the free cash flow target was increased to £ 300 million per year. The overall emphasis was on growth and management was given additional incentives to focus on promoting economically profitable growth through innovation. This formula applied equally to developed and emerging markets.

Leadership Capability and Sharpening the Culture

Sunderland was convinced that only strong, forward-thinking, internationally oriented and entrepreneurial managers who had the ability to motivate teams would be able to achieve their objectives and deliver results. Based on the premise that Management for Value is only 20 % about quantifiable data and 80 % about people, GfV set new behavioral aims for the deployment, appraisal and development of incumbent and newly recruited managers.

Top-Down Implementation

CS adopted a pragmatic approach by recommending that the cost of capital to be used for all units in the Western world should be pegged at 10 % uniformly. Spending time on cost of capital adjustments was not considered a productive use of time, as real benefits would come from elsewhere.

Ongoing Search for Value Creating Activities

In addition to identifying and defining the exact sources of value creation (and destruction), GfV was also a tool to identify the 10 biggest "value at stake" issues – the areas of significant value creation potential. The top management would focus on the areas of highest priority, and to engage in a more profound discussion on a handful of issues with significant value creation potential.

Developing New Business Management Process

The central philosophy of the GfV program was to decentralize strategic thinking capabilities as far down in the organization as possible. The business units' role was to initiate and take ownership of strategic actions, while being held accountable for their outcomes. The use of economic profit provided a common language and framework for both the Group Office and business units, thereby enhancing the quality of communication between them.

Key Performance Indicators

Within the business units, introducing the so-called "Key Performance Indicators" (KPIs) linked the activities of managers, at levels where economic profit could not be measured directly, with shareholder value. KPIs for each product and channel were identified in the economic profit analysis. They were cascaded down along the organization and individual employees committed to a certain set of specific KPIs, which would then be measured and acted upon if necessary. The use of KPIs would change the behavior of individual managers and employees and shift their actions toward long-term value creation.

Extensive Communication and Training

To educate people in the GfV philosophy and train people in VBM techniques, a series of workshops was established at various levels of the organization.

During these workshops, the executives jointly developed a new vision of the capabilities that the ideal manager of Cadbury Schweppes should possess according to the MfV philosophy. Once formally defined, these Leadership Imperatives served as a basis to put each executive through an audit of his profile and capabilities. Each individual manager received feedback from the audit, and an individual personal development plan was agreed upon for every executive.

The managers were also asked to put together an action plan with self-committed deliverables. For example, management information system managers committed to upgrade the business unit's IT system to the level necessary for implementing VBM, and accounting managers set a goal of introducing activity-based costing by a certain date.

To help spread the new culture through the organization, a communication pack on GfV was developed and distributed to all employees.

Aligning the Interests of the Whole Organization

GfV was based on the premise that the process of creating shareholder value depended on aligning the interests of employees became closely with those of shareholders. Accordingly it encouraged share ownership amongst employees, so that they increasingly thought and behaved as business owners.

The company encouraged employees at all levels to invest heavily in Cadbury shares by participating in a variety of newly developed stock purchase plans (three-to-five-year programs that entitled each employee to purchase shares of CS at a discount).

To support the alignment of self- and shareholder interests on the executive level, top managers became eligible to participate in a long-term investment plan that linked rewards with CS' share price performance indexed to the share price performance of CS' peer group. Second-tier top managers were eligible to receive stock options and to participate in an incentive program, ranging from 0% to 100% of base salary, which went toward further CS share purchases. Stock options were granted annually to a further 1,000 managers worldwide.

The Next Challenge

John Sunderland and the assembled executives were satisfied with the progress of the GfV program in its first year. The holistic approach had led to overall cost savings, higher morale, and breakthrough advances in process improvement throughout the whole Group. In the context of the present acquisition they were also convinced that CS's combined internal and growth strategy was well aligned with its portfolio of brands and distribution channels.

And yet, they were aware that these advances had been gained in a relatively short time, through intensive campaigns that had addressed three issues: repositioning the global brands, streamlining management processes and eliminating operational inefficiencies. In the years ahead, sustaining a progressive rate of value creation would be more difficult. The giant competitors in Atlanta and Chicago were sharpening their focus, and new entrants from the alcoholic beverage and from the tobacco industry were waiting in the wings.

A recurring topic in the informal conversations was the flamboyant Austrian maverick, Dietrich Mateschitz. The CS executives were impressed by the fact that his quasi-guerrilla marketing strategy had that tangy energy drink in the slim can flying off the shelves, generating $ 1.3 billion revenues. Besides sponsoring exciting events that fit his brand image – from soapbox races, and snowboarding competitions to Formula One motor racing – he had pioneered several interesting viral marketing techniques. Cultivating a new-age brand ethos, he didn't rely so much on mass marketing as on a gut feel for bringing people to the product, for instance throwing parties around seemingly weird themes, or persuading students to drive cars with an oversized can strapped on top.

Launching new formulas for the emerging Millennium Generation, the maturing Generation X, and the geriatric Baby-Boomers represented a huge challenge.

Sunderland and his entourage agreed to arrange a strategy meeting to discuss how to maintain the momentum of GfV in going for diversification, acquisitions, R&D, and brand formulation for the next five years.

Appendix:

CS's beverages business is centered around three strong regional businesses in North America, Continental Europe and Australia. The company operates across the non-alcoholic beverage market with a range of branded carbonated drinks, fruit flavored still drinks, fruit juices, flavored teas, water and flavored milks.

(1) Dr Pepper: the oldest major soft drink in the United States and the principal brand of Dr Pepper/Seven Up. It was first made and sold in 1885 in Waco, Texas from a closely guarded formula defining a blend of fruit flavors. It has been one of the fastest growing soft drinks in the US for well over ten years.

(2) Snapple: became part of CS in October 2000. This relatively young brand has been around since 1972 and has aimed to excite consumers with its huge range of zany and innovative natural flavors.

(3) Schweppes: Confidence, sophistication, maturity and humor have been the intended message of Schweppes' advertising since the early 1900s. One of the most notable hallmarks of Schweppes' advertising has been the creative use of the brand name. Since 1998, a sophisticated talking leopard in over 20 countries has successfully fronted the brand.

(4) Motts: has been making apple products since 1842 in Bouckville, NY. Today, Mott's make over 13 million cases of Mott's branded apple sauce and apple juice every year.

(5) Canada Dry: Canada Dry "Pale Dry" Ginger Ale was launched in 1904 in Toronto. Today Canada Dry is the No 1 ginger ale, No 1 club soda.

(6) European Regional Brands: TriNa is a product, bottled and distributed only in France and Belgium. Oasis is a fruity soft drink available in France.

(7) North American Regional Brands

(8) Australian Regional Brands: launched in 1973, Solo has developed to be an Australian icon brand. Spring Valley is a premium juice and nectar brand and is the number one selling single serve juice brand nationally.

(9) Orangina: acquired in September 2001, Orangina is a top international orange carbonated brand, and the leading orange carbonated soft drink in France. Created in Algeria in 1936, today over 1.5 billion Orangina bottles are sold worldwide. Orangina has a sophisticated and vibrant marketing heritage with a particular focus on the youth consumer.

Beverage Acquisition History 1997 – 1999

(1) 1997: the Group's 51 % interest in Coca-Cola & Schweppes Beverages was sold for £ 622. million.

(2) 1998: through a partnership with The Carlyle Company, acquired two leading independent bottlers in the US for $ 724 million to form The American Bottling Company (ABC) to strengthen CS's route to market in the US. ABC subsequently acquired Cotton Club Bottling.

(3) 1999: sold soft drinks brands in over 160 countries for nearly $ 1 billion, retaining a No 3 presence in the US, the world's largest soft drinks market, and also beverage operations in Europe and Australia. Sold Dutch own-brand confectionery production facilities, in order to focus on building branded business in Dutch and Scandinavian markets. Acquired Hawaiian Punch, America's leading fruit punch brand. Together with The Carlyle Group, acquired the Dr Pepper Bottling Company of Texas. Combined with The American Bottling Company, this forms the largest independent soft drinks bottler in the US.

Managing For Value – Phase 1

Results: 1997 – 2000

	1997	1998	1999	2000	Average	Total
Underlying EPS Growth	10 %	11 %	8 %	13 %	11 %	49 %
Free Cash Flow	£ 157 m	£ 157 m	£ 292 m	£ 401 m	£ 252 m	£ 1,007 m
TSR Growth	+ 14 %	+ 57 %	+ 2 %	+ 2 %	+ 16 %	+ 84 %

EPS (Earnings per share) at constant currencies and excluding restructuring, goodwill amortization and exceptional items

TSR (Total shareholder return)

Cadbury Schweppes Group: Turnover / Trading Profit

	2001 £m	2000 £m	% As reported	% At constant exchange rates
Turnover	5,519	4,575	+21	+19
Trading Profit	930	775	+20	+18
	2001 £m	2000 £m	2001 £m	2000 £m
North America Beverages	2,168	1,522	541	403
Europe Beverages	571	481	91	78
Europe Confectionery	1,532	1,427	212	200
Americas Confectionery	312	304	44	44
Asia Pacific	639	561	109	98
Africa, India and Middle East	288	272	33	28
Central and Other	9	8	(100)	(76)

B 14 | Integrating the Total Concept

Financial Highlights	2001	2000	% change as reported	% change at constant exchange rates
Turnover (a)	£ 5,519 m	£ 4,575 m	+21	+19
Trading profit (a)	£ 930 m	£ 775 m	+20	+18
Trading margin (a)	16.9 %	16.9 %	–	–
Profit before tax and disposals (a)	£ 886 m	£ 792 m	+12	+10
Basic earnings per share	27.0 p	24.8 p	+9	+7
Underlying earnings per share (a)	30.0 p	25.8 p	+16	+14
Net dividend per share	11.0 p	10.5 p	+5	n/a
Capital expenditure	£ 240 m	£ 124 m	+93	+93
Marketing expenditure	£ 1,081 m	£ 887 m	+22	+18
Free cash flow	£ 397 m	£ 401 m	–1	n/a
Group employees	38,489	36,437	+6	n/a

(a) Excluding restructuring costs, goodwill, amortization & gains or losses on disposals of subsidiaries and investments

C

Business Correspondence

Preview – Part C
Business Correspondence

1. Anfragen (Enquiries)
2. Angebote (Offers)
3. Bestellungen (Orders)
4. Zahlung (Payment)
5. Versand und Transport (Despatch and transport)
6. Verzögerungen (Delays)
7. Mangelhafte Lieferung (Bad delivery)
8. Mahnungen (Reminders)
9. Memos
10. Berichte (Reports)
11. Bewerbungen (Applications)
12. Die 13 Incoterms

C Business Correspondence

Layout of business letters

Sender's address: Place sender's address at top right hand corner.

Date: Place date at top right hand corner below sender's address.

Recipient's address: Place recipient's address beneath date on left hand side.

Salutation: If you know the person's name use "Dear (name)".

If you don't know the person's name write "Dear Sir/Madam".

If you are writing to a company or organization use "Dear Sirs".

Complimentary close: After "Dear (name)" finish with "Yours sincerely".

After "Dear Sir/Madam" and "Dear Sirs" use "Yours faithfully".

Signature: Sign the letter beneath complementary close on left hand side.

Typed Signature: Place printed name of sender beneath the signature.

Position/Department: State the position/department beneath the printed name.

Tips for writing business letters

- State the purpose or subject right away.
- When replying to a letter, identify that letter by its subject and date in the first paragraph.
- Use paragraphs to structure your letter.
- List or itemize contents whenever possible.
- Place important information strategically.
- Include all the relevant information.
- Leave out irrelevant information.
- Find positive ways to express bad news.
- Focus on the recipient's needs and interests.
- Give your letter an "action ending" whenever appropriate.
- Check spelling, grammar, and punctuation.

Example of layout

	Sender's address PC Planet GmbH Bergstraße 12 40215 Düsseldorf GERMANY

Date 6 April 2003

MoreStore plc
24 Meadow Lane   *Recipient's address*
London N17 9LN
UNITED KINGDOM

Dear Sir/Madam   *Salutation*

Information about data storage solutions   *Subject line*

Please send us your current catalogue and price-list. We are especially interested in your new range of data storage solutions.

We look forward to hearing from you soon.

Yours faithfully   *Complimentary close*

Angelika Steffek   *Signature*

Angelika Steffek   *Typed signature*
IT Coordinator   *Position/Department*

The main objective of information management is to make sense of ambiguous information. In general, the more ambiguous the information, the more communication cycles are needed to reduce uncertainty. The overall goal in managing information should be to maintain diverse communication channels in order to suppress groupthink and complacency.

Because information exchange is a social activity, communication typically evolves in a slow process, starting with minor transactions, in which all parties involved can prove their trustworthiness, and eventually progressing to expanded relations. Communication links represent an investment that would be lost if either party behaved in a way that would erode the relationship. But, cultivating expanded communication channels may also produce adverse results by promoting excessive cohesion at the expense of opinion diversity.

In conditions of uncertainty, some individuals are so focused on maintaining contacts within their respective communication cluster that they do not invest in relations with individuals in other clusters. A communication cluster may be considered as a single source of information because people connected to one another tend to have the same information. Consequently, bridging this gap in order to connect the different flows of information could provide added network benefits. Furthermore, information benefits can be generated by expanding communication networks to a more diverse set of contacts.

In general, networks with many disconnected contacts provide rich opportunities for entrepreneurs. A manager can create value by acting as an information broker between disconnected contacts, and by controlling the information flow. For instance, in the diagram below, agent "B" obtains more information than agent "A", because (a) indirectly, he reaches more people, and (b) due to the higher diversity of his contacts, he also achieves a higher information quality.

Entrepreneurial Opportunities for Information Brokers

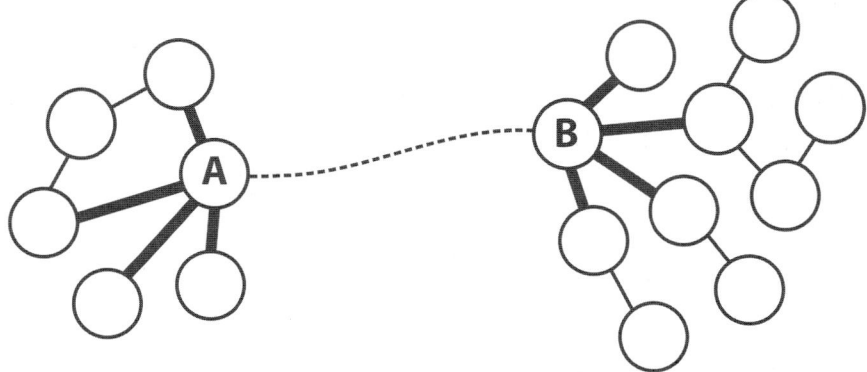

C 1   Anfragen (Enquiries)

Key Vocabulary

> **supplier** – Lieferant
> **advertisement** – Anzeige, Werbeanzeige
> **trade fair** – Messe, Handelsmesse
> **sales representative** – Handelsvertreter
> **to forward** – schicken, senden
> **current** – aktuell
> **offer** – Angebot
> **quotation** – Preisangebot, Angebot
> **delivery** – Lieferung
> **discount** – Rabatt

Key Phrases

Einleitung (Opening)

- Our company is a leading wholesaler/retailer ...
- We are a medium-sized manufacturer of ... specializing in ...
- We have received your name from the *German Embassy* in Dublin.
- We have received your name from the *London Chamber of Commerce* as suppliers of ...

Informationen anfordern (Requesting information)

- With reference to your advertisement in yesterday's *New York Times,* could you please send us a copy of your latest catalogue.
- With reference to your advertisement in *PC*-World of 12 February 2003 we would be glad if you could let us have an offer for the goods listed below.
- Further to our telephone conversation of 7 July 2003 ...
- Further to our visit to your stand at the *Hanover* trade fair, we would be grateful if you could forward us an offer for the following: ...
- With regards to the visit of your sales representative, we would be grateful if you could forward us an offer for the following: ...

Anfragen (Enquiries) | C 1

- With reference to your current catalogue, we would be grateful if you could let us have additional information on …
- Please forward us a copy of your current catalogue and additional information on …
- According to your website/leaflet/brochure …

Angebote einholen (Requesting an offer)

- We would be grateful if you could forward us a quotation for the following items: …
- We would be glad if you could arrange to let us have an offer for … as soon as possible.

Zusätzliche Anfragen (Additional requests)

- All prices should include delivery to …
- Please quote all prices CIF Bremen / FOB Hamburg.
- Delivery should take place by not later than 17 March 2003.
- We hope that you will be willing to grant us a trade discount of 10 % on list price.
- As discussed on the telephone, we understand that you will grant us an additional discount of 3.75 %.
- Please confirm that the equipment meets the requirements of DIN/ISO …

Schlussformulierungen (Closing sentences)

- We look forward to hearing from you soon.
- We look forward to receiving your catalogue.
- Thank you for your efforts, and we look forward to receiving your quotation.

C 1   Anfragen (Enquiries)

Sample letter – Enquiry

DV-Advance GmbH
Lange Straße 68
86167 Augsburg
GERMANY

2 April 2003

TTX Systems Services
12 South Clerk Street
Edinburgh
Midlothian EH8 9PS
UNITED KINGDOM

Dear Sir/Madam

Enquiry

With reference to your advertisement in last week's issue of *Hardware Direct*, we would be grateful if you could forward us a quotation for the following:

– 8 Rack Servers/Quad Processor 1.0 GHz or higher

– 4 Tower Servers/Single Processor 2.0 GHz or higher

We look forward to hearing from you soon.

Yours faithfully

Patrick O'Connell

Patrick O'Connell
Procurement – IT Services

ANFRAGEN (ENQUIRIES) | **C 1**

Exercise 1

Ihre Firma, *FlexPort AG, Lange Allee 168, 20355 Hamburg*, möchte die Büros der Mitarbeiter neu gestalten und benötigt neue Möbel, insbesondere Schreibtische, Stühle und Aktenschränke.

Vor 2 Monaten haben Sie auf einer Möbelmesse in Essen ein interessantes Sortiment eines neuen Herstellers, *NiceDesign, 16 Waterhouse Square, London N12 8LN*, gesehen, welches Ihnen sehr gut gefallen hat.

Schreiben Sie an den Hersteller und bitten Sie um die Zusendung eines aktuellen Kataloges sowie einer Preisliste. Erkundigen Sie sich darüber hinaus über die üblichen Liefer- und Zahlungsbedingungen.

Exercise 2

Sie arbeiten für die Firma *Meier & Wolf KG, Corneliusstraße 79, 40215 Düsseldorf*, und haben in der letzten Ausgabe der Zeitschrift *Office Today* eine Anzeige der Firma *StarSoft Ltd, 46 Longstone Rd, Edinburgh, Midlothian EH12 8NP*, gesehen, welche eine neue Software (*"StarProject"*) für das Projektmanagement anbietet.

Schreiben Sie an das Unternehmen und fragen Sie an, ob von der Software eine Demo-Version verfügbar ist. Bitten Sie ferner um einen Termin mit einem Vertreter des Unternehmens, um weitere Einzelheiten zu besprechen.

Erkundigen Sie sich nach Rabatt für Mehrfachlizenzen (*multi-user licenses*) und den Preisen für Schulung, Wartung und Service.

Exercise 3

Ihr Unternehmen, *Argus Computer Großhandel GmbH, Sonnenweg 40-42, 52070 Aachen*, hat von der Industrie- und Handelskammer die Adresse eines neuen Lieferanten für Computerzubehör, *ProPC Ltd, 117 Swanston St, Glasgow, Lanarkshire G40 4HW*, erhalten.

Schreiben Sie an den Lieferanten und bitten Sie um die Zusendung eines Kataloges sowie einer Preisliste.

Lassen Sie sich darüber hinaus ein Angebot über 450 PC-Mäuse, 450 Tastaturen und 80 Paar Lautsprecher schicken.

Betonen Sie, dass eine Lieferung bis Ende des nächsten Monats erfolgen müsste. Alle Preise sollen einschließlich Lieferung angegeben werden; ein entsprechender Handelsrabatt wird erwartet.

Erwähnen Sie, dass im Falle einer erfolgreichen Geschäftsabwicklung weitere Aufträge folgen werden.

C 2 Angebote (Offers)

Key Vocabulary

> **to submit an offer** – ein Angebot unterbreiten
> **to enclose** – beifügen, beilegen
> **Terms and Conditions of Business** – Geschäftsbedingungen
> **to despatch** – absenden, versenden
> **valid** – gültig

Key Phrases

Einleitung (Opening)

- Thank you for your enquiry of 19 October 2003.
- Thank you for your letter of 6 April 2003 enquiring about …
- I refer to your letter of 17 February 2003 concerning …
- Further to your enquiry of 19 October 2003, we have pleasure in submitting an offer on the following terms: …
- As discussed on the telephone, we quote you for the supply of … as follows: …
- I am writing to confirm our telephone conversation of 2 April 2003 regarding …

Anlagen (Enclosures)

- Please find enclosed …
- Enclosed you will find …
- We have pleasure in enclosing …
- We enclose …

Geschäftsbedingungen (Terms and Conditions of Business)

- Our usual Terms and Conditions of Business apply.
- The goods remain the property of the seller until such time as they have been paid for in full.
- Products subject to availability, while stocks last.
- Errors and omissions excluded.

Angebote (Offers) | C 2

Preis (Price)

- All prices are net and subject to payment within 30 days of receipt of the goods.
- We are prepared to offer you a discount of 20 % on list price.
- On an order of this size, we are willing to increase our usual trade discount of 20 % by a further 5 %.
- In addition to this volume discount, we allow a further cash discount of 2 % on condition that invoices are settled within 14 days of receipt of the goods.

Transport und Lieferung (Transport and delivery)

- All prices are (quoted) EXW.
- All prices are (to be understood) FOB Bremen/CIF Hamburg.
- The goods will be despatched from our stores as soon as we have received your formal acceptance of this offer.
- As agreed, the consignment will be delivered within 14 days of receipt of order.
- The order will be delivered to your premises by 19 October 2003 at the latest.

Gültigkeit (Validity)

- This offer remains valid for a period of 4 weeks as from the above date.
- This offer is valid until 19 October 2003.

Zusätzliche Informationen (Additional information)

- We would also like to inform you …
- Please note that …
- We would like to point out that …
- In answer to your question …

Schlussformulierungen (Closing sentences)

- Should you have any questions, please do not hesitate to contact us.
- If you require any further information, please do not hesitate to contact us.
- Thank you for your interest, and we hope to hear from you in due course.
- We look forward to receiving your order.
- We look forward to welcoming you as our client (customer).

C2 | Angebote (Offers)

Sample letter – Offer

TTX Systems Services
12 South Clerk Street
Edinburgh
Midlothian EH8 9PS
UNITED KINGDOM

14 April 2003

DV-Advance GmbH
Patrick O'Connell
Lange Straße 68
86167 Augsburg
GERMANY

Dear Mr O'Connell

Quotation

Thank you for your letter of 2 April 2003 enquiring about our range of servers. We have pleasure in submitting an offer on the following terms:

- **8 Rack Servers TX 1000**
  Quad Processor 1.6 GHz/16GB RAM/5 x 36 GB HDD   € 272,000.00

- **4 Tower Servers TT 800**
  Single Processor 2.4 GHz/8 GB RAM/8 x 36 GB HDD   € 47,600.00

All prices are EXW and subject to payment within 30 days of receipt of the goods.

We are prepared to offer a discount of 2.5% on condition that invoices are settled within 14 days.

This offer remains valid for a period of 4 weeks as from the above date.

Our usual Terms and Conditions of Business apply.

If you require any further information, please do not hesitate to contact us.

We look forward to welcoming you as our customer.

Yours sincerely

John Sullivan

John Sullivan
Sales Manager

ANGEBOTE (OFFERS) | **C 2**

Exercise 1

Sheila O'Donoghue von der Firma *Walsh Bros Ltd, 12 Broadwick Street, London W1A 2HG*, hat bei Ihnen (*Weinberg & Partner, Birkenweg 4, 54294 Trier*) einen Katalog angefordert.

Bedanken Sie sich für das Interesse an Ihren Produkten. Teilen Sie mit, dass ein Katalog und eine Preisliste dem Schreiben beiliegen.

Betonen Sie, dass Sie gerne weitere Informationen schicken, falls dieses gewünscht oder erforderlich ist.

Exercise 2

Die Firma *NetLog plc, Regents Place, 311 Euston Road, London NW1 3BT (Eileen O'Sullivan)*, hat bei Ihnen (*CMC Hardware-Center, Kastanienweg 38, 63067 Offenbach*) gestern telefonisch ein Angebot über 180 DVD-Laufwerke (*DVD drives*) angefordert.

Unterbreiten Sie dem Unternehmen ein Angebot über 180 Laufwerke vom TYP DSX 6000 zum Preis von € 119,00 pro Stück – alle Preise verstehen sich ab Werk.

Beziehen Sie sich dabei auf das Telefonat und bestätigen Sie die folgenden Details: Zahlung per Überweisung innerhalb von 30 Tagen, 3 % Skonto bei Zahlung innerhalb von 10 Tagen, 12,5 % Handelsrabatt, weitere 5 % Mengenrabatt bei Abnahme von mindestens 220 Laufwerken, Eigentumsvorbehalt bis zur vollständigen Bezahlung, Lieferung innerhalb von 14 Tagen nach Annahme des Angebots, Geltung der üblichen Geschäftsbedingungen, Angebot gültig für 6 Wochen.

Exercise 3

Sie arbeiten in der Vertriebsabteilung der Firma InfoMedia KG, Nobelstraße 16, 93059 Regensburg. Die Firma *OfficeLink, 12 Denny Street, Tralee, Co Kerry, Irland (Patrick Nolan)*, hat bei Ihnen ein Angebot über 100 *InfoShare XL Organizer* angefordert. Die Produktion des *InfoShare XL* wurde jedoch vor einigen Wochen eingestellt, da ein Nachfolgemodell geplant ist.

Teilen Sie dem Unternehmen mit, dass dieses Produkt nicht mehr hergestellt wird. Es wird jedoch in 2 Monaten das Nachfolgemodell geben, welches zu einem sehr attraktiven Einführungspreis angeboten werden wird.

Fügen Sie hinzu, dass Sie dem Unternehmen weitere Informationen zukommen lassen werden, sobald das Produkt erhältlich ist.

C 3   Bestellungen (Orders)

Key Vocabulary

> to confirm – bestätigen
> to supply – liefern
> sample – Muster, Probe
> trial order – Probeauftrag, Probebestellung
> to place an order – eine Bestellung aufgeben
> consignment – Lieferung, Sendung
> to acknowledge – bestätigen
> of utmost importance – von größter Wichtigkeit
> catalogue price – Listenpreis
> cash discount – Skonto

Key Phrases

Einleitung (Opening)

- Thank you for your offer of 13 March 2003.
- With reference to your offer dated 19 October 2003., we have pleasure in …
- I refer to our telephone conversation of 6 April 2003, and would like to confirm the following details (order): …
- We would like to confirm our telephone order for the following items: …

Bestellungen aufgeben (Placing orders)

- We would be grateful if you could supply the following goods at catalogue price/ at the agreed price.
- Please supply the following items, as listed in your catalogue: …
- We enclose our order for …
- Thank you for letting us have the samples so promptly. We would now like to place the following trial order.
- We were very satisfied with the trial order of … and would now like to place the following order.
- We would like to add that delivery by the due date is of the utmost importance.
- We would like to add that prompt delivery is essential.
- As agreed, you are willing to allow us a discount of 20 %.

- We understand that you are willing to allow an additional discount of 12% on volume orders.
- As stated in your quotation/letter/fax/catalogue …

Anfragen über Bestellungen (Requests about orders)

- Please let us know when the consignment is ready for delivery.
- Please let us know when the goods are ready for shipment.
- Perhaps you would be kind enough to confirm that you are willing to give an additional cash discount of 2.5 % for payment within 15 days of receipt of goods.

Bestellungen bestätigen (Acknowledging orders)

- We acknowledge receipt of your order No. 1204 of 27 May 2003.
- We would like to acknowledge your order for … of 6 April 2003, and confirm that we can deliver by the date requested.

Schlussformulierungen (Closing sentences)

- Thank you for your efforts, and we look forward to receiving the goods by the due date.
- We look forward to receiving your acknowledgement of this order shortly.

C 3   BESTELLUNGEN (ORDERS)

Sample letter – Order

DV-Advance GmbH
Lange Straße 68
86167 Augsburg
GERMANY

28 April 2003

TTX Systems Services
John Sullivan
12 South Clerk Street
Edinburgh
Midlothian EH8 9PS
UNITED KINGDOM

Dear Mr Sullivan

Order

Thank you for your offer of 14 April 2003. Please supply the following items at the agreed price:

- 8 Rack Servers TX 1000

- 4 Tower Servers TT 800

We would like to add that prompt delivery is essential.

We look forward to receiving your acknowledgement of this order shortly.

Yours sincerely

Patrick O'Connell

Patrick O'Connell
Procurement – IT Services

Exercise 1

Ihr Unternehmen *(Vector Gerätebau OHG, Opernweg 31, 63225 Langen)* hat ein Angebot für die Anfertigung von kundenspezifischen Gerätekomponenten *(customized device components)* erhalten.

Bedanken Sie sich für das Angebot. Bringen Sie zum Ausdruck, dass Sie mit dem Angebot sehr zufrieden sind und Sie es zu den vereinbarten Bedingungen annehmen. Bitten Sie das Unternehmen *(BlueLine Electronics, 27 Castle St, Eye, Suffolk IP23 7AW)* um eine Auftragsbestätigung und um eine Benachrichtigung, sobald die Waren zum Versand bereit sind.

Exercise 2

Sie haben von der Firma *Milestone Systems Ltd, 6 Birmingham One Business Park, Clement St, Birmingham, West Midlands B11 2AA,* ein Angebot für 25 PC-Komplettsysteme erhalten.

Teilen Sie dem Unternehmen mit, dass Sie das Angebot nur zu geänderten Bedingungen annehmen würden.

Fordern Sie eine bessere Ausstattung der Rechner (größere Monitore, bessere Laufwerke, mehr Speicher) und verlangen Sie einen Rabatt von 15 %. Teilen Sie dem Unternehmen darüber hinaus mit, dass Sie *(Q-Tel Kommunikationssysteme GmbH, Am Neumarkt 23, 79115 Freiburg)* eine Übernahme der Lieferkosten erwarten.

Exercise 3

Antworten Sie auf das Schreiben der Firma *Q-Tel Kommunikationssysteme GmbH.*

Teilen Sie dem Unternehmen mit, dass die geänderten Bedingungen nicht akzeptabel sind und Sie den Auftrag daher nicht annehmen können.

Betonen Sie, dass Ihr ursprüngliches Angebot sehr konkurrenzfähig ist und ein ausgezeichnetes Preis-Leistungs-Verhältnis bietet. Sie wären allenfalls bereit, die Lieferkosten zu übernehmen.

C 4 Zahlung (Payment)

Key Vocabulary

> **bill of exchange (B/E)** – Wechsel
> **letter of credit (L/C)** – Akkreditiv
> **documents against payment (D/P)** – Dokumente gegen Zahlung
> **documents against acceptance (D/A)** – Dokumente gegen Akzept
> **cash in advance** – Vorkasse, Vorauszahlung
> **cash with order** – Zahlung bei Auftragserteilung
> **cash on delivery** – Zahlung bei Lieferung, gegen Nachnahme
> **payment on receipt of goods** – Zahlung bei Erhalt der Waren
> **payment on receipt of invoice** – Zahlung bei Rechnungserhalt
> **crossed cheque** – Verrechnungsscheck
> **remittance/transfer** – Überweisung

Key Phrases

Einleitung (Opening)

- With reference to our order No. 17/280, we would like to suggest the following method of payment: ...
- With reference to your order No. 17/280, we would be happy to offer you the following terms of payment: ...

Zahlungsbedingungen (Terms of payment)

- With reference to your letter (fax) dated 6 April 2003, we are willing to agree to the terms of payment you suggest.
- With reference to our telephone conversation of 26 October 2003, we are sorry to have to inform you that we are unable to offer more favourable terms of payment at this stage.
- We would like to inform you that deliveries to countries outside the European Union are only possible against irrevocable letter of credit arranged through a bank of good standing.

Zahlung (Payment) | C 4

Zahlungen tätigen (Making payments)

- We enclose our crossed cheque No. 355678895 for € 72,860 on the AIB Bank, Dublin, in settlement of your invoice.
- We have asked our bank to transfer the sum of € 24,710 to your account with the Dresdner Bank, Frankfurt.

Zahlungen erhalten (Receiving payments)

- Please remit the invoice amount to our account No. 344 771 with the Commerzbank, Alsfeld, Bank Code 51343224.
- We confirm receipt of your remittance of € 32,000.
- Thank you for your cheque in payment of our invoice No. 221/7840/03.

Wechsel (Bill of exchange – B/E)

- This is to inform you that we have drawn on you a 2 months' sight draft to the value of € 28,000.
- We would be grateful if you could accept the enclosed draft and return it to us as soon as possible.
- Please find enclosed our invoice No. 221/7840/03 for € 12,370. We agree to accept your draft at 30 d/s (days' sight) for the outstanding amount.

Akkreditiv (Letter of credit – L/C)

- We have asked the Deutsche Bank, Wiesbaden, to open and confirm an irrevocable letter of credit to the value of € 36,450 in your favor.
- We have instructed our bank to release the shipping documents against acceptance/payment of our draft.

C 4 | Zahlung (Payment)

Sample letter – Acknowledgement

TTX Systems Services
12 South Clerk Street
Edinburgh
Midlothian EH8 9PS
UNITED KINGDOM

5 May 2003

DV-Advance
GmbH
Patrick O'Connell
Lange Straße 68
86167 Augsburg
GERMANY

Dear Mr O'Connell

Acknowledgement

We acknowledge receipt of your order No. 337/03 of 28 April 2003.

Quantity	Description	Total
8	TX 1000 – Quad CPU 1.6/16 GB RAM/5 x 36 GB HDD	€ 272,000.00
4	TT 800 – Single CPU 2.4/8 GB RAM/8 x 36 GB HDD	€ 47,600.00

Terms of payment:

Payment by bank giro transfer.

All prices are net and subject to payment within 30 days of receipt of the goods.

2.5 % cash discount on condition that invoices are settled within 14 days.

Please remit the amount to our account No. 887 447 338 021 with the Lloyds TSB Bank, Edinburgh.

Yours sincerely

John Sullivan

John Sullivan
Sales Manager

Exercise 1

Die Firma *PC Perfect, 31 Brearly St, Hockley, Birmingham, Westmidlands B19 3NS*, hat bei Ihnen *(Taunus PC Zubehör GmbH, Feldgasse 17, 65222 Taunusstein)* 160 Scanner vom Typ SCX 4000 bestellt.

Erstellen Sie ein Bestätigungsschreiben unter Berücksichtigung der folgenden Details: Auftrag Nr. 388753/10, 160 Scanner vom Typ *SCX 4000* zum Preis von 129,00 € pro Stück, Lieferkosten 68,00 €, Zahlung mittels Überweisung auf das übliche Konto.

Exercise 2

Sie haben von der Firma *SellCertified plc, Woodhall Business Park, Sudbury, Suffolk CO10 1WH*, Schulungsunterlagen für die Durchführung von Seminaren für Vertriebsmitarbeiter erhalten, welche Sie vor einer Woche angefordert hatten.

Bedanken Sie sich für die prompte Lieferung. Teilen Sie mit, dass dem Schreiben ein Verrechnungsscheck über 2.870,00 € beiliegt.

Bitten Sie um die Zusendung weiterer Broschüren für andere Mitarbeiterschulungen an Ihr Unternehmen *(ProActiv Vertriebsgesellschaft mbH, Grundbergweg 48, 35428 Cleeberg)*.

Exercise 3

Das Unternehmen *ProCert Solutions, 9 Cathedral Rd, Cardiff, South Glamorgan CF11 9HB*, hat bei Ihnen um die Lieferung von 40 Notebooks vom Typ *SilverLine K7 CDL* auf Rechnung gebeten.

Teilen Sie dem Unternehmen mit, dass eine Lieferung auf Rechnung in diesem frühen Stadium der Geschäftsbeziehung nicht üblich ist. Nach der erfolgreichen Abwicklung der nächsten Aufträge sind Sie *(Hardware Center Dorsten, Industriestraße 22, 46284 Dorsten)* jedoch gerne bereit, eine Lieferung auf Rechnung in Erwägung zu ziehen. Bis dahin müssen die Aufträge leider gegen Vorkasse abgewickelt werden.

C 5 Versand und Transport (Despatch and transport)

Key Vocabulary

> air waybill – Luftfrachtbrief
> bill of lading (B/L) – Konnossement, Seefrachtbrief, Ladeschein
> certificate of origin – Ursprungszeugnis
> insurance certificate – Versicherungsschein, Versicherungszertifikat
> rail consignment note – Bahnfrachtbrief
> shipping note – Schiffszettel

Key Phrases

Abholung und Versand veranlassen (Initiating collection)

- We wish to send a consignment of hard disks to Dublin.
- Can you accept a consignment of 200 PC monitors (19") for immediate collection?
- The consignment must arrive in Cork by 17 March 2003 at the latest.
- Please let us know your charges for collection and delivery.
- Please advise us of your current freight rates.
- We would be grateful if you could let us have your tariffs.
- We would like to know about your rates for urgent/bulky/large consignments.
- Please let us know the extra charges for express goods.

Transport (Modes of transport)

- Which mode of transport would you recommend?
- Please let us know any differences between air freight and transportation by train or a combined mode of transport.
- Do you think air freight is suitable for the consignment?
- What is the fastest route from Glasgow to Frankfurt?
- How much more expensive is rail compared with road.
- How long will the container take to reach Amsterdam by sea?

Versand und Transport (Despatch and transport) | **C 5**

Zusätzliche Informationen (Additional information)

- The goods are packed in crates measuring 60 x 80 x 60 cm.
- Please collect the goods from our Manchester plant by 0500 hrs on Friday.
- The consignment should be ready for collection by Monday, 25 August 2003.
- We will take care of all formalities.
- We will clear the goods through customs on your behalf.
- We would like you to look after insurance and customs formalities.
- Please make sure that we have the documents by 3 November 2003.
- Our rates include all handling charges.
- Our prices are door-to-door rates.
- Prices and terms of offer may change without notice.
- Taxes and shipping charges vary and are not subject to discount.
- All pricing, shipping and payment information is subject to change without notice.

C 5 | Versand und Transport (Despatch and Transport)

Sample letter – Enquiry about collection and delivery

TTX Systems Services
12 South Clerk Street
Edinburgh
Midlothian EH8 9PS

phone   0131 355 1188
fax   0131 355 1199

15 October 2003

ProPlus Haulage Ltd
34 Castlebank Ind Est
Castlebank Crescent
Glasgow
Lanarkshire G11 6DU

Dear Sirs

We need to send an urgent consignment of 200 PC monitors to Waterford, Ireland.

Could you accept a consignment for immediate collection?

Please let us know your tariffs for collection and delivery. Rates should include all handling charges and we would ask you to look after insurance and customs formalities.

We look forward to receiving your quotation by fax as soon as possible.

Yours faithfully

Liam McCarthy

Liam McCarthy
Despatch Manager

Versand und Transport (Despatch and transport) | C 5

Exercise 1

Ihr Unternehmen *(GreenLine Furniture plc, Fairgate House, 205 Kings Rd, Tyseley, Birmingham, West Midlands B11 2AA)* muss 300 Stühle für die Ausstattung eines Tagungszentrums versenden. Beauftragen Sie die Spedition *LongHaul Ltd, 58 Brearley St, Hockley, Birmingham, West Midlands B19 3NS,* mit dem Versand der Güter.

Die Stühle müssen nächste Woche Freitag am *Northwood Conference Centre, 164 Ashley Rd, Lee Valley Technopark, London N17 9LN,* angeliefert werden.

Weitere Details bezüglich der Anlieferung sind beim Tagungszentrum zu erfragen. Die Rechnung soll an *GreenLine Furniture plc* geschickt werden.

Exercise 2

Ihre Firma *(Desktop Software Vertrieb KG, Alter Markt 1, 74072 Heilbronn)* beabsichtigt eine große Anzahl an Softwarepaketen zu importieren. Der Transport soll von einer Spedition *(O'Connell Cargo Company, 64 Abbey St, Dublin)* übernommen werden, welche die Waren in Dublin *(RTC Software Engineering, 29 Grafton St, Dublin)* abholen und nach Deutschland transportieren soll.

Erkundigen Sie sich nach der am besten geeigneten Transportmethode, den Preisen und Geschäftsbedingungen der Spedition.

Fragen Sie an, welche Dokumente für die Abwicklung erforderlich sind. Die Spedition soll alle notwendigen Formalitäten erledigen.

C 6 Verzögerungen (Delays)

Key Vocabulary

> **to promise** – versprechen, zusagen
> **serious delays** – gravierende Verzögerungen
> **dissatisfied** – unzufrieden
> **due date** – Termin, Fälligkeitsdatum
> **condition** – Bedingung
> **delivery date** – Lieferdatum
> **to cancel an order** – einen Auftrag stornieren
> **unsatisfactory** – unbefriedigend
> **urgent** – dringend
> **breakdown** – Störung, Betriebsstörung, Ausfall
> **shortage** – Engpass, Mangel
> **haulier** – Spediteur, Frachtführer

Key Phrases

Einleitung (Opening)

- We are contacting you concerning our order No. 17/280, which has still not arrived.
- Although delivery was agreed for 8 June 2003, we are still waiting for our order No. 17/280.
- Unfortunately we have to write to you yet again about delays in delivery.

Beschwerden (Complaints)

- As our own customers are waiting for deliveries, we are extremely concerned about the situation.
- We have to point out that delivery by the due date was an essential condition of the order, and you accepted this.
- Please let us know when we can expect delivery
- It is essential that the goods arrive by 2 July 2003 at the latest. We would be grateful if you could confirm this revised delivery date by fax.

Verzögerungen (Delays) | C 6

- Unless you are able to deliver by the revised date of 2 July 2003, we will have to cancel the order.
- If this extremely unsatisfactory situation does not improve, we will have to find alternative suppliers.
- The financial loss caused by the delay in delivery must be made good by the supplier.

Schlussformulierungen (Closing sentences)

- I would be grateful if you would look into this matter as soon as possible.
- I trust that you will give this matter your urgent attention.
- We are sure you understand our position, and look forward to an improvement in future.
- Please confirm receipt of this letter and your agreement to its contents.

Auf Beschwerden antworten (Replying to complaints)

- We apologize for the delay in delivery.
- We were concerned to hear that your order No. 17/280 has still not arrived.
- We are sorry to say that we will not be able to deliver your order No. 17/280 until 14 August at the earliest.
- The delay has been caused by factors completely outside our control.
- The delay has been caused by a strike…
- The delay was due to technical breakdowns/materials shortages at our Manchester plant.
- We are doing all we can to keep delays as short as possible.
- We will complete the order as soon as possible.
- As this delay has been caused by transport problems, we can only refer you to the hauliers/shipping company.

Sample letter – Complaint about delay in delivery

Duggan & Sons Ltd
7 Penston Rd
Glasgow
Lanarkshire G33 4AG

phone   0141 417 8210
fax   0141 417 8211

21 November 2003

TTX Systems Services
12 South Clerk Street
Edinburgh
Midlothian EH8 9PS

Dear Sirs

Delay in delivery of order No. 17044/03

We are writing about our order No. 17044/03 which has still not arrived.

It is essential that the goods arrive by 12 December 2003. We would be grateful if you could confirm this revised delivery date by fax.

Unless you are able to deliver by the above mentioned date, we will have to cancel our order.

I trust that you will give this matter your urgent attention.

Yours faithfully

Kathleen Lynch

Kathleen Lynch
Purchasing Department

Exercise 1

Sie arbeiten bei der *ProTec Maschinenbau AG, Industriestraße 76, 42651 Solingen,* und warten seit 3 Tagen auf eine Lieferung von Komponenten für die Fertigung, welche noch immer nicht angekommen ist.

Schreiben Sie an den Lieferanten *(Feeney Engineering Equipment plc, 6 Fitzroy Place, Glasgow, Lanarkshire G3 7RH)* und bitten Sie um eine umgehende Stellungnahme per Fax. Bestehen Sie ferner auf einer Lieferung innerhalb der nächsten sieben Werktage.

Exercise 2

Nach acht Werktagen hat sich das Unternehmen *Feeney Engineering Equipment plc* noch immer nicht gemeldet. Teilen Sie dem Unternehmen mit, dass Sie die Komponenten anderweitig beschaffen werden und Sie den Auftrag leider stornieren müssen.

Exercise 3

Als Leiter der Kundenbetreuung der Firma *Feeney Engineering Equipment plc* haben Sie von dem Vorfall mit der *ProTec Maschinenbau AG* erfahren.

Antworten Sie auf die Beschwerde des Unternehmens. Entschuldigen Sie sich für die Verspätung und begründen Sie die Verzögerung mit technischen Problemen, die in der Zwischenzeit beseitigt wurden.

Betonen Sie, dass derartige Verspätungen in Zukunft nicht mehr auftreten werden.

Ferner haben Sie mit den verantwortlichen Mitarbeitern in den Bereichen Beschaffung, Logistik und Versand gesprochen, um Verbesserungen anzuregen.

Bringen Sie darüber hinaus Ihre Hoffnung zum Ausdruck, das Unternehmen trotz der Probleme weiterhin als Kunden begrüßen zu können.

C 7 Mangelhafte Lieferung (Bad delivery)

Key Vocabulary

> dissatisfaction – Unzufriedenheit
> to complain – sich beschweren, reklamieren
> packing – Verpackung
> damaged – beschädigt
> to comply with – entsprechen, erfüllen
> missing – fehlend
> to return – zurückschicken
> to expect – erwarten
> refund – Rückerstattung
> to replace – ersetzen, austauschen

Key Phrases

Einleitung (Opening)

- I am writing to inform you that …
- We wish to inform you that ….
- I am writing to complain about …
- I wish to draw your attention to …
- We are writing to express our dissatisfaction with ….

Problem beschreiben (Describing the problem)

- The packing was damaged.
- The supplied components are damaged/defective/faulty/of poor quality.
- The supplied items did not comply with our quality specifications.
- On checking the consignment, we found that it is incomplete. The following items are missing: …
- You have obviously made a mistake and sent us the wrong articles.

Forderungen stellen (Making claims)

- We have arranged for the goods to be returned to you and expect a full refund without delay.
- Please send us the missing items as soon as possible.
- We have arranged to obtain the missing items elsewhere and will deduct them from your invoice.
- We have arranged for the defective items to be returned to you at your expense and hope to receive replacements without delay.

Ansprüche akzeptieren (Accepting claims)

- We are sorry about our mistake/the problem, and we have already despatched the correct articles.
- We regret that you have received the wrong articles/substandard goods/faulty components and we will of course replace them at our expense.
- We apologize for any inconvenience caused.

Ansprüche ablehnen (Rejecting claims)

- There seems to have been a misunderstanding. According to our records (order No. 17/280), the consignment is complete.
- Our department has examined the components and they conform to specification in every way.
- We are sure that you will understand our reasons for not accepting your claim.

Schlussformulierungen (Closing sentences)

- Please let me know as soon as possible what action you propose to take.
- I hope we can settle this matter to our satisfaction.

C 7 — Mangelhafte Lieferung (Bad delivery)

Sample letter – Complaint about defective goods

Synott IT Solutions
7 Clash Rd
Tralee
Co. Kerry
IRELAND / EIRE

27 June 2003

TTX Systems Services
12 South Clerk Street
Edinburgh
Midlothian EH8 9PS
UNITED KINGDOM

Dear Sirs

Complaint about defective items

We are writing to express our dissatisfaction with your latest delivery.

On checking the consignment, we found that almost half of the supplied components were badly damaged.

We have arranged for the defective items to be returned to you at your expense and hope to receive replacements without delay.

Yours faithfully

Maureen O'Kelly

Maureen O'Kelly
Purchasing Manager

MANGELHAFTE LIEFERUNG (BAD DELIVERY) | **C 7**

Exercise 1

Ihr Unternehmen *(Westland IT GmbH & Co KG, Schlossallee 16, 89231 Neu-Ulm)* hat von einem Zulieferer 60 Hauptplatinen *(main boards)* eingekauft.

Bei der Wareneingangskontrolle mussten Sie jedoch feststellen, dass 17 der Platinen beschädigt sind, was vermutlich auf eine unzureichende Verpackung zurückzuführen ist.

Schreiben Sie an den Lieferanten *(ICB Circuit Boards Ltd, 9 Wicklow St, Dublin, Ireland)*, reklamieren Sie die Lieferung und fordern Sie Ersatz für die beschädigten Platinen.

Exercise 2

Antworten Sie auf die Reklamation des Unternehmens *Westland IT GmbH & Co KG*. Entschuldigen Sie sich für die mangelhafte Lieferung und sichern Sie dem Unternehmen eine umgehende Ersatzlieferung zu.

Exercise 3

Letzte Woche hat Ihre Firma *(DuraPrint OHG, Am Südhang 18, 66121 Saarbrücken)* von Ihrem Händler eine Lieferung Druckerzubehör erhalten. Beim Auspacken mussten Sie jedoch feststellen, dass die falschen Druckerpatronen *(printer cartridges)* geliefert wurden. Die darüber hinaus bestellten Druckerkabel fehlten komplett.

Schreiben Sie an den Händler *(O'Grady Print Supplies Ltd, 4 Breydon Avenue, Cusworth Lane, Doncaster DN5 8LA)* und beanstanden Sie die Falschlieferung.

Exercise 4

Sie haben von der Firma *CD Centre, 510 Oxford St, London W1C 2PZ* eine Reklamation über eine Falschlieferung erhalten. Der zuständige Sachbearbeiter in Ihrem Unternehmen, *Kevin Breen*, hat Ihnen jedoch versichert, dass die Bestellung ordnungsgemäß abgewickelt wurde.

Antworten Sie *(Remmert Audio Technik KG, Nordring 7, 38102 Braunschweig)* auf die Reklamation und teilen Sie dem Unternehmen mit, dass alle bestellten Artikel (Bestellung Nr. 221/498/0703) ordnungsgemäß verpackt und verschickt wurden. Alle Sendungen werden darüber hinaus vor dem Verlassen des Lagers noch einmal überprüft.

C 8   Mahnungen (Reminders)

Key Vocabulary

> **invoice** – Rechnung
> **to settle** – begleichen, bezahlen
> **to overlook** – übersehen
> **despite** – trotz
> **outstanding** – offen stehend, ausstehend, unbezahlt
> **to insist on** – bestehen auf
> **to start proceedings** – gerichtliche Schritte unternehmen
> **matter** – Angelegenheit
> **solicitor** – Anwalt, Rechtsanwalt
> **immediate settlement** – sofortige Begleichung

Key Phrases

Einleitung (Opening)

- We are contacting you regarding our invoice of 25 May 2003, which you still have not settled.
- We are writing concerning our invoice of 25 May 2003, which we feel sure you have overlooked.
- You may have overlooked our statement of account.
- Please note that your invoice No. 883/03 is overdue.
- You may have overlooked that a balance of € 625.00 is still open on your account.
- It has come to our attention that you still have not settled our invoice of 25 May 2003, despite our reminder.
- We are writing for a third time concerning our invoice of 25 May 2003, which is still outstanding.

Zahlung verlangen (Demanding payment)

- We are sure that you will settle the invoice now that we have reminded you about it.
- Now that we have reminded you a second time we confidently expect your remittance.

Mahnungen (Reminders) | C 8

- After this second reminder, we expect payment by 30 June 2003.
- We must ask you to remit the amount covering your current due account.
- You have not reacted to our previous reminders, although we gave you ample time to pay. Now we must insist on payment in full within 10 days.

Weitere Maßnahmen (Further action)

- Unless we receive payment in full by 21 July 2003 we will start proceedings without further notice.
- Unless we receive payment in full by 21 July 2003 we will have no choice but to place the matter with our solicitors.
- Unless we receive payment in full by 21 July 2003 it is with regret that the matter will be placed with our solicitors.

Schlussformulierungen (Closing sentences)

- If you have settled the invoice in the meantime, please ignore this letter.
- We look forward to receiving payment within the next few days.
- We look forward to receiving your remittance soon.
- We are sure that no further reminder will be necessary and look forward to an immediate settlement.

C 8 | Mahnungen (Reminders)

Sample letter – Reminder

TTX Systems Services
12 South Clerk Street
Edinburgh
Midlothian EH8 9PS

10 March 2003

O'Brien Office Services
Eileen O'Brien
27 Windsor Rd
Manchester
Lancashire M19 2EB

Dear Ms O'Brien

Non-payment of invoice No. 44719/EOB/03

We are writing concerning our invoice No. 44719/EOB/03 of 12 February 2003, which is still outstanding.

Please remit the invoice amount of £ 320.00 to our account No. 499 732 110 with the Abbey National, Edinburgh.

If you have settled the invoice in the meantime, please ignore this letter.

Yours sincerely

Deirdre McNamara

Deirdre McNamara
Customer Accounts

Mahnungen (Reminders) | C 8

Exercise 1

Sie arbeiten in der Buchhaltungsabteilung der Firma *Huber & Co. KG, Finkenweg 9, 90489 Nürnberg*.

Ein langjähriger Kunde, *Sean Murphy, 11 Bridle Lane, London W1R 3HL*, hat seine Rechnung vom letzten Monat noch nicht bezahlt.

Schreiben Sie eine erste Zahlungserinnerung und bitten Sie um die Überweisung des ausstehenden Betrages von 310,00 €.

Exercise 2

Sie sind Geschäftsführer der Firma *Fischer Büromaschinen OHG, Am Wall 23, 23554 Lübeck*.

Schreiben Sie eine zweite Mahnung an das Unternehmen *FX Supplies Ltd, P.O Box 37, Manchester, Lancashire M60 1BZ,* bezüglich der noch ausstehenden Rechnung (Nr. 6231/3) über 12.340,00 €.

Fordern Sie das Unternehmen auf, die Rechnung innerhalb von 3 Wochen zu begleichen.

Exercise 3

Schreiben Sie als Geschäftsführer der Firma *Fischer Büromaschinen OHG* eine letzte Mahnung an das Unternehmen *FX Supplies Ltd* bezüglich der noch ausstehenden Rechnung (Nr. 6231/3) über 12.340,00 €.

Drohen Sie dem Unternehmen mit Konsequenzen und machen Sie deutlich, dass Sie umgehend gerichtliche Schritte einleiten werden, falls die Zahlung nicht innerhalb der nächsten 10 Tage erfolgt.

Exercise 4

Sie arbeiten in der Buchhaltung der Firma *ProShop GmbH, Ringstraße 81, 91052 Erlangen*.

Sie haben von dem Unternehmen *ComLine plc, 82 Barrack Rd, Guildford, Surrey GU2 9ZW,* irrtümlicherweise eine Mahnung bezüglich der Rechnung Nr. 112/84603 erhalten.

Teilen Sie dem Unternehmen mit, dass die Rechnung bereits vor 3 Wochen beglichen wurde.

C 9 Memos

Layout of memos

Memos are used for internal communication, e.g. writing to staff, department heads and so on. A memo is usually fairly short and the language is more direct than in a letter. Focus on relevant information and leave out unnecessary details, but be polite.

Memo

To: All Department Heads

From: Imelda Mc Dermott, IT Coordinator

Subject: IT meeting on 10 April 2003

Date: 6 April 2003

Please note that the IT meeting will take place in the conference room on 10 April 2003 at 1400 hrs.

Attendance is mandatory, as you will receive new user IDs and passwords.

If you are unable to attend, please contact me immediately.

Exercise 1

Sie sind als Leiter der Controlling-Abteilung beschäftigt. In den letzten Wochen haben Sie einen erheblichen Anstieg bei den Spesen für Außendienstmitarbeiter festgestellt.

Schreiben Sie an den Leiter der Vertriebsabteilung, *Kevin Foley*. Bitten Sie ihn seine Mitarbeiter daran zu erinnern, dass die vereinbarten Höchstgrenzen für die Abrechnung von Spesen nicht überschritten werden dürfen.

Exercise 2

Ihr Unternehmen hat sich entschlossen, ein neues Firmenlogo zu verwenden. Schreiben Sie an das Verkaufspersonal des Unternehmens und weisen Sie die Mitarbeiter darauf hin, dass vom nächsten Monat an nur noch das neue Logo verwendet werden darf.

Die Mitarbeiter im Verkauf sollen sich daher die neuen Materialien (Visitenkarten, Broschüren, Kataloge, Briefpapier, Kugelschreiber etc.) in den nächsten Tagen abholen.

Exercise 3

Sie arbeiten als Koordinator in der IT-Abteilung. In der nächsten Woche werden in dem Unternehmen die Datenbank-Server *(data base servers)* ausgetauscht.

Schreiben Sie an alle Abteilungen und weisen Sie die Mitarbeiter darauf hin, dass aufgrund der Arbeiten ein Zugriff auf Kundendaten vorübergehend (von Freitag, 13.00 Uhr bis Montag, 8.00 Uhr) nicht möglich sein wird.

Exercise 4

Sie sind als Assistent der Geschäftsleitung tätig. Ihr Chef hat Sie beauftragt, ein Memo an die Belegschaft zu verfassen, um folgende Probleme anzusprechen: häufige private Nutzung der Fotokopierer, zahlreiche private Telefongespräche auf Kosten der Firma und eine zunehmende private Nutzung des Internets während der Arbeitszeit.

Weisen Sie die Mitarbeiter darauf hin, dass dieses Verhalten zum Nachteil des Unternehmens und damit zum Nachteil aller Beschäftigten ist. Bringen Sie zum Ausdruck, dass ein kooperatives Verhalten der Mitarbeiter erwartet wird. Andernfalls werden disziplinarische Konsequenzen unumgänglich sein.

Exercise 5

Schreiben Sie an alle Abteilungen und weisen Sie die Mitarbeiter darauf hin, dass sich das für Freitag, 14.00 Uhr, geplante Seminar „Internet-Sicherheit" leider auf Mittwoch, 16.00 Uhr, verschiebt. Alle anderen Details (Raum 22, 2. Stock, West-Gebäude) bleiben bestehen.

C 10 Berichte (Reports)

Layout of reports

A report contains the following 5 sections:

Terms of reference: Outline <u>what</u> the report is about and <u>who</u> it is for.

Proceedings: Explain how the information was obtained, e.g. interviews, questionnaires, statistics etc.

Findings: Present the facts provided by the information.

Conclusions: Explicate what the facts mean.

Recommendations: Suggest suitable measures or solutions.

Tips for writing reports

- Reports have to be clear, concise, and matter-of-fact.
- Language should be factual and neutral.
- Provide an appropriate heading.
- The report has to be signed and dated.

Example of layout

Computer Training Seminars

Terms of reference
The Managing Director, Sean O'Brien, has asked me to write this report on the proposed computer training seminars for members of staff.

Proceedings
A sample of workers and superiors was questioned and asked for their opinions.

Findings
- Most workers thought PC training seminars were a good idea.
- The majority of superiors expected an increase in productivity and efficiency.
- Some members of staff would prefer vouchers for external training seminars.
- A few workers suggested time off instead.

Conclusions
In general most workers and superiors were in favour of the proposed training seminars.

Recommendations
The proposed PC training seminars should be introduced for a trial period of 4 weeks.

(signature)
(today's date)

BERICHTE (REPORTS) | C 10

Exercise 1

Sie arbeiten in einem Unternehmen, das Drucker für den *Consumer*-Bereich herstellt. In den letzten Monaten sind die Umsätze merklich zurückgegangen. Ihr Vorgesetzter, Thomas Burke, hat Sie beauftragt, einen Bericht bezüglich der rückläufigen Umsätze zu erstellen.

Benutzen Sie die folgenden Informationen, um den Bericht zu erstellen:

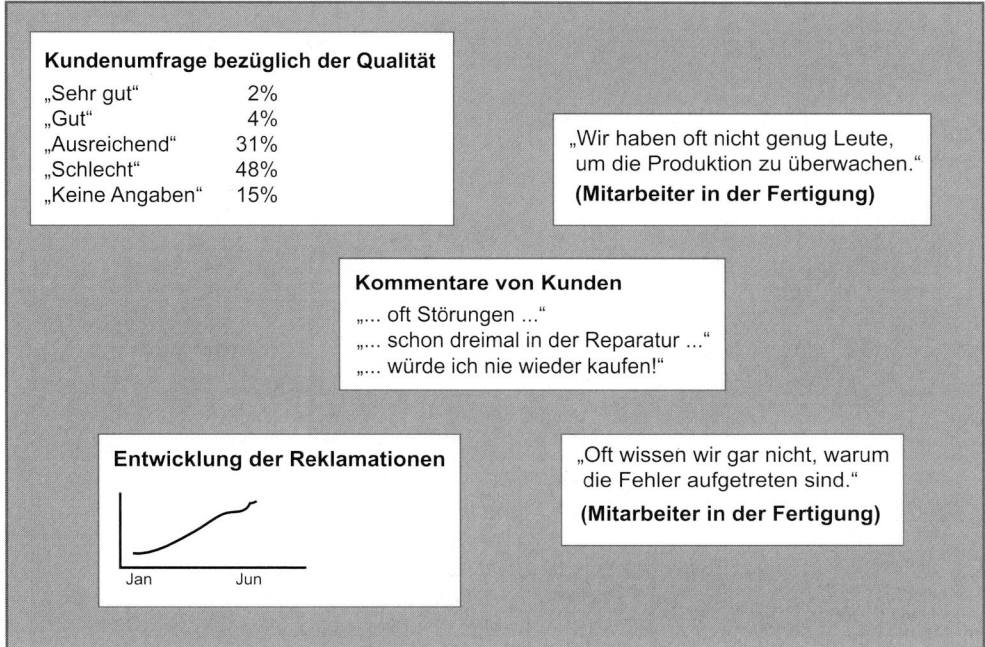

Exercise 2

Ihr Unternehmen erwägt eine Fusion mit einem Konkurrenzunternehmen. Der Vorstand hat Sie beauftragt, einen Bericht über die gegenwärtige Lage zu erstellen.

Benutzen Sie die folgenden Informationen, um den Bericht zu erstellen:

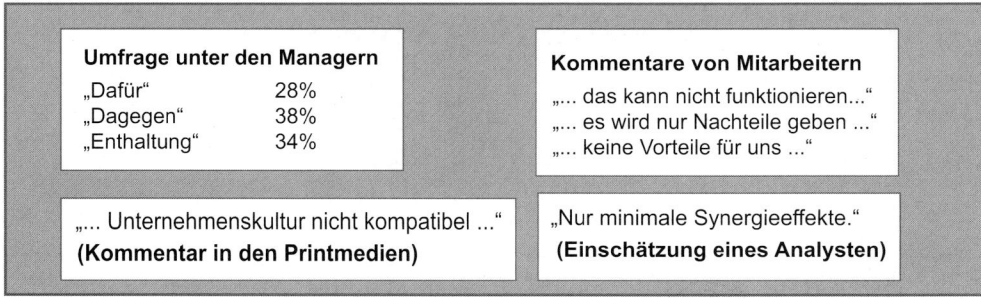

C 11 Bewerbungen (Applications)

Sample Cover Letter

Claudia Becker
Bekscher Berg 79
33100 Paderborn
GERMANY

13 April 2003

ITS Systems Ltd
c/o Mr Sean Murphy
12 Grafton Street
Dublin
IRELAND

Dear Mr Murphy

Application for the position of Assistant Marketing Manager

With reference to your advertisement in *The Times* of 12 April 2003, I am applying for the position of Assistant Marketing Manager. The position seems to fit very well with my education, experience, and carrer interests.

According to the advertisement, your postition requires excellent communication skills, computer literacy, and a university degree in marketing. I will be graduating from the University of Paderborn in July with a degree in business studies.
My studies included courses in marketing, computer science, economics, and international management. I understand the position also requires a candidate who works well under pressure, and is able to deal with people in departments throughout the firm. These are skills I developed both in my course work and in my recent internships.

My background and goals seem to match your requirements well. I am confident that I can perform the job effectively, and I am excited about the idea of working for a dynamic, internationally recognized firm.

Thank you for your consideration. I would appreciate a personal interview at your convenience, and look forward to hearing from you.

Yours sincerely

Claudia Becker

Sample Curriculum Vitae (CV)

Curriculum Vitae

Claudia Becker
Bekscher Berg 79
33100 Paderborn
GERMANY
phone   0049 5252 941296
email   claudia.becker@web.de

Personal Details

Date of Birth	19 October 1971
Place of Birth	Paderborn, Germany
Nationality	German
Marital Status	Single

Work Experience

09/99 – present	Market Research Assistant, WebNet GmbH
10/98 – 08/99	Part-time Sales Representative, Schmitt & Co KG
07/98 – 09/98	Freelance Lecturer, EDV Akademie Paderborn

Education

10/94 – 06/98	University of Paderborn, Degree in Business Studies
09/91 – 09/94	Apprenticeship – Bank Clerk, WestLB, Dortmund
09/82 – 07/91	Grammar School, Schloß Neuhaus, A-Level

Internships / Projects

07/96 – 09/96	Web Design Project, WebNet GmbH
07/95 – 09/95	Internship – Sales Department, Schmitt & Co KG

Skills

Computing	Windows 2000/XP, Office 2000/XP, Lotus Notes
Languages	English – fluent
	Spanish – good knowledge
	French – basic knowledge

Sample Resume

Resume

Claudia Becker
Bekscher Berg 79
33100 Paderborn
GERMANY
0049 5252 941296
claudia.becker@web.de

Objective
Position of Assistant Marketing Manager

Summary of Qualifications
Over three years of broad-based experience as Market Research Assistant. Proven track record of successfully managing IT projects.

Professional Experience
More than three years of experience as Market Research Assistant at WebNet GmbH. Streamlined the tracking of customers. Worked with interdisciplinary team on various projects. Promoted for outstanding work within 6 months.

Education
University of Paderborn, Degree in Business Studies (June 1998). Courses included marketing, computer science, economics, and international management.

Skills
Excellent IT skills – Microsoft Windows 2000/XP, Microsoft Office 2000/XP Microsoft Certified Professional, Microsoft Office User Specialist Master Certificate, Lotus Notes. Extensive language skills: Fluent in German, English, and Spanish.

Personal Interests / Leisure Activities
Triathlon, Diving, Mountaineering

C 12 Die 13 Incoterms

Incoterms are standardized trade definitions used in international sales contracts.

The 13 Incoterms	
EXW Ex Works Ab Werk	"Ex-Works" means that the seller delivers when he places the goods at the disposal of the buyer at the seller's premises or another named place (warehouse, factory etc.). The buyer has to bear all costs and risks.
FCA Free Carrier Frei Frachtführer	"Free Carrier" means that the seller delivers the goods, cleared for export, to the carrier specified by the buyer at the named place.
FAS Free alongside Ship Frei Längsseite Schiff	"Free alongside Ship" means that the seller delivers when the goods are placed alongside the vessel at the named port of shipment. The buyer has to bear all costs and risks of loss of or damage to the goods from that moment. The seller has to clear the goods for export.
FOB Free on Board Frei an Bord	"Free on Board" means that the seller delivers when the goods pass the ship's rail at the specified port of shipment. The buyer has to bear all costs and risks of loss of or damage to the goods from that point.
CFR Cost and Freight Kosten und Fracht	"Cost and Freight" means that the seller delivers when the goods pass the ship's rail at the specified port of shipment. The seller has to pay the costs and freight necessary to bring the goods to the named port of destination. The buyer has to bear the risk of loss of or damage to the goods, as well as any additional costs due to events occurring during the transport, after the time of delivery.
CIF Cost, Insurance, Freight Kosten, Versicherung, Fracht	"Cost, Insurance, Freight" means that the seller delivers when the goods pass the ship's rail at the specified port of shipment. The seller has to pay the costs and freight necessary to bring the goods to the named port of destination. The buyer has to bear the risk of loss of or damage to the goods, as well as any additional costs due to events occurring during the transport, after the time of delivery. The seller, however, has to insure the goods against loss or damage.

CPT **Carriage Paid to** Frachtfrei	"Carriage Paid to" means that the seller delivers the goods to the specified carrier. The seller has to pay the cost of carriage necessary to bring the goods to the named destination. The buyer has to bear all risks and any other costs after the time of delivery.
CIP **Carriage and** **Insurance Paid** Frachtfrei versichert	"Carriage and Insurance Paid" means that the seller delivers the goods to the specified carrier. The seller has to pay the cost of carriage necessary to bring the goods to the named destination. The buyer has to bear all risks and any other costs after the time of delivery. The seller, however, has to insure the goods against loss or damage during the carriage.
DAF **Delivered at Frontier** Geliefert Grenze	"Delivered at Frontier" means that the seller delivers when he places the goods at the disposal of the buyer on the arriving means of transport – not unloaded, and not cleared for import – at the specified frontier, but before the customs border.
DES **Delivered Ex Ship** Geliefert ab Schiff	"Delivered Ex Ship" means that the seller delivers when he places the goods at the disposal of the buyer on board the ship – not cleared for import – at the named port of destination.
DEQ **Delivered Ex Quay** Geliefert ab Kai	"Delivered Ex Quay" means that the seller delivers when he places the goods at the disposal of the buyer on board the ship – not cleared for import – on the quay (wharf) at the named port of destination. The buyer has to clear the goods for import and pay for all formalities, duties, taxes and charges involved.
DDU **Delivered Duty** **Unpaid** Geliefert unverzollt	"Delivered Duty Unpaid" means that the seller delivers when he places the goods at the disposal of the buyer on the arriving means of transport – not unloaded and not cleared for import – at the named place of destination. The buyer has to clear the goods for import and pay for all formalities, duties, taxes and charges involved.
DDP **Delivered Duty Paid** Geliefert verzollt	"Delivered Duty Paid" means that the seller delivers the goods to the buyer, cleared for import, and not unloaded from any arriving means of transport at the named place of destination. The seller has to bear all costs and risks, clear the goods for import and pay for all formalities, duties, taxes and charges involved.

C 12 | Die 13 Incoterms

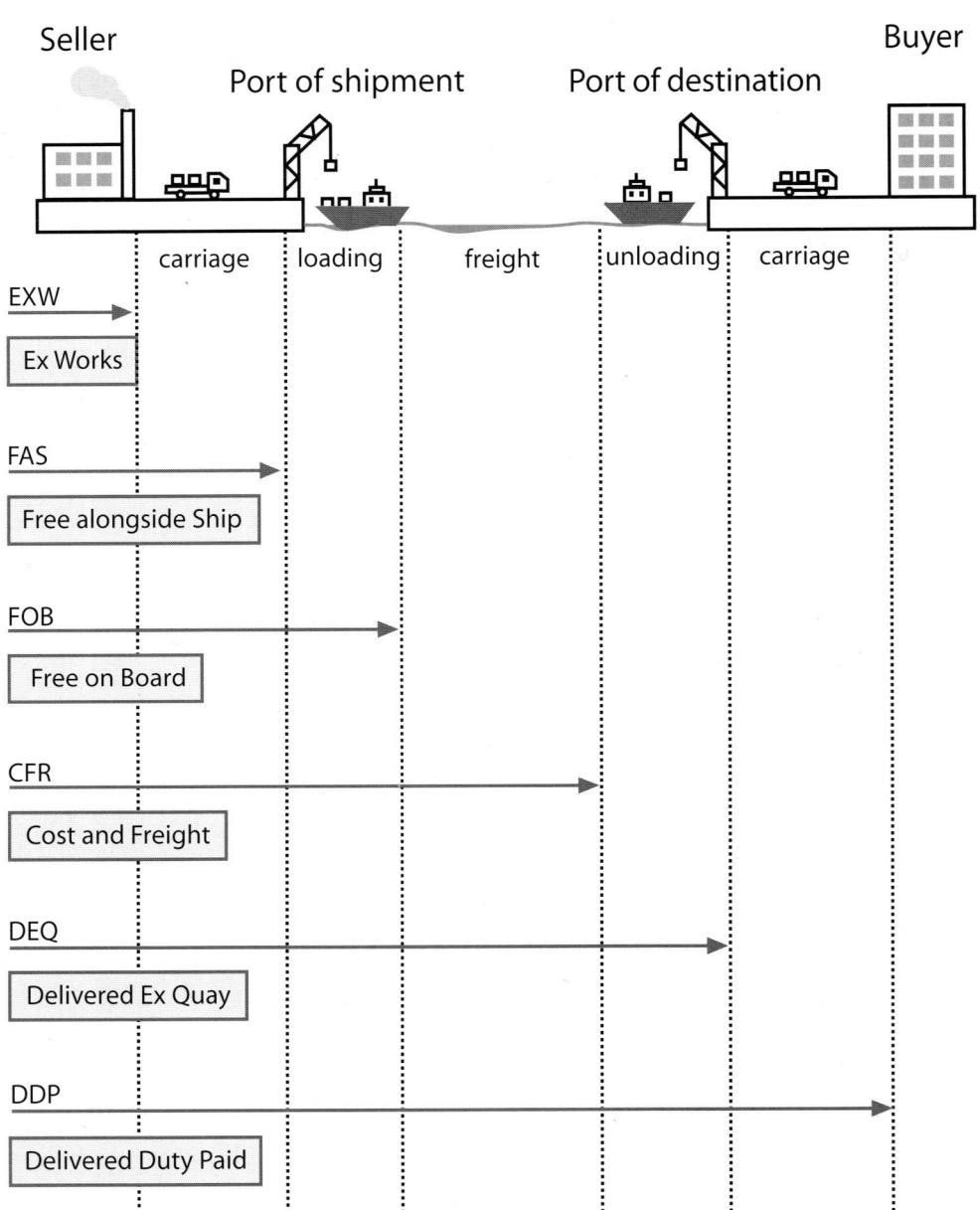

D

Answer Key

D | Answer Key

> **Answer Key A**

A 1 Exercise – Scheduling reservations

Customer	Event	Suite	Staff	Time
Aran Mills	Fashion Show	Munster	Patrick	1630 hrs
Irish Crystal	Product Launch	Leinster	Patricia	1400 hrs
Kelly's Brewery	AGM	Ulster	Patrick	1000 hrs
Tara Books	Press Reception	Connacht	Christina	0900 hrs

A 1 Exercise – Calling a meeting

To: All Department Heads
From: Managing Director
Subject: Meeting – Restructuring of business units
Date: [today's date]

The meeting regarding the restructuring of business units will take place on the 28th of next month at 2.10 pm in room 19 (3rd floor).

The meeting will take approximately $1\,^1/_2$ hours. Please make sure you are on time and remember to bring the latest quarterly report.

A provisional agenda is attached.

Please send a short note if you are not able to attend.

A 2 Exercise – Deciding on a conference venue

1. Meadowlands
2. 2
3. 2
4. The Brandon
5. 2
6. 3
7. Horan's
8. 4
9. 2
10. 4 miles
11. Yes
12. Benner's
13. Benner's
14. No
15. Benner's
16. 2
17. 1
18. The Brandon
19. 3
20. No

A 2   Exercise – Requesting information

To: info@ccc.ie
Subject: Information about conference facilities

Dear Sir/Madam

Please forward us your latest brochure and price-list.

We look forward to hearing from you soon.

Yours faithfully

A 3   Exercise – Arranging hotel reservations

Company	Town	Hotel	Arrival	Departure	Consultant
Bewley's	Dublin	Oakfield Arms	22nd	26th	John
Data Tec	Tralee	Brandon	4th	6th	Declan
ITC Ltd	Galway	Horan's	17th	20th	Kate
OfficeLine	Limerick	Benner's	8th	9th	Steve

A 3   Exercise – Booking a hotel room

To: bookings@oakfield-arms.ie
Subject: Booking, O'Sullivan, 22nd – 26th

Dear Sir/Madam

We would like to book a room for Mr John O'Sullivan from the 22nd to the 26th of this month.

Furthermore, we would be grateful if you could provide a rental car.

Please confirm the booking by fax.

We look forward to hearing from you soon.

Yours faithfully

A 4 Exercise – Scheduling job interviews

Applicant's Name	Age	Present Employer	Starting Time
Caffrey, Ann	23	OfficeWorks	0900 hrs
Casey, Noel	21	TrendLine	0930 hrs
Connell, Bridget	25	Giles	1000 hrs
O'Donovan, Mary	22	presently without job	1045 hrs
O'Shea, John	25	OfficeWorks	1115 hrs
Sullivan, Maureen	26	Parker Smyth	1145 hrs

A 4 Exercise – Arranging an interview

To: bridget.connell@webmail.com
CC: helen.smyth@pc-company.ie
Subject: Job interview – 9. April 2003

Dear Ms Connell

We would like to invite you for an interview on Wednesday, 9 April 2003 at 10 am.

Please remember to bring all relevant certificates.

Your sincerely

A 5 Exercise – Making a reservation

Hotel Booking Form

COMPLETE IN BLOCK CAPITALS

Hotel	MEADOWLANDS	Fax	00353 21 377 855
Town	CORK		
Name	MS HELEN O'BRIEN		
Company	SOUTHBRIDGE INVESTMENTS PLC		
Address	12 KINGSWAY		
	LONDON WC2B 6XF		
Telephone	020 7648 7410		

☑ single room Check-in 21ST 7 PM
☐ double room Check-out 23RD
☐ twin-bedded room Other requirements:
(Please tick)
– BATH AND SHOWER
– RENTAL CAR
– INTERNET ACCESS

Date _____
Signature _____

D Answer Key

A 5   Exercise – Finalizing details

Please call the Meadowlands Hotel on 021 377 888 to discuss the details of the rental car.

A 6   Exercise – Selecting a supplier

1	10	11	TMT Ltd
2	Smyth & Co	12	4 miles
3	5	13	6
4	6	14	Smith & Co
5	No	15	4
6	5	16	4
7	2	17	Yes
8	Yes	18	Smyth & Co
9	No	19	2
10	2	20	4

A 6   Exercise – Delegating tasks

To: John Carrol, Purchasing Manager
From: Managing Director
Subject: Appointment with new supplier
Date: [today's date]

We have decided in favour of Smyth & Co as our new supplier.

Please make an appointment for next week. Their phone number is 061 322 749 55.

Answer Key | D

A 7 Exercise – Processing orders

DELIVERY NOTE

COMPLETE IN CAPITALS

Company	PC PLANET
Account No	7109224
Ordered on (date)	25 MARCH 2003
Ordered by (name)	THOMAS HARP
Delivery Address	47 HENRY STREET
	DUBLIN
Delivery Date	28 MARCH 2003
Payment Method (please tick)	cash ☐ credit card ☐ cheque ☐ account ☑

Catalogue No	Description	Quantity	Unit Price in €
PR1219	PRINTER	10	169.00
CA8801	CABLE	10	3.50
SO3648	SILVERLINE OFFICE SOFTWARE	15	49.90
ME4486	DVDs – RECORDABLE	20	38.90

A 7 Exercise – Problems with deliveries

To: thomas.harp@pcplanet.ie
Subject: Ordered printers PR1219

Dear Mr Harp

The printer model PR1219 is temporarily out of stock. Therefore, we will supply the model PR1239 at the same price.

If you are not satisfied with the printers, we will certainly change them next week.

Yours sincerely

D | Answer Key

A 8   Exercise – Managing performance records

TRAINING REPORT

Company   ITS Ltd.

Course Title Office Applications

Course Length 2 weeks

D = Distinction
C = Credit
P = Pass
F = Fail
A = Absent

Candidates	Word Processing	Spreadsheet Calculation	Data Base	Presentations	Internet and Email
Michael O'Donnell	C	P		C	
Ted O'Neill			F		
Maureen O'Brien			F	D	C
Mary Burke	C	C			
Patricia O'Leary		D	C	D	D
Patrick O'Carroll	F	A		F	
Brian Gallagher	D		C	D	
Fiona Doyle		P			

(Exam Results)

A 8   Exercise – Requesting resources

To: Training Officer
From: Managing Director
Subject: Additional examination room
Date: [today's date]

We will need an additional examination room for 12 people on Thursday next week. Windows XP (operating system) and Office XP have to be installed on all PCs.

A 9   Exercise – Organizing the collection of guests

Pick-up Time	Guest	Flight	From	To
0830 hrs	Ted Murphy	EI 698	Cork	Gatwick
1130 hrs	Pat Mahony	TW 8346	New York	Stansted
1400 hrs	Owen Carrol	LH 412	Frankfurt	Heathrow
1600 hrs	Anne McCarthy	EI 502	Dublin	Heathrow
2020 hrs	Mary Lynch	RA 704	Milan	Luton

A 9   Exercise – Changing arrangements

Due to a delay in Milan I will arrive in Luton at 8.20 pm on flight RA 704 and not as planned in Heathrow at 11 am on BA 5869.

➤ Answer Key B

B   Introduction

Model SWOT Structure: STMicroelectronics

Case Study Topic: Analyze the factors impacting ST's response to cyclical changes in demand

S. ST have spread their R&D and manufacturing operations over the whole world, in order to better adapt to local customers' needs.

W. The company has no standard guiding the development and production of new systems, and there is no coordinated workflow to optimize the global supply chain. This decentralized approach leads different departments to waste millions of dollars and much time in working out similar solutions. As the supply chain

D | Answer Key

operations aren't standardized, hundreds of managers will be unaware of effective solutions that colleagues in similar positions all over the world may have developed.

O. The diversified operations support close relationships with both customers and suppliers, while limit the threat of relying closely on a few suppliers for highly sensitive material.

T. However, the decentralized structure is preventing global solutions for bundling purchasing power, and for smoothing demand across geographic areas.

Model SWOT Analysis (75 words)

S. ST is World's No. 3 chipmaker. It is an innovative company (with a company-wide award system), and also rates high in efficiency and effectiveness benchmarks.

W. No standards to the development and production of new systems; no coordinated workflow linking the global supply chain; various departments are wasting time and resources in working out similar solutions.

O. R&D and manufacturing facilities are spread over geographic areas, in order to better adapt to local customers' needs, and to source local talent; distributed political risk.

T. Overall, the doughnut structure is preventing competitive global solutions both for bundling purchasing power, and for smoothing demand across geographic areas.

B 1.2

(1) Explain what an economic system is.

An economic system is a society's cultural, and legal framework for producing, distributing, and marketing the goods and services desired by its members.

(2) State the object of antitrust policy.

Government enforces rules and regulations to foster competition.

(3) Identify four realities of the Global Network Economy (GNE).

(a) The competitive price in a GNE market is often ill defined.

(b) The difference between price and cost is no longer useful as a measure of market power.

(c) The changing nature of products and services makes it difficult to define relevant markets for antitrust.

(d) The contemporary rise of winner-take-all markets makes it harder to identify illegitimate monopoly power and foul competitive practices.

B 1.5 Discursive Case Solution – Nortel

1. Key Issue

(a) Problem Identification

When Nortel's senior management realized that the customer base was shifting away from copper wire to fiber optic networks they decided to change their strategy. The company decided to go from "vertical to virtual". In essence, the company's managers realized that their corporate effectiveness was outdated. They had a "low cost leadership" structure, which actually slowed them down. This style had strong central authority and tight cost controls. They had focused on frequent and detailed reports, standard operating procedures and close supervision. The changing environment however sent them a strong signal to change their organizational structure to a more flexible and customer focused one. The current problems have arisen because Nortel underwent this wrenching change in the space of only two years. Rather than managing this transformation piecemeal, Nortel bit the bullet with a very aggressive plan.

(b) Claim

The restructured Nortel have to act looser and less rigid with strong coordination between the departments. They also have to measure their costs, maintain customer loyalty and push empowerment to its employees with customer contact. This suggested "Focus" approach is a combination of the "Low-cost leadership" and "Differentiation" structures.

2. Analysis

Some of Nortel's first steps involved were to identify what exactly needed to change. They looked at their internal processes and realized that companies failed because their processes weren't correct and that in order to go from a $20 billion company to a $40 billion one, they had to change those existing processes and systems. Their operative goals now focused on Innovation. They had to make their internal structure more flexible and ready to adapt to changes in the triple-digit growing industry of telecommunications. They decided to aggressively sell off its production facilities to contract manufacturers in order to revamp its production & supply chain management processes. This allowed them direct communication and response links to their customers and suppliers.

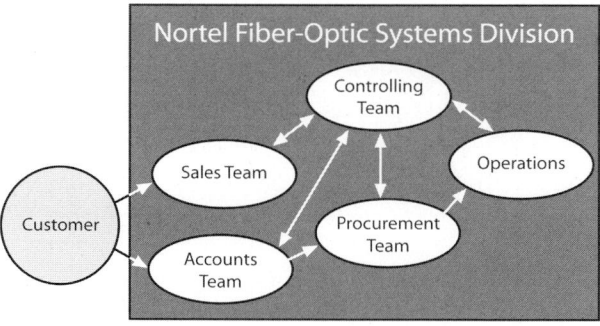

Old Nortel Order House Process

Part of their innovation strategy was through Supply-Chain Management. This involved building new relationships with all their suppliers. Nortel's impressive conquest of the optical Internet equipment market is a classic case of how the allianced organizational and operational model helped a traditional manufacturer achieve rapid and transformative change.

Nortel also wedged its foot in the door for routers and specialized computers that direct traffic on a network by buying Bay Networks, Inc. Bay Net-works was the number two maker of computer networking equipment. Nortel stuck by the stock option plans that were a major part of the employee's compensation. The stock options gave the employees a direct cut in the success of their hard work. Next, Nortel spent over $11 billion in nine months to acquire various technology companies. It was buying the technology and the talented employees of the purchased firms, but not the production capacity. In fact, Nortel started selling off 15 of its manufacturing sites and transferred 9000 employees over to contract manufacturers. This secured Nortel's position away from the traditional manufacturer status.

Supply Chain Management therefore became crucial to Nortel's future success. They started by throwing out the five lines of business and incorporating a new "customer-centric" model, which placed each major customer with its own dedicated supply chain management team called an "order house". The order house was a virtual unit with team members spread out geographically with no physical plant. Communication is in real time from customer to Nortel to supplier. The Internet became a central force to make everything happen quickly. Suppliers in turn, felt more confident in Nortel because they were able to see Nortel's plans as well as, Nortel's customers' needs immediately. This in turn pushed the supplier to work more closely with Nortel to give their (now mutual) customers what they needed. Their customer-centric structure also enabled them to predict future needs – dependent on their level of access to the information. Nortel also pushed their suppliers by getting them involved in an "end-to-end fulfillment perspective" which had them involved in every aspect of a particular customer design. Instead of trying to bargain with multiple sources for the best prices, now they work as a link between their customers and suppliers. This required more trust, demanded loyalty and seemed to be exactly what the company was looking for. Unfortunately for Nortel, revenue and earnings continued to fall below Wall Street expectations sending their stock prices downward.

New Nortel Order House Process

Supply Chain Management Team

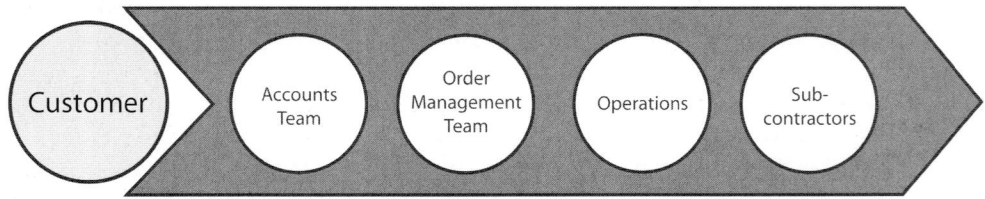

Nortel's strength lay in their ability to make a paradigm shift from old world, traditional type thinking to new world, quick and flexible thinking. They achieved this in only 24 months. They utilized a supply-chain management approach, which allowed them to break down walls that were between the all the players. When Nortel dropped the proverbial "wall" and allowed the suppliers to access the same information they had for their customers, they allowed faster and more accurate service to their customers needs. The suppliers also felt more loyal to Nortel because they were a part of the process rather than just a tool. The customers were able to benefit from having both Nortel and Nortel's suppliers working on their problems at the same time. They were also able to adjust for potential needs or problems based on recommendations from suppliers who were able to readily access the customer information. This benefited all parties. Notwithstanding their current difficulties, Nortel's overall strategy is strategically sound.

However, Nortel's reliance on the company stock plans in order to "empower" their employees has backfired with the sudden drop in the stock market. Because the stock options were such a large part of the employee compensation package, the employees benefited when the company was successful. Unfortunately, the employees are affected when the stock market loses faith in the company as well. They may have to rearrange the entire compensation package in order to retain good workers. If employees are not properly compensated for their work for the company, Nortel may end up losing key players or having to spend millions on revamping a potentially failing benefit program.

3. Alternative Solutions

Nortel's future opportunities may come out of the volatility in the market. Although most companies are having a hard time right now, it's feasible to say that the more focused, yet flexible, Nortel become, the better the chance is that they will be able to take up some of the market share of their failing competitors. One of their competitors, Lucent Technologies, lost its focus and credibility with customers and shareholders. Nortel have a good chance of winning over lost customers because they have the right tools in place and are ready to adapt to anything their customers throw at them. They just need to stay afloat in this storm on Wall Street. Therefore, instead of shedding more skilled personnel, the most important asset in a web-based network, the company should consider divesting some acquisitions that have not been fully integrated into their supply chain, like Bay Networks.

Although Nortel have succeeded in driving down inventory levels on their balance sheet, the present slowdown in telecommunication networks has created bottlenecks in the equipment sold customers' networks, waiting to be turned on. Despite their dedication to transparent communications, this surplus inventory sitting on their customers' balance sheets demonstrates that Nortel's interaction with customers has not always been effective. Therefore, Nortel's supply chain staff could expand their communications links between the company's customers and its suppliers by working from a common database, to determine proactively where the constraints are and find ways to work around them. Nortel must realize that their focus on new technology is right, but the logistics are just as important.

> D | ANSWER KEY

4. Recommended Solution

Competitive threats won't come from the giants, like Cisco Systems or Juniper, but rather from the small, unknown entrepreneur who is probably 18 years old, sitting at his computer between his undergraduate math and gym classes. The future threat is going to come from the younger generation who are building quickly on the Internet foundations that are in place. They don't think inside a box but instead try to find creative ways to make things happen. Many times it's by accident. Nortel need to spend money on developing its industry, employees and new technologies in their industry to stay ahead of their competitors. Being in one of the fastest changing industries ever, they need to "stay ahead or be dead". They can't ever go back to sitting idol. Changing to a "supply chain management" approach was only the first step. They have to make the future for themselves.

(1400 words)

B 2.2 Knowledge Check

(1) Explain the factors driving and limiting a company's size.

A company's size is determined by profit-maximizing motives. Some activities can be performed more efficiently within a company than in the marketplace. The higher monitoring costs associated with greater size offset the aim of a company to undertake more activities itself.

(2) Which monitoring and controlling activities help secure a company's effectiveness?

A company must decide how to organize itself internally to generate employee commitment and to prevent opportunistic behavior and bad decisions. The multidivisional structure evolved to help companies monitor and control employees' actions more efficiently.

(3) How does a company secure the loyalty of its managers?

If managers do not run a company efficiently or maximize profits, it may be driven out of business or taken over by others. Therefore, the company must design incentives and controls to ensure that managers operate to maximize profits and not to pursue different goals.

B 2.4 Model Case Solution – Enron Corp. – Out-of-the-Money

Case Study Topic: Applying the Transaction Cost Model, Does Enron's Disintegrated Structure Fit Its Strategy?

1. Enron has suffered a steep fall in revenue, due to increasing competition and customer defection. The resulting liquidity squeeze led to a further loss of confidence within the financial community. For Enron, the most pressing issue is regain investor trust by increasing revenue and strengthening its financial position.

2. To regain credibility, Enron must reduce transaction costs and solve agency problems. The company enjoys huge economies of scale as an energy trader and has successfully pioneered the development of online trading platforms. Therefore, it could leverage these competencies to boost revenue, and cut costs by divesting or outsourcing non-core activities which other companies can perform more efficiently. Enron would prosper by pursuing a focused strategy of cost leadership in global energy trading. To communicate this focused strategy to investors, Enron must slim down. It could achieve a leaner structure by exiting from loss-making domains, such as telecommunications, and outsourcing the non-core stages of the value chain, such as generating electricity to business partners.

3. An appropriate exit strategy could be to sell or to spin-off the non-core activities, and to retain the know-how and talent of the traders by focusing exclusively on energy trading domain. The resulting lean structure would reduce agency problems, and enable Enron to purchase resources and to sell its products at market prices.

   An alternative strategy would be to form strategic alliances with cash-rich suppliers and customers. By jointly consolidating the value chain, Enron could achieve economies of scope and become more independent of short-term market fluctuations.

4. To counter the immediate liquidity crisis, we would recommend divesting non-core businesses. In the long run, Enron should establish strategic partnerships with strong partners in other stages of the value chain. Together, they could develop innovative products for globally distributed public utility markets.

   (292 words)

B 3.2 Knowledge Check

(1) Discuss the two main types of partnerships.

A general partnership is owned by partners who are equally liable for the business' debts. A limited partnership is owned by at least one general partner, who runs the business. Limited partners are passive investors who are only liable for the amount of their investment.

(2) Explain the legal identity of a corporation.

A corporation is similar to an individual in that it can own and dispose of property, borrow money, enter into contracts, and sue and be sued.

(3) List the four groups governing a corporation, and describe the role of each.

Shareholders are the owners of the corporation. They elect the board of directors who in turn appoint the officers of the corporation who carry out the decisions of the board. In practice, shareholders and board members usually support the decisions of the CEO. Employees may influence the governance of the corporation through stock ownership (ESOP).

D | Answer Key

B 3.4 Model Case Structure – KirchMedia – Game Over?

Case Study Topic: Discuss Kirch Group's outlook for obtaining funds on the capital market

1. Key issue is lack of transparency in corporate structure and governance.
2. To attract funds, the Kirch Group must improve investor relations. This involves (a) publishing detailed financial reports and forecasts for all subsidiaries, (b) applying arm's length relationships to all transactions among subsidiaries (c) divesting loss-making operations, and (d) widening corporate governance by co-opting outside experts into the board of directors.
3. (a) Building on improved investor relations to attract and join forces with a strong partner in the media industry;
   (b) Maintaining family control by divesting subsidiaries and concentrating on trading media content.
4. To escape capital-intensive competition in the media industry, Kirch should focus on leveraging his expertise in trading media content.

B 4.2 Knowledge Check

(1) **Explain (a) how a company can predict environmental changes, and (b) how a company can achieve an environmental fit.**
   (a) Scan the external environment for threats, changes and opportunities, bundling elements in the external environment into ten sectors for analysis and focusing on volatile sectors;
   (b) fit the structure to the external environment; match a stable environment with a mechanistic structure, and an unstable, changing environment with an organic structure.

(2) **List suitable actions for controlling the environment.**
   Control external sectors that threaten needed resources, e.g. by advertising, public relations, political action, trade associations or change of domain. Establish interorganizational links through ownership, strategic alliances, long-term contracts, joint ventures or cooptation.

(3) **Recommend a strategy for survival in the process of "natural selection".**
   In line with its capabilities, a new company must discover a niche for the products and services it provides, and should prepare itself to compete for scarce resources.

Solution for Group Exercise "Nonstop Point-Point Flight"

Rankings: 9, 12, 3, 11, 14, 7, 6, 15, 13, 10, 16, 2, 5, 4, 18, 17, 8, 1

ANSWER KEY | **D**

B 4.4 Model Case Structure: Iridium LLC – Steering into a Descending Orbit

Case Study Topic: Does Iridium have a future developing its market niche in cooperation with partners?

1. - Large financial losses lead to Chapter 11 bankruptcy regime.
   - High operational complexity and low subscriber growth call for changes.

2. Iridium's survival depends on adapting to its dynamic environment:
   - **General (Industry) Environment:**
     - The exponential growth of cellular market reduces business outlook for Iridum's domain (handheld satellite communications).
     - Investors, worried about long-term prospects, now insist on meeting short-term targets.
   - **Task Environment**
     - Iridium's products are demanded by very specialized customer groups.
     - Projected high network density is not achieved due to technical problems and slow sales.
   - **Internal Environment**
     - Difficulties in coping with fast rate of technological change.
     - Cooperation with incompetent consortia partners hamper technological development.
     - The organic structure of a consortium – adapted to coping with high environmental uncertainty – is not effective for fulfilling well-defined technological requirements. A programmed structure would provide both more transparency, and efficiency, thereby reducing investors' uncertainty.

3. (a) Restructure, consolidate operations, and enter into a strategic alliance with a large cellular operator.
   (b) In each chosen domain (maritime, aeronautical, remote communications) link the value chain closely with the environment by entering into strategic alliances with large customers and suppliers.

4. Alternative (b) chosen because:
   - Concentrating on the communication needs of specific industries requires close relationships between suppliers and customers.
   - Development of boundary spanners with a deep knowledge of each industry is facilitated by linked value chain.

   whereas:
   - Cooperating with a large cellular operator would dilute Iridium's narrow strategic focus.

D | Answer Key

B 5.2 Knowledge Check

(1) **State how (a) government affects business, and (b) companies influence government.**

(a) Government acts as a regulator for company activities that might destroy competition or harm the public; it also acts as a tax collector, a customer, and a financial backer;

(b) Companies form lobbies in order to influence legislation, and donate money to political groups.

(2) **List five revenue-raising taxes and two regulatory taxes.**

Revenue-raising taxes include personal and corporate income taxes, property taxes, sales taxes, and value-added taxes. Regulatory taxes include excise taxes and customs duties.

(3) **State the difference between statutory and common law.**

Statutory law arises from legislation, administrative law from government's interpretations of statutory law, whereas common law is developed in courts.

(4) **Name (a) six areas of law related to companies; (b) seven elements of a valid contract.**

(a) Torts, product liability, contracts, agency, property transactions, and bankruptcy.

(b) A clear offer, a clear acceptance of the offer, consideration from both parties, genuine assent from both parties, competency, legality, and proper form.

(5) **Distinguish between real, personal, and intellectual property.**

Real property is land and anything that is permanently attached to it. Personal property is anything that is not real property. Intellectual property is the result of mental creativity.

B 5.4 Model Case Structure: Dimon Inc. – Treading Carefully

Case Study Topic: What strategy should Dimon plan as a result of changing consumer markets and looming product liability claims?

1. ■ Tobacco industry in trouble; product liability claims, bans on smoking and tobacco advertisement, consideration of new excise tax on cigarettes, etc.;
   ■ industry/market changes Dimon's adaptations;
2. ■ Changing consumer markets;
   ■ product liability claims: product liability claims (developing our of tort law; holds companies responsible for their products, etc.); legal and financial pressure for tobacco companies, but: Dimon does not sell directly to end-consumer, i.e. no direct involvement in manufacturing and selling tobacco products to consumers; problem: close partnerships with major customers (e.g. Phillip Morris Companies), therefore Dimon might be considered as an accessory;

- New excise tax on cigarettes: excise tax (tax originally raised to suppress potentially harmful practices); on manufacturer or retailer, but it is ultimately the consumer who pays; consequences: prices increase, less demand (?), less profits for Dimon Inc. (?);
- Dimon could be legally and financially in trouble, but: Dimon adapts to environment: diversification (flower business), responding to shifts in consumer habits (light tobacco blends), merging (share risks and costs).

3. (a) Restructuring: more diversified, more non-tobacco businesses;
   (b) Concentration on tobacco business, extend competitive advantages; expand to other markets, e.g. East-Europe (laws less strict, expanding market); lobbying, trying to avert stricter laws on advertisement, etc.
4. Recommended solution (b): selling of Florimex, acquisition of Intabex (4th largest leaf merchant) increase of market share, augmentation of company's sourcing capabilities.

B 6.2 Knowledge Check

(1) **Which steps must a company take to: (a) achieve legitimacy; (b) resolve goal conflicts?**

(a) Communicate corporate mission and goals to external stakeholders, and communicate operational goals to provide direction, guidelines, and standards of performance for employees.

(b) Identify competing goals of a company, and establish priorities. Achieve multiple goals through bargaining, satisficing, sequential attention, and priority setting.

(2) **Distinguish between alternative effectiveness approaches.**

The goal approach, the internal process approach, and the resource approach are used to assess effectiveness; stakeholder satisfaction represents perspectives on effectiveness.

(3) **Discuss the factors involved in the choice of a strategic goal.**

Environmental conditions, goal measurability, and leader preferences all influence preferred outcomes. The strategies should fit the goals, environmental needs and opportunities.

(4) **Discuss the suitability of different control strategies.**

Use bureaucratic control in large firms which use routine technology in a stable environment. Use market control with outputs which can be priced, and where there is a market. Use peer-group control in a turbulent environment.

(5) **Describe strategies for controlling the sequential stages of the transformation process.**

Use management control systems to monitor, evaluate, and influence activities. While the budget controls resource inputs, performance appraisals, and standard operating procedures control work activities. Profit and loss, and statistical reports control the output.

D Answer Key

B 6.4 Strategy Case: Expedia Inc. – Courting a Virtual Third Party

Case Study Topic: Based on a Stakeholder Approach, design an effective generic strategy for Rent-A-Holiday

1. The start-up Rent-A-Holiday is the largest European company in the independent leisure lodging segment with a focus on villas and bed & breakfast. Since RAH wants to become a global player, it is time to define an effective generic strategy. But there are several problems: improving the internal process structure, and managing a prospective merger.

2. To develop a focused strategy, RAH could, for instance, aim for a low-cost leadership position by emphasizing cost reduction and efficiency. In contrast, it could follow a differentiation strategy by offering customized customer solutions. RAH could also combine both strategies by focusing on a niche market and becoming a cost leader.

   Currently, operations are not run efficiently. Although the two owners are good in acquiring listings the burn rate is high and a good IT-infrastructure is missing. A joint-venture could help to overcome these disadvantages but negotiations with VS highlight new problems, such as a low valuation of RAH and a relocation to the United States.

3. Becoming a global player is not a realistic option. Alternatively,
   (a) merging with an established online travel agent, such as Expedia, would enable RAH to pursue a strategy of cost-leadership.
   (b) Another solution would be a joint-venture with VS. This would make sense because of the complementary geographical focus, the similar business models and VS's sophisticated IT infrastructure.

4. Based on a stakeholder approach it would be better to merge with VS. In this case the merger would hinge on retaining the two owners of RAH with long-term management contacts. A merger with Expedia is not recommended, because the two owners of RAH would probably be eclipsed.

   (257 words)

B 7.2 Knowledge Check

(1) **Describe the context of (a) the rational approach, and (b) the political model.**
   (a) Use a rational decision approach, when a problem situation is well understood.
   (b) The political model emphasizes the need for building a coalition and maintaining agreement about goals and problems when company goals and problem priorities are in conflict.

(2) **Describe the activities in the incremental approach.**
   Take risks and move the company ahead incrementally when a problem is defined, but solutions are uncertain. Try solutions in a step-by-step manner to learn whether they work.

(3) **Discuss decision-making in a turbulent environment.**

Apply both the political model and the incremental process model in situations with low goal consensus and low technical knowledge. Also consider employing intuitive procedures.

(4) **Outline an approach for (a) generating acceptance; (b) for avoiding escalating commitment for mistaken decisions.**

(a) Monitor quantitative and qualitative information, and try to involve everyone.

(b) Encourage administrative learning by readily trying new alternatives. Seek information that indicates when a course of action is failing, and allocate resources to new choices.

B 7.4 Model Case Structure: CEMEX – Global, Nimble … & In the Money

Case Study Topic: Based on the rational decision approach, recommend a growth strategy for CEMEX in Asian markets

1. CEMEX, the third largest cement company world-wide, have the aim to become number one in the world by going to Asia. They have begun the expansion to Asia, but now there are some difficulties which force CEMEX to design a new strategy.

2. To analyse the problem of CEMEX, a systematic problem analysis like the rational approach is needed. Therefore it is necessary to discuss the two steps of the rational approach: the problem identification stage and the solution stage.

   To identify the problem, it is important to characterise the geographical areas.

   In Japan, Korea and Taiwan, there is a mature market, which means that there is a saturation and no more or little growth. The middle East cannot be considered as a growth market because of the political instability. In China and India, there is a huge growth potential, but it is long-termed because it is difficult to overcome government. In south-east Asia, there is a huge growth market.

   After having identified the problem, it is necessary to find solutions. They have to concentrate on one area, which has a growth potential like south-east Asia. Accordingly, CEMEX have the choice how to enter this market: Greenfield projects, acquisitions or a merger.

3. One alternative is to concentrate on Indonesia, because they have already experience and a base there and then they can go to other countries like Thailand.

   Another alternative is to expand to all these countries at once because assets are cheap at the moment.

4. I would recommend the second solution because CEMEX want to grow fast and the company is a risk taker, so that they should take the risky, but more promising solution. Moreover, CEMEX have enough money to choose the second solution.

D | Answer Key

B 8.2 Knowledge Check

(1) **Define (a) a career path, and (b) a lateral career path.**
   (a) A career path is a progression of jobs, linked together, to furnish the competence necessary for promotion to the next job.
   (b) A lateral career path is a series of jobs that are not interdependent, and exist on the same level of hierarchy.

(2) **Explain the phenomenon of career plateauing.**
   Even though an employee begins on a career path, there is no assurance that he or she will advance to a high level. Many careers stall, a phenomenon known as career plateauing.

(3) **Discuss the unstable in-and-out system of human resource flow.**
   This type of work system tends to be found in companies where performance is considered to be a function of the individual and highly variable, due to external factors.

(4) **(a) List the factors that must be considered in choosing a compensation policy, and (b) discuss the difference between hourly pay and pay-for-performance.**
   (a) Factors that affect compensation, and must be considered by management, include supply and demand for labor, the company's ability to pay and its productivity.
   (b) The hourly wage is paid for the time an employee works regardless of output. The pay-for-performance wage is paid based on number of units produced regardless of hours put in.

B 8.4 Model Case Solution: Pharmacia – Merging People, not Firms

Case Study Topic: Integrate the different work systems, or not?

1. Pharmacia Corp. is facing high complexity and competitive pressure. Due to the many interpersonal conflicts resulting from the post-merger integration process involving two different business cultures and work systems, Pharmacia has to review its global human resource strategy.

2. Being a diversified multinational enterprise, Pharmacia needs a differentiated organizational culture. Specifically, it must think about combining P&U's sales-driven business culture and its hierarchically organized operations with the research-driven, decentralized work systems of Monsanto Co. By establishing a network of empowered research facilities, and linking programmed local workflows into a global network, the group could achieve synergy effects. In addition, a strong corporate culture could align the different work attitudes in teams composed of foreign specialists. In the long run, promoting learning and innovation will replenish and sustain the pipeline of high revenue-drugs. In manufacturing, operations should also be linked across geographies. This would require transforming vertically controlled operations into horizontally linked work systems. To achieve responsiveness, the programmed workflows should be regrouped into

team-controlled processes, with more broadly defined jobs. Also, a formal policy of job rotation could enhance skill variety and increase intercultural communication.

3. Pharmacia could realize the full potential of both companies by divesting P&U's non-core activities and personnel in the agricultural business, and just integrating Monsanto's research teams, and high performers in marketing and sales.

   Alternatively, the company could pursue a global strategy based on economies of scope, integrating Monsanto with all its product lines, and human resources. This broadly based growth strategy would require unifying the two cultures under a centralized global corporate culture.

4. The international drug industry being highly competitive it will be necessary to focus on achieving economies of scale in high-revenue products. Divesting and outsourcing of non-core operations and personnel would increase efficiency and reduce agency costs. In R&D and in sales, Pharmacia should foster innovation through combining high commitment work systems with market-related rewards.

B 9.2 Knowledge Check

(1) **Define the goal of advances in production technology.**

   Competitiveness, or maximizing the efficiency and the quality of the production process, is the goal of most advances in production technology.

(2) **Cite the four technological advances that made mass production possible.**

   Mass production became possible after the development of mechanization, standardization, the assembly line, and automation.

(3) **Explain three innovations in materials management.**
   - Material requirements planning (MRP) determines when materials are needed, when they should be ordered, and when they should be delivered.
   - Just-in-time (JIT) is the practice of limiting the quantity of materials on hand by making them available only when they are actually required for the production process.
   - Enterprise resource planning is a computerized system that brings together data from all parts of a company (including financial and design departments). These data automatically generate inventory-control information, and simulate "what if" analysis.

(4) **Identify the three main production layouts.**

   Process layout, assembly-line layout, and fixed-position layout are the three main classifications. They apply to both the manufacture of goods and the production of services.

(5) **Describe a technique for improving scheduling.**

   Scheduling may be improved with the use of the critical path method (CPM), which identifies the sequence of tasks expected to take the longest in order to control the project completion time.

D | Answer Key

B 9.4 Model Case Solution: Smithfields Foods – Sensing a Gut Feeling

Case Study Topic: Responding to the operational challenge for Smithfields Foods

1. Smithfields Foods is one of the largest hog producers and hog processors in the world. Their aim is to increase productivity and variety, but should they keep the old technology or should they introduce advanced technology? Significantly, the American consumption of pork has shrunk.

2. To create an efficient continuous flow in response to shifting consumer demand, Smithfields must align process-related factors, financial aspects and market conditions.

   If you consider the suppliers, you can recognise risks and uncertainties: the input factors should be available, you should think about the prices of live hogs and raw materials, and you should contemplate environmental and health standards.

   Internally, Smithfields have to improve their skills to achieve the efficiencies and flexibility they need. The pork conversion process is very complicated. There are many steps, and some steps are hand-operated. Therefore, Smithfields Foods must concentrate on increasing the productivity in the internal business, and produce the high quality products just-in-time.

3. The 1st alternative would be to implement new technology, e.g. automated meat cutting systems (CIM) and enterprise resource planning (ERP) to link the supply chain with customer demand. Alternatively, they could reengineer the existing assembly line both to improve efficiency and to achieve flexibility to changing market conditions.

4. Smithfields Foods should introduce automated meat cutting systems and ERP. The advanced technology improves cycle time, quality, hygiene, and enhances work safety. Also, as the workflow and the work relationships will undergo change, the employees have to be part of the change process: they should feel involved and empowered.

B 10.2 Knowledge Check

(1) Explain (a) the purpose of the balance sheet and identify its three main sections, and (b) explain the purpose of an income statement and identify its three main components.

    (a) The balance sheet provides a snapshot of the business at a particular point in time. Its main sections are assets, liabilities, and owners' equity.

    (b) The income statement reflects the results of operations over a period of time. Its main components are revenues, expenses, and net income or loss.

(2) Define the position of public accountants.

    Public accountants monitor and certify a company's financial statements, but operate independently of the companies they serve.

(3) **Explain the purpose of the statement of cash flows.**

The statement of cash flows summarizes receipts and disbursals of cash (and cash equivalents) in three areas: operations, investments, and financing.

(4) **Identify four areas in which accountants may exercise considerable discretion.**

The four areas where accountants have maximum discretion are in (a) the timing of revenue recognition, (b) the choice of a depreciation method, (c) the choice of an inventory valuation method, and (d) the method of disclosing extraordinary or unusual items. The choices made in these areas may greatly affect a company's earning record.

(5) **List the four main categories of financial ratios.**

Most of the important ratios fall into one of four categories: profitability ratios, liquidity ratios, activity ratios, or debt ratios.

B 10.4 Model Case Solution: Elan Corp.

Case Study Topic: Based on the Balanced Scorecard Model, how can Elan defuse its accounting minefield?

1. Elan is accused of using its joint ventures to hide R&D costs and to overstate revenues. To reverse the resulting loss in shareholder value, Elan must improve its control system by balancing financial ratios with critical operational measures.

2. The accounting scandal does not affect customers directly, but the bad press will negatively influence customers' perceptions, lessening the demand for Elan's products.

   The accounting scandal has already resulted in a general lack of trust, which is reflected in class action lawsuits of investors against the company. This uncertainty will create future difficulties in raising funds, impairing the financial perspective (for example, by reducing ROI, market share, cash flow).

   The loss of customer confidence will also lead to reduced sales, which in turn will result to operational inefficiencies (such as under-utilization of assets, lack of funding in R&D, etc.).

   A simultaneous drive to improve customers' perceptions, investors' confidence, and the efficiency of business processes will enhance learning and growth processes. Elan can reinforce the change process by focusing on the continuous improvement in the use of its resources.

3. One possible solution would be to change accounting techniques, making them more transparent to investors (especially controversial items like joint venture structure and related accounting techniques). This transparency would help to regain the trust of customers and investors, thereby increasing shareholder value.

   The alternative strategy would be to retain the creative accounting techniques (as long as nothing else is ruled by court) and intensify investor relations. Consistently high revenues and an improved public image would facilitate the search for new investors, and help Elan regain trust of customers.

4. The customer and financial perspectives will affect Elan most immediately: failure to regain trust will reinforce the vicious circle of less demand, less financial assets, lower asset utilization, decreased competitive advantage resulting in lower shareholder value. Therefore, creating financial transparency is recommended as the safer alternative.

B 11.2 Knowledge Check

(1) **List the five steps involved in the financial-planning process.**

The financial manager estimates the monthly flow of funds out of/into the business, compares inflows/outflows and plans how to use excess funds or meet shortfalls, selects the optimum mix of outside funding and establishes a system for tracking financial performance.

(2) (a) **State the matching principle.**

(b) **Explain the chief advantages of debt versus equity.**

(a) The timing of a company's borrowing should roughly match the timing of its spending.

(b) Debt is cheaper than equity because debt payments can be deducted from a company's income tax and dividend payments on stock are paid with after-tax revenues.

(3) **Name three major types of short-term debt.**

The three major types of short-term debt are trade credit, loans, and commercial paper.

(4) **List four major long-term financing options.**

The four major long-term financing options are loans, leases, bonds, and equity.

(5) **Explain the guiding principle of cash management.**

The principle of cash management is to limit the amount of cash on hand to the minimum necessary to cover immediate expenses, and employ all available money productively.

(6) **State the financial manager's primary goal in handling receivables and payables.**

The aim is to shorten cycles between collection of receivables and payment of payables.

(7) **Define the objective of the capital-budgeting process.**

Capital budgeting aims to optimize cash flows and rates of return on investments.

B 11.4 Model Case Structure: Egg plc – Not Fully Hatched Yet

Case Study Topic: How should Prudential provide Internet services in future? Recommend a strategy using the Balanced Scorecard Model.

1. Prudential has founded Egg plc, and has continued to hold 79 % of share capital; problems: Egg plc faces strong competition, fast market changes, financial problems.

2. Costly loss-leader strategy, anxious investors, backlash against Internet services; vicious circle: more competition, anxious investors, less funds, lower competitive advantage, lower shareholder value, even more difficult position in market;

   - **Customer Perspective:** customers' eagerness concerning the Internet overrated/ decreased; customer complaints (e.g. poor customer service); loss-leader strategy attracts customers, but: costly; market changes (e.g. demographic shift of customer base); danger of losing customers to competitors; in case of losing customer: decrease of demand for products, under-utilization of assets, lower competitive advantage, lower shareholder value;

   - **Internal Process Perspective:** innovative products; synergy potential: growth in cross-holdings; ideas of organizational change: Prudential had intended to sell majority of its stake, but: Egg plc in risk of running out of cash (anxieties of investors mean less investment);

   - **Learning and Growth Perspective:** innovative ideas; but quick changes in market (customer demands) require need of continuous R&D, learning, innovating; growth: growth towards different areas dangerous: e.g. by becoming a portal and e-shopping site, Egg plc faced even stronger competition.

3. **Alternative (a):** "stay on track", keep majority of stake in Egg plc and keep its business concept: four main areas (banking, investments, insurance, online shopping), keep strategy of loss-leader; try to calm investors; successively integrate Prudential's and Egg's activities & promote both brands for cross-selling;

   Alternative (b): change business model: dual e-commerce site and Internet portal, i.e. continuously change Egg plc's business concept according to market demands/ changes.

4. **Recommend (a):** combine the "one-stop-shopping" and multi-channel distribution options by successively integrating Egg plc and Prudential's operations, while maintaining two separate brands, thus achieving economies of scope and scale at a minimum of cost and risk.

D | Answer Key

B 12.2 Knowledge Check

(1) What is the relationship between the PLC and the Product Portfolio Matrix (BCG)?

Questions Marks (BCG) are usually within the infancy stage of their product life cycle (PLC). Star are within the adolescence stage; Cash Cows are within the maturity stage; Dogs are within the aging stage.

(2) What is the difference between the PLC and the Product Portfolio Matrix (BCG)?

The Product Life Cycle illustrates the development of ONE product. The Product Portfolio Matrix (BCG) is used to display a SELECTION of products.

(3) What are the corresponding strategies for the Product Portfolio Matrix (BCG)?

question mark – observe; star – promote; cash cow – milk/harvest; dog – divest/eliminate.

B 12.4 Model Case Structure: The Algonquin Hotel – Still Executive Suite?

Case Study Topic: What strategy should The Algonquin pursue in future? Base your analysis on the Market Portfolio Matrix!

1. DH&R' acquisition of the New York hotel, "The Algonquin",

   industry in general suffering from a general economic slowdown (i.e. is losing revenues)

   main issue: to remain a premier business hotel, or target other segments?

2. Diversification: in this case not an option

   - **Portfolio Development:** Algonquin differentiates itself already from most hotels (a premier business hotel, i.e. focus on its reputation for excellent restaurant facilities and gathering place for New York writers); developing its portfolio to an even higher extent is impossible; the question is: should it keep this strategy?
   - **Market Development:** only an option to a very low extent, e.g. by expanding marketing activities to new markets; how would the revenues be affected by promotions in new markets? Are there any new markets that promise an increase in revenues (the hotel industry being very international anyway)?
   - **Market Penetration:** losing differentiation (mainly business hotel), trying to attract wide range of customers, problem: differences in price sensitivity (leisure segment is more price-sensitive than business segment), in booking behaviour (business customers often book at short notice), in services required, in fees for services (packaged fees vs. itemised charges), etc. in order to increase revenues, The Algonquin must accurately forecast demand, revenue and contribution produced by these segments.

3. (a) remain a business hotel, keep the portfolio strategy, try to increase revenues by Customer Relationship Management;

(b) focus on a broad customer base (strategy of market penetration), i.e. Mass Marketing;

(c) combination of business and leisure hotel, i.e. pursue Target/Niche Marketing, or Key Account Marketing.

4. Recommend (c): combination, Target/Niche Marketing or Key Account Marketing; reasons: both segments (business and leisure) are important to The Algonquin, the hotel cannot afford to disregard and lose one of the segments; by using the technique of Key Account Marketing or Target/Niche Marketing, it can serve both the business segment and the leisure segment to their satisfaction; however, it has to regard the differences of those segments (i.e. different treatment without displeasing customers).

B 13.2 Knowledge Check

(1) **Distinguish between an absolute and a comparative advantage in global trade.**

A country with an absolute advantage can produce a given product more efficiently than any competitor, whereas a country with a comparative advantage can produce a given product more efficiently than any other product.

(2) **List five common forms of international business activity.**

International business activities include importing/exporting, licensing, franchising, joint ventures, and wholly or partly owned subsidiaries.

(3) **List and describe three types of international trade pacts.**

Trade pacts may take the form of free trade areas, customs unions, common markets, the form of large-scale agreements (e.g. WTO), or the form of bilateral agreements between countries.

(4) **Identify four techniques that countries use to protect their domestic industries.**

Common forms of protectionism are tariffs, quotas, subsidies, and restrictive standards.

B 13.4 Model Case Structure: Tesco – Ever on Piling High & Selling Cheap?

Case Study Topic: Design an organizational framework for Tesco's global strategy

1. Tesco: close to market saturation in UK, hence strategy of globalization; (potential) problems: increased overhead and complexity;

2. Tesco's organizational structure has to match their growth factors on the international market and their global strategy:
   - **Structure, Strategy and Competition:** high competition → on the one hand global competition (with global brands), on the other hand national competition (with local brands, adaptation to local needs); strategy of exporting the UK format and fine-tuning it to local markets → high complexity, costly;

D | Answer Key

- **Customer Needs:** differences in demographic factors, buyer sophistication, purchasing power requires differentiated products → problem: complex, costly;
- **Related Industries and Services:** existence of support industries within countries, e.g. transport companies;
- **Factors of Production:** similar work attitudes, skills in countries facilitate globalization; certain standard of infrastructure required.

3. The right choice of countries/regions on the basis of mentioned factors have potential to reduce complexity and costs of globalization:
   (a) Different patterns of hypermarkets for different regions/localization according to regions (i.e. cluster of regions & organization on the basis of cluster);
   (b) Organization on the basis of types of businesses → online retailing, hypermarkets, etc. (i.e. standardization of hypermarkets/products).

4. Recommend solution (a): localization has been successful; by structure of clusters, attempt cost reduction. Reap two advantages (localization & cost reduction) combined.

► Answer Key C

C 1   Exercise 1

Dear Sir/Madam

Enquiry – office furniture

Two months ago we saw your range of products at the furniture trade fair in Essen.

We were impressed by your selection and are especially interested in your desks, office chairs and filing cabinets as we intend to redesign our offices.

Please let us have a copy of your current catalogue and price-list and include details regarding your terms of delivery and payment.

We look forward to hearing from you soon.

Yours faithfully

C 1   Exercise 2

Dear Sir/Madam

Enquiry – "StarProject"

With reference to your advertisement in the last issue of "Office Today", we would like to know if a demo version of your software "StarProject" is available.

Furthermore, we would be grateful if you could let us have additional information on discounts for multi-user licenses and prices for training, maintenance and service.

Additionally, we would like an appointment with one of your sales representatives to discuss further details.

We look forward to hearing from you soon.

Yours faithfully

C 1   Exercise 3

Dear Sir/Madam

Enquiry

We have received your address from the Chamber of Commerce and Industry as suppliers for computer equipment.

Please let us have your current catalogue and price-list. Furthermore, we would be grateful if you could forward us a quotation for the following:
- 450 PC mice
- 450 keyboards
- 80 pairs of speakers

All prices should include delivery, a corresponding trade discount is expected and please confirm that delivery could take place before the end of next month.

If this transaction is successful we will place further orders in future.

We look forward to hearing from you soon.

Yours faithfully

C 2   Exercise 1

Dear Ms O'Donoghue

Catalogue and price-list

Thank you for your letter enquiring about our range of products.

Please find enclosed our current catalogue and price-list.

If you require any further information, please do not hesitate to contact us.

We look forward to hearing from you soon.

Yours sincerely

D | Answer Key

C 2   Exercise 2

Dear Ms O'Sullivan

Quotation – DVD drives

With reference to our telephone conversation of 11 May 2003, we have pleasure in submitting an offer on the following terms:

- 180 DVD drives (DSX 6000) € 119.00 each

All prices are EXW and subject to payment by remittance within 30 days.

We are prepared to offer a discount of 3.0 % on condition that invoices are settled within 10 days.

Furthermore, we are willing to grant a 12.5 % trade discount and an additional quantity discount of 5.0 % on orders of more than 220 units.

The consignment will be delivered within 14 days of receipt of order.

The products remain the property of the seller until such time as they have been paid for in full. Our usual Terms and Conditions of Business apply.

This offer remains valid for a period of 6 weeks as from the above date.

We look forward to welcoming you as our customer.

Yours sincerely

C 2   Exercise 3

Dear Mr Nolan

Enquiry – InfoShare XL

Thank you for you enquiry about our InfoShare XL Organizer.

Unfortunately, this model is no longer in production, but we would like to point out that the successor of our popular InfoShare XL Organizer will be available in 2 months' time and this latest model will be on offer at an extremely attractive introductory price.

We will let you have additional information once our new product on sale.

Thank you for your interest and if you require any further information, please do not hesitate to contact us.

Yours sincerely

C 3   Exercise 1

Dear Sir/Madam

Order – customized device components

Thank you for your offer dated 5 May 2003 regarding the production of customized device components according to our specifications.

We are very pleased with your quotation and would be glad if you could supply the components at the agreed price.

Please let us know when the consignment is ready for delivery.

We look forward to receiving your acknowledgement of this order shortly.

Yours faithfully

C 3   Exercise 2

Dear Sir/Madam

Quotation – PC systems

Thank you for your offer of 6 May 2003 for the supply of 25 PC systems.

In consideration of the details we have to emphasize that we expect PC systems with first-class equipment before we are willing to accept an offer.

We require larger monitors, high-quality drives and more memory than specified in your quotation. Additionally, we hope that you are willing to grant a 15.0% trade discount and delivery free of charge.

Thank you for your cooperation in this matter, and we look forward to receiving your revised quotation.

Yours faithfully

C 3   Exercise 3

Dear Sir/Madam

Quotation – PC systems

Thank you for your letter of 12 May 2003.

Unfortunately, we are unable to supply you with an improved offer within this price range.

We would like to emphasize that our prices and conditions are very competitive and we offer excellent value for money.

However, we are willing to deliver the goods free of charge.

D | Answer Key

Should you have any questions, please do not hesitate to contact us.

Yours faithfully

C 4 Exercise 1

Dear Sir/Madam

Acknowledgement

We acknowledge receipt of you order No. 388753/10 of 14 May 2003.

Quantity	Description	Price per Unit	Total
160	Scanner SCX 4000	€ 129.00	€ 20,640.00
	Shipping and handling	€ 68.00	€ 68.00
			€ 20,708.00

Please remit the amount to our usual account.

Yours faithfully

C 4 Exercise 2

Dear Sir/Madam

Additional training material/enclosed cheque

Thank you very much for your prompt delivery of the training material.

We enclose our crossed cheque No. 36885247 for € 2,870.00 in settlement of your invoice.

We would be grateful if you could forward us additional information regarding other material for training courses.

Yours faithfully

C 4 Exercise 3

Dear Sir/Madam

Your order/terms of payment

With reference to your order of 14 May 2003, we regret having to inform you that it is not our usual procedure to accept payment on receipt of invoice for initial transactions.

We would like to suggest cash with order or alternatively payment by remittance in advance.

We are sorry that we are unable to offer more favourable terms of payment at this stage. However, this will certainly be open to negotiation at a later date in our business relationship.

We look forward to hearing from you soon.

Yours faithfully

C 5   Exercise 1

Dear Sir/Madam

Consignment of 300 chairs

We wish to send a consignment of 300 chairs to the

Northwood Conference Centre, 164 Ashley Rd, Lee Valley Technopark, London N17 9LN

The consignment has to arrive at the conference centre **by Friday, next week.**

Please contact the Northwood Conference Centre for further details regarding the delivery.

The invoice is to be made out to GreenLine Furniture plc.

We look forward to hearing from you soon.

Yours faithfully

C 5   Exercise 2

Dear Sir/Madam

Import of software packages

We would like to import a large number of software packages from Ireland to Germany.

The consignment would have to be collected at

RTC Software Engineering, 29 Grafton St, Dublin

We would be grateful if you could advise us of a suitable mode of transport and which documents are required for the transaction.

Please let us know your tariffs for collection and delivery. Rates should include all handling charges and we would ask you to look after the necessary insurance and customs formalities.

We look forward to hearing from you soon.

Yours faithfully

D | Answer Key

C 6   Exercise 1

Dear Sir/Madam

Delay in delivery

We are contacting you concerning our order No. 123/xyz, which has still not arrived.

The components are 3 days overdue and as the ordered parts are urgently required for production, we are extremely concerned about the situation.

We expect an immediate clarification by fax and have to point out that delivery has to take place within the next 7 working days. Unless you are able to deliver by the revised date, we will have to cancel our order.

I would be grateful if you could look into this matter as soon as possible.

Yours faithfully

C 6   Exercise 2

Dear Sir/Madam

Cancellation of order/Delay in delivery

Unfortunately we have to write to you again concerning our order No. 123/xyz.

As you have not replied to our letter of 2 June 2003, emphasizing the urgency of the delivery, we will have no choice but to cancel our order and purchase the parts elsewhere.

Yours faithfully

C 6   Exercise 3

Dear Sir/Madam

Delay in delivery

We apologize for any inconvenience caused by the delay in delivery.

The delay was due to technical problems which have been dealt with in the meantime.

Regarding future deliveries we would like to assure you that such an incident will not occur again as we have upgraded our quality systems.

Furthermore, we have taken steps within procurement, logistics and despatch to improve our services and we look forward to providing an efficient and reliable service in future.

Yours faithfully

Answer Key | D

C 7   Exercise 1

Dear Sir/Madam

Complaint about defective goods

We are writing to inform you that your latest delivery contained defective items.

On checking the consignment we found that 17 of the 60 main boards were damaged due to insufficient packaging.

We have arranged for the defective items to be returned and hope to receive replacements without delay.

We look forward to hearing from you soon.

Yours faithfully

C 7   Exercise 2

Dear Sir/Madam

Complaint about defective goods

We regret that some of the items were damaged and we will certainly replace them at our expense without delay.

We apologize for any inconvenience caused.

Yours faithfully

C 7   Exercise 3

Dear Sir/Madam

Delivery of incorrect printer cartridges

On checking last week's consignment, we found that it contained the wrong printer cartridges.

Moreover, the printer cables which we ordered were missing.

We have arranged for the items to be returned and hope to receive the missing printer cables and the cartridges specified in our order.

We look forward to hearing from you soon.

Yours faithfully

D | Answer Key

C 7   Exercise 4

Dear Sir/Madam

Complaint regarding the delivery of incorrect items

With reference to your complaint of 2 June 2003 regarding the delivery of incorrect items we would like to clarify that all items listed in your order No. 221/498/0703 were packed and despatched according to your specifications.

In addition, all consignments are crosschecked before leaving our storage facilities.

If you have any further questions regarding the delivery, please do not hesitate to contact us.

Yours faithfully

C 8   Exercise 1

Dear Mr Murphy

Invoice No. 123/xyz

We are writing concerning our invoice of 10 May 2003, which we feel sure you have overlooked.

Please remit the invoice amount of 310.00 € to our account.

If you have settled the invoice in the meantime, please disregard this letter.

Yours sincerely

C 8   Exercise 2

Dear Sir/Madam

Non-payment of invoice No. 6231/3

It has come to our attention that you still have not settled our invoice No. 6231/3, despite our letter of 30 May 2003.

Now that we have reminded you a second time, we confidently expect your remittance of 12,340.00 € within the next 3 weeks.

If you have settled the invoice in the meantime, please ignore this letter.

Yours faithfully

Answer Key D

C 8   Exercise 3

Dear Sir/Madam

Final reminder regarding non-payment of invoice No. 6231/3

We are writing for a third time concerning our invoice No. 6231/3, which is still outstanding.

Unless we receive payment in full within the next 10 days we will have no choice but to place the matter with our solicitors.

Yours faithfully

C 8   Exercise 4

Dear Sir/Madam

Reminder regarding your invoice No. 112/84603

We are writing to inform you that the above mentioned invoice was settled 3 weeks ago.

Yours faithfully

C 9   Exercise 1

To:	**Kevin Foley, Head of Sales**
From:	**Controlling Department**
Subject:	**Limit on company expenses for sales staff**
Date:	**16 June 2003**

Over the past weeks we have noticed a significant increase in expenses for our sales representatives.

Please remind the sales staff of the agreed limit on company expenses.

C 9   Exercise 2

To:	**All Sales Staff**
From:	**PR**
Subject:	**New Company Logo**
Date:	**16 June 2003**

Please note that we will introduce our new corporate design.

From next month on you should only use material displaying the new company logo.

Please pick up the new material (business cards, brochures, catalogues, stationery, biros etc.) within the next few days.

D | Answer Key

C 9   Exercise 3

To: All Departments
From: IT Coordinator
Subject: Data Base Server Maintenance
Date: 16 June 2003

Please note that the data base servers will be replaced next week.

Therefore, it will not be possible to access customer data

from   Friday, 1 pm
to   Monday, 8 am

We apologize for any inconvenience caused.

C 9   Exercise 4

To: All Staff
From: Managing Director
Subject: Personal Use of Company Facilities
Date: 16 June 2003

It has come to our attention that recently the photocopier, the telephone and the internet have been increasingly used for personal purposes during working hours.

This is unacceptable and leads to increasing costs which are counterproductive for the company's financial performance.

We ask for your cooperation in this matter.

If the situation does not improve, disciplinary measures have to be taken.

C 9   Exercise 5

To: All Departments
From: Training Department
Subject: Seminar "Internet Security"
Date: 16 June 2003

Please note that the seminar on "Internet Security" scheduled for Friday, 2 pm has been postponed.

The seminar will now take place on **Wednesday** at **4 pm**.

Room 22 – 2nd Floor – West Building

C 10   Exercise 1

Decline in sales of printers (B2C)

- **Terms of reference**

  Thomas Burke has asked me to write a report on the decline in sales of printers (B2C).

- **Proceedings**

  A sample of customers and workers was questioned and asked for their opinions.

- **Findings**
  - Most customers are not satisfied with the quality of the printers.
  - Several customers complained about malfunctions and frequent repairs.
  - Some customers said that they wouldn't buy the product again.
  - There seems to be a lack of staff in the production department.

- **Conclusions**

  Apparent quality control problems lead to decreasing customer satisfaction and declining sales.

- **Recommendations**

  Quality control measures will have to be improved. More personnel should be assigned to monitor production. A more detailed investigation regarding the malfunctions is required. Marketing measures are needed to restore customer confidence.

C 10   Exercise 2

Planned merger with competitor

- **Terms of reference**

  The Board of Directors has asked me to write a report on the current situation regarding the planned merger.

- **Proceedings**

  A sample of managers and workers was questioned. Print media articles were examined.

- **Findings**
  - Only a third of the managers agrees to the planned merger.
  - The majority of the workers is sceptical and opposed to the merger.
  - The staff is afraid of possible drawbacks and doesn't see any advantages.
  - Analysts expect little benefits and question the compatibility of the corporate cultures.

D | Answer Key

- **Conclusions**

  The majority of the staff is highly sceptical which might lead to possible resistance and motivational problems.

- **Recommendations**

  It is advisable to provide more information about the benefits and the necessity of the planned merger. More managers and workers should be involved in a campaign to promote the merger. Further PR measures will be required to influence public opinion.

E

The
"Handy 500"

The "Handy 500": Glossary of 500 fundamental business terms

"Handy 500" word	Brief explanation	Translation
Absenteeism	Failure to show up for work	Personalfehlzeiten, Absentismus
Access	(1) Approach, channel (2) Right or means of approaching	(1) Zugang (2) Zugangsberechtigung
Accessory	Additional (1) item or (2) person with supporting function	(1) Zubehör (2) Gehilfe
Accommodation	Occurs when the parties' goals are compatible and the interaction between groups is relatively unimportant to the goals' attainment	Anpassung
Account payable	An amount owed to a supplier for goods or services purchased on credit; payment is due within a short time period, usually 30 days or less	Verbindlichkeiten aus Lieferungen und Leistungen
Account receivable	A current asset representing money due for services performed or merchandise sold on credit	Forderungen aus Lieferungen und Leistungen
Accrual method of accounting	Revenues are counted during the time they're earned, and expenses are counted during the time they're incurred. Cash does not need to change hands for transactions to be recorded	Entstehungsprinzip
Accrued revenue	Revenue that has been earned and must be accounted for but is not received by the end of the reporting period; also recorded as an accrued asset. The accrued asset is shown separately under current assets as part of accounts receivable in the Balance Sheet.	Sonstige Forderungen
Accumulated depreciation	The total depreciation recorded on an asset since its acquisition; a contra account deducted from the original cost of an asset on the balance sheet	Kumulierte Abschreibungen
Activity based costing (ABC)	An accounting method that allocates costs to specific products based on breakdowns of cost drivers	Prozesskostenrechnung
Advance payment	Trading method in which the buyer pays for the goods before they are sent out, method is used when buyer is of unknown credit worthiness	Vorauskasse
Affiliate	Branch company of a controlling corporation	Tochterunternehmen

"Handy 500" word	Brief explanation	Translation
Agency costs	The costs of monitoring management and ensuring that it acts in the best interest of other stakeholders	Kontrollkosten
Agency temporaries (Temps)	People employed by a temporary help agency and supplied to the contracting firm	Zeitarbeitskräfte
Agent	(1) In corporate governance: management is the agent of the principal stakeholders in a principal-agent relationship. (2) In sales: a person who acts on behalf of a company or individual to sell its products or services. An agent is typically compensated on a commission only basis	(1) Beauftragter (2) Vertriebsbeauftragter
Aggregate demand	The total demand of all potential buyers of a commodity or service. Includes all individuals and organizations who have the ability, willingness, and authority to purchase such products	Gesamtnachfrage
Agreement	(1) Mutual understanding (2) Contract legally binding on parties	(1) Vereinbarung, Absprache (2) Vertrag
Air waybill	A non-negotiable instrument of domestic and international air transport which functions as a bill of lading	Luftfrachtbrief
Alignment	Taking position of agreement or alliance with others	Ausrichtung, Anpassung
Allocational efficiency	The efficiency with which a market channels capital toward its most productive uses	Allokationseffizienz
Allowance for bad debt	The amount of debt a company expects not to collect. This is subtracted from what the company is owed for goods it sold on credit	Abschreibungen auf Forderungen
Amenities	Non-monetary benefits; perquisites, or "perks"	Annehmlichkeiten
Amortization	A method of debt reduction in which a borrower pays off a portion of the interest and principal periodically.	Amortisation
Annual General Meeting	Yearly held assembly of stockholders	Hauptversammlung
Annual report	A document that summarizes the result of operations and financial status of a company for the past year and outlines plans for the future	Geschäftsbericht

"Handy 500" word	Brief explanation	Translation
Anti-dumping laws	Laws that are enacted to prevent dumping-offering prices in the overseas market that is lower than that at which a product is sold in its home domestic market	US-Dumpinggesetz
Antitrust laws	Sherman-Clayton Act outlawing cartels and conspiracies against competition	US-Kartellgesetz
Application service provider (ASP)	A software solution used by the customer where the solution itself is developed, hosted and managed by an outside company (generally implies a lower implementation cost)	Anbieter von Software-Dienstleistungen per Datennetz
Arbitrage	The process of purchasing and selling foreign exchange, stocks, bonds and other commodities in several markets intending to make profit from the difference in price – a transaction which generates a risk-free profit	Arbitrage
Arbitration	Process by which two parties to a dispute agree in advance to abide by the decision of an independent referee or quasijudge	Schiedsgerichtsverfahren
Arm's length relationship	Dealing with a subunit of one's own company as if it were a third party	Simuliertes Marktverhalten
Assets	Economic resources that are owned or controlled by an entity	Aktiva
Attrition rate	Rate of workforce turnover	Natürlicher Personalabbau
Auction	Buyers bid against each other to win a seller's business	Versteigerung
Audit	The result of an independent accountant's review of the statements and footnotes to ensure compliance with generally accepted accounting principles and to render an opinion on the fairness of the financial statements	Prüfbericht
Avoidance (negative reinforcement)	The opportunity to avoid or escape from an unpleasant circumstance after exhibiting behavior. Avoidance occurs when the interacting parties' goals are incompatible and the interaction between groups is relatively unimportant to the attainment of the goals	Ausweichen
Bad debt	An uncollectable account receivable	Uneinbringbare Forderung

"Handy 500" word	Brief explanation	Translation
Balance of Payments	The balance of payments is a statistical summary of international transactions. These transactions are defined as the transfer of ownership of something that has an economic value measurable in monetary terms from residents of one country to residents of another (Balance on – : – Current account; – Goods, services, and income; – Investment income; – Merchandise trade; – Services; – Unilateral transfers)	Zahlungsbilanz
Balance sheet (Statement of financial position)	The financial statement that shows the assets, liabilities and owners' equity of an entity at a particular date	Geschäftsbilanz
Balanced scorecard (BSC)	A strategic, measurement-based management system, which provides a method of aligning business activities to the strategy, and monitoring performance of strategic goals over time	BSC, strategisches Management- und Leistungsmessungssystem
Banker's Acceptance	A banker's acceptance is a draft drawn on and accepted by a bank. Depending on the bank's creditworthiness, the acceptance becomes a financial instrument which can be discounted	Bankakzept
Bankruptcy	Inability to pay their debts. Companies filing for protection under Chapter 7 of the bankruptcy code are shut down and their assets transferred to the creditors. Under Chapter 11, companies try to rework their debts and stay in business	Konkurs
Barter	An exchange of products and/ or services for other products and/ or services	Tauschverkehr
Basis point	One-one-hundredth of a percent	Zehntelprozent
BCG Framework	An approach to product portfolio planning. It has two controlling aspects namely relative market share and market growth. Each of the four cells has its own name as follows: Dogs, Cash Cows, Question Marks, Stars	BCG-Portfolio-Matrix
Benchmarking	The process of comparing one set of measurements to another. This may be done for various reasons, such as to determine trends in a process over time, or to compare one organization's efficiency to another's	Vergleich mit Klassenbestem

E | The "Handy 500"

"Handy 500" word	Brief explanation	Translation
Beta Factor	A measure of systematic risk, whereby the volatility of a an asset is related to the cohort	Betafaktor
Bidding	Suppliers or contractors of goods and services participate in a procurement process by invitation or advertisement, All parties are informed about the rules and about the specifications of the items to be procured	Ausschreibungsverfahren
Bill of Lading	Contract between the owner of the goods and the carrier. There are two types. A straight bill of lading is nonnegotiable. A negotiable or shipper's order bill of lading can be bought, sold, or traded while goods are in transit.	Konnossement, Seefrachtbrief
Bill of material	A listing of components, parts, and other items needed to manufacture a product, showing the quantity of each required to produce each end item	Stückliste
Board of directors	Individuals elected by the stockholders to govern a corporation	Vorstand
Bond	A type of security that pays a fixed amount of interest at a regular interval over a certain period of time	Festverzinsliches Wertpapier
Bottleneck	The production resource that limits the capacity of the overall process. This is usually the production	Engpass
Bounded rationality	The idea that decision makers cannot deal with information about all the aspects and alternatives pertaining to a problem and therefore choose to tackle some meaningful subset of it	Begrenzte Rationalität
Brainstorming	A technique used in the idea-generation phase of decision making that assists in the development of numerous alternative courses of action	Kreativitätsübung
Brand	(1) Trademark, goods of particular make (2) Class of particular goods	(1) Warenzeichen, Markenartikel (2) Sorte
Bribery	Paying someone to facilitate a deal	Bestechung
Broker	A person who acts on behalf of a company to sell its products or services. A broker is typically compensated on a commission only basis	Makler

"Handy 500" word	Brief explanation	Translation
Budget	The amount of money available for use to a salesperson or purchasing agent for a particular time period or a particular project. The term can also be used to describe a sales target in specified time period (also referred to as a quota, goal or forecast)	Haushalt, Ausgaberahmen, Verkaufsziel
Buffer	Interim storage where work-in-process can be stored between steps in a process	Puffer
Bumping	Occurs in situations where senior employees whose jobs have become obsolete transfer into jobs of less senior workers	Abschieben
Burnout	A general feeling of exhaustion that develops when an individual simultaneously experiences too much pressure and has too few sources of satisfaction	Ausgebranntsein
Business expenses	Expenses that have been paid or incurred in the course of business and that are ordinary, necessary and reasonable in amount	Betriebliche Aufwendungen
Business plan	A description of the company and its products or services for potential investors, encompassing a budget, an overview of current and projected financing, a market analysis and strategy, and projected profits and losses	Geschäftsplan
Business service providers (BSPs)	Software developers that rent business applications. Rather than purchasing software, a company can access applications via the Internet. A BSP's offerings are hosted by a computer service provider, and are often tailored to a specific industry	Anbieter von Software-Diensten per Datennetz (ASP)
Business-to-business (b2b)	Communications and transactions conducted between businesses, as opposed to between businesses and consumers. Expressed in alphanumeric form, it refers to such transactions conducted over the Internet	B2B, Geschäftskundenbereich
Buying signal	A communication from a prospect or customer that indicates s/he is strongly considering making a purchase (typically delivered in the form of a question (i.e., Can I have it delivered tomorrow?)	Signalisiertes Kaufinteresse

E | The "Handy 500"

"Handy 500" word	Brief explanation	Translation
Capital Asset Pricing Model	A model for valuing financial assets based upon their systematic risk. The objective is to limit exposure to only a few uncorrelated risk factors	CAPM, Modell zur Beschreibung von Anlagemärkten, Markowitz-Modell
Capital budget	Overview of planned purchases of long-term assets with estimates for the costs of those purchases	Investitionsplan
Capital stake	Invested stock with which company or person enters into business	Kapitaleinlage
Career development	Encompasses career management by which organizations select, assess, assign, and develop employees & the process through which individual employees identify and implement steps to attain career goals	Karrierepfad
Case study	An in-depth analysis of one setting	Fallstudie
Cash Against Documents (CAD)	A term denoting that payment is made when the bill of lading (or other document transferring title) is presented	Zahlung gegen Dokumente
Cash flow	A measure of the cash receipts and cash payments a company makes over a given time period. If a company has negative cash flow, the company must borrow money to operate its business. If a company has positive cash flow, the company has money available to spend on research and development, to expand operations, and to pay dividends to investors	Cashflow
Cash In Advance (CIA)	A method of payment for goods in which the buyer pays the seller in advance of the shipment of the goods. Usually employed when the goods are built to order, such as specialized machinery	Vorauskasse
Cash-basis accounting	A system of accounting in which transactions are recorded and revenues and expenses are recognized only when cash is received or paid	Ein- und Ausgabenbuchhaltung
Cell phone	Mobile phone	Handy
Centralization	A structural policy in which decision-making authority is concentrated at the top of the organizational hierarchy	Zentralisierung
CEO	Chief Executive Officer (Chairman of the Board of Directors)	Vorstandsvorsitzender

"Handy 500" word	Brief explanation	Translation
Change agent	A person responsible for managing a change effort	Promotor
Channel	The means used by companies to make their products and services available to their target market... examples include direct channel (sold by the company's sales force), distributors, retail stores, manufacturers' reps and value added resellers	Distributionskanal
Charity	Institution for helping those in need	Wohltätigkeitsverein
Chart of accounts	A systematic listing of all accounts used by a company	Kontenplan
Charter (Articles of Incorporation)	A document issued by a state that gives legal status to a corporation and details its specific rights, including the authority to issue a certain maximum number of shares of stock.	Gründungsurkunde für Kapitalgesellschaft
Clearinghouse	(1) Bankers' institution where payable and receivable bills are exchanged, so that only the balances need be paid in cash (2) Agency for collecting and distributing information	(1) Verrechnungsstelle (2) Informationszentrale
Close	The point at which either the prospect makes a commitment to purchase a particular product or service, or the salesperson asks or encourages the prospect to make a commitment to purchase a particular product or service	Käuferzusage, Aufforderung des Verkäufers zum Vertragsabschluss
Coercive power	The extent to which a person has the ability to punish or physically or psychologically harm someone else	Bestrafungsmacht
Cognitive dissonance	The anxiety a person experiences when he or she simultaneously possesses two sets of knowledge or perceptions that are contradictory or incongruent	Innere Zerrissenheit
Collaboration	Occurs when the interaction between groups is very important to goal attainment and the goals are compatible	Zusammenarbeit auf der Basis von kompatiblen Zielen
Collaborative filtering	The process by which a software component sifts through the profiles or usage patterns of users who visit a Website, and makes recommendations based on purchasing habits or other preferences	Kundenprofilierung

"Handy 500" word	Brief explanation	Translation
Collateral	Assets held to secure an obligation	Kreditsicherheit
Collectivism	The extent to which people emphasize the good of the group or society	Solidarität
Collusion	Conspirative cooperation	Konspirative Zusammenarbeit
Commercial paper	Short term debt typically issued by a company to raise cash. These instruments mature in less than one year and are backed by the issuer's credit line	Kurzfristiges Handelspapier (z. B. Wechsel)
Commission	Compensation paid to a salesperson following the successful completion of a sale to a customer… typically a percentage of the gross sales revenue but can be linked to units or margin as well	Provision, Courtage
Commodity	Product for trade	Fungibles Gut
Common stock	Regular stock. Owners of this class of stocks have a share of the company and a vote for the board of directors and on corporate policy. But they rank behind owners of preferred stock both to receive dividends and, usually, to receive assets if a company is liquidated	Stammaktien
Comparative financial statements	Financial statements for which data for two or more years are shown together	Bilanzvergleich
Compensation	(1) Money given to make amends for damage caused (2) The total array of money (wages, salary, commission), incentives, benefits, perquisites, and awards provided by the organization to an employee (3) Offsetting deficiency or frustration by developing another trait	(1) Entschädigung; (2) Entgelt; (3) Psychologisches Kompensieren
Competitive strategy	An outline of how a business intends to compete with other firms in the same industry	Wettbewerbsstrategie
Component	A part, ingredient, or subassembly that is both a component to a higher level part, and a parent part to other components	Teil
Compounding	A process whereby the value of an investment appreciates exponentially over time as interest is earned on interest	Zinseszinsverfahren
Compromise	Occurs when the interaction is moderately important to meeting goals and the goals are neither completely compatible nor completely incompatible	Kompromiss

The "Handy 500"   E

"Handy 500" word	Brief explanation	Translation
Confidence trick	Fraud based on misuse of trust (i.e. to "con" someone by deceiving him or her to engage in a transaction as a sign of trust)	Vertrauensmissbrauch in betrügerischer Absicht
Configuration	An organization's shape, which reflects the division of labor and the means of coordinating the divided tasks	Organisationsmodell
Conglomerate	Corporation formed by merging firms in unrelated businesses	Mischkonzern
Constraint	Limitation imposed on action	Einschränkung des Handlungsraums
Consumer profiling	The process of assembling a comprehensive database regarding consumer shopping habits, motivations, and product/service preferences. Information is captured from online and offline transactions, including supermarket loyalty cards scanned at checkout, cookies, credit cards, and other means	Modellierung eines Verbraucherprofils
Content provider	An organization that provides and updates information on the Internet. Content simply means any type of information	Online-Programmgestalter
Contingency	An event that may or may not occur	Kontingentes Ereignis
Contingency approach	An approach to organization design where the desired outcomes for the organization can be achieved in several ways	Kontingenzansatz
Contingency plans	Alternative actions to take if the primary course of action is unexpectedly disrupted or rendered inappropriate	Alternativplan
Continuous improvement	Describes the many management practices and techniques used to find and eliminate waste and to general improvements in business processes, quality or costs	Kontinuierliche Verbesserung
Contract work	Products or services provided by a separate organization (such as cleaning, security, consulting, and catering)	Zukauf, Fremdbeschaffung
Contractor	Contract manufacturer who designs and makes gadgets but leaves the marketing to companies with famous brands, producing either according to prespecified plans (electronic manufacturing services, EMS) or as an original design manufacturer (ODMS)	Vertragsunternehmer

"Handy 500" word	Brief explanation	Translation
Contribution	Pay, furnish (to common fund)	Beitrag
Controlling	The process of monitoring and correcting the actions of the organization and its members to keep them directed toward their goals	Controlling
Cooptation	A manipulative form of participation and involvement in a change, whereby key opponents are given what appear to be (but are not really) important roles	Kooptierung
Core competencies	The set of the most strategically significant and value-creating skills within an organization. CCs must be distinctive of the organization and representative of existing strengths and unique capabilities. CCs must lead to competitive advantage, be growth oriented and difficult to imitate	Kernkompetenzen
Corporate culture	The set of key values, beliefs, and understandings that are shared by the members of an organization	Unternehmungskultur
Corporate governance	Exercise of control over an organization	Spitzenverfassung, Unternehmensaufsicht
Corporation	A legal entity formed by one or more persons. A corporation is formed under the laws of a specific state and is legally defined as having a separate existence from that of its founders or owners	Kapitalgesellschaft
Cost, Insurance and Freight (CIF)	Under this term, the seller quotes a price for the goods (including insurance), all transportation, and miscellaneous charges to the point of debarkation for the vessel (CIP, or carriage and insurance paid to, is a term used for shipment by modes other than water)	Kosten, Versicherung, Fracht (CIF)
Counterparty	A party with whom one transacts business	Vertragspartner, Gegenpartei
Countertrade	Trade in which the seller agrees to accept goods, services, or other instruments or trade, in partial or whole payment for its products. Forms include barter, buy-back or compensation, offset requirements, swap, switch, or triangular trade, evidence or bilateral clearing	Tauschhandel
Credit	An entry on the right side of the account	Haben-Buchung
Credit exposure	Total amount of exposure to possible default by a counterparty	Ausfallrisiko

"Handy 500" word	Brief explanation	Translation
Credit risk	The probability that a counterparty may fail to perform on its obligations	Kreditrisiko
Cross-channel marketing	Marketing effort in which a company uses one of its sales channels to promote another	Cross-Channel-Marketing
Current assets	Cash and assets that are expected to be used, sold or converted to cash in the near future, usually one year	Umlaufvermögen
Current liabilities	These liabilities must be paid in a relatively short time, usually one year (e.g. Taxes)	Kurzfristige Verbindlichkeiten
Current ratio	A company's current assets (typically cash + receivables + inventory) divided by its current liabilities (debt due within a year). This ratio gives you a sense of a company's ability to meet all short-term liabilities with liquid assets, should it need to	Goldene Bilanzregel (eng gefasst)
Customer base	Portfolio of buyers	Kundenstamm
Customer relationship marketing (CRM)	A one-to-one marketing model in which information gathered throughout the history of the customer's relationship with the company is used to market to that customer in a way that promotes trust, loyalty, and, therefore, increased sale	Beziehungsmarketing
Cycle time (CT)	Average time between completion of successive units	Durchlaufzeit
Debit	An entry on the left side of an account	Soll-Buchung
Debt financing	Acquiring funds by borrowing money from creditors in the form of long-term notes, mortgages, leases or bonds	Langfristige Fremdfinanzierung
Debt-assets ratio	The ratio of a company's liabilities to its total assets. Long-term debt-assets is the ratio of long-term liabilities (those that won't be paid off in one year) to total assets. Total debt-assets is the ratio of long-term and current liabilities (debt that will be paid off within one year) to total assets	Goldene Bilanzregel (weit gefasst)
Debt-equity ratio	The ratio of a company's liabilities to its equity (total value of stock). Long-term debt-equity is the ratio of a company's long-term liabilities (debt that won't be paid off in one year) to its equity. Total debt-equity is the ratio of a company's	Fremdkapitalquote

"Handy 500" word	Brief explanation	Translation
	long-term and current liabilities (debt that will be paid off within one year) to its equity	
Deed	Certificate embodying a value	Urkunde
Default	Failure to pay back loan on maturity	Rückzahlungsverzug
Delegation	The transfer to others of authority to make decisions and use organizational resources	Übertragung von Kompetenzen
Demographics	Study of total size, sex, regional distribution, age, and other characteristics of human populations	Demografie
Deployment	Activation	Einsatz
Depreciation	The process of cost allocation that assigns the original cost of plant and equipment to the periods benefited	Abschreibung, Absetzung für Abnutzung (AfA)
Deregulation	Substituting public regulation by market rules	Deregulierung
Derivative instrument	A type of financial instrument which derives its value from the value of other financial instruments	Derivat
Developmental Change	Organizational change essentially limited to improving what currently exists rather than making radical changes. Examples include team building, most quality improvement efforts, enhancing internal communications, increasing technical expertise or core competencies, or basic expansion of services and products	Inkrementeller Wandel
Deviation	Difference between planned and actual position	Abweichung
Differentiation	Specialization of operations and separation of those operations within specific work units	Differenzierung
Discharge	Termination of employment relationship because of harmful employee behavior	Auflösung eines Arbeitsvertrages
Disintegration	Separation into component parts or fragments	Aufteilung, Zerschlagung
Disintermediation	Cutting out, or displacing, the middleman, or intermediary, between producers and consumers in transactions	Ausschaltung des Zwischenhändlers

"Handy 500" word	Brief explanation	Translation
Dismissals	Separation decisions initiated by the employer (occurring either as discharges or layoffs)	Massenkündigung
Disruption	Interrupt flow or continuity of (e.g. work)	Zerreißen, Zerrütten
Diversification	A technique for managing risk where risk is divided among multiple, uncorrelated exposures	Diversifizierung
Divest	To sell or liquidate (for instance, sale by one corporation of large blocks of stock it holds in another corporation)	Unternehmensteil veräußern
Divisional structure	Traditional organization structure based on departmentalization along product lines	Spartenorganisation
Donation	Present, grant, gift (esp. of money to an institution)	Spende, Zuwendung
Double entry accounting	A system of recording transactions in a way that maintains the equality of the accounting equation	Doppelte Buchführung
Dow Jones Industrial Average	A stock market indicator which measures the performance of 30 industrial stocks on the NYSE	Dow-Jones-Index
Downsizing	The process of purposely becoming smaller by reducing the size of the workforce or shedding divisions or businesses	Verschlanken
Earnings before interest, tax, depreciation and amortization (EBITDA)	This measure is related to cashflow, but it takes no account of a firm's capital spending and gives no indication of how much profit is actually turned into cash – as opposed to, for example – remaining tied up in receivables	Ebitda, Jahresüberschuss vor Zinsen, Steuern, AfA und Tilgung
Earnings per share (EPS)	The net income (or earnings) of a company for the past 12 months divided by the current number of shares	Gewinn pro Aktie
E-commerce	The activity of buying and selling over an electronic data interchange... typically referred to when describing the activity of buying and selling over the Internet and a web interface	E-Business
Economic Order Quantity (EOQ)	The size of an order that minimizes the total inventory cost, under a given set of circumstances, obtained by trade off analysis between the cost of placing an order and the cost of holding stock	Optimale Bestellmenge

E | The "Handy 500"

"Handy 500" word	Brief explanation	Translation
Economies of scale	Achieving reduction of unit costs through mass production and benefiting from the experience curve	Skaleneffekte, Größenvorteile
Economies of scope	Achieving synergy effects	Synergie-Effekte
Effectiveness	(1) Degree to which a strategy is successful in achieving the vision (outcome) (2) Degree to which activities of a unit achieve the unit's mission or goal faster, better (as defined by the customers), and cheaper	Grad der Zielerreichung
Efficiency	Measure of production or productivity relative to input resources	Effizienz
Employee benefits	Indirect form of total compensation, including paid time away from work, insurance and health protection, employee services, and retirement income	Geldwerte Nebenleistungen
Employee leasing	Long-term arrangement whereby an employer dismisses its employees, who are then hired by the leasing company and leased back to the original employer	Personal-Outsourcing
Employee performance	The degree to which employees accomplish job requirements	Leistungsgrad
Employee separations	Ending of employment relationships. Employee separations may be initiated by employer (as discharges or layoffs) or by employees (as quits or retirements) affecting the composition and characteristics of the retained workforce	Personalumsatz
Empowerment	The process of enabling workers to set their own work goals, make decisions, and solve problems within their sphere of responsibility and authority	Selbstverantwortung
Enterprise Requirement Planning (ERP)	A further extension of Material Resource Planning (MRPII) whereby a single system embraces and integrates all aspects of business operations into a single database application	PPS (Produktionsplanung und -steuerung), integrierte softwaregestützte Unternehmenssteuerung
Entitlement	Giving person or firm a rightful claim	Berechtigung, berechtigter Anspruch
Entity	An organizational unit (a person, partnership or corporation) for which accounting records is kept and about which accounting reports are prepared	Betriebsstätte

"Handy 500" word	Brief explanation	Translation
Entrepreneur	Business person risking own money	Unternehmer
Equity	(1) Ownership, e.g. of stock in a corporation (2) In the case of real estate, home equity equals the down payment plus any principal repaid on the mortgage (3) The belief that we are being treated fairly in relation to others	(1) Eigenkapital (2) Eigenanteil (3) Fairness
Equity risk	The risk of owning stock or having some other form of ownership interest	Eigenkapitalrisiko
Equity theory	Focuses on people's desire to be treated with what they perceive as equity and to avoid perceived inequity (also Contribution-Benefit Theory)	Anreiz-Beitrags-Theorie
Escalating commitment	The tendency to persist in an ineffective course of action when evidence reveals that the project cannot succeed	Kontern
ESOP (Employee Share Ownership Plan)	A qualified retirement plan designed to give employees an ownership stake in the company. Companies contribute shares of stock without requiring employees to invest their own money	Belegschaftsaktienplan
Executive	Senior or middle-level manager	Leitender Angestellter
Expectancy theory	Suggests that people are motivated by how much they want something and the likelihood they perceive of getting it	Erwartungshaltungstheorie
Expenses	Costs incurred in the normal course of business to generate revenues	Betriebsausgaben
Experience Curve	Cost reductions due to learning derived from production process	Erfahrungskurve
Extraordinary item	Non-operating gains and losses that are unusual in nature, infrequent in occurrence and material in amount	A. o. Aufwendungen
Factoring	The discounting of a foreign account receivable. The exporter transfers title to its foreign accounts receivable to a factoring house for cash at a discount from the face value. Export factoring allows an exporter to ship on "open account," by which goods are shipped without guarantee of payment (that is, a letter of credit). The factor assumes financial ability of the customer to pay and handles collections on the receivables	Factoring, Auf-/Verkauf von Forderungen

E | The "Handy 500"

"Handy 500" word	Brief explanation	Translation
Fair market value	The current value of an asset, e.g., the amount at which an asset could be sold or purchased on an arm's-length transaction	Theoretischer Marktwert
Field survey	Typically relies on a questionnaire distributed to a sample of people selected from a larger population	Feldforschung
Filter program	This is a program that accepts incoming data, processes it based on programmable criteria, and then moves it to the next appropriate location for action	Filterprogramm
Financial accounting	The area of accounting concerned with reporting financial information to interested external parties	Geschäftsbuchführung
Financial Accounting Standards Board (FASB)	The private organization responsible for establishing the standards for financial accounting and reporting in the United States	FASB, US-Wirtschaftsprüferkammer
Financial risk	Financial exposure to uncertainty.	Finanzrisiko
Financial statements	Reports such as the balance sheet, income statement and statement of cash flows, which summarize the financial status and results of operations of a business entity	Geschäftszahlen
First-in, first-out (FIFO)	(1) Stock Valuation – The method of valuing stocks which assumes that the oldest stock is consumed first and thus issues are valued at the oldest price. (2) Stock Rotation – The method whereby the goods which have been longest in stock are delivered (sold) and/or consumed first.	(1) FIFO bei Bewertung des Lagerbestands (2) FIFO als sequentielles Vorgehen bei Lagerumschlag
First-mover advantage	Gaining a powerful competitive edge by being the first or an early successful-player to identify and establish yourself in a market	Vorteil, als erstes Unternehmen am Markt zu sein
Fiscal Year	An entity's reporting year, covering a 12 month accounting period	Geschäftsjahr
Flattening (Organizational):	The intentional reduction or streamlining of processes by eliminating waste and redundant functions, often while decentralizing decision-making	Verschlankung
Flexible work schedules (flextime)	These schedules give employees more personal control over the hours they work each day	Flexible Arbeitszeiten

"Handy 500" word	Brief explanation	Translation
Flotation	(1) Starting of company or enterprise (2) Issue of stock or bonds	(1) Gesellschaftsgründung (2) Wertpapieremission
Formalization	The degree to which rules and procedures shape the jobs and activities of employees	Formalisierung
Forward (or Future)	An agreement to execute a transaction at some time in the future	Termingeschäft
Franchise	A relationship that allows a business owner to license its property, trademarks, and concepts to another entity. Most franchises are national or widely recognized "chains" operated by licensees or franchisees, overseen by the franchiser	Franchise
Free Alongside Ship (FAS)	Under FAS, the seller quotes a price for the goods that includes charges for delivery of the goods alongside a vessel at the port of departure. The seller handles the cost of unloading and wharfage; loading, ocean transportation, and insurance are left to the buyer. FAS is also a method of export and import valuation	Frei Längsseite Schiff (FAS)
Free on Board – Free On Board (FOB)	The seller quotes the buyer a price that covers all costs up to and including delivery of goods aboard a vessel at a port. FOB is also a method of export valuation	Frei an Bord (FOB)
Freelancer	Self-employed contract worker for an organization	Freier Mitarbeiter, Freiberufler
Fulfillment	The entire process of completing transactions such as sales orders, requests for information, and redemption of coupons, premiums, giveaways, rebates, and refunds. Fulfillment can be outsourced so that an outside company handles part or all of the order-fulfillment process.	Abwicklung
GAAP (Generally Accepted Accounting Principles)	Authoritative guidelines that define accounting practice at a particular time	GAAP, Rechnungslegungsstandard in den USA, US-GoB
Gainsharing	Linked employee suggestion and bonus pay program	Erfolgsbeteiligung
General partnership	Joint business	OHG
Global Company	Company with worldwide reach that continuously balances centralized strategies and local responsiveness	Global agierendes Unternehmen, Global Player

"Handy 500" word	Brief explanation	Translation
Goal	A goal should provide a sense of what level of performance is expected but it should not specify how the organization is to achieve the level of performance. Generally, there should be a Goal assigned to each Critical Issue or programmatic area within the organization. Goals link "downward" to Objectives. Every Goal should have at least one Objective	Ziel
Grievance	Formal dispute between an employee and management on the conditions of employment	Beschwerde, Arbeitsstreitigkeit
Gross Domestic Product (GDP)	The value of all the goods and services produced by a country in a given period of time (formerly called Gross National Product, or GNP)	Bruttonationaleinkommen
Groupthink	Occurs when a group's overriding concern is a unanimous decision rather than critical analysis of alternatives	Kollektivdenken
Guarantee agreement	A guarantee of the borrower's credit provided by the guarantor	Bürgschaft
Guerrilla marketing	Aimed at small businesses with limited resources, guerrilla marketing has been described as a "take-no-prisoners" approach to marketing that encompasses a wide range of creative, lively, low-cost techniques"	Unkonventionelles Marketing
Haulage	Road transport of goods	Straßentransport, Güterverkehr
Hedge	To take offsetting risks	Ausgleichsrisiko
Horizontal vertical structure	A process form of management utilizing the concept of focusing on common objectives that transcend traditional departmental boundaries to meet customer or stakeholder requirements	Prozessorganisation
Hostile takeover	Acquisition forged against the will of the top management of the target company	Feindliche Übernahme
Impairment	Loss of goodwill assessed by auditor	Beeinträchtigung des Firmenwerts
Impression management	A direct and intentional effort by someone to enhance his or her own image in the eyes of others	Imagepflege
Incentive systems	Plans in which employees can earn additional compensation in return for certain types of performance	Anreizsysteme

"Handy 500" word	Brief explanation	Translation
Income statement	The financial statement that summarizes the revenues generated and expenses incurred by an entity during a period of time	G & V (Gewinn- und Verlustrechnung)
Incremental decision-making	Iterative approach based on making many small decisions	Schrittweises Vorgehen
Industrial clusters	Groups of interrelated industries that drive wealth creation in a region, primarily through export of goods and services	Industrielle Ballungsräume
Inequity	The belief that one is being treated unfairly in relation to others	Benachteiligungsgefühl
Infomediary	A hybrid of "information" and "intermediary"; the term describes a new kind of online middleman – between consumer and vendor – who brokers consumer Internet data in exchange for vendor concessions on goods and services. The term infomediary is increasingly used to refer to Websites that facilitate business-to-business (B2B) e-commerce by offering information about suppliers and other businesses	Online-Broker
Initial public offering (IPO)	A company's first sale of stock to the public	Erster Börsengang
Injunction	Courts issue these to stop a person or group from doing something that might cause future harm	Einstweilige Verfügung
Input measure	Resource expended on a given activity. Input measures are useful for tracking status of available resources with no consideration of the results	Inputbezogene Leistungsmessung
Intangible	A long-lived asset without physical substance that are used in business, such as licenses, patents, franchise and goodwill	Immaterielles Gut
Interest rate	The cost of using money, expressed as an annual percentage	Zinssatz
Intermediate product	A product for which independent demand can exist and for which there is also demand as part of another higher level product e.g. a sub-assembly spare and the major assembly of which it forms part	Zwischenprodukt, Halbfertigerzeugnis

"Handy 500" word	Brief explanation	Translation
Internal process control	Focuses on internal activities and assesses effectiveness by indicators of process efficiency	Operative Leistungsmessung
International Company	Company which produces and sells standardized products around the world	Internationales Unternehmen
Intrapreneurship	Entrepreneurial activity that takes place within empowered strategic business units of corporations	Innerbetriebliches Unternehmertum
Intrinsic reward	Inherent compensation residing in the performance of a task	Intrinsische Belohnung
Investor relations (IR)	The function or department within a publicly traded company that acts as its intermediary with investors and the financial community. IR is generally responsible for communicating with shareholders, analysts, the business and financial media, and the investment community at large. A successful IR also ensures public disclosure of relevant information, prepares annual and quarterly reports, organizes annual shareholder meetings, and looks for opportunities to show the company in the most positive light	Pflege der Beziehungen zu Investoren
Inventory	Products ready for sale and the materials needed to make them	Inventar
Job enlargement	Involves giving workers more tasks to perform	Arbeitserweiterung
Job enrichment	Entails giving workers more tasks to perform and more control over how to perform them	Arbeitsbereicherung
Joint venture	Subsidiary established jointly by several companies aiming to enter a specific market by pooling resources	Gemeinschaftsunternehmen, Gelegenheitsgesellschaft
Junk bond	A fixed-interest security, not backed by collateral, with a low credit rating (usually compensated by high interest)	Ungesicherte Schuldverschreibung
Just-in-Time (JIT)	A dependent demand inventory control philosophy which views production as a system in which all operations, including the delivery of materials needed for production, occur just at the time they are needed. Thus, stocks of material are virtually eliminated	Fertigungssynchrone Beschaffung

"Handy 500" word	Brief explanation	Translation
Kiosk	A stand-alone, boxlike unit that houses a computer and monitor for public display. Generally, users make selections through a touch screen or a built-in keyboard and pointing device	Öffentlicher Internet-Terminal
Labor relations	Continuous relationship between organized group of employees (represented by a union) and an employer, including negotiation of contract governing conditions of employment and their interpretation over its period of coverage	Sozialbeziehungen
Lateral career path	Transferring horizontally to different functions, programs or projects within the organization	Rotation
Layoffs	Workforce reduction caused by poor business conditions	Massenentlassungen
Lead	A person or organization that has shown an interest in a particular product or service	Interessent
Lead-time	The time between the decision to place a replenishment order until its availability for use	Lieferzeit
Lease	Contract granting the use of fixed assets for a period of time in exchange for payment, usually as rent	Pacht
Legitimate power	Power that is granted by virtue of one's position in the organization	Funktionsmacht
Letter Of Credit	A financial document issued by a bank at the request of the consignee guaranteeing payment to the shipper for cargo if certain terms and conditions are fulfilled. Normally it contains a brief description of the goods, documents required, a shipping date, and an expiration date after which payment will no longer be made	Akkreditiv
Letter of intent	Preliminary agreement on the scale and scope of a planned project subject to further negotiation on details	Vorvertrag
Leverage	(1) The compounding of risks (2) Ratio of debt to equity	Hebelwirkung
Leveraged buyout (LBO)	The purchase of a company using borrowed money. Usually the buyer secures the loan with the assets of the company to be purchased	Fremdfinanzierte Übernahme

"Handy 500" word	Brief explanation	Translation
Liabilities	Obligations measurable in monetary terms that represent amounts owed to creditors, governments, employees and other parties	Verbindlichkeiten
Liaison	An individual who serves as a bridge between groups, tying groups together and facilitating the communication flow needed to integrate group activities	Verbindungsstelle
Licensing	Official or legal permission to own or do something, such as the permission to utilize intellectual property, patents, trade secrets, or copyrights under a contract or agreement	Lizenzierung
Limited partner	An owner in a limited partnership who's liable only up to the amount of money invested	Kommanditist
Liquidity	A company's ability to meet current obligations with cash or other assets that can be quickly converted to cash	Liquidität
Litigation	Settling a legal dispute in a court of law.	Prozessieren
Long position	A position which entails ownership or effective ownership of an asset	Kaufposition
Low-cost leadership	Competitive strategy focused on achieving cost efficiency	Kostenführerschaft
Machine bureaucracy	This structure is typical of large, well-established organizations. Work is highly specialized and formalized, and decision making is usually concentrated at the top	Hochformalisierte Unternehmensorganisation
Management accounting	The area of accounting concerned with providing internal financial reports to assist management in making decisions	Finanzbuchhaltung
Management by objectives (MBO)	A collaborative goal-setting process through which organizational goals cascade down throughout the organization	Führen durch Zielvereinbarung
Manufacturing Resource Planning (MRP II)	A method for the effective planning of all the resources of a manufacturing company. Ideally it addresses operational planning in units, financial planning in money, and has a simulation capability to answer what if questions	PPS (Produktionsplanung und -steuerung), softwaregestützte Unternehmenssteuerung

"Handy 500" word	Brief explanation	Translation
Margin	The difference between the selling price of a product or service and the cost of producing, delivering or acquiring the product or service	Gewinnspanne
Marginal cost	The cost of producing an additional unit	Grenzkosten
Market capitalization	The share price times total shares outstanding for a particular company	Börsenwert einer Unternehmung
Market risk	Risk from changes in market prices	Preisrisiko
Market share	A measure of how dominant a company is in its industry. Market share is determined by expressing a company's revenues, sometimes for a specific product or service, as a percentage of the industry's overall revenues for similar products or services	Marktanteil
Market value	The value at which an asset trades, or would trade in the market	Marktpreis
Marketable securities	Securities, like government bonds, that can be sold easily. On balance sheets, they are listed as current assets because they're expected to be converted to cash in the near future, usually one year	Börsenfähige Wertpapiere
Marketing	A set of activities that assist in driving sales of a product and/or service	Marketing
Matrix design	Combines two different designs to gain the benefits of each; typically combined are a product or project departmentalization scheme and a functional structure	Matrixorganisation
Maturity	The date on which a note or obligation becomes due	Fälligkeit
Maturity stage	The career stage defined as the time to hold on to one's place in the chosen field of work	Reifephase
Mechanistic structure	This structure is primarily hierarchical. Within it, interactions and communications are typically vertical, instructions come from the boss, knowledge is concentrated at the top, and loyalty and obedience are required to sustain membership	Linienorganisation
Mentoring	Occurs when a more experienced person helps a younger employee grow and advance by providing advice, support, and encouragement	Coaching, Patenschaftsmodell

"Handy 500" word	Brief explanation	Translation
Merger	The acquisition of one company by another company whereby the companies combine as one legal entity, with the acquired company going out of existence	Fusion
Mindset	An individual's self-perception of skills, interests and personal agendas which shape activities at work	Denkstil, interessengeleitete Denkweise
Mission Statement	A statement of the role, or purpose, by which an organization intends to serve its stakeholders. Describes what the organization does (current capabilities), who it serves (stakeholders), and what makes the organization unique (justification for existence)	Unternehmensleitbild
Mortgage	A written promise to pay a stated amount of money at one or more specified future dates that is secured by the pledging of certain assets, usually real estate, as collateral	Hypothek, Grundschuld
Multidomestic Enterprise (MDE)	Company with area structure which produces and sells localized products worldwide	Dezentral operierende multinationale Unternehmung
Multilateral agreement	An international compact in which three or more parties participate	Mehrseitige Übereinkunft
Multinational Enterprise (MNE)	Company which produces and sells products across different countries	Multinationale Unternehmung
Mutual fund	A group of securities owned by a group of investors. It is managed by investmentprofessionals who make buy and sell decisions for the group	Investment Fonds
Negative reinforcement (avoidance)	The opportunity to avoid or escape from an unpleasant circumstance after exhibiting behavior	Anpassungsdruck
Negligence	Lack of appropriate care or perspicacity	Fahrlässigkeit
Net assets (Owners equity)	The ownership interest in the assets of an equity; equal total assets minus total liabilities	Eigenkapital
Net income	The amount of a company's total sales (revenue) remaining after subtracting all of its costs, in a given period of time (also referred to as "net earnings"	Betriebsergebnis
Net proceeds	The difference between maturity value and discount when a note receivable is discounted	Barwert

"Handy 500" word	Brief explanation	Translation
Net sales	Gross sales less sales discounts and sales returns and allowances	Nettoverkaufswert
Network effect	Law of increasing returns	Netzwerkeffekt
Non-cash item	Item included in the determination of net income on an accrual basis that does not affect cash; examples are depreciation and amortization	Rechnerischer Posten
Nonprogrammed decision	A decision that recurs infrequently and for which there is no previously established decision rule	Situative Entscheidung
Note payable	A debt owed to a creditor, evidenced by an unconditional written promise to pay a certain sum of money on or before a specified future date	Schuldwechsel
Note receivable	A claim against a debtor, evidenced by an unconditional written promise to pay a certain sum of money on or before a specified future date	Besitzwechsel
Notes to financial statements	Explanatory information considered an integral part of the financial statements	Eventualverbindlichkeiten, Bilanzerläuterungen
Objectives	Specific and measurable targets for accomplishment during the stated time frame. Objectives link "upward" to goals, link "downward" to strategies	Operationalisierte Ziele
Obligation	(1) Binding agreement (2) Deed by which company or government promises to repay borrowed money, usually with interest	(1) Vertragliche Verpflichtung (2) Festverzinsliches Wertpapier
Offsite storage	A Web-based service that lets individuals and companies store electronic documents on the Provider's computer system	Ausgelagerte Datenspeicherung
Open system	A system that interacts with its environment	Offenes System
Open transaction	A transaction that is not completed at the end of an accounting period; a purchase that has not yet been paid for or a sale where payment is yet to be collected when the accounting period ends	Rechnungsabgrenzungsposten
Operating activities	Transactions and events that enter into the determination of net income	Betriebliche Aktivitäten

E | The "Handy 500"

"Handy 500" word	Brief explanation	Translation
Operating assets	Long-term or non-current assets acquired for use in the business rather than for resale; includes property, plant and equipment; intangible assets and natural resources	Anlagevermögen
Operating system	Any part of an organization that takes inputs and transforms them into outputs of greater value to the organization than the original inputs.	Fertigungsbereich, operativer Bereich
Operational risk	Risk from mistakes or failures in operations	Betriebsbedingte Risiken
Option	The right to buy or sell an investment instrument, usually a security, at a previously agreed price known as the strike price	Wahlrecht, Option
Organic structure	This structure is set up like a network. Within it, interactions and communications are horizontal, knowledge resides wherever it is most useful to the organization, and membership requires a commitment to the organization's tasks	Gewachsene Organisation
Organizational structure	Lines of authority and responsibility	Organisationsstruktur
Original equipment manufacturer (OEM)	Term that originally defined a manufacturer who produced a product to be sold under other company's brands (now used also to describe when a company makes a product and sells it to other companies so that they can sell it under their label	Vertraglicher Zulieferer
Other revenues and expenses	Items incurred or earned from activities that are outside, or peripheral to, the normal operations of a firm	Außerbetriebliche Aufwendungen und Erträge
Outcome measure	An assessment of the results of a program, project or work task compared to its intended purpose to produce a specific desired effect or result which can be qualitatively measured	Soll-Ist-Vergleich
Out-of-the-money	A condition where an option has no intrinsic value. It is opposed to the In-the-money condition where an option has a positive intrinsic value	Wertlos gewordene Option
Output control	Focuses on measurable employee outputs and productivity	Ergebnisorientierte Unternehmenssteuerung

"Handy 500" word	Brief explanation	Translation
Output goal	A tactical or short-term quality or efficiency indicator for a business process	Effizienzziel, Produktivitätsziel
Output measure	The tabulation of activity or effort that can be expressed in a quantitative or qualitative manner. Output measures are useful for tracking volumes or levels of work when tracking of quality or effectiveness is typically less important than tracking costs	Effizienzmessung
Outsource	To have a service performed or a function completed by others outside of own company	Auslagern
Over the counter	Not traded on an exchange	Tafelgeschäft
Parent company	Company in control of subsidiary companies	Muttergesellschaft
Pareto chart (80/20 rule)	A form of Pareto analysis applied to a group of products in order to apply selective inventory management controls. The inventory value for each item is obtained by multiplying the annual demand by unit cost and the entire inventory is then ranked in descending order of cost	ABC-Analyse
Participation	The process of giving employees a voice in making decisions about their own work	Mitwirkung
Partnership	A business enterprise comprised of two or more individuals. Liability is shared between partners. Income and expenses related to the partnership must be reported on each partners' individual personal income tax	OHG
Path dependence	Dependence of further steps on the actual path taken by an underlier over a specified period	Iteratives Vorgehen
Payee	The person (entity) to whom payment on a note is to be made	Zahlungsempfänger
Penalize	Make subject to penalty or comparative disadvantage	Bestrafen
Pension plan	A contract between a company and its employees whereby the company agrees to pay benefits to employees after their retirement. For example: A 401(k) plan – its name taken from the section of the US Internal Revenue	Steuerbegünstigte betriebliche Altersversorgung

E | The "Handy 500"

"Handy 500" word	Brief explanation	Translation
	Code – is a retirement savings plan that is funded by employee contributions and (often) matching contributions from the employer. The major attraction of these plans is that the contributions are taken from pre-tax salary, and the funds grow tax-free until withdrawn. Also, the plans are (to some extent) self-directed, and they are portable. A 401(k) plan that created them	
Perception	The set of processes by which an individual becomes aware of and interprets information about the environment	Wahrnehmung
Performance assessment	Is the process that measures employee performance	Leistungsbewertung
Performance goal	Target level of performance that is expressed by a tangible, measurable objective against which actual achievement can be compared	Leistungsziel
PLC	Public Limited Company	Aktiengesellschaft (UK)
Policy surrender	The early termination of an insurance product by the policyholder	Kündigung von Versicherungsvertrag
Portfolio theory	A body of theory relating to how investors optimize portfolio selections	Portfolio-Theorie
Position power	Resides in the position, regardless of who is filling that position. People who possess this trait are upbeat and optimistic, have an overall sense of well-being, and see things in a positive light	Vorgesetztenmacht
Positive reinforcement	A reward or other desirable consequence that a person receives after exhibiting behavior	Verhaltensbelohnung
Power distance	The extent to which less powerful persons accept the unequal distribution of power	Unterordnungsbereitschaft
Prepayment	The payment of a debt prior to its being due	Vorauszahlung
Price/Earnings Ratio (P/E)	An indicator of a stock's value, calculated by dividing the stock's price by its earnings per share for a 12-month period. Stocks with high P/Es compared to the overall market are typically growth stocks	KGV (Kurs-Gewinn-Verhältnis)

"Handy 500" word	Brief explanation	Translation
Prior tax	VAT on purchased inputs credited to companies	Vorsteuer
Problemistic search	Pragmatic approach to problem-solving	Pragmatisches Vorgehen
Procurement	Purchase	Beschaffung, Einkauf
Product life cycle	Concept suggesting products follow a predictable trajectory, patterned on the life cycle	Produktlebenszyklus
Production lead time	The time taken to manufacture or produce an item after an external order has been received until the item is available for packing	Produktionszeit
Productivity	Value added by the process, factored against the value of all labor, capital or other resources consumed by processes	Produktivität
Profit	Financial gain, or revenues minus expenses	Gewinn
Profit margin	Determined by dividing net income by net sales during a time period (usually the past four quarters) and is expressed as a percentage. Net profit margin is a measure of efficiency	Gewinnspanne
Proliferation	Dispersion	Verbreitung
Property, plant and equipment	Tangible, long-lived assets acquired for use in business operations; includes land, buildings, machinery, equipment and furniture	Anlagevermögen
Proprietary	Owned by a person or organization	Im Eigentum befindlich
Prospect	(as noun) An individual or organization with a need for a particular product or service; (as verb) To proactively seek out potential buyers of a product or service and approach them through personal contact with the intent to sell should a need exist	Potenzieller Kunde; akquirieren
Provision	Providing against accrued possible future expenditure	Klausel; Rückstellung
Proxy	A shareholder's written statement designating someone else to vote for him or her at a corporate meeting	Stimmrechtsvollmacht
Public law	Regulates relations between persons and State	Öffentliches Recht

"Handy 500" word	Brief explanation	Translation
Public relations	Any form of communication designed to promote goodwill or prestige for a company or organization	Öffentlichkeitsbeziehungen
Pull system	A system where orders for an end item are pulled through the facility to satisfy demand for the end item. An examples of pull system is the JIT Kanban process	Nachfrageorientierte Steuerung
Push system	A system where orders are issued for completion by specified due dates, based on estimated lead-times, or where the flow of material in a product structure is controlled and determined by the lower levels	Angebotsorientierte Steuerung
Put option	An option to sell an asset	Verkaufsoption
Quick ratio	A measure of a company's ability to meet its short-term financial obligations with its liquid assets. The company's liquid current assets (cash, accounts receivable, marketable securities) is divided by its current liabilities. The quick ratio is similar to the current ratio, but does not include inventory as a current asset	Goldene Bankregel
Rating agency	Professional organization (such as Moody's, and S&P) that on demand assesses the default risk of debts and the volatility of financial instruments on a letter scale ranging from AAA to D (default). Many investment institutions must by charter put their money into investment –grade instruments (between AAA and BBB). Many loan agreements stipulate that if there is a downgrade, interest rates will be increased or the debt must be repaid immediately	Rating-Agentur
Reach	The number of different persons or households exposed to a particular media vehicle or media schedule at least once during a specific time period	Erreichte Zielgruppe
Reactive strategy	Refers to the actions that take place in response to events that occur (are typically less effective than proactive and intentional strategies)	Abwartende Strategie
Real Property	Immovable property, such as land, houses	Immobilien
Receivables	Claims for money, goods or services	Forderungen

"Handy 500" word	Brief explanation	Translation
Recruiting	Activity to identify AND attract a pool of candidates for employment, from which some may later be selected to receive offers	Personalbeschaffung
Reengineering	The radical redesign of organizational processes to achieve major gains in cost, time, and provision of services	Prozesserneuerung
Referent power	Exists when one person wants to be like or imitates someone else	Vorbildmacht
Reliability	The extent to which a measure is consistent over time	Reliabilität
Resource approach	Focuses on organizational effectiveness in obtaining scarce and valued resources	Steuerung durch akquisitorisches Potenzial
Resource power	Power derived from the control of vital employees, money, equipment, customers, etc.	Verteilungsmacht
Resume	Curriculum Vitae (CV)	Lebenslauf
Retailer	Seller of goods not for resale	Einzelhändler
Retaliatory measure	Action taken by a country, whose exports are adversely affected by the raising of tariffs or other trade restricting measures by another country. The WTO permits an adversely affected contracting party (CP) to impose limited restraints on imports from another CP that has raised its trade	Vergeltung
Return on equity (ROE)	A percentage that indicates how well common stockholders' invested money is being used. The percentage is the result of dividing net earnings by common stockholders' equity. The ROE is used for measuring growth and profitability	Aktienrendite
Return on investment (ROI)	A measure of how well a company's management is performing. ROI is calculated by dividing earnings before taxes (EBIT) by total assets at the end of the year	Eigenkapitalrendite
Revenue	The dollar amount of annual sales, net of allowances (discounts, returned merchandise). It is the "top line" figure from which costs are subtracted to determine net income	Umsatz, Einnahmen
Reward power	The extent to which a person controls rewards that another person values	Belohnungsmacht

"Handy 500" word	Brief explanation	Translation
Risk aversion	The degree to which a person is unwilling to take chances and make decisions under conditions of uncertainty	Risikovermeidung
Risk propensity	The degree to which a person is willing to take chances and make risky decisions	Risikobereitschaft
Risk-free rate	A theoretical interest rate at which an investment may earn interest without incurring any risk	Natürlicher Zins
Role ambiguity	Arises when a role is unclear	Fehlende Rollenklarheit
Routinization	Standardization and formalization of procedures	Standardisierung von Abläufen
Sample	In promotion, a trial size of a product to be distributed free to potential customers. In research, a small representation of a larger universe or market used to study that audience	Muster
Sarbanes-Oxley Act	This Act of 2002 aims to improve the quality and transparency in financial reporting and independent audits under the oversight of the PCOAB. Also, it directs the SEC to set rigorous rules for the internal controls, financial disclosure, and personal responsibility of board members in public corporations	Sarbanes-Oxley-Gesetz
Satisficing	Examining alternatives only until a solution that meets minimal requirements is found	Minimalisieren
Scalability	The ability of computer hardware, software, and applications to adapt to increased demands and continue to function well	Kapazitätsreserven
Scarcity	Demand for a good outruns the supply	Knappheit
Scenario	Possible set of future events	Szenario
Secondary market	Where securities are traded after their initial issuance. Money from trades goes to dealers and sellers, not to the company that originally issued the security. Secondary markets include exchanges, as well as virtual marketplaces (such as the over-the-counter markets of computer and telephone lines)	Handelsmarkt

"Handy 500" word	Brief explanation	Translation
Secured bonds	Bonds backed by collateral or a lien (pledged assets – such as real estate) if borrower defaults	Schuldverschreibungen
Securities	A general term for publicly traded stocks, bonds, and other financial instruments.	Wertpapiere
Securitization	The creation of security interests in an asset	Verbriefung von Forderungen
Segmentation	Process of subdividing customers into groups sharing characteristics and needs	Aufgliederung
Selective perception	The process of screening out information that we are uncomfortable with or that contradicts our beliefs	Selektive Wahrnehmung
Self-efficacy	The extent to which we believe we can accomplish our goals even if we failed to do so in the past	Selbstvertrauen
Self-esteem	The extent to which a person believes he or she is a worthwhile and deserving individual	Selbstwertgefühl
Sensitivity	Exposure to a risk factor	Verwundbarkeit
Settlement risk	Risk from possible default by a counterparty at the time an obligation is to be settled	Delkredere-Risiko
Share price	The price of a unit of ownership in a company (a share). The most recent trade in the stock is typically used as the "quoted" share price	Kurswert
Shareholder value	Increase in the market value of a company's stocks, as quoted on the stock exchange	Marktwert des Aktienkapitals, Aktienwert
Shelf life	The maximum time an item may be stored before use	Lagerungsdauer
Shrinkage	The decrease in inventory quantities over time from loss or theft	Schwund
Slack	Underused resources	Ungenutzte Reserven
S–O Actions	Referring to the SWOT-MPM, a term that is used to discuss those actions that use organizational strengths to take advantage of existing opportunities	Analyse der inneren Stärken und der externen Chancen
Social loafing	The tendency of some members of groups to put forth less effort in a group than they would when working alone	Trittbrettfahren

"Handy 500" word	Brief explanation	Translation
Sole proprietorship	A business owned by an individual who is completely liable for its actions and income	Einzelfirma
Solvency	Having the money to meet all eventual liabilities	Solvenz
Span of control	The number of people who report to a manager	Kontrollspanne
Spare parts	Components or parts, either consumable or repairable, from the associated bill of material used to maintain or repair machinery or equipment	Ersatzteile
Specific risk	Risk which is unique to a particular asset or liability	Anlagebedingtes Risiko
Spin-off	(1) A corporate divestiture in which a subsidiary or division becomes a separate corporate entity (2) A dividend made up of assets (e.g. another company's stock) that is distributed to stockholders	(1) Auslagerung eines Unternehmensteils (2) Aktienspaltung
Spinout	A strategy in which a company develops businesses based on its noncore emerging technologies and sells minority stakes to public investors. The venture-capitalized spinouts remain within the corporate orbit or structure	Eigeninduzierte Konzernbildung
Spot market	Where goods are traded for immediate delivery	Kassamarkt
S–T Actions	Referring to the SWOT, a term that is used to discuss those actions that use organizational strengths to minimize or avoid existing or potential threats	Analyse der internen Stärken und externen Risiken
Staffing	Activities that determine the composition of an organization's workforce	Personalbeschaffung und Personaleinsatz
Stakeholder	Those individuals, groups, and parties that either affect or who are affected by the organization	Unternehmenspartner
Standard & Poor's 500 (S&P 500)	A stock-market indicator based on the performance of 500 popular common stocks	S & P 500
Standard operating procedures (SOP's)	Explicit directives that tell employees exactly what is or is not appropriate on the job	Arbeitsrichtlinien

"Handy 500" word	Brief explanation	Translation
Startup	A business that has recently begun operation	Neugründung
Statement of earnings (Income statement)	The financial statement that summarizes the revenues generated and the expenses incurred by an entity during a period of time	G & V (Gewinn- und Verlustrechnung)
Statutory law	Written law enacted by legislature, as opposed to case and common law	Gesetztes Recht
Stock	(1) A share of ownership, or equity, in a corporation (2) All the goods and materials stored by an organization and retained for future use	(1) Aktie (2) Lagervorrat
Stock option plan	This plan allows employees to buy a set number of shares of their company's stock at a future date and at a set price (at or below the market price at the time the option is granted) for a specified period of years	Belegschaftsaktienprogramm
Strategic management	The process by which an organization determines its long-run direction and performance by ensuring that careful formulation, effective & efficient implementation, and continuous evaluation of strategy and performance takes place	Strategisches Management
Strategic planning	The process by which an organization formulates and implements important decisions across different levels and functions of the organization	Strategische Planung
Strategies	Are the specific methods, processes, or steps used to accomplish Goals and Objectives. Strategies impact resources (Inputs) in some positive or negative way and they are executed in a tactical manner so as to link Goals and Objectives to day-to-day operations	Strategien
Strategy	A general direction set for the organization and its various components to achieve a desired state in the future, resulting from the detailed strategic planning process. Strategy in this general sense should not be confused with Strategies	Langfristiger Unternehmensplan
Subsidiary	Company controlled by another company on basis of share ownership	Tochtergesellschaft

E | The "Handy 500"

"Handy 500" word	Brief explanation	Translation
Sunk cost	Nonswitchable investment	Irreversible Investitionen
Supervisor	Manager at operational level	Operativer Vorgesetzter
Supply chain management (SCM)	Organization of the overall business processes to enable the profitable transformation of raw materials or products into finished goods and their timely distribution to meet customer demand	Steuerung der Lieferantenbeziehungen bzw. der Logistikkette
Support activities	Internal business activities that enable achievement of mission activities and strategic activities, but that are permanent and not directly linked to specific goals	Zuarbeitung
Swap	(1) Exchange by way of barter (2) A type of derivative instrument	(1) Tauschgeschäft (2) Swapgeschäft
Systematic risk	(1) Risk which is common to an entire class of assets or liabilities; (2) Risk which threatens an entire financial system	(1) Klassenspezifisches Risiko (2) Systemisches Risiko
Tangible personal business property	Depreciable operating assets of a business, other than real property, including machinery, furniture and fixtures, automobiles and trucks and equipment	Bewegliche Anlagegüter
Targeted marketing	(1) A technique in which marketers mine computerized databases of customer information to create profiles of prospects who will be most receptive to their messages (also known as database marketing) (2) Tapping information specific to one prospect to develop personalized messages	(1) Sozio-demografische Segmentierung (2) Database Marketing
Task	Assignment	Aufgabe, Auftrag
Task environment	This environment includes specific organizations, groups, and individuals that influence the organization	Geschäftsumwelt
Telecommuting	A work arrangement in which employees spend part of their time working off-site	Telearbeit
Tender	Offer to execute work or supply goods at a fixed price	Festpreis
Tipping point	Point of no return	Kipppunkt
Tit-for-tat behavior	Any perceived unfriendly act is answered by a similar unfriendly act	Abstrafendes Verhalten

"Handy 500" word	Brief explanation	Translation
Toll	Tax or duty paid for use of facility or service rendered	Nutzungsgebühr
Tort	A wrongful act, resulting in injury or damage, on which a civil action may be based	Unerlaubte Handlung
Total Quality	Degree to which a product or service meets or exceeds a customer's requirements and expectations	Ganzheitliche Qualität
Total revenue	The dollar amount of annual sales, net of allowances (discounts, returned merchandise). It is the "top line" figure from which costs are subtracted to determine net income.	Umsatzerlöse
Trade union	Representative organization of workers	Gewerkschaft
Transaction costs	The costs of transacting trades	Transaktionskosten
Transfer	(1) Hand over (2) Make over of possession (e.g. of money) (3) Move	(1) Übertragen (2) Überweisen (3) Verlegen
Transformational Change	Involves implementation of an evolutionary new state, which requires major and often on-going shifts in organizational strategy. Examples include reengineering, major restructuring, downsizing, consolidation, and major shifts in business focus	Grundlegende Veränderung, Wende
Transit time	The time taken to move goods physically between different locations in a supply chain or laterally to another facility	Transportzeit
Transitional Change	Involves implementation of a new state which requires dismantling the present ways of operating and introducing new or replacement ways of operating. Examples include reorganization, minor restructuring, utilization of new operational techniques/methods/procedures, or introduction of new services or products	Neuausrichtung
Turn around time	The total time taken to service a component at the service location, including waiting time but excluding transit time	Wartungszeit
Turnover	When people quit their jobs	Personalfluktuation
Unbundle	Separate a diversified company or a package into its constituent parts	Aufspaltung

"Handy 500" word	Brief explanation	Translation
Uncertainty	Condition under which the decision maker lacks enough information to estimate the probability of possible outcomes	Ungewissheit, Unsicherheit
Underground economy	Business sectors that either finance their operations with laundered money or engage in illegal activities, such as tax evasion and product piracy	Schattenwirtschaft
Unit cost	The cost to an organization of acquiring one unit, including any freight costs, if obtained from an external source or the total unit production cost, including direct labor, direct material and factory overheads, if manufactured in-house	Stückkosten
Useful life	The term used to describe the life over which an asset is expected to be useful to the organization; cost is assigned to the periods benefited from using the asset	Wirtschaftliche Lebensdauer
Utility	(1) Usefulness (2) Organization providing a public service (e.g. gas, water)	(1) Nutzen, Nützlichkeit (2) öffentlicher Versorgungsbetrieb
Validity	The extent to which a measure actually reflects what it was intended to measure	Validität
Valuation	Estimating or appraising the value of a business	Bewertung
Value chain	View that classifies organizational activities as being either primary activities (that create, transfer or support something of value) or as support activities (that assist the primary activities by providing resources or infrastructure)	Wertschöpfungskette
Value-added-tax (VAT)	Taxes increase in value of an article at each stage of production	MwSt
Value-at-risk (VAR)	A measure of the potential price volatility of assets	Potenzieller Wertverlust
Value-chain management	The process of adding value in every step of the manufacturing process: from raw materials to delivery of the product to the end user to the end user's disposal of the packaging. The goal of value-chain management is to optimize that network to deliver maximum value to the end user at the least possible cost (Supply-chain management is a subset)	Steuerung der Wertschöpfungskette

"Handy 500" word	Brief explanation	Translation
Values	Set of beliefs or standards that the organization (i.e., organizational values) and its stakeholders (i.e., personal values) believe in and operate from	Werte
Vendor	Supplier	Zulieferer
Venture	Business undertaking	Unternehmerisches Vorhaben, Projekt
Vertical Hierarchical Structure	Traditional hierarchical pyramid structure, vertically oriented and using traditional concepts such as division of labor, standardization of parts and products, mass production and control as basic or primary function of management	Linienorganisation
Vertical integration	All value chain activities related to a product are transacted within the organization	Vertikale Integration
Vested interest	Possession of a stake established through long association and giving rise to the expectation of a profit	Berechtigtes Eigeninteresse
Viability	Ability to survive in business	Leistungsfähigkeit, Erfolgsaussichten
Violation	Breach of a contract or law	Verstoß, Verletzung
Viral marketing	The act of marketing a product or service using tactics that encourage individuals to pass along a marketing message to others	Schneeballmarketing
Vision	Long-term goal of strategy. Answers the question, "How would things be different if your mission were fully successful?"	Strategisches Gesamtziel
Volatility	Measurement of the propensity of a stock, bond, mutual fund, commodity, or market to rise or fall sharply in price	Volatilität
Vulnerability	Risk exposure	Anfälligkeit, Verletzbarkeit
Warrant	(1) Thing or person that authorizes action (2) A long-term option	(1) Vollmacht, Garantie; Garant (2) Berechtigungsschein
Warranty	Guarantee of vendor that the product sold fulfils specified conditions	Herstellergarantie
Wealth	Total assets owned by an individual or society	Wohlstand, Reichtum

E | The "Handy 500"

"Handy 500" word	Brief explanation	Translation
Wholesaler	Seller of large quantities of goods for resale	Großhändler
Winner takes all market	Only one company survives competitive struggle and captures the whole domain	Aus Wettbewerb hervorgehendes Monopol
W-O Actions	Referring to the SWOT, a term that is used to discuss those actions that take advantage of existing or future opportunities by improving areas of weakness	Analyse der internen Schwächen, welche die Nutzung neuer Chancen bremsen
Work in progress (WIP)	The total amount of work in processing, between production stages or subject to a waiting time	Bestand an Halbfertigerzeugnissen
Workforce diversity	The similarities and differences in such characteristics as age, gender, ethnic heritage, physical abilities and disabilities, race, and sexual orientation among the employees of organizations	Heterogenität der Arbeitnehmer
Working capital	Current assets minus current liabilities	Betriebskapital, Nettoumlaufvermögen
Works	Plant, factory	Werk, Anlage
Worst-case	A measure of potential credit exposure	GAU (größter anzunehmender Unfall)
W-T Actions	Referring to the SWOT, a term that is used to discuss those actions that are largely defensive and that seek to minimize weakness by avoiding or mitigating existing or potential threats	Analyse zum Ziel der Risikominimierung durch Vermeidung oder Absenkung externer Risiken
Yield	The interest earned on a bond, or the dividend paid on a stock or mutual fund. Total return is the combination of yield plus any change in the underlying value of a security	Ertrag
Yield curve	A description of yields for multiple horizons	Ertragsspektrum
Yield management	The science of segmenting the price sensitive customers from their price-insensitive counterparts – for instance when airline charges $399 for a seat four weeks in advance, but $1.655 on the day of flight	Preisdifferenzierung gemäß individueller Nachfrageintensität
Zero coupon bond	A bond which pays no coupons	Zinslose Industrieobligation mit abgezinstem Ausgabekurs

F Index

Abbreviations 8f.
Abkürzungen 8f.
Accounting 200 ff.
Active listening 196 f.
Agency 135
AGM 106
Anfragen 286 ff.
Angebote 290 ff.
Annual general meeting 106
Anschreiben 322
Applications 322 ff.
Arousal and wellness 270
Artful persuasion 197
Auditing process 170

Bad delivery 310 ff.
Balanced scorecard 208
Bankruptcy 136
Berichte 320 f.
Bestellungen 294 ff.
Bewerbungen 322 ff.
Board of directors 107
Bounded rationality 162
Budgets 207
Bureaucratic control 150
Business etiquette 48
Business skills 40 f.

Capital budgeting 221 f.
Career movement 174 f.
Case study approach 78
Certification of financial statements 205
Company of the future 104
Competitive framework 266

Conference centres 24
Conflict management 128
Conglomerate 93
Constitution of business 102 ff.
Contingency framework for decision-making 164
Contracts 132 ff.
Control 149 f., 190
Control function 149 f.
Controlling role 156
Conversation skills 44
Corporate culture 120 f.
Corporate governance 106 f.
Corporations 105 f.
Cover letter 322
Cultures 120 f.
Curriculum vitae 323
Customer management framework 245
Customer service 52

Decision support system approach 162
Decision-making processes 160 ff.
Delays 306 ff.
Delegating 114
Despatch 302 ff.

Effectiveness 148 f.
Efficiency 148, 187 f.
Empowerment 126
Enquiries 286 ff.
Enterprise resource planning 188
Environment, external 117 ff.
Environment, internal 119
Environment, task 119

413

Exercise – Arranging an interview   38
Exercise – Arranging hotel reservations   30
Exercise – Booking a hotel room   31
Exercise – Calling a meeting   23
Exercise – Changing arrangements   59
Exercise – Deciding on a conference venue   25
Exercise – Delegating tasks   47
Exercise – Finalizing details   43
Exercise – Making a reservation   41
Exercise – Managing performance records   53
Exercise – Memo "Please report to work on Saturday"   171
Exercise – Organizing the collection of guests   58
Exercise – Problems with deliveries   51
Exercise – Processing orders   49
Exercise – Requesting information   27
Exercise – Requesting resources   55
Exercise – Scheduling job interviews   36
Exercise – Scheduling reservations   22
Exercise – Selecting a supplier   45
Experiential Case: Feeling Sidetracked   85 f.
Experiential Case: Negotiating Objective Criteria   198 f.
Experiential Case: Skilled Incompetence   156 ff.
Experiential Case: The Group Decision   128 f.
Experiential Case: The Stress-Challenged Manager   99 f.
Experiential Case: The Temperamental Networker   114 f.
Experiential Exercise 1: Organizational Design Preference   211 f.
Experiential Exercise 2: Corporate versus Professional Identity   214
Experiential Exercise: ACME Role-Play   246 f.
Experiential Exercise: Creativity-Relevant Skills   182 ff.
Experiential Exercise: Giving and Receiving Feedback   141 f.

Experiential Exercise: The Confrontation Meeting   228 f.
Experiential Exercise: The Glass Cubicle   259 ff.

Financial Accounting   201
Financial analysis   204 f.
Financial Management   216 ff.
Financial plan   217 f.

Global company   249 ff.
Global competition   248 ff.
Global competitive advantages   251 f.
Global Network Economy   74 ff.
Globalization, barriers   253
GNE   74 ff.
Goal approach   148
Goals, managing conflicting   147 f.
Goals, official   145 f.
Goals, operative   146 f.
Group decision-making   162 ff.

Horizontal merger   93
Human Resource Management   172 ff.

Incoterms   9, 326 ff.
Incremental decision process model   164
Individual decision-making   161
Information, analyzing   170
Information, filtering   170
Information management   285
Information, presenting   171
Internal process approach   148
Intuitive Model   164

Layout of business letters   283 f.
LBO   107
Lebenslauf   323

Legal forms   104 ff.
Legitimacy   145
Leveraged buyout   107
Linked mindsets framework   84 f.

M&A   93
Macho culture   121
Macroenvironment   117, 265
Mahnungen   314 ff.
Management accounting   207
Mangelhafte Lieferung   310 ff.
Market control   149
Market research   233
Market segmentation   233
Marketing   230 ff.
Marketing management process   231 f.
Marketing mix   234
Materials management   188
Meetings   20 ff.
Memos   318 f.
Merger and acquisition   93
Mindset   83 ff.
Mindset management   83 ff., 268 f.
Mindset, administrator   155 f.
Mindset, advocate   126
Mindset, auditing   170 f.
Mindset, collaborative   259
Mindset, entrepreneurial   196 f.
Mindset, informating   212
Mindset, intrapreneurial   98 f.
Mindset, proactive   245
Mindset, risk-managing   227 f.
Mindset, visionary   181
Mindsets, aligning   268 f.
Mindsets, switching   269
Mission statement   145
Monitoring costs   93

Motivation   98
Motivational modes   86 f.
Multidivisional organization structure   93

Network organization   104
Nonstop – Point-Point Flight   126 f.

Offers   290 ff.
Open system   117
Opportunistic behavior   91 f.
Orders   294 ff.
Organic structure   119, 121
Organizing role   156

Partnerships   105
Payment   298 ff.
Peer-group control   150
Personal productivity   98
Planning   155, 189, 207
Planning role   155
Pleasure principle   269 f.
Political model   162 f.
Presentations   28 f.
Process organization   121, 267
Product liability   134 f.
Product life cycle   234 f.
Product portfolio matrix   236 f.
Production and operations
    management   189 f.
Programmed Structure   119, 121

Quality   170, 188

Rational approach   161
Rational decision-making   161
Reminders   314 ff.

Reports   320 f.
Resource approach   149
Resume   324
Reward system   175
Risk management   218
Routing   189 f.

Sample balance sheet   202 f.
Sample income statement   204
Scheduling   190
Scorecharting   207 f.
Shareholders   106
Socio-technical systems model   190
Sole proprietorships   105
Staffing   173 f.
Stakeholder approach   149
Strategies, generic   146
Strategy Case: Cadbury Schweppes   271 ff.
Strategy Case: CEMEX   165 ff., 349
Strategy Case: Dimon Inc.   135 ff., 346 f.
Strategy Case: Egg plc   223 ff., 355
Strategy Case: Elan Corp.   209 ff., 353 f.
Strategy Case: Enron Corp.   94 ff., 342 f.
Strategy Case: Expedia Inc.   151 ff., 348
Strategy Case: Iridium LLC   122 ff., 345
Strategy Case: Kirch Media   109 ff., 344
Strategy Case: Nortel   79 ff., 339 ff.
Strategy Case: Pharmacia   177 ff., 350 f.
Strategy Case: Smithfields Foods   191 ff., 352
Strategy Case: STMicroelectronics   66 ff., 337 f.
Strategy Case: Tesco   254 ff., 357 f.

Strategy Case: The Algonquin Hotel   240 ff., 356 f.
Stress management   98 f.
Structural variety   119
Supply chain   187 f.
SWOT Analysis   64 f.

Taxes   131 f.
Telephoning   32 ff.
Theory of the firm   88 ff.
Tips for writing letters   283
Torts   134
Transaction costs   90 ff.
Transport   302 ff.
Trend and ratio analysis   205 f.

UK Airports   56 f.

Value Chain   63, 92
Versand   302 ff.
Vertical integration   90
Vertical merger   93
Verzögerungen   306 ff.

Work system   175 f.

Yield management   220, 243

Zahlung   298 ff.